Global Management

Business Strategy and Government Policy

Yoshi Tsurumi

Copley Publishing Group
Acton, Massachusetts 01720

Fourth Printing 1994

ISBN 0-87411-379-2

To Evan and Andrea

Contents

1 The U.S. Trade Deficit with Japan: Putting America's House in Order

By now it should be clear that a lower dollar is no panacea for America's trade imbalance. Two years after it peaked in early 1985, the dollar has declined more than 40 percent against the Japanese yen, the German mark, and other major currencies. Yet the dollar's plunge has done little to reduce the trade deficit, which last year reached a record $148 billion.

No single country has taken as much blame for this widening imbalance as Japan, which last year registered a $56-billion trade surplus with the United States. Japan's share of the U.S. trade deficit has remained more or less constant since the 1970s, at around 30 percent. But, lately, resentment over this large surplus, which critics attribute partly to unfair trade practices, has been mounting. "The level of frustration with Japan is higher than I have ever seen," Clayton Yeutter, the United States trade representative, said in March.[1] This frustration is evident in calls for more "voluntary" restrictions on the export of Japanese goods, White House efforts to block the sale of an electronics subsidiary — foreign-owned — to one of Japan's electronics giants, and a bill before Congress that would require the president to retaliate against countries whose large trade surpluses are determined to be the result of practices that close markets to U.S. products. Japan is also under pressure to open more of its markets to U.S. goods and to help buy the United States out of its trade slump through increased consumption of those goods.

The tendency to blame Japan first may be politically convenient but it does not go to the heart of the matter and, more important, it is likely to exacerbate the problem. In April 1987 the Reagan administration finally joined the congressional chorus for bashing Japan and slapped punitive import tariffs on an assortment of electronic goods. In turn, Japan is poised to take retaliatory measures. No one doubts that the playing field of U.S.-

Yoshi Tsurumi is professor of international business at Baruch College, City University of New York and president of the Pacific Basin Center Foundation.

Japanese trade relations is not entirely level, but which way does it slope? For if Japan restricts its imports of U.S. agricultural products, the United States protects its steel, automobile, textiles, and microchip industries against Japanese competition. According to the Institute of International Economics, about $5 billion worth of Japanese exports are being restrained by various U.S. quotas and regulations.[2] Were Japan to drop all barriers to trade, this same study concludes, its trade surplus with the United States would only be trimmed by about the same amount. In other words, if all were perfectly fair, little difference would it make.

U.S. pressures on Japan are already proving to be counterproductive. The rising yen has left Japan vulnerable to other export-oriented Asian economies whose currencies have not appreciated against the dollar. As its volume of exports declines, Japan is even resorting to plant closings, layoffs, and relocation overseas—measures it has traditionally avoided.[3] Unemployment rose to 3 percent in January—the highest level since 1953.[4] Such conditions only aggravate social tensions and strengthen the hand of "localists" against any further accommodations. To cope with this economic slowdown, Japan, naturally enough, is not increasing its consumption of American-made goods but rather is buying fewer imports generally.[5]

The clues to America's worsening trade deficit with Japan lie closer to home. The United States has long believed that economic success does not require any special effort, a belief perhaps understandable for a nation that was catapulted into a position of economic hegemony at the end of World War II. This belief is now gradually giving way to an increasing recognition of the need to enhance U.S. competitiveness, evident in calls for more research and development, expanded investment, and worker retraining. Yet, as we shall see, even these proposals skirt the central issue: the need for the federal and state governments to assume a more active role in managing economic development. In this and other respects, learning from the Japanese is likely to prove more useful than blaming them.

A Changed World Economy

The fact that the United States has been able to run large trade deficits for the past six years defies conventional economic wisdom. According to laissez-faire logic, which has largely governed the Reagan administration's approach to global commerce, the U.S. trade imbalance should have corrected itself: bulging trade deficits should have depressed the U.S. economy and triggered a general decline in the value of the dollar, thereby making U.S. goods less expensive relative to those of foreign competitors. This automatic adjustment of U.S. trade flows would have been further aided by a depressed U.S. economy buying less from abroad and selling more to the growing economies of trade-surplus countries. In reality, however, it did not work that way; the dollar never really fell but had to be "talked down" through agreements among the leading industrialized countries. And when the dollar was finally lower, the long-awaited improvement in trade did not materialize.

What kept the dollar so high for so long relates to one feature of a changed world economy: the emergence of a money-game economy of capital movements, currency speculation, and credit flows. Spurred by developments as various as the shift from fixed to floating exchange rates, the massive flow of funds to OPEC during the 1970s, the surging growth of Eurodollar markets, the deregulation of domestic financial markets, and the application of new technologies that permit instantaneous transfer of funds across the globe, the money-game economy now dwarfs the "real" economy of goods and services.[6] By conservative estimates, the value of international money-game transactions is at least 20 times greater than that of goods and services. Moreover, the money-game economy operates largely independently of the real economy, allowing currencies, for instance, to attain greater value than the performance of their national economies would suggest.

When money-game transactions overwhelm merchandise transactions in this fashion, international money flows and foreign exchange rates become extremely sensitive to money-market rates and other short-term financial yield differentials among trading nations, as well as to perceptions of a country's stature as a political leader. This is precisely what occurred with the dollar. Interest rates were kept high in the United States to attract capital from abroad, thus enabling the country to finance its budget and trade deficits. These large inflows of capital, in turn, pushed the dollar's value upward, where it would remain in spite of ever-larger deficits.

It took the intervention of the leading industrialized countries to finally drive the dollar down. But even with a 40 percent decline in the dollar's value since then, U.S. trade deficits remain staggeringly high. One reason for this is the hollowing-out of America's nondefense manufacturing sector—a trend that has been apparent for some time but that has accelerated under the Reagan administration. Pentagon spending, which doubled from $150 billion in 1981 to over $300 billion in 1986, lured many American manufacturers away from civilian manufacturing with lucrative defense contracts shielded from foreign competition. Also, many U.S. manufacturers were convinced to relocate in low-wage countries where the high dollar reduced labor costs even further. The resultant hollowing-out effect is most visible in such traditional export-generators as machine tools, transportation equipment, and electronics, leaving the United States with fewer "Made in America" products to export or to substitute for imports at home. As foreign competitors, notably the Japanese, have increased their share of the U.S. market, they have also increased their profits. This has made it easier for them to weather the dollar's decline and retain their market share; they have simply reduced their profit margin. And where a higher yen has left Japanese firms less able to compete, the rising export-led countries of the Pacific, whose currencies have not appreciated against the dollar, have been only too glad to fill the vacuum.

Another reason the lower dollar has done little to correct the trade imbalance is that the United States has always relied on agriculture to offset its deficit in manufactures. But we live at a time when the world is suffering an embarrassment of riches: a chronic and, likely, permanent glut of primary commodities. Agricultural production, in particular, has greatly increased with the application of new scientific and bioengineering technologies — not only in the United States but the world over. Thus, once the United States lost its traditional export markets for agricultural products as a result of the Carter grain embargo of 1980 and the high-dollar years of 1981–85, it experienced difficulty regaining them. Moreover, abundance of supply has encouraged buyers such as the Soviet Union to no longer purchase from any single source but to diversify their sources, thereby assuring greater reliability of supply. All told, the U.S. agricultural sector registered a $20-billion trade surplus in 1981 by exporting $38 billion and importing $18 billion. By 1986, U.S. exports of agricultural products plummeted to $21 billion while U.S. imports reached an all-time high of $25 billion. The agricultural sector can no longer be counted on to produce net trade surpluses.

Another factor in America's lingering trade deficit is the erosion of America's economic leadership, which has left it unable to play its traditional role of both lender and market of last resort. And neither Japan nor West Germany — today's powerhouse economies — has been willing or able to assume the responsibilities relinquished by the United States. Indeed, Japan, now the world's largest creditor, has invested much of its trade surpluses in financing U.S. trade and budget deficits at the expense of capital-starved nations in Africa, Latin America, and Asia. Consequently, these countries have been left to struggle with rising debt-servicing burdens, falling commodity prices, and increasingly closed industrialized country markets. Third World economic stagnation has in turn reduced world demand for U.S. exports, contributing to the U.S. trade deficit.

America's Trade Deficit with Japan

Efforts to understand the U.S. trade deficit often do not take these over-arching factors into account. They tend, instead, to focus narrowly on bilateral trade relations. But even then, a closer examination of the U.S. trade deficit with Japan reveals a picture quite different from the one that is commonly perceived. To casual observers, Japan appears to buy little from the United States and to sell it much. In reality, Japan buys quite a lot from the United States. After Canada, Japan is the second largest importer of U.S. goods, purchasing about 14 percent of America's total exports. Japan imports more U.S. goods than Mexico, the United Kingdom, and West Germany combined. Thirty-three percent of all U.S. agricultural exports are purchased by Japan—three times more than the Soviet Union buys—including 70 percent of America's beef exports, 40 percent of its citrus fruit exports, and 18 percent of its tobacco exports. Moreover, although Japan's share of America's $148-billion trade deficit amounted to $56 billion last year, this was partly offset from U.S. net surpluses of about $10-$15 billion in the service-trade sector with Japan: receipts from technical royalties, investment income, transportation fees, and tourism. (Over 7 million Japanese tourists visited the United States in 1986 alone.)

A closer look at the U.S. trade deficit with Japan also reveals that it has less to do with foul play and more to do with such things as comparative advantage and differences in product quality, consumer preference, levels of consumer spending, and the relative importance the two countries place on defense spending. On the basis of technological complexity, U.S. and Japanese products fall into three categories: low-tech goods, including agricultural products and other primary commodities such as coal, forestry products, scrap iron, and processed foods; medium-tech products, including consumer and industrial goods like automobiles, steel, machine-tools, textiles, photocopiers, and cameras; and high-tech products, including pharmaceuticals, computers, industrial robots, precision medical equipment, biotech-related products, telecommunication equipment, microchips, and aircraft.

In terms of price and quality, the United States commands absolute advantage over Japan in most low-tech products; it generates a $16-billion annual trade surplus with Japan in this group. Japan generally commands absolute advantage over the United States in many medium-tech products, enjoying a $70-$80 billion surplus in this area. The United States and Japan split their relative advantage among high-tech products. The United States exports many passenger aircraft to Japan, and American-made satellites and accompanying high-speed communication gears are still largely superior to Japanese brands. Cray Corporation, an American firm, outsells Fujitsu and Hitachi supercomputers, even in Japan. However, Japan enjoys comparative advantages in microchips and in the field of civilian telecommunications equipment, such as telephones and electronic switchboards. In fact, it was largely on the basis of Japan's dominance of the U.S. microchip market that it generated a $6-$7 billion trade surplus in high-tech products last year.

In the utopian world of free trade and comparative advantages, the United States would export mostly low- and some high-tech products to Japan, and Japan would export mostly medium-tech products to the United States. If mutual demand for these products were the same, if there were no market restraints, and if American-made low- and high-tech products were internationally competitive in price, quality, delivery, and other customer services, there would be no U.S. trade deficit with Japan. But these conditions, of course, do not prevail. First of all, Japanese consumers traditionally have been low spenders, saving more than twice as much of their personal disposable income as their American counterparts. Moreover, the United States has a population twice as large as Japan's, which means its absolute demand for goods is greater. It also means that, on a per-capita basis, both countries actually import about the same amount from each other.

As for market restraints, both the United States and Japan restrict imports of many low- and high-tech products. In the area of high-tech products, where the two countries enjoy rough trade parity, the United States often restricts imports because many of these products are closely related to defense procurements. On the other hand, Japan is suspected of erecting barriers to the importation of U.S. supercomputers: despite its acknowledged technological lead over Japan in this area, the United States has only 23 percent of the Japanese market. Since both liberals and conservatives in the United States are anxious about the future of U.S.-Japanese high-tech competition, they are pressuring Congress and the White House to further limit Japanese access to the American market and, at the same time, to pry open the Japanese market.

Most of Japan's trade barriers affect imports of low-tech products. Twenty-two out of the 23 product categories restricted for import to Japan are

6

mainly agricultural products. In Japan, farmers wield a disproportionate amount of influence, given that they constitute only about 10 percent of the total population. They benefit from the fact that the power of elected national officials in Japan derives from the Lower Diet, whose seat allocation has changed very little since 1947 when much of the country's population was living out the war in rural regions. Japan's farmer-bureaucrat alliance is not only powerful but quite prepared to jeopardize the country's overall relations with the United States in pursuit of its interests. To the consternation of the Rice Millers Association, the Japanese rice lobby bans all foreign rice imports, including the less costly rice that California produces. The United States trade representative is therefore requesting that Japan discuss rice as part of the GATT (General Agreements on Tariffs and Trade) negotiations in 1987.

The Japanese market for medium-tech products is wide open to U.S. imports. The problem here is that few American products can compete with Japanese products in terms of price, quality, and delivery requirements. For instance, in 1985 Nippon Telephone and Telegraph Corporation (NTT), the government-owned communication monopoly at the time, chose to import Motorola's cellular mobile telephones, pocket bells (beepers), and telephones to placate rising anti-Japanese sentiment in the U.S. Congress. The quality of Motorola's products was so poor, however, that NTT had to recall most of them due to consumer complaints. Subsequently, NTT refused to reorder them—a decision that prompted Motorola to charge that its products were being treated unfairly by NTT.

At the heart of these differences are two very distinct management cultures. American manufacturing firms frequently set lower standards for quality. Even 98 percent quality, though it seems high, permits two defective products for every 100. Their Japanese counterparts, on the other hand, have designed quality control systems that reduce defects to one per one million finished products.[7] (Most American managers and engineers do not even believe such a high level of product quality is feasible.) Japanese manufacturers can therefore count on parts suppliers to deliver zero-defect products promptly. As a result, Japanese manufacturers have been able to develop more efficient "just-in-time" and "zero inventory" systems that allow them to make swift changes in production schedules and product specifications. Because parts suppliers can accommodate these changes "just in time," manufacturers avoid the expense of maintaining inventories and are not bound by the design requirements of that inventory.[8] Many American manufacturing firms are unable to serve the Japanese market because they cannot adapt to its manufacturers' flexible production needs.

The United States, on the other hand, is increasingly dependent on Japan for medium-tech products, either because those products are no longer available domestically or because their quality is inferior. Today, over 30 percent of machine tools, about 25 percent of passenger cars, and over 80 percent of semiconductors sold in the United States are made in Japan. Consumer products that American companies like RCA, General Electric, Motorola, and Zenith invented, such as color television sets and stereo equipment, are now being manufactured by Japanese firms. American consumers eagerly snap up Toyotas, Hondas, Sony compact disc players, Nikon cameras, Canon copiers, and Ricoh telefax machines, whereas Japanese consumers show very little enthusiasm for Chevrolets, Fords, and Zenith color televisions. Even such standard industrial materials as construction steel products flow from Japan to the United States. The timely completion of New York City's Javits Convention Center, for example, was only possible because the center ultimately turned to Japanese steel mills, frustrated with the shoddy quality and delivery of U.S.-made steel construction materials.

Japan is blamed for "unfair" and "unlevel" competition but, as a former assistant U.S. trade representative commented, "Japan is the metaphor for the loss of our competitive edge."[9] Japan, it is true, needs to eliminate its obsolete and cumbersome requirements for product specifications, product tests, and customs clearance procedures that handicap many medium- and high-tech imports; eventually it will have to open all its markets, especially in the agricultural sector. For these restrictions inevitably and unnecessarily politicize U.S.-Japanese economic relations. But even by the most optimistic reckoning, the removal of all Japanese tariff and nontariff barriers might increase U.S. annual exports to Japan by $10-$15 billion.[10] This would still leave a bilateral trade deficit of $40-$45 billion. Moreover, this assumes, among other things, that the United States would be the only beneficiary of a more open Japanese market. But, for instance, if all barriers to primary commodities were removed, the United States would still face severe competition from Canada, Thailand, and Argentina, among others.

As for medium-tech products, which account for most of the trade deficit with Japan, the only real barriers to U.S. imports are quality and consumer satisfaction, and these obviously cannot be negotiated away. Moreover, any gains by the removal of Japanese barriers in this area would be offset by increases in Japanese exports to the United States with the removal of voluntary export restraints. Finally, in the area of high-tech products, one of the greatest barriers to increased U.S. sales is Pentagon

8

distortions of the commercial market and restrictions on the sale of sensitive technology. America's trade problems, in other words, cannot be solved by quarreling over trade barriers because these problems are largely made in America, born of twin failures: a defense-first style of planning and obsolete management practices.

The Failure of a Defense-first Policy

Strategic economic planning has long been anathema to an American public weaned on the virtues of an unfettered marketplace. But there is little reason to expect much improvement in America's competitive position so long as there is such hostility to planning. In today's world economy, the federal government's active role as arbiter and allocator of scarce resources is necessary and useful for setting the competitive framework within which market competition works best to reward performance that meets the national goal of improved international competitiveness. This is especially needed now that the United States has run into a chronic shortage of many critical resources.

Until recently the United States has not had to worry about scarce resources. It has enjoyed ready access to natural resources, capital, technology, foreign exchange, a trained work force, and a political culture conducive to industrial growth. Japan, on the other hand, has had to contend with a persistent scarcity of resources. Just as felicitous conditions allowed the United States to indulge its aversion to economic planning, scarcity led the Japanese to perceive the need for an active government role allocating resources and structuring the nation's industries. By this arrangement, the Japanese government, in cooperation with business, has fashioned an overall framework for national development. To the advocate of a laissez-faire approach, government-led industrial planning would seem to be a clear prescription for inefficiency. However, within Japan's overall national framework, corporations engage in fierce competition at home and abroad to exploit new technologies commercially, thereby weeding out the weaker firms.

This principle of "survival of the fittest" has come to characterize the industrial policy framework of Japan.[11] More precisely, the promotion of market competition is achieved through government orchestration of joint R & D (research and development) activities among competing Japanese firms for very basic projects like the development of prototype designs and manufacturing systems. All participants in joint R & D projects are then encouraged to compete with one another for the commercialization of these projects. In Japan, this joint R & D program is viewed as promoting competition rather than stifling it. It enables Japan to have at least two competing firms with basic technological capabilities. The "survival of the fittest" principle forces these firms to improve their common prototypes and compete fiercely in markets at home and abroad.

The United States may have no strategic plan as such, but the priorities of defense spending constitute a de facto industrial policy. And the defense-first approach of Reaganomics, in particular, has placed the United States at a severe disadvantage with respect to Japan and other industrial countries. If we examine the industrialized nations over the past decade, the greater their defense spending in proportion to gross national product, the smaller has been their economic growth and the greater their industries' loss of international competitiveness.[12] Underinvestment has long plagued the U.S. economy; the declining steel, automobile, and electronics industries are among its many casualties. One reason for this, albeit not the only reason, is that high levels of military spending have tended to crowd out productive investment; for example, in recent years, the high interest rates that have been necessary to finance runaway defense spending have also discouraged borrowing to invest in America's productive assets.

The negative effects of runaway defense spending on international competitiveness, however, run deeper than the crowding out of nondefense firms from capital markets. In this technology-driven age, a highly skilled work force is vital to a competitive economy. What we find, however, is the United States graduating only half the number of college-trained engineers as Japan.[13] Furthermore, the study of engineering in the United States has become less and less oriented to the manufacturing needs of nondefense industries as defense-related industries have come to claim seven out of ten new engineering and science graduates.[14] American non-defense firms are finding it increasingly difficult to compete with Japanese firms that have ready access to many more and better trained engineers and scientists suited to nondefense manufacturing assignments. It is no small wonder that the productivity and quality of American manufacturing industries have deteriorated markedly.

It is not the number of Nobel Prize–winning scientists but the average quality of high school graduates that determines the economic strength of a nation today, and a policy of defense-first spending has meant less money available for even this basic investment. As compared with their Japanese, Korean, Chinese, and German counterparts, American high school graduates fall short in their literacy and communication skills, as well as in their knowledge of science, mathematics, foreign languages, world history, and geography.[15] For a leading industrial nation this is tantamount to unilateral economic disarmament.

But that's not how America's policy elite sees it. The defense-first stance is sold to the American public as providing stimulus to civilian industry. In reality, this stance has not only contributed to the hollowing out of America's medium-tech manufacturing sector, it is also eroding America's high-tech sector. And without a strong medium-tech manufacturing sector, the best results of advanced technological innovations can find no application for industrial purposes. Contrary to popular belief, many of the higher paid "service" jobs such as engineering, design, management, transportation, and marketing are closely tied to a strong manufacturing base of medium-tech nondefense products. High-tech jobs are already disappearing because American firms do not possess the manufacturing base to withstand Japanese competition.

Nearly three-quarters of all federally funded R & D is earmarked for defense purposes, but there is little evidence here, either, of many benefits to civilian industry.[16] For instance, despite generous Pentagon subsidies, American microchip firms have been outdistanced by their Japanese counterparts, who are producing chips of greater quality and more memory. By 1985 Japanese suppliers had captured over 90 percent of the U.S. market for 256K RAM chips and were quickly moving into one mega (1,024K RAM) chips, well ahead of the American competition. When, in 1986, the Japanese were poised to enter the microprocessor and erasable-memory chip market long dominated by American firms, the Pentagon finally began to suspect that its involvement might actually be hindering development.[17] For about 10 years, it discovered, U.S. military specifications for semiconductors had been lower than what had come to be acceptable in the civilian market. Because American microchip producers had been locked into a limited volume production of older generation semiconductors for military use, they were shielded from dynamic market competition. Consequently, they had no incentive to upgrade product quality or production facilities.

While it is true that radar, integrated circuits, jet engines, optical fibers, and other products may be counted among the spinoffs of defense-led R & D, such spinoffs are becoming rarer as commercial and military needs diverge. Even when Pentagon-led efforts produce a patentable breakthrough, commercial exploitation is often costly and time-consuming. The Commerce Department found that it takes 10 man-years of civilian R & D to produce a commercial patent as opposed to 1,000 man-years of defense R & D.[18] Furthermore, defense R & D is shrouded in secrecy, which often inhibits scientists and engineers from freely exchanging mutual criticism and technical information vital to pioneering new technologies.

The situation is not helped by the fact that, overall, the United States is spending less and less on R & D than Japan. In 1960 Japan spent 1.2 percent of its gross national product for R & D activities as opposed to 2.7 percent in the United States. This pattern has changed markedly: today Japan spends over 2.7 percent of its GNP on R & D compared to America's 2.3 percent. And while the U.S. government allocates nearly three-quarters of its R & D for defense-related purposes, the government-supported one-third of Japan's total R & D is largely for commercial exploitation of new technology.

There is some evidence of efforts to redress this disparity. In the hope of regaining the lost technological and commercial lead in microchips from Japan, for instance, IBM has organized a group of semiconductor firms including Intel, Motorola, and Texas Instruments into a consortium. The Semiconductor Manufacturing Technology Institute, or Sematech, as it is called, will pool the resources of American semiconductor manufacturers, universities, and the Pentagon to exploit frontier manufacturing technologies.[19] IBM is rightfully worried that any further decline of the U.S. semiconductor industry could be a fatal blow for American manufacturers. And without American microchip manufacturers, IBM would become dependent on Japanese competitors, severely handicapping the firm in its competition with Japanese computer companies. It is highly questionable, however, that Sematech will be able to accomplish its goals. Pentagon participation in the project means it may suffer some of the same pitfalls that have already marred defense-first management of this technology. But, just as critical, while IBM may be able to share a prototype manufacturing system of new four mega chips with the other Sematech firms, it cannot impart its successful management practices to these firms, which points to another root cause of America's declining international competitiveness.

The Failure of American Corporate Management

The Japanese have not only recognized the need for strategic planning, they have also fostered a unique management culture that has both facilitated the rapid absorption of technology and promoted industrial growth through a quality-first approach—factors that have been key to Japan's postwar economic expansion. Japanese management thinking has tended to favor long-term growth over the short-term bottom line, the idea being that once Japan became a world economic leader the profits would follow. Moreover, Japanese firms generally treat employees not as disposable costs but as some of their most valuable assets. Workers are kept keenly aware of all aspects of the company, market competition, and customer needs. In return, they exhibit a remarkable degree of commitment to the firm and adapt more willingly to the changes—technological, occupational, and otherwise—that a volatile economic climate requires.[20]

The contrast to American management practices is evident in the response of each country's firms to recent recessionary pressures. Since September 1985, Japan has had to cope with economic dislocation produced by a rapidly appreciating yen, much as the United States faced hardship during the high-dollar days of 1981–85. If the crisis was similar, the response has been very different. In the belief that a firm needs to preserve its trained human resources if it is to bounce back from periods of economic hardship, many Japanese firms have been adjusting by first cutting executives' salaries and bonuses. Layoffs have indeed occurred, but overall unemployment has been kept at a relatively low 3 percent, mainly because Japanese firms are keeping on hundreds of thousands of idle employees in anticipation of renewed opportunities. New markets and new products are being developed—at home and abroad—so that, wherever possible, trained human resources will not be wasted.

When it has been necessary to permanently discharge workers, as Nippon Steel, Nihon Kohan, and other heavy industrial firms have done, these firms have assumed primary responsibility for retraining and relocating their workers elsewhere. When that has not been possible, government and corporations have worked together to distribute the social and economic costs fairly among management, discharged workers, local communities, and the banks and suppliers of affected companies. Unemployment insurance and worker retraining programs administered by the government further ease the burden.[21]

American management, on the other hand, is so obsessed with the short-term bottom line that it often takes a quick-fix approach to meeting the competition: cost-cutting. And for many American executives, that means layoffs. During the economic slump, over five million people were permanently discharged in the consumer electronics, machine-tool, automotive, steel, and computer industries. When an improved economy brought renewed demand for these products, hollowed-out American industries were caught without the necessary manpower to meet that demand—a void that was quickly filled by Japanese imports. Furthermore, while American executives were asking sacrifices of their workers and communities, they were voting themselves generous raises: during the recession of 1981–83, compensation for chief executives nearly doubled while national unemployment passed the 11 percent mark. In light of such conduct, is it any wonder that American workers respond with absenteeism, shoddy workmanship, drug abuse, and a stubborn resistance to the introduction of technological innovations?

American management's penchant for maximizing quarterly earnings expresses itself in other unproductive ways. Such wasteful actions as hostile takeovers and stock buybacks are justified on the grounds that they reallocate financial resources from less efficient to more efficient entities. In fact, leveraged buyouts often dismantle the physical assets of acquired firms or saddle the acquiring firm with whopping debts. When firms lay off workers or forgo necessary investments to pay for such financial burdens, the only ones who benefit are accountants, lawyers, arbitragers, investment bankers, and other money-game specialists. The overall outcome is nothing short of disaster for the U.S. economy. In March 1987, General Motors suddenly announced that it would spend $5 billion to buy back 20 percent of its own shares merely to prop up its stock prices. That money would be better spent solidifying the manufacturing and technological base of the firm. In 1986 alone, the money spent for corporate stock buybacks exceeded $37 billion — a nearly tenfold increase over 1981.[22]

A management culture that is not responsive to consumer demand cannot meet the challenge of foreign competition that is. In 1974, a year after the first oil crisis, Lee Iacocca, then president of Ford, refused to produce the fuel-efficient, front-wheel drive models that American consumers wanted. "The public can't see the front wheel drive," Iacocca claimed. "I say give 'em leather. They can smell it."[23] But the public wanted fuel-efficient cars, so it turned to the Japanese instead. Similarly, if General Motors had been willing to spend a mere $100 more per car on the Corvair's suspension system and other improvements, the company might have won America's loyalty toward efficient compact cars rather than forcing it to turn to the Japanese. The problem is captured in a joke one hears in Detroit: "When the federal government first enacted air pollution regulations, Honda hired 200 engineers while American auto firms hired 200 lawyers and public relations specialists."

A management culture unable to adapt to the challenges of foreign competition can hardly be expected to increase American exports even if the U.S. government succeeds in opening more foreign markets. The rigid, bureaucratic management structures of many American firms are poorly suited to cultivating and maintaining export markets. Developing mutually trusting relationships, an element especially critical to international business transactions, requires a continuity of the individuals involved. But this requires time, which the typical American firm, oriented to short-term profits, is often unwilling to invest.[24] It also requires flexibility—yet many American export managers are bound by rigid instructions and have little authority to make quick executive decisions. Moreover, their relative lack of foreign language skills and their inadequate understanding of world history and geography put American export managers at a severe disadvantage with respect to the competition.

Nowhere is the failure to manage exports more visible than in the failure of the Export Trading Company Act of 1982. At the height of the Reagan recession, in 1982, Congress enacted this law to encourage banks, manufacturers, transportation firms, and retailers to develop export trading companies patterned after the successful Japanese general trading companies.[25] It was hoped that such companies would help American manufacturers capture new export markets. Scores of trading firms were created but, by 1986, many had disappeared, unable to meet their profit objectives. The two leading export trading companies, Sears World Trade and General Electric Trading Company, have all but dismantled their exporting activities.[26]

As U.S. business executives bemoan America's loss of international competitiveness, their Japanese challengers are coming to the United States in droves to produce high-quality products with high-wage American labor, thereby demonstrating what adaptive corporate behavior can achieve. In the wake of an American manufacturing exodus overseas, Japanese companies have bought up, either partly or wholly, more than 600 factories in the United States and have turned them into rousing successes. The "Japanese paradox" makes clear that all the excuses American executives use to account for their failures—the overvalued dollar, high labor costs, restrictive union work rules, government regulations—are largely irrelevant.[27]

In perhaps the most celebrated example of the Japanese paradox, Toyota revived a unionized auto plant in California that had been virtually abandoned by General Motors. Toyota pledged that management would cut its own salaries before rank-and-file employees would be asked to accept temporary concessions during economic downturns. Accepting this pledge, the United Automobile Workers allowed Toyota to reduce over 26 rigid job categories to four broad classifications, thereby facilitating more flexible rotational assignments among workers. Furthermore, hundreds of plant workers and managers underwent training at Toyota's factories in Japan so that they could familiarize themselves with Toyota's zero-inventory, zero-defect, and flexible manufacturing systems. Workers continue to receive training to handle changing work assignments.

Similarly, in 1973 General Electric sold a unionized, deteriorating, special alloy plant in Michigan to Hitachi Metal. In less than two years, Hitachi Metal was operating it successfully, using the same workers and the same plant manager. During the 1974-76 recession, Hitachi Metal opened its books to the United Automobile Workers and asked employees to choose between a 20 percent reduction in the work force or a 20 percent temporary pay cut from the top down. Workers were more willing to make a sacrifice—they chose to accept the pay cut—because they had been invited to participate in a process from which they are generally excluded.

Illustrations of the Japanese paradox can be found increasingly across America's industrial landscape.[28] A common thread runs throughout: management, in cooperation with labor, restoring the vigor of firms abandoned by American executives as uneconomical. The Japanese are successful because they understand that sustained improvements in competitiveness and productivity can only be achieved by a long-term investment in automation and people, and not by quick-fix remedies like migration to low-wage countries. Indeed, the Japanese are finding that the introduction of new manufacturing technologies is well-suited to countries like the United States, where high wages also mean a highly skilled work force.

Moving production facilities abroad may permit American companies to cut labor costs, but in the long run it proves self-defeating. For one thing, it is vital to have good communication between those who develop, those who market, and those who manufacture a product, but these links are attenuated when production facilities are moved abroad. Furthermore, there is no substitute for constant exposure to market demands. Isolated from their markets, overseas factories become less responsive to customer needs. And low-wage employees in a distant land cannot be expected to make the same contribution to a firm as employees not only familiar with the domestic market but encouraged by a corporate rewards system to take a keen interest in a company's overall competitive standing.

The decision of the American microchip industry to move its operations abroad has more to do with the demise of that industry than most people realize. Overseas American plants were slow to respond to demand for more powerful microchips. U.S.-based laboratories had new chip designs but the plants, out of touch with the market and seduced by the call of cheap labor, resisted switching from labor-intensive processes to the more automated processes these new designs required. The Japanese, with no such hesitations, captured the market.

The United States and Japan at a Crossroads

America's trade problems, then, are deeply rooted and not remedied by quick-fix solutions. In fact, as Japan makes greater strides in the area of high-tech products and as the newly industrialized countries further refine their manufacturing processes and adopt Japanese-style approaches to doing business, the United States can expect greater deterioration, not improvement, of its trade balance. Viewed in this light, the ad hoc responses of the Reagan administration and Congress do not address the problem and may, in fact, do more harm than good. Whatever specific action they try to force Japan to take — accepting "voluntary" export restrictions, guaranteeing a portion of its domestic market for U.S. goods, suffering stiff penalties as a trade-surplus nation, or living with a higher yen — the basic intent is always the same: to shift the burden elsewhere. These piecemeal approaches all ignore the underlying problems afflicting U.S. competitiveness and thus distract attention from more painful but necessary policy changes.

Over the years the United States has obtained agreements from Japan to limit its exports of steel, automobiles, textiles, apparel, machine goods, and microchips. These may placate American industry demands for protection but, in the end, they benefit no one. American consumers are forced to pay perhaps $25 billion more in higher prices. Restrictions governing the import of lower-priced Japanese cars, for instance, have increased the average purchase price of a new car by at least $1,500.[29] This means that, in 1984 alone, over 9 million American purchasers of new cars were forced to pay hidden automobile subsidy taxes totaling $13 billion. Nor does industry really benefit from the protection of export restraints; on the contrary, shielded from foreign competition, management and labor lose their incentive to abandon the uncompetitive ways that inspired these restraints in the first place.[30]

Market-oriented sector-specific (MOSS) negotiations can be a more promising approach than export restraints, especially when they are used to pry open Japan's remaining protected markets. This allows the United States to export those products — such as rice, coal, and petroleum — in which it enjoys a genuine advantage. But too often MOSS arrangements acquire the worst features of export restraints with, predictably, many of the same ill effects. In August 1986, for example, the Japanese agreed

17

to price their microchips sold outside Japan higher than American chips, in response to charges of dumping. Although intended to protect the American microchip industry, the pricing agreement has actually contributed to its virtual extinction. As prices of the highly valued Japanese chips increased 400 percent, Motorola and Texas Instruments, the last remaining U.S. chip makers, quickly abandoned their own production to sell imports from Japan. The pricing agreement also meant that manufacturers and other producers requiring high-grade microchips could now look forward to inflated chip prices and limited availability, thus placing them at a further disadvantage relative to their Japanese competitors.

MOSS negotiations also do more harm than good when, like voluntary export restraints, they are conducted to the benefit only of the United States and not of all nations. Exclusive market concessions create economic blocs that threaten to undermine the world trading system. It is this same preoccupation with bilateral trade deficits that bedevils proposals for remedial legislation, particularly the Rostenkowski, Bentsen, and Gephardt trade bills currently before Congress. These proposals would penalize a chronic trade-surplus nation like Japan unless it agrees to reduce its surplus with the United States by a designated amount each year. Supporters of such protectionist measures assume that a trade-surplus nation will choose to increase imports exclusively from the United States to cut its surpluses. In reality, trade-surplus nations like Japan, Taiwan, and South Korea are more likely to restrict their exports to the United States if they are forced to meet a surplus reduction target. They may also retaliate against U.S. exports. The end result will be a dramatic shrinkage of trans-Pacific and worldwide trading, which will have adverse effects for the U.S. economy as well.

Moreover, given today's multilateral, interdependent trading systems, it makes little economic sense to single out bilateral trade deficits such as the one between the United States and Japan. The trans-Pacific trading structure is already so intertwined among nations that a unilateral reduction in U.S. imports of Japanese goods could, for instance, wipe out the U.S. trade surplus with Australia. With fewer goods to export to the United States, Japan might reduce its imports of industrial raw materials from Australia. Australia, in turn, would have less to spend on goods from the United States because of reduced income from exports to Japan. All would suffer. Similarly, if Japan were to retaliate for U.S. actions by shifting its purchases of grain from the United States to Thailand, Australia, or Canada, the overall U.S. trade deficit would grow and the U.S. agricultural sector would plunge deeper into recession.

The Reagan administration is placing an increasing emphasis on talking down the dollar, not just as a way of making U.S. goods more competitive but also in the hope of forcing Japan to reflate its economy. This is proving to be counterproductive. U.S. pressure for a weaker dollar and a stronger yen plays into the very hands of those in Japan who resist any further accommodation with the United States. Rapid yen appreciation has damaged the export competitiveness of many firms and regions that make standard crafts and manufactures. Here Korea, Taiwan, Singapore, and other Asian nations whose currencies have not appreciated against the dollar now enjoy a competitive advantage. This situation has not only depressed the Japanese economy—GNP grew by only 2.5 percent in 1986, well below the 4.7 percent of the previous year—but is creating a rift between "localists" and "internationalists." Small to medium-sized manufacturers, local merchants, and employees whose export-related interests are crushed by the rising yen are joining the coalition of farmers and bureaucrats who stand to lose most by opening Japan's markets and dismantling its consumer and industrial regulations.

If the United States continues to talk down the dollar against the yen, the bureaucrat-farmer-localist alliance that holds enormous political power in Japan could very well seek retaliation against the United States, perhaps through the financial leverage Japan now wields with its massive investments in that country. If Japan were to abruptly curtail its capital outflows to the United States, this would put upward pressure on U.S. interest rates and possibly plunge the U.S. economy into a recession. For that reason, the United States needs to be more mindful of the imperiled internationalists, who are increasingly represented in the ruling Liberal Democratic party (LDP). Even though the LDP won an overwhelming victory in elections held last July, candidates in rural areas encountered heightened opposition. Liberal Democrats, as a result, are turning increasingly for support to internationalist-oriented urban voters. But continued demands on the part of the United States for export restraints and a strong yen could work against this budding realignment that, in the end, offers the best chance for improved U.S.-Japanese relations.

This is not to say that an adjustment of the dollar-yen relationship is unnecessary or unwelcome, only that it must be more carefully managed. A dollar-yen exchange rate stabilized around the 165-yen level would benefit both the United States and Japan. It would allow Tokyo to put into effect stimulative domestic measures to offset any deflationary effects of reduced export activity. And without the uncertainty that now hangs over the yen, Japanese industries would be able to plan for a more orderly expansion

19

of their overseas manufacturing and service activities, including those in the United States.

Such expanded Japanese operations in the United States would mean greater U.S. job creation and more competitive American-made products. As it is, Japanese firms lead all other foreign firms in the United States in their export of U.S.-made products, accounting for 12 percent of total exports.[31] Unfortunately, the American business and political leadership treats this expansion of Japanese business activity in the United States somewhat as an enemy invasion. Consider, for example, Congress and the Pentagon's reaction to Fujitsu's offer to purchase the ailing Fairchild Semiconductor Corporation, a subsidiary of Schlumberger Ltd. When Schlumberger, a French firm, acquired Fairchild in 1979, there was no outcry in the United States. But Fujitsu's recent offer triggered sudden concerns that the sale would jeopardize U.S. security interests, since Fairchild supplies the military with computer chips. Bowing to pressure, Fujitsu announced it would not proceed with the purchase. Ironically, this decision may now make U.S. national security even more dependent on the import of microchips, whereas Fujitsu's purchase of Fairchild might have helped bolster the company's sagging technological capabilities.

Increased Japanese business activity in the United States would also be likely to increase the sale of U.S.-made goods and services to Japanese firms operating here and to their subsidiaries abroad. This could help restore balance to multilateral trading in the Pacific Basin and throughout the world. Meanwhile, continued outflows of capital and technology from Japan to the United States would foster stronger ties between American and Japanese firms in the Pacific and elsewhere. A stable dollar-yen rate would also benefit Pacific nations who rely on Japanese purchases of their goods to service their debts. For such countries as Korea and the Philippines, which have yen-based debts, a lower yen is especially crucial if they are to avoid the austerity measures and consequent economic contraction that the high dollar has meant for Latin America — contraction that has closed one market after another to U.S. exports.

Toward a More Competitive U.S. Economy

The debate on U.S. competitiveness needs to shift its focus from Japan-bashing to the root causes of America's economic difficulties. The Japanese challenge should be met with the same seriousness that Sputnik was 30 years ago, when the Soviet satellite launching shocked the United States out of complacency. Congress and the federal government subsequently cut loose from laissez-faire dogma and initiated a nationwide effort to improve the quality of science education, to accelerate space and scientific research, and to work jointly with business and universities to put a man on the moon before the Soviet Union did. By contrast, few Americans today even recognize the seriousness of the "microchip shock" and its home-grown causes.

The United States must understand that it cannot regain its competitiveness without adopting new ways of doing business. There is nothing wrong with pressing Japan to open markets that remain closed, but the United States cannot expect simply to bully its way to competitiveness. The United States needs to recognize that it can no longer dictate the rules of international competition, especially now that it is so dependent on Japanese capital to revive its industries. In fact, by virtue of its economic efficiency and manufacturing dominance, Japanese-style strategic planning and corporate management practices are being adopted by Asia's newly industrializing countries. Rather than fight these rules, the United States would be wise to adapt them to its own particular needs.

At a minimum, a stronger government role is required to encourage more flexible and competitive behavior on the part of labor and management, to set national goals and priorities for the allocation of scarce resources, to ensure that the different components of a competitive strategy—from worker retraining to research and development—are properly funded and well coordinated with each other, and to assist those parts of the country that lag behind other parts. These are all aspects of what can be called strategic planning.

If the federal government does not assume a larger planning role, the ideas now offered for enhancing U.S. competitiveness—increasing R & D, improving education, expanding worker retraining—will not be effective. For example, unless the government sets clearer national spending priorities and cuts defense spending, the federal budget deficit cannot be reduced and capital and human resources cannot be freed to meet more urgent civilian industrial goals. Similarly, as long as lower education is financed locally, industrial dislocations and regional economic downturns will continue to devastate public schools: the federal government must take over the financial burden of primary and secondary education if there is to be much hope for improving the general educational level in this country or eliminating widespread regional differences in the quality of education. It is also clear that unless the United States accepts the goal of full employment, the best efforts at job retraining will be of little avail. Massachusetts succeeded in getting tens of thousands of welfare recipients back to work only because the state had a full-employment policy and a development plan that drew on the concentration of high-tech firms in the region.

While there is much the federal government can accomplish in these areas, there is a limit to what any government can do to remedy the uncompetitive behavior of management or labor. Nevertheless, there is no reason for government to reward uncompetitive behavior, as it now does when it offers tax and other financial incentives for hostile takeovers, stock buybacks, and leveraged buyouts. Instead, the government might consider a penalty tax on loans used for these purposes or on the resulting "greenmail" windfall profits. Once we accept the fact that taxes are not neutral, we can begin to consider such useful applications of taxes as the Polluter Pay Principle: if hostile takeovers cannot be entirely discouraged, those who engage in this and other forms of economic pollution should at least be forced to pay a price. Similar measures could be taken to discourage the hasty and needless resort to worker layoffs; for example, executive bonuses and salary increases awarded within less than three years of substantial worker layoffs could be taxed at higher rates.

The government could also use its granting of subsidies and import restrictions as a leverage point. Management, labor, banks, and suppliers of industries that seek import restrictions should be required to make their own concessions and mend their uncompetitive ways. To this end, Congress might consider empowering the International Trade Commission and the special trade representative to negotiate and oversee the implementation of plans to revive the international competitiveness of firms and other groups that seek protection, much as the courts oversee the reorganization of companies that declare bankruptcy.

Ultimately, of course, only corporations can learn to manage themselves better. Rather than knocking Japanese companies' success, U.S. firms would do better to learn from the Japanese example. This is not as alien as some would believe. American firms are already demonstrating that it is not essential to be Japanese to become competitively lean and productive. IBM, Johnson & Johnson, Procter & Gamble, Black & Decker, Lincoln Industries, and Xerox have all responded effectively to the challenge of foreign competition by making fundamental changes in corporate behavior. Black & Decker, for instance, galvanized its managers and employees to work together bringing out new products more quickly and at more competitive prices. And Xerox's copier division underwent the corporate equivalent of a cultural revolution, cutting its component rejection rate from a whopping 8,000 parts per million in the early 1980s to 1,300 parts per million by 1985.

Getting America's own house in order, of course, will not solve all the problems of U.S.-Japanese trade. But it will allow whatever trade complaints there are to be addressed on their merits. It will also facilitate the type of U.S.-Japanese cooperative management that the growing trans-Pacific economy now requires.

Notes

[1] Clyde H. Farnsworth, "Mounting Conflict over Trade Looms for U.S. and Japan," *New York Times*, March 9, 1987.
[2] C. Fred Bergsten and William R. Cline, "U.S.-Japan Economic Problems," Policy Analysis Series #13 (Washington, DC: Institute for International Economics, 1987).
[3] For a discussion of these trends, see Charles Smith, "The Yen Strikes Home," *Far Eastern Economic Review*, December 25, 1986.
[4] Clyde Haberman, "Japan Jobless Rate at Record 3%, Stirring Worries of Worse to Come," *New York Times*, March 4, 1987.
[5] "Trade Surplus of Japan Rises," *New York Times*, March 11, 1987.
[6] This analysis owes much to Peter F. Drucker's "The Changed World Economy," *Foreign Affairs*, Vol. 64, No. 4 (Spring 1986), pp. 768–791. Drucker distinguishes between the "symbol" economy and the "real" economy.
[7] Yoshi Tsurumi, "Managing Consumer and Industrial Marketing Systems in Japan," *Sloan Management Review*, Fall 1982.
[8] Nakane and Hall, "Management Specs for Stockless Production," *Harvard Business Review*, May-June 1983.
[9] Farnsworth, (fn. 1).
[10] Bergsten and Cline, (fn. 2).
[11] Yoshi Tsurumi, "The Case of Japan: Price Bargaining and Controls on Oil Products," *Journal of Comparative Economics*, No. 2 (1978), pp. 126–143.
[12] Paul Lewis, "Military Spending Questioned," *New York Times*, November 11, 1986.
[13] Yoshi Tsurumi, "The Challenge of the Pacific Age," *World Policy Journal*, Vol. 2, No. 1 (Fall 1984), pp. 72–73.
[14] Jonathan Rowe, "Why the Engineers Left the Shop Floor," *Washington Monthly*, June 1984.
[15] A 17-nation study by the U.S. Department of Education, cited in "In Math, We Don't Make Grade," *Newsday*, February 17, 1986.
[16] See Jay Stowsky, "Competing with the Pentagon," *World Policy Journal*, Vol. 3, No. 4 (Fall 1986), pp. 697–721.
[17] Hajime Karatsu, a Japanese expert on quality control, was invited by the Pentagon in April 1986 to address this issue. See Karatsu's *Amerika eno Chokugen* [Tough Words for American Industry] (Tokyo: PHP Publications, 1986).
[18] Rowe (fn. 14).
[19] David E. Sanger, "Compromise Expected on Chip Consortium," *New York Times*, March 3, 1987.

[20] "Employees Go to the Rescue," *New York Times*, August 14, 1986.

[21] Yoshi Tsurumi, "Labor Relations and Industrial Adjustment in Japan and the U.S.: A Comparative Analysis," *Yale Law & Policy Review*, Spring 1984, pp. 256–271.

[22] Winston Williams, "Corporate America Buys Itself Back," *New York Times*, August 17, 1986.

[23] Quoted in Rowe (fn. 14).

[24] Tsurumi (fn. 7).

[25] Yoshi Tsurumi, *Sogoshosha* (Montreal: Institute on Public Policies, second edition, 1984).

[26] Charles F. McCoy, "Sears to Close Part of World Trade Unit, Underscoring Dismal Picture for Exports," *Wall Street Journal*, October 29, 1986.

[27] Yoshi Tsurumi, "Explaining the 'Japanese Paradox': Made in America, Managed by Japan," *New York Times*, November 16, 1986.

[28] Al Blik, "What Japanese Firms in the U.S. Think of Labor," *New York Times*, February 11, 1982; "Factory Magic in a Plant in Memphis, Japanese Firms Show How to Attain Quality," *Wall Street Journal*, April 29, 1983.

[29] Yoshi Tsurumi, "Congress Urged Not to Push for Continued Voluntary Export Restraints on Japanese Automobiles," *Pacific Basin Quarterly*, No. 12 (Spring-Summer 1985).

[30] "The Consumer Cost of U.S. Trade Restraints," *Quarterly Review*, New York: Federal Reserve Bank, Vol. 10, No. 2 (Summer 1985); Gary Hufbauer, *Trade Protection in the U.S.* (Washington, DC: Institute for International Economics, 1986).

[31] *Handbook on U.S.-Japan Economic Relations* (Tokyo: Japan Trade Center, 1985).

2 RECORDING AND DIAGNOSING INTERNATIONAL TRANSACTIONS

1. WHAT IS MULTINATIONAL MANAGEMENT?

Multinational management can best be understood by clarifying what we mean by management and then identifying how these management functions should be refined to meet the challenges of multinational business. Managers deploy such scarce managerial resources as capital, foreign exchange, technology, manpower, and industrial raw materials (purchases from outside their firm) to a limited number of specific business activities according to priorities dictated by the competitive business environment. At any given time, managers must have in mind clear-cut strategies and a keen sense of timing to be able to carry out these allocation problems.

Problems invariably arise for managers as the firm grapples with the disparity between its collective ability to produce and deliver goods and services and the conditions of the outside world—those political, economic, and social elements that constitute the firm's broadly defined "market." Accordingly, managers must recognize the gap between the firm's ability to produce and the outside environment's demand. Managers must evaluate and ultimately choose the interim solution that would be the most appropriate for the company's continued success.

In order to hone this skill, managers must begin by understanding the dynamic changes in their business environment and then assessing the shortcomings of available managerial resources to cope with changes in that environment. Furthermore, managers can evaluate and implement the appropriate solutions only with the help of their staff. In the final analysis, interpersonal skills including consulting, motivating, and learning from and developing other persons are among the most important acquired attributes of any manager.

What is multinational about management functions? The business environment that any firm, small or large, faces today is global. No company can remain immune to political, economic, and social changes anywhere in the world. Technological innovations in the areas of transportation and communication have reduced the physical distance of travel and transport of goods and communication. In the years to come, we can count on further shortening of this distance as the technological frontiers of transportation and communication expand. Furthermore, we are already witnessing recurring, acute shortages of technology, capital, natural resources, managerial skills, and other necessary elements of sustained industrial and mercantile growth. These worldwide shortages have made all nations far more interdependent than ever before.

Any example of this interdependency is an incident that occurred in a remote corner of the world and that came to haunt small, "papa-mama" soybean cake (tofu) peddlers tucked away in the neighborhood alleys of Japanese towns and villages. From 1971 to 1972, schools of anchovies (miniature herring) suddenly disappeared from the familiar fishing grounds off the Chilean coast. The anchovy fishermen were, of course, the first to be hardest hit. Then the effect spread to American manufacturers who used to import and grind the dried anchovies into cheap protein additives for animal feed. Feed makers scrambled for the next cheapest source of protein additives—soybeans. A sudden increase in demand for American soybeans drove up the world price of this commodity, to the wrath of animal feed manufacturers and cattle farmers who had successfully lobbied then President Nixon to impose an embargo on American soybean exports. Japan, which still relied on soybean-related foods for a substantial portion of her population's daily protein intake, was next to suffer from the shortage.

Not only did the price of soybean cakes soar beyond the reach of Japan's general population, but it created a near crisis since the sheer physical shortage of soybeans drove many "papa-mama" soybean cake makers to bankruptcy. The boomerang effect did not end there. This sudden embargo of the leading U.S. export commodity further weakened the U.S. dollar and aggravated stagflation in the United States.

In the 1980s and 1990s, we will frequently witness similar incidents. We may not be able to prevent such events from happening, but we can certainly avoid spreading such repercussions from one industry to another and from one country to another. All that it would take is a better understanding of the delicate balance in which the world economic and political systems coexist. There is no longer any nation or company that can indulge in the obsolete and imaginary dichotomy of domestic and foreign markets. All industrial and merchantile activities are not only economically interrelated but also globally interdependent.

We do not have to look far to find examples of how managers' self-serving views of the separateness of domestic and foreign markets have inflicted a severe blow. From 1979 to 1981, amidst Chrysler's deepening crisis and Ford's near crisis, the United States braced itself for the end of two of the "Big Three" automakers. In fact, as late as 1979, American auto manufacturers and their observers habitually talked of the Big Three and ascribed 100 percent of the auto market to them—with 55 percent, 30 percent, and 15 percent going to General Motors, Ford, and Chrysler, respectively—as if the world auto industry in general and the American auto market in particular consisted only of these three firms. Consequently, it was no surprise when the Big Three that once dominated the world automobile industry were caught unprepared by the persistent shift in American consumer demand from large cars to fuel efficient subcompacts. The demand gap left untouched by the Big Three was filled by Japanese imports.

2. THE FUNCTIONS OF MULTINATIONAL BUSINESS

Since 1978 the United States has embarked on a Pacific Age. Pacific Asian connections have become the leading trading partners and markets for U.S. exports and imports. Many in business, political, academic, and journalistic circles in the United States, however, have remained unaware of this fundamental turn of events. With this shift in exports and imports of agricultural commodities as well as manufactured goods, the banking community in the United States began to adjust its focus toward exploiting growing opportunities in the Pacific Basin. This turnabout took place before the People's Republic of China became an active participant in Pacific Basin trade. Now and in the future, managers must be on the lookout for the opportunities and challenges posed by this Pacific Age.

27

Let us identify the key functions of multinational business using a condensed version of the least complex international venture: importing purchases from foreign countries for resale purposes. Mary Anne Peterson established her own business in 1982, importing women's apparel made of Indonesian batik to New York City. Until then she had built a successful ten-year career as chief buyer of women's fashion with a leading department store in New York. She rented an office and warehouse combination in Long Island City (just across the East River from Manhattan) for $1,500 a month plus utilities. She hired Sally Sanchez for $250 a week as the secretary-clerk who would handle correspondence and order processing. For the initial capital of the firm, Peterson put up her personal savings of $15,000 and her used Chevy van valued at $4,000. In addition, she borrowed $30,000 yen equivalent at the prevailing rate of 240 yen (¥) to 1 U.S. dollar from her Japanese friend in Tokyo, Jiro Tanaka. The loan was to be denominated in Japanese yen and carried an interest rate of 12 percent per year on the unpaid balance, payable in yen. The loan principal was to be paid back in five equal installments due in five years starting in 1983.

Peterson also made an arrangement with an Indonesian friend, Uben Parhusip, who had studied with Peterson in the United States and who subsequently returned to Jakarta, where his father handled exports and imports of manufactured goods and agricultural commodities. Parhusip would ship Peterson's purchases, c.i.f. New York. In order to finance the letter of credit (L/C) for the imports, Peterson arranged a $100,000 revolving line of credit with Citibank, N.Y. at 3 percentage points above the prevailing prime rate.

Managers like Peterson, Tanaka, and Parhusip must always hold a realistic picture of the rate and direction of change in the economic value of their venture. Since their own economic and personal fortunes are closely tied to the performance of Peterson's company, they should all want to know how well or how poorly the firm has performed so far and how it could and should improve its economic performance in the future. This task requires that managers be able to intelligently read two basic financial statements: the balance sheet (B/S) and the profit and loss (P/L) statement. These financial records are twins born of the systematic recording of economic transactions of the firm. To read and analyze these statements, managers must know how they are compiled according to the basic rules of the "double entry" method of accounting.

The double entry accounting method was invented by Catholic monks in Renaissance Italy and was refined by the great houses of international business of the period, the Rothschilds and the Medicis.

These European practices were brought to the United States by immigrants long before the American Revolution. Japan formally adopted this method in the 1920s, long after the industrial and mercantile activities of Japanese firms had become too complex to be recorded by the traditional single entry accounting method. Today, many developing nations are now adopting the double entry bookkeeping method.

3. EVALUATION OF THE ECONOMIC PERFORMANCE OF A FIRM

Step 1: Selecting Accounting (Reporting) Period

Peterson created her new firm on July 1, 1982. Now it is January 1983. To discover how well her firm has fared during the past year, she should arbitrarily select a time period during which her firm was in operation and summarize all of the company's economic transactions during this period into a balance sheet and profit and loss statement.

In this case, the economic performance of Peterson's company from July 1, 1982 through December 31, 1982 should be reviewed as if her firm "died" on the last day of the year. When a firm is in fact a going concern, it is theoretically killed from time to time just to close the book on it. The balance sheet reveals how large the firm's assets and liabilities were on balance as of December 31, 1982. The profit and loss statement shows how much profit (or loss) the firm made from July 1 to December 31, 1982.

Step 2: Double Entry Bookkeeping

Each economic transaction (sales, purchases, borrowing, etc.) *always* involves two "offsetting" transactions, for example, the sale of goods and the receipt of payment for that sale. When we know from the outset that there are always two offsetting entries for each economic transaction, it is expedient to record them from the beginning under two separate headings or accounts. For example, if on October 1, 1982 Peterson's company sold $100 worth of merchandise and received $100 in cash payment at the same time, $100 should be entered in the "sales account" and another $100 in the "cash account." On which side of sales and cash accounts should this $100 be entered?

For each account, two opposite types of transactions should be recorded: debits and credits or "in" and "out." Imagine that the cash account is a cash register. You put money into the register and also take it out of the register.

Rule 1: The cash account should be divided into a T-shaped space. The left hand side (debit entry) denotes an "in" action and the right hand side (credit) an "out" action.

Rule 2: Since Peterson's cash receipt of $100 should be entered on the left hand side of the cash account, the firm had no choice but to enter $100 of sales on the right hand side of sales account. When it is not clear whether or not a specific transaction should be recorded on the right hand side or left hand side of any account, it is best to imagine the simplest cash transaction and check the entry in the cash account first as "in" or "out." Then you know your correct offsetting entry in the other account is on the opposite side of the cash entry.

If, for example, M Company paid its April telephone bill with $200 cash, the following entry should be made:

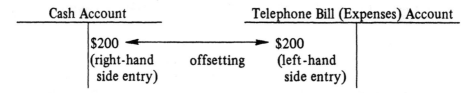

Cash Account		Telephone Bill (Expenses) Account
$200 (right-hand side entry)	offsetting	$200 (left-hand side entry)

Rule 3: When you do not know the name of an appropriate account to record certain transactions, you should feel free to create one. For your convenience, however, try to create some general heading (account) such as Office Equipment rather than one with too finely defined products such as Typewriter.

For each economic transaction, continue to record the date of the transaction and two offsetting entries in two separate accounts. This procedure is called "journalizing" in accountants' jargon. Some economic transactions are straightforward; others have to be estimated. For example, the wear and tear of the Chevy van that Peterson used for transporting imported merchandise will have to be estimated for the accounting period. This expense is called "depreciation" and should be arithmetically estimated by the firm. To approximate this noncash expense the company has to select a depreciation method. This method assumes that the value of the equipment declines every year by a constant amount. The amount is arrived at by dividing the depreciable value (the initial value minus the estimated salvage value at the end of the depreciation period) by the number of depreciation periods.

As of December 31, 1982 (or any other date you choose) you will choose the accounts and compile the balance sheet and profit and loss statement.

Rule 1: All accounts that are related to sales, costs, expenses (including depreciation charges), and resultant profit figures should be compiled in the profit and loss statement.

Rule 2: The remaining accounts must then be related to assets and liabilities and capital accounts (including profit for the period and retained earnings up to that period).

Rule 3: In order to estimate the cost of goods sold, you will need three figures: beginning inventory, purchases during the period, and final inventory.

After physically counting the ending inventory, and estimating it as the summation of physical value, we make the adjustment shown in Table 2-1.

According to the accounting convention, any loans and unpaid expenses that mature within one year of the date of the balance sheet are treated as short-term liabilities. Any debts that do not fall due within one year are treated as long-term liabilities.

4. THE ECONOMIC PERFORMANCE OF PETERSON'S FIRM

By applying these rules, we can compile the balance sheet and profit and loss statement of Peterson's company for the year 1982. Just to round out the economic transactions of the firm, let us assume the following additional information for the period July 1 to December 31, 1982.

1. Purchases (imports) from Parhusip totaled $80,000, c.i.f. N.Y.;
2. Custom clearing fees of $1,200 paid in cash;
3. Sales to specialty fashion stores in New York area, $145,000 (all but $45,000 paid by December 1980);
4. The Japanese yen depreciated to ¥280 to $1.00 by December 31, 1982;
5. The company borrowed $90,000 from Citibank on October 15 to finance the L/C (import payments) at 18 percent per year and the entire amount will be due on January 15, 1983;

Table 2-1. Filing Financial Statements: A Presentational Format.

<table>
<tr><th colspan="4">Inventory Account</th></tr>
<tr><td>Beginning inventory</td><td>$100</td><td rowspan="2">(Beginning inventory + Purchases
– Ending inventory = Cost of goods
sold) $100 + $500 – $50 = $550</td></tr>
<tr><td>Purchases totaled</td><td>$500</td></tr>
<tr><td>Ending inventory</td><td>$ 50</td><td></td></tr>
</table>

Typical profit and loss statement
From July 1, 1982 to December 31, 1982
(always from one date to another)

Sales	xxx
Cost of goods sold	xx
Gross profits	xx
Administrative and sales expenses	
Salaries and wages	xxx
Utilities	xx
Telephone and mail	xx
Advertising	xx
– – – – – – – –	
Depreciation	xx
Interest	
Profit before taxes	xx
Taxes paid	xx
Profit after taxes*	xx

*to be added to the retained earnings
of the balance sheet after deducting
dividends paid, if any.

Typical balance sheet As of December 31, 1982
(always as of a certain date)

Assets		*Liabilities*	
Cash	xx	Accounts payable	xx
Accounts receivable	xx	Short term loan	xx
Inventory	xx	Unpaid expenses and taxes	xx
Current assets	xx	Current liabilities	
Fixed assets (buildings and equipment, etc.)	xx	Long term loans	xxx
		Capital	
		Paid in capital	xxx
		Retained earnings	xxx
Total assets	xxx	Total liabilities and capital	xxx

6. Repairs, gasoline, and insurance bills for the Chevy van came to $4,300 (all but $700 paid by December 31, 1982);
7. Utilities and heating bills were $2,400 (all but $200 were paid by the end of the year;
8. Typewriter rental was $100 a month, paid in cash; telephone, telegrams, and mailing costs were $5,600 (all but $600 were paid by December 31, 1982);
9. Peterson withdrew $15,000 from the firm as her salary;
10. The depreciation method chosen for the Chevy van was the five-year straight line method with no salvage value assumed;
11. On December 31, 1982, Peterson actually took an inventory of the imported merchandise that remained unsold; they were valued at $12,000 purchase price.

Sample journalized records are produced in Table 2-2.

Table 2-2. Sample Journalized Records.

Date	Accounts	Debit (Left side)	Credit (Right side)
7/1/82	Cash	15,000	
	Capital (Peterson)		15,000
7/1/82	Vehicle	4,000	
	Capital (Peterson)		4,000
7/1/82	Cash	30,000	
	Long-term loans (Tanaka)		30,000
7/1/82– 12/31/82	Cash	90,000	
	Bank loans (Citibank)		90,000
	Imports (purchases)	80,000	
	Cash (payment to Parhusip)		80,000
7/1/82– 12/31/82	Interest (owed to Citibank)	3,375	
	Accrued interest		3,375
7/1/82– 12/31/82	Cash	100,000	
	Accounts receivable	45,000	
	Sales		145,000
7/1/82– 12/31/82	Vehicle expenses	4,300	
	Cash		3,600
	Accounts payable		700
7/1/82– 12/31/82	Utilities	2,400	
	Cash		2,200
	Unpaid expenses		200

5. ANYTHING INTERNATIONAL?

The preceding recording for Peterson Company do not account for anything particularly international in nature. This should not surprise anyone. The managerial skills of international business consist of everything required for performing domestic business and something additional that is inherent in international business transactions.

Peterson Company launched its wholesale women's apparel business successfully only because the founder accomplished the following things: First, Mary Anne Peterson was quick to sense that the urban customers of women's fashion were increasingly attracted to the mystique of the Orient, and she had realized that the traditional Indonesian batik designs could be adapted to modern fashion. Second, she knew that Indonesia would be the most suitable supplier in terms of production costs and availability of indigenous batik making—in economists' jargon, the most "efficient" supplier of internationally traded products. Third, she recognized that her unique strength, relative to Indonesians for example, was that she had intimate knowledge of the ins and outs of the women's fashion business in New York. Besides, she had accumulated valuable business contacts among potential buyers of women's fashions in and around New York. In addition, Peterson had the rare advantage of knowing Uben Parhusip. To exploit her advantages in the New York market with the Indonesian suppliers before competitors beat her to it, she had to move quickly.

Peterson had known for some time that she did not have to limit the funding sources of her new venture in the United States. Foreign currencies such as the Japanese yen and the Deutsche mark were easily converted into U.S. dollars in New York. She also knew that in 1982 Japan had much lower interest rates than did the United States. Luckily, she was able to persuade Jiro Tanaka in Tokyo to loan her $30,000 at 12 percent a year, which was higher than what he would earn by investing in Japan but lower than the prevailing interest rate in New York.

The final step for ensuring the success of Peterson's venture was to set up detailed transportation arrangements for the batik apparel, which would be sewn according to the designs supplied by Peterson. All of the cumbersome problems of controlling product quality and guaranteeing timely delivery to the port of New York would be handled by Uben Parhusip. The remaining details of financing the imports through letters of credit and clearing the shipments through U.S. Customs were managed by Citibank and any one of the forwarders (customs agents) listed in the Yellow Pages of the Manhattan Telephone Directory.

A letter of credit is a device through which a bank in Indonesia designated by Citibank (probably Citibank's Jakarta branch) guarantees the payments to Uben Parhusip (the exporter). The necessary financing would be arranged between Citibank in New York and Peterson Company. From the point of view of the exporter, it merely allows the financial risks of the foreign customer (Peterson) to be assumed by a well-known financial institution. The recent spread of worldwide branch networks of U.S., European, Japanese, and other multinational banks have eased export–import financing even for fledgling firms like Peterson Company.

This hypothetical narrative illustrates the basic managerial skills inherent in international business. Above all, the manager has to expand his or her business horizon beyond the home base even while seeking new domestic opportunities. Once this basic attitude is learned, the manager must investigate both potential markets for their products and services and the best possible suppliers. Managers also must develop a keen interest in foreign culture and international economic and political affairs. Compared with managers who ignore the international marketplace, global-minded entrepreneurs like Mary Anne Peterson would survive better even in domestic market competition.

Familiarity with export–import procedures, letter of credit financing, and customs clearances can easily be gained by reading pamphlets available through a number of multinational banks. Abbreviations such as f.o.b., f.a.b., c.i.f., L/C, D/A, and D/P can easily be added to a manager's vocabulary. Definitions of the most commonly used abbreviations are as follows:

Free on Board (f.o.b.) or Free Alongside Board (f.a.b.): Sometimes called ex-factory or ex-country price, this is the sales price of merchandise quoted before transportation and other charges are added. If you buy foreign merchandise f.o.b., you are responsible for paying for the necessary transportation and other costs to bring it to your place.

Cost, Insurance, and Freight (c.i.f.): This is sometimes called landed value at the port of entry of foreign merchandise. If the price is quoted as c.i.f. New York, the price includes the merchandise plus transportation and shipping charges to bring the product to New York. Import tariffs, if any, and custom clearing charges at the port of entry are additional expenses usually borne by the importer.

35

Documents Against Acceptance (D/A) and Documents Against Payments (D/P): These designations indicate the terms of how the shipment is going to be physically released to the importer by the shipper (and its designated warehouse). The D/A designation permits the importer to take possession of the shipment merely on his or her acceptance and subsequent presentation of such bills as bills of lading or marine insurance certificates. The D/P designation requires that the importer pay for the shipment before taking possession of it. Accordingly, depending upon the exporter's evaluation of the importer's credit, the exporter may require either D/A or D/P release condition. The exporter is free to sell or ship the merchandise on "open account" by mailing all of the necessary documents in toto to the importer in advance. Exporting on open account is functionally the same as selling on credit domestically. The exporter assumes all the risk of collecting the payment from the buyer.

Documentation procedures and preparation of necessary papers can be easily subcontracted to forwarders for a fee or may be mastered after some practice with sample documents by any secretary-clerk. Transportation firms can also teach how to prepare necessary export–import documents. This kind of factual knowledge is easy for a manager to learn.

6. RISKS OF INTERNATIONAL BUSINESS

Is the Peterson Company fail-safe? Is the 12 percent annual interest rate of the original $30,000 loan really cheap when both interest payments and principal amortization are made in Japanese yen?

Peterson Company successfully exploited business opportunities that were opened up and expanded by import strategies. However, as profit opportunities increase so do business risks. Peterson Company is now exposed to the political and economic risks associated with Japan and Indonesia, which provide its financing and supply its products. In addition, there are risks inherent in the political and economic systems of the United States, where Peterson is operating. The art of managing these other risks is the secret of multinational management.

When Peterson Company expanded its business horizon to Indonesia and Japan, it exposed itself to the opportunities and risks associated with the fluctuations in the Indonesian rupiah and the Japanese yen vis-à-vis the U.S. dollar. In fact, this kind of direct exposure to foreign exchange fluctuations versus the domestic currency of the firm separates fundamentally domestic from international operations. Therefore, global-minded managers must familiarize themselves with the ways in which the fluctuations of foreign exchange rates affect their overall business performance (see Chapter 3).

When we record (journalize) the economic transactions of Peterson Company, we must record $4,286 in foreign exchange gains. In Chapter 3 we will deal with the foreign exchange market and the balance of payments, which managers must master if they are to become successful international business operators. In the example of Peterson's company, the $4,286 foreign exchange gains were made when the Japanese yen depreciated from 240 yen per U.S. dollar in July 1982 to 280 yen per U.S. dollar by December 31, 1982 and when Peterson's debts to Tanaka in Tokyo were denominated in Japanese yen and not in U.S. dollars.

Tanaka loaned Peterson Company ¥7,200,000, which the company converted into $30,000 at the then prevailing exchange (spot rate) of ¥240 to U.S. $1.00. When this spot rate changed to ¥280 to U.S. $1.00 by December 31, 1982, the original debt of ¥7,200,000 became the equivalent of $25,714. In other words, Peterson would have needed $4,286 less than the initial dollar equivalent of $30,000 if the firm had to pay back the debt immediately. The foreign exchange loss on the principal of the loan denominated in the currency of the creditor is computed as follows:

$$\left(\frac{L}{S_x} - \frac{L}{S_f} \right)$$

where

L = the initial amount of the loan denominated in the currency of the creditor;

S_x = the spot exchange rate (the prevailing exchange rate) at the time of the loan transaction between the currency of the creditor and the currency of the debtor; and

S_f = the spot exchange rate prevailing at the final period of the debtor's fiscal year (the last date of compiling the balance sheet) or at the time of loan repayment.

Tanaka also requested that his interest earnings be paid in Japanese yen. While the interest rate remained at 12 percent per year, it was 12 percent of ¥7,200,000, not of $30,000. Accordingly, in addition to the foreign exchange gain, Peterson's interest payment obligations in terms of U.S. dollars decreased on paper in absolute amount when the Japanese yen became cheaper with respect to the U.S. dollar.

According to the standard recording form of the double entry bookkeeping method, we record the foreign exchange gains (on paper) and accrued interest payment obligations of Peterson to Tanaka as follows:

	Debit	Credit
December 31, 1982		
Foreign exchange gains		$4,286
Long-term debt	$4,286	
Interests	$1,542	
Accrued interest		$1,542

Readers should be able to compile the profit and loss statement and balance sheet of Peterson Company by transferring all the journalized entry records respectively to either one of these two financial statements. Tables 2-3 and 2-4 summarize them.

Table 2-3. Peterson Company's Profit and Loss Statement (from July 1, 1982 to December 31, 1982).

Sales	$145,000	
Cost of goods sold	68,000	
Gross profit	77,000	
Sales and general administrative		
General expenses:		
Salaries	15,000	
Wages	6,500	
Vehicle	4,300	
Depreciation	400	
Custom Clearance	1,200	
Typewriter	600	
Telephone, etc.	5,600	
Rent	9,000	
Utilities	2,400	$45,000
Financial expenses:		
Interests		4,917
Profit before taxes		27,083
Taxes at 30% rate		8,125
		(to be paid in 1983)
Profit after taxes		18,958
Dividends		0
To be added to retained earnings of the balance sheet		$18,958
Foreign exchange gains (to be added to retained earnings)		4,286

Table 2-4. Peterson Company's Balance Sheet (as of December 31, 1982).

Cash	$111,900	Accounts payable	$ 1,500
Accounts receivable	45,000	Bank loans	90,000
Inventory	12,000	Unpaid interest	4,917
		Unpaid taxes	8,125
Current assets	168,900	Current liabilities	104,542
Fixed assets	3,600	Long-term debts	25,714
		Capital	19,000
		Retained earnings	23,244
Total assets	172,500	Total liabilities and capital	172,500

7. BREAK EVEN AND CASH FLOW ANALYSIS

Peterson Company made a $23,244 net profit ($18,958 of cash profit and $4,286 of a paper profit) for the first six months of its operation. If the firm can accomplish at least a similar feat in 1983, it can theoretically expect to have the projected "cash inflow" of $47,288 [($23,244 of net profit + $400 of depreciation) × 2 to annualize the six-month figure]. When this projected cash inflow is added to the beginning cash position of $111,900 and to the expected collection of $45,000 of accounts receivable during 1983, the firm seems to have adequate cash inflows to cover the outstanding current liabilities of $104,542.

If we want to check just how vulnerable Peterson Company may be to sales fluctuations, we can apply simple break even point analysis to the basic economics of the firm. As usual, let us lump together the fixed costs and expenses that do not seem to vary with the level of business activities such as sales level. In the case of Peterson Company, sales and administrative expenses plus interest payments minus $400 of depreciation (the only noncash fixed expense) appear to be fixed for the next twelve months of operation. Accordingly, the annual fixed expenses are estimated at $99,834 ($49,917 × 2) if Peterson does not add any new fixed expenses such as new salaried sales personnel. If the firm maintains the same percentage of gross sales margin (the ratio of gross profits to sales, 53 percent, also called contribution to sales dollar) the firm will have to generate at least $188,366 ($99,834 divided by 0.53) of sales in 1983 merely to break even, indicating that $188,366 of sales are required to cover the fixed and variable costs of the firm.

Assuming about a 15 percent rise in fixed costs due to inflation, and that the firm cannot pass these cost increases to its customers

39

through increased prices of its batik merchandise (a reasonable assumption for a small firm like Peterson operating in a brutally competitive market), the break even sales for 1983 are projected at around $216,620. This is how to arrive at the estimate of the minimum sales target that serves as a sales planning guide for 1983.

8. CURRENCY RISKS: A BUSINESS OPPORTUNITY

International business managers like Peterson should realize that the increased risks of currency fluctuations can be managed and simultaneously turned into expanded business opportunities. All that Mary Anne Peterson must do now is to generate earnings denominated in Japanese yen. How? Export sales of Indonesian batik apparel to Japan would be ideal. The increased earnings from these exports could be used to pay back Tanaka's loans plus interest. By matching the yen denominated debt obligations with the yen denominated revenues, Peterson can become free from the risks associated with the fluctuations of the yen to U.S. dollar rate. Furthermore, if and when the Indonesian rupiah depreciates, Peterson can negotiate anew with Parhusip to request more supplies for a given dollar-based amount of purchases (imports) from Indonesia. At minimum, once she recognizes the economic impact of the appreciating yen aupon her profit performance, Peterson can increase her sales target in the United States to cover higher currency risks.

The heightened risks of international business are also the source of additional business opportunities. The import strategy that Peterson used to expand the firm's profit opportunities in the United States soon motivates the company to the next stage in multinational management – export–import activities. Further risks and opportunities associated with exports are also likely to encourage the firm to expand its stake in international business by engaging in direct management of manufacturing, marketing, and other service activities abroad (foreign direct investment).

9. A FULLY GROWN MULTINATIONAL FIRM

Limited as it was, Peterson Company exploited its relatively unique strength vis-à-vis American and foreign competitors to develop a profitable business. Once the firm acquires the managerial skill to handle expanded opportunities and risks of the import business, it is likely to be lured into exports. Export–import activities are likely to lead the firm into the third stage of multinational activities: foreign direct investment.

However, Peterson Company may not be able to move up the ladder of international business automatically. What is required of the firm at the various stages of international activities is distinctly different from one stage to the next. Even if the firm chooses to remain as an importer or at any other stage, its capacity invariably weakens as more and more competitors catch up. Accordingly, to preserve the firm's position, perpetual updating and expansion of its strength are necessary for various stages of international operations.

When a firm becomes fully multinational, it acquires the following characteristics. It operates manufacturing, marketing, and other activities directly in more than one country on the basis of common strategies and a common pool of such crucial resources as management skills, technology, capital, and foreign exchange.

To manage a multitude of risks associated with a wide range of business activities across many national boundaries, the multinational firm has to train its managers and even rank and file employees to develop a strong interest in political, social, economic, and cultural affairs of the key foreign countries in which the firm is involved. Otherwise, the company will find it difficult to readily identify the rippling effect that sudden political, economic, and natural occurrences anywhere in the world have on the economic performance of a business. These sudden shocks are also compounded by the company's competitors at home and overseas.

EXERCISE QUESTIONS

1. What is the management function? What are the minimum requisite skills that managers must acquire? What are the additional skills that multinational managers should acquire?

2. Why are the risks of international business likely to offer business opportunities?

3. Explain the following terms. What kind of international trading risks (collection of payments, pricing fluctuations, etc.) are mitigated by the uses of the following devices?

    a. f.o.b. (or f.a.b.) pricing;
    b. c.i.f. pricing;
    c. D/A account transactions;
    d. D/P account transactions;
    e. open account transactions;
    f. L/C transactions

4. In the fall of 1982, the Mexican government successively devalued the peso vis-à-vis the U.S. dollar. Johnson & Johnson, a leading pharmaceutical firm based in New Jersey, had outstanding accounts receivable with its Mexican subsidiary. If these accounts receivable were denominated in the Mexican peso, who absorbed the currency fluctuation losses?

5. Analyze the international business problems of the attached case, *Pacific Trading Company*.

   Follow the recording examples of Peterson Company, and compile the profit and loss statement and the balance sheet of Pacific Trading Company. Identify and evaluate the risks and opportunities inherent in the ways in which Pacific Trading Company set up its business operations and financial structure. What should the firm do to improve its business performance?

CASE 1:
PACIFIC TRADING COMPANY

On April 1, 1978, Josef Devonski and his younger brother, Malcom, founded Pacific Trading Co. in East Los Angeles, California. For the initial capital of the firm, Josef put up his savings of $4,000 and Malcom contributed his personal savings of $2,000. In addition, Josef contributed his electric typewriter that was valued at $1,000. Malcom's VW van, valued at $4,000, was also contributed as a payment in kind to the initial capital of the firm. Josef also paid the lawyer's fees of $1,000 for registering Pacific Trading Co. incorporated as a California-based corporation. This fee was to be amortized as soon as possible once the firm got off the ground. Josef's contribution of $1,000 was credited to his share of the initial capital of the firm. The ownership of the firm was equally divided between the two brothers.

In order to augment the fund available to the firm, Josef borrowed from his old friend in Japan, Akai, the U.S. dollar equivalent of $50,000 (Akai's loan in the Japanese yen was converted early in April 1978, at the rate of ¥240 to the U.S. dollar). Akai's loan was to be paid in five years with one year of deferred payment. Annual interest rate of the loan was agreed to be at 11 percent on the unpaid balance. Both principal and interest payments were to fall due in the Japanese yen once a year on the anniversary of the loan agreement, April 10.

Pacific Trading Co. was the importer of ladies' dresses, skirts, men's shirts, and other specialty apparel made of Indonesian batik. Josef and Malcom had known for some time that Indonesia produced batik cloths of very fine quality. Lately, batik craft industries of Indonesia were also producing silk batik in addition to traditional cotton cloth batik. However, their designs were very much tradition bound and were dominated by dark colored patterns. However, Josef

goal

and Malcom believed that modern designs and colors could be applied to batik without losing enough of the Indonesian traditional touch.

From December 1977 through February 1978, both Josef and Malcom visited Indonesia, Malaysia, and Singapore, searching local merchant-entrepreneurs who would produce batik apparel to fit the modern designs and patterns. Josef and Malcom were to supply the local producers with modern designs and patterns which Josef and Malcom believed would go very well with the upper middle class clients of fashion retail chains in southern California. All the travel expenses, which came to $5,000 for the two brothers, were to be carried over to the Pacific Trading Co. as organizational expenses of the firm. Meanwhile, this sum was to be treated as owed to Josef and Malcom.

Fortunately, Josef and Malcom found a local merchant, Hoki Tanunjaya, in an old part of Jakarta, Kota, who graduated from a leading business school in the United States. He was starting up his own exporting firm. Hoki was to purchase necessary cotton and silk cloths locally which would, in turn, be dyed according to the designs supplied by Pacific Trading Co. All the necessary batik dyeing and subsequent sewing operations were to be subcontracted out to Indonesian housewives in and around Jakarta and JogJakarta on a piece rate arrangement. Then, Hoki was to have all the merchandise crated and shipped, c.i.f. Long Beach, California, to Pacific Trading Co. All the necessary forwarding and shipping arrangements including cumbersome custom house procedures in Indonesia were to be handled by Hoki. All the payments to Hoki were to be negotiated every year. Once agreed upon, the payments were to be made in U.S. dollars.

On the confirmation of Hoki's loading the merchandises to freighters bound for Long Beach by a Jakarta branch of American or Japanese banks, Hoki was to be paid 90 percent of value of merchandises previously agreed upon between Hoki and Pacific plus necessary shipping and insurance costs. The remaining 10 percent was to be released by the bank to Hoki upon Pacific's acceptance of the merchandises. Pacific had two weeks after its inspection of the merchandises to file necessary claims, if any, with the bank that in turn held the remaining 10 percent of total value of the shipped merchandises as a buffer against possible claim settlements. In order to pay for the imports from Indonesia, Pacific arranged revolving short-term line of credit of $100,000 for six months with a medium-sized American bank headquartered in Los Angeles.

Don't use "shouldn't have..."

In order to make the deadline for Christmas sale stockups of most retail stores, all the merchandises needed to be shipped to Long Beach by the end of October 1978. This meant that Pacific needed to place a firm order of merchandises from Hoki before the end of June 1978. Partly emboldened by $30,000 (ex-Pacific) worth of orders that Josef and Malcom were able to sign up in the Los Angeles area by mid-June 1978, Pacific committed itself to $100,000 worth of batik dresses and shirts, c.i.f. Long Beach by the end of June 1978. Then, Josef and Malcom spent from July through October for drumming up additional sales of about $90,000. They hoped that last minute sales work would sell off the entire *goal* merchandises before Christmas 1978. Pacific intended to make about 50 percent markups on the imported value of merchandises.

During the first week of January 1979, Josef and Malcom were wondering how well or badly they had fared in 1978. They were hoping that the profit and loss statement and balance sheet of the firm for 1978 would help them plan a new strategy to improve the firm's performance in 1979. This was particularly important because orders for summer fashion sales had to be placed with Hoki before the end of February. Josef and Malcom were also wondering how the strength of the U.S. dollar vis-à-vis the Japanese yen and the Indonesian rupiah would affect their business. Indonesia devalued its rupiah by 50 percent suddenly in November 1978 from Rps. 415 to Rps. 625 per U.S. dollar. The Japanese yen appreciated rapidly from the second to the fourth quarter of 1978, reaching 175 yen to the U.S. dollar in the end of October. On December 31, 1978, the yen spot rate was hovering at 195 yen to the U.S. dollar. Many businesses were predicting that the yen would further appreciate to ¥180 to the U.S. dollar by the summer of 1979.

Before Josef and Malcom were there following piles of receipts, bills, and other records of their business transactions from April 1 through December 31, 1978. The balance of their firm's checking account showed, as of the end of December 1978, $58,220.

1. Received $100,000, c.i.f. Long Beach, worth of merchandises on October 20, 1978. Custom clearance and warehousing at Long Beach cost $280 which Pacific paid in check. Merchandises were found to meet the expected quality and Malcom moved the merchandise by VW van to Pacific's store room adjacent to its office in East Los Angeles.

2. In order to pay Hoki on September 1, 1978, a line of credit of $100,000 was fully utilized at the annual interest rate of 12 percent falling due together with the full repayment of the loan. The breakdowns of the total value of the shipment were as follows: merchandise ($85,000) and insurance, transportation, and handlings ($15,000).

3. On November 2, 1978, Pacific delivered $30,000 (ex-Pacific) to Brentwood Fashion Store on thirty-day payment term. On December 15, Pacific received a full payment of $30,000 from the store.

4. On November 20, Westwood Batik purchased $20,000 (ex-Pacific) worth of women's dresses and shirts on sixty-day payment term.

5. On December 1, Pacific sold $60,000 (ex-Pacific) worth of merchandise to a large chain of fashion stores in southern California on sixty-day payment term.

6. On December 10, Josef and Malcom delivered $10,000 worth of merchandise (ex-Pacific) for $7,000 to a dry good broker in Los Angeles who drove a hard bargain in exchange for outright cash payment.

7. On December 31, 1978, Pacific estimated that there remained in the store room $15,000 worth, c.i.f. Long Beach, of merchandises.

8. Repair and gasoline bills of the VW van totaled $1,750 from April through December. Additionally, the firm paid $800 for auto insurance. All were paid in cash.

9. Utility bills of the firm came to $450 from April through December. All were paid in cash.

10. The rent of the office space and store room amounted to $300 per month. All were paid in cash.

11. Telephone and telegraph costs were $7,500 from April through December. All but $1,100 had been paid in cash.

12. Josef and Malcom had withdrawn $10,000 each as their salaries from April through December. Income taxes that were estimated to be $1,500 each remained owed to the Internal Revenue Service.

13. The lease costs of one Dodge passenger automobile for business use had cost $150 per month from April through December. Only the bill for December remained unpaid. Gasoline and other operating costs including mileage charges amounted to $1,200 for the same period. All were paid in full.

14. The following schedules were considered prudent for the depreciation of office equipment and VW van:

> Typewriter: Five-year straight line method (5 equal amounts of write-offs of the estimated initial value minus estimated salvage value) and salvage value of $100 at the end of the fifth year.

> VW van: Five-year straight line method with salvage value of $500 at the end of the fifth year.

3 BASIC INTERNATIONAL FINANCE FOR MULTINATIONAL MANAGERS
Foreign Exchange Markets and Balance of Payments

1. INTERNATIONAL POLITICS OF MONEY

On August 15, 1971, the anniversary of Japan's defeat in World War II, President Nixon shocked Japan with a declaration of the U.S. government's unilateral decision to no longer honor requests by foreign governments to cash surplus U.S. dollars into gold. This withdrawal of the U.S. government's political commitment to the convertibility of foreign governments' U.S. dollars into gold marked the end of the fixed exchange rate for the post World War II period and triggered a volatile appreciation of Japanese yen and other key foreign currencies. The Japanese yen, which was pegged to the U.S. dollar at a rate of ¥360 to $1.00 under the fixed exchange system, floated to ¥300 to $1.00 by the end of 1971. With some temporary depreciation of the yen after the oil crisis of 1973, it came under persistent pressures to appreciate further. In October 1978, it hit the ¥175 to $1.00 level. This all-time high occurred amid persistent rumors that the U.S. government was attacking the yen in the foreign exchange market to blunt the effects of mounting imports of color television sets, steel products, and automobiles from Japan.

As the Reagan administration ran up unprecedentedly large amounts of budget deficits from 1981 to 1983, and as the Federal Reserve Board of the United States maintained a tight money policy from August 1979 to September 1982, U.S. interest rates soared. Meanwhile, the Israel–PLO war fought on Lebanese soil from May through August of 1982 triggered massive flights of capital from the

46

Middle East region into the United States, which was considered a safe heaven. The war between Britain and Argentina over the Falklands from April to June 1982 also increased capital flights from the Latin American nations into the United States. All these effects combined had one dramatic effect, namely, a rapid strengthening of the U.S. dollar against other currencies. From the first quarter of 1981 to the fourth quarter of 1982, the U.S. dollar appreciated on the average about 25 percent against fifteen major currencies. This had a predictable impact on the merchandise trade of the United States: a record trade deficit. Since one-half of this trade deficit was with Japan, whose currency depreciated by about 24 percent against the U.S. dollar, there arose untrue but politically sensitive allegations in the United States about Japan's manipulation of the yen value.

From the fall of 1982 to the spring of 1983, five financial ministers of advanced economies—the United States, Japan, the United Kingdom, France, and Germany—were busy finding ways to shore up the lending capacities of the International Monetary Fund (IMF) to rescue such external debt-ridden countries as Mexico, Brazil, Argentina, and Chile. The debt service requirements (payments of interests and principals) of these countries ranged annually from 200 percent of total export earnings for Brazil to 70 percent for Mexico and Argentina (the debt-service ratio). Korea, with 40 percent of the debt-service ratio, was demanding a large amount of economic aid from Japan.

The preceding accounts illustrate the political and economic factors at work to produce volatile movements of key currencies in the world foreign exchange markets. In the years ahead, internationally minded managers will have to deal with numerous uncertainties of foreign exchange markets that are collectively caused by the conflicting interests of key actors in these markets. These protagonists include the central banks of non-Socialist governments of both developed and developing nations, OPEC nations, the Soviet Union, multinational banks and firms, arbitrageurs, speculators, the IMF, and foreign exchange traders. Wars, natural calamities, epidemics, abnormal climatic changes, and depletion of fish and other marine life all have a tremendous effect on the fluctuations of currencies.

2. A RELEVANT HISTORY: INTERNATIONAL LIQUIDITY AND THE IMF

Just as most firms need to maintain a certain level of cash and near cash funds (called liquid funds or assets) to meet payment obligations and to amass investment funds locally, from time to time com-

47

panies and governments engaged in international trade and investment also require liquid funds to finance their trade and investment activities. National currencies are used internationally as vehicles of diverse economic transactions. Since at any given moment, cash inflows and cash convertible funds are not always expected to be adequate for meeting outflow obligations, companies and individuals in domestic markets maintain a minimum cash reserve as a buffer against sudden cash shortfalls. Likewise, in each of the some 148 IMF member nations (in 1982), demand for and supply of respective national currencies to satisfy both vehicle and reserve requirements are routinely managed by individuals, banks, firms, government agencies, and ultimately, central banks such as the Bank of England, the Bank of Japan, and the U.S. Federal Reserve System.

Until recently, most people considered gold and silver the ultimate means of exchange (currency) because there was no central bank or government powerful enough to regulate the national money supply and win the trust of its populace. Even when paper money was printed by the government and by private banks to facilitate these transactions, it was specifically backed by gold reserve. This was the basic system of the "gold standard."

However, especially after the Industrial Revolution spread from England to other nations, the growth of industrial and mercantile activities outstripped the rate of gold and silver production and supplies. Rather than accepting the restrictions imposed by the availability of gold and silver on economic growth, one nation after another went off the gold standard, replacing gold and silver with paper money, *fiat*, as the medium of exchange. Today, there are still ideological conservatives who argue for a return to the gold standard. The only drawback is that they are unprepared to limit their own living standard to what our ancestors knew in the days of the gold standard—the days of horse and buggy.

Internationally, gold survived much longer as the ultimate means of exchange because there was no global body, central government, or bank strong enough to enforce the nongold standard. As international trade and investment activities multiplied, such domestic currencies as British sterling began to supplement gold in providing international liquidity and in serving as a vehicle and reserve currency. Since Britain stood at the apex of the political, industrial, and mercantile powers of the pre-World War II era, few doubted her ability to defend the value of pound sterling. The U.S. dollar, the Japanese yen, and other national currencies were tied to British sterling. After all, by then the United Kingdom had amassed over two-thirds of the world's total gold reserves.

48

The Great Depression of the 1930s and World War II eclipsed the economic and political power of the United Kingdom and propelled the United States to a world leadership position. The virtual collapse of domestic and international money markets during the depression years were inadvertently precipitated as one nation after another scrambled for economic gain at the expense of the others by erecting prohibitive tariff and nontariff trade barriers and simultaneously resorting to competitive devaluations of their own currencies. As nations retaliated against one another, the policy of "beggar thy neighbor" developed. Each nation tried to shift the costs of coping with shrinking economic activities to its neighbors. In the end, every nation became poorer.

In 1944, as the defeat of the Axis powers—especially Japan, Germany, and Italy—became imminent, the United States and the United Kingdom began to plan the international monetary system for the postwar era so that the disastrous experience of the Great Depression would not be repeated. What emerged was the International Monetary Fund, popularly called the Bretton Woods Agreement after the American town in New Hampshire where the treaty was signed in July 1944.

The IMF was given the mandate to act as the ultimate clearing agency and the credit (liquidity) granting body for the signatory nations so that they would avoid self-defeating competitive devaluations of their currencies. The IMF would also promote freer flow of capital and goods among member nations. The United States pledged to tie the U.S. dollar to gold at $35 per troy ounce. The other signatory nations would tie their currencies to the U.S. dollar.

The U.S. dollar was considered as sound as gold because most nations wanted U.S. dollars in order to purchase goods and services from the United States, which was the only source of goods and services for the war torn economies of Europe and Asia. Besides, the bulk of gold that used to be held by the Bank of England was physically moved during the war to the United States and was held as U.S. government property. With a cash-and-carry method of selling foods, arms, and other products to England during the initial phase of the war, the United States came to hold about three-quarters of the world's monetary gold reserves.

Under the fixed exchange rate system, the par value of other national currencies was pegged to the U.S. dollar and was permitted to fluctuate only within a narrow band ($\pm 1\%$ first, expanding in steps to $\pm 10\%$ in 1971). When the signatory nations of the IMF wanted to change the par value of their currencies, they needed IMF permission. In order to defend fixed exchange rates, the member

49

countries were able to draw upon their own accounts (the same as deposits) with the IMF and then borrow from the IMF. The IMF would make its loans (stand-by credit etc.) conditional on the execution of the mutually agreed upon monetary and fiscal policies that the borrowing nations promised to impose to remedy inflation, balance of payments deficits, and other causes of the weakening values of their currencies.

This fixed exchange rate system lasted until 1971, when President Nixon unilaterally disavowed the foundation of the Bretton Woods Agreement, specifically the convertibility of foreign governments' holdings of U.S. dollars for gold. The U.S. government had been experiencing difficulty since about 1958 in honoring its commitments for converting foreign governments' U.S. dollar holdings into gold. The amount of U.S. dollars held by foreigners exceeded the gold held by the U.S. government (converted into the dollar equivalent at $35 per troy ounce). The dollar shortage that existed from the mid-1940s to the 1950s had turned into a dollar glut as European nations and Japan recovered from the war and reemerged as exporters of many products to the United States and other markets at the expense of U.S. exports.

As the U.S. dollar lost its luster as the coveted "vehicle" and "reserve" currency of world trade and investment, the IMF sought to create additional liquidity that would be accepted by IMF members as the final medium of settling IMF accounts among IMF members. Special Drawing Rights (SDRs), which were created in 1970, were apportioned among member countries in 1970, 1971, and 1972. Initially, the SDR was linked to gold. However, its value soon came to be determined as a weighted average of a basket of sixteen national currencies. Up until mid-1978 the reference currencies and their assigned weights were: U.S. dollar, 33 percent; West German mark, 12.5 percent; British pound, 9 percent; Japanese yen and French franc, 7.5 percent each; Canadian dollar, Italian lira, and Dutch guilder, 5 percent each; Belgian franc, 4 percent; Saudi Arabian riyal, 3 percent; Iranian riyal and Swedish kroner, 2 percent each; Austrian schilling, Australian dollar, Norwegien krone, and Spanisn peseta, 1.5 percent each. Since these relative weights and national currencies reflected the trading importance of these currencies, it was highly conceivable that the ingredients of the currency basket and their assigned weights would change subsequently. With the world's acceptance of the European common currency unit – the European Monetary Unit (EMU) – consisting of six reference currencies of the original members of the European Economic Community, it is likely to be included in the currency basket but, more importantly, will function as a useful reserve and liquidity vehicle to supplement the U.S. dollar and other key national currencies in world markets.

As the IMF experienced the difficulty of having the SDR accepted as the new international liquidity by bankers and other international money managers, the IMF decided to reduce the number of reference currencies. From January 1, 1981, the SDR was pegged to the five most widely used currencies, namely, the U.S. dollar, 42 percent; German mark, 19 percent; British pound, 13 percent; French franc, 13 percent; and Japanese yen, 13 percent. This simplification immediately led some London banks to sell certificates of deposit (CDs) denominated in SDRs, which were aimed at attracting especially oil-exporting nations intent on diversifying their asset holdings out of the U.S. dollar. As more and more international bankers and multinational money managers come to use SDRs as their composite currency unit for managing assets and liabilities, the SDR will become one important international liquidity. The ultimate acceptance will come, however, only when the prices of such internationally traded commodities as oil, wheat, and mineral ores are denominated in the SDR.

The primary source of the IMF's lending capabilities is its quotas (paid-in funds) by the member nations. Despite intermittent increases in the IMF's quotas from the mid-1960s to the mid-1970s, its resource drastically declined relative to total world reserves held by individual member nations. During the 1960s, IMF quotas stood at about 60 to 70 percent of total world reserves. In 1982, even after the increase in quotas in 1980, quotas were barely equivalent of 20 percent of the total world reserves.

Financially and politically, the IMF is still maintained by the industrialized nations which contributed about 61 percent of its quotas. In June 1982, at the Ottawa meeting of the IMF member nations, developing countries, Europe, and Japan urged the United States to agree to increase the IMF quotas once again in order to cope with the predictable loan demands from the debt-ridden Latin American nations. However, the Reagan administration resisted this dire demand until November 1982, when the United States was caught unprepared to rescue external debt service problems of Mexico and Brazil. Since American banks held the largest amounts of such external debts of Latin American nations, the Reagan administration was forced to recognize the imminent danger of the collapse of the American financial markets if the panic of the collapse of foreign credits spread to the United States. Of about 1,400 billion dollars of foreign loans of the world, the United States alone held about

370 billion dollars. The Citibank, Bank of America, Chase Manhattan, and other leading banks of the United States would have been the first casualties of the collapse of international financial systems. By the end of 1982, the IMF member nations worked out an emergency increase of $20 billion to the fund's quotas, and the United States was organizing the IMF and other industrialized nations to join the rescues of Mexico, Brazil, Argentina, and Chile initiated by the United States.

3. FOREIGN EXCHANGE MARKETS

National currencies are traded internationally in the same way as are other commodities, like soybeans, wheat, copper, cotton, gold, silver, nickel, coffee, and tin. As in the case of other internationally traded commodities, national currencies are traded not only for today's sales and purchases but for future sales and purchases. Just as there are prices quoted for soybean futures, so there are selling and buying prices for future delivery of key national currencies.

(1) Foreign Exchange Glossary

Many institutions develop their own jargon to facilitate communication among their "in" members; the foreign exchange market is such an institution. The following glossary of foreign exchange market terms is a useful guide for managers interested in international trade.

Foreign Exchange: This refers to foreign currency that is held (or used) by traders and governments for business transactions.

Foreign Exchange Rate: This is the price of one currency expressed in terms of another currency. Unlike commodities like soybeans, national currencies can only be traded against other currencies. The classic definition of the price is nothing but the exchange (barter) rate between two given commodities. If one bride is traded for two horses, the price of bride expressed in terms of horse is two; conversely, the price of horse expressed in terms of bride is one-half.

Spot Rate: The current (today's) price of one currency expressed in terms of another currency that is offered in the spot (today's) market for transaction on any given day for delivery within 1 business day (same-day delivery).

52

Forward Rate: The future price of one currency that is quoted "firm" today in the forward (future) market. If you buy Japanese yen at the 90-day forward rate of yen to the U.S. dollar quoted today in the New York market at ¥230 to U.S. $1.00, you will receive 230 yen for every U.S. dollar you deliver at ninety days from today regardless of the actual spot rate ninety days from now.

Appreciation: When one currency becomes dearer in terms of another currency under the floating exchange rate system, the currency is "appreciating." Under the fixed exchange rate system, the upward movement of the par value is called "revaluation."

Depreciation: The opposite of appreciation and revaluation is called "depreciation" and "devaluation."

(2) Foreign Exchange Transactions

Consider the following example. Yamato of Japan imports $100,000, f.o.b. Illinois, worth of soybeans from the Illinois Farming Cooperative. The Illinois farmers demand payment in U.S. dollars. At the same time, Ford Motor of the United States imports $100,000, f.o.b. Japan, worth of auto transmissions from Toyokogyo, Japan. Toyokogyo needs Japanese yen to pay its employees and suppliers in Japan. Suppose that the spot rate of the yen quoted in Tokyo is ¥200 to U.S. $1.00.

In essence, Yamato obtains $100,000 by giving 20 million yen to Toyokogyo in exchange for $100,000 that is paid by Ford. In reality, however, the foreign exchange traders (banks and other dealers) intervene and act as intermediaries matching the needs of importers like Yamato and exporters like Toyokogyo. Depending upon where these needs arise, the foreign exchange market transactions could take place anywhere in the world. Reflecting the importance of such trading volume, such international money market centers as New York, London, Tokyo, Singapore, Hong Kong, Basel, Dusseldorf, Montreal, and Amsterdam have emerged as leading foreign exchange markets.

In the preceding example, we assumed not only that the timing of Yamato's payment and Toyokogyo's receipt coincided but also that the amounts involved were the same. In reality, timing of expected receipts and payments in diverse currencies does not always correspond exactly. In addition, there are many speculators who buy and sell national currencies in both spot and forward markets, depending upon their personal views of the future movements of foreign exchange rates quoted in these markets. Accordingly, there is no guarantee that the demand for a given currency in a given foreign exchange market is equal to the supply of that currency. Prices of over-supplied commodities fall and prices of overdemanded commodities rise until the market is cleared.

Under the present floating (flexible) exchange rate system, which includes an increasing number of national currencies, the values of national currencies relative to one another (cross rates are determined by the value of each currency to the U.S. dollar) are determined in the spot and forward markets depending upon their supply and demand. Through the central banks, many governments also participate in spot and forward markets to influence, at the margins, the value of their own currencies. The central banks of the industrialized nations have a de facto understanding to support one another if one of their currencies is under attack in the markets. Because of these government interventions in the supposedly free foreign exchange markets, the present system is often called a "dirty" float system.

The *Wall Street Journal* and the *New York Times* print daily the "selling rates" of forty-eight currencies against the U.S. dollar, quoted by a leading bank in New York. Banks and other foreign exchange traders deal in other currencies as well. If one wished to buy the U.S. dollar in exchange for foreign currency, one would be quoted a "buying rate." The spread between the two rates is the bank's commission. Among the forty-eight listed, for such key currencies as the British pound, Canadian dollar, French franc, Japanese yen, Swiss franc, and German mark, the spot rates and the forward rates for up to 180 days are quoted in newspapers for the benefit of the general public. Banks and foreign exchange traders are able to quote many more forward rates even up to 365 days ahead for other currencies.

How are the rates quoted in Tokyo, London, and New York, for example, brought into equilibrium with one another? Does it pay for buyers to shop around among foreign exchange traders and different markets? There are many traders who specialize in exploiting even small differences in the foreign exchange rates quoted by different intermediaries in various markets. They are called "arbitrageurs," and they arbitrate the differences in the prices of the same commodity from one market to another. They try to buy one currency low in one place and offer it for sale in other markets where its quoted price still permits them to sell it high. For example, you can buy Deutsche marks in Tokyo for Japanese yen, sell marks for British pounds in Dusseldorf, and buy back Japanese yen in New York by selling British pounds for yen. If you are lucky and can deal in multiples of

$250,000 units and upward, you might make one-tenth of one percent profit in three minutes through this three-point transaction.

Because of these shrewd deals by arbitrageurs, exchange rates quoted in different world markets and among different traders are brought into equilibrium with one another. Therefore, the foreign exchange markets are in reality the trading networks of different money market centers of the world that are linked with one another by the telex, telephone, cable, and mail networks of foreign exchange traders.

4. FORECASTING FOREIGN EXCHANGE RATES

The example of Peterson Company in Chapter 2 showed how necessary it was for the manager to follow future spot rates of Japanese yen against the U.S. dollar to evaluate the effective cost of yen-based debts. Importers and exporters also would like to know what the future trends of exchange rates will be for the currencies they are using so that they might make proper pricing, purchasing, and other marketing decisions.

As we discussed in preceding sections of this chapter, both spot and forward rates are determined by supply and demand conditions of currencies in the marketplace. Therefore, managers need to know how to keep track of key political, economic, and social factors influencing the supply and demand conditions of the currencies in question. Which economic fundamentals should global-minded managers watch periodically? How do these economic conditions affect the movement in daily exchange rates? How do exchange rate fluctuations influence such economic fundamentals as prevailing interest rates, price, production, exports and imports, and national employment?

There are unending controversies among academics and practitioners about the interactions between exchange rate movements and changes in macroeconomic fundamentals. For a reasonable fee, managers can even subscribe to a number of foreign exchange rate forecasting services. Invariably, these soothsayers use explicit or implicit models of forecasting the future movements of foreign exchange rates. Some models are explicitly expressed in arrays of simultaneous equations. Each equation is a mathematical summary of the forecaster's beliefs about the causal relationships between the exchange rate and a preselected number of independent variables such as foreign trade volume and national economic growth rates. Others merely rely on their implicit and intuitive understanding of how complex world affairs hang delicately in balance.

It is beyond the scope of this book to go into the technical details of forecasting foreign exchange rates. Instead, we will highlight a few important concepts and analytical paradigms that multinational managers must understand to avoid undue anxiety about fluctuating movements in foreign currencies.

First, we should recognize that all decisions to buy or sell any commodity including foreign currency on the exchange market are basically financial decisions. Financial decisions are crucially dependent on the decisionmakers' expectations of future movements in exchange rates. In short, we must analyze how expectations are likely to be influenced by the movements in selected economic indicators. In the case of the September 1980 war between Iran and Iraq, the sudden fall of the Japanese yen against the U.S. dollar signaled that bearish speculators and traders outperformed bullish buyers of Japanese yen. The bearish traders anticipated that the war would affect Japan's economy far more adversely than that of the United States, since Japan imports practically 100 percent of her oil needs, a bulk of which comes from the Middle East.

(1) Spot, Forward, and Interest Rates

At the beginning of this chapter, we observed that soaring short-term interest rates in the United States strengthened the U.S. dollar against other currencies. At that time spot and forward rates moved in the same general direction. The difference between the two rates seemed generally related to interest rate differentials between the United States and Japan. These movements were not altogether coincidental.

Upon closing on January 20, 1983, the New York Foreign Exchange Market quoted the following spot and forward rates for Japanese yen (always expressed in terms of one U.S. dollar unless otherwise defined).

Spot rate	236.65
90-day forward rate	235.26

Forward exchange rates are also quoted at a discount from or premium on spot exchange rates. As noted above, the 90-day forward rate of Japanese yen could be quoted outright as a 139 points (1.39 yen) discount from the spot rate. Similarly, it could be expressed as a 2.35 percent discount (annualized rate) from the spot rate. To compute the annualized percentage discount or premium of the forward rate over and above the prevailing spot rate, the following formula should be used:

$$\text{Discount or premium of forward rate (\%)} = \frac{(Fx - Sx) \times 100}{Sx} \times \frac{360}{Fx\text{-Day}}$$

where

Sx = spot rate (236.65);
Fx = forward rate (235.26); and
Fx-Day = period for which Fx is quoted (90).

When two currencies are mutually and freely convertible – that is, when there are no legal, political, or economic restrictions on the purchase and sale of the currencies – spot and forward rates are likely to be determined simultaneously. Barring strong expectations of fundamental changes in the factors that determine exchange rates (e.g., devaluation or revaluation, war, or sudden crop failure of key exporting or importing commodities) changes in forward rates are immediately transmitted to changes in spot rates and vice versa. The remaining difference between the two rates reflects the interest rate differentials prevailing between the two countries involved. Why is this so?

(2) Interest Rate Parity Theory of Foreign Exchange Rates

Consider this scenario. The prevailing interest rate in the United States is eight percentage points higher than in Japan. The 360-day forward rate of Japanese yen happens to be at a two percentage point discount. Under these circumstances, anyone who has a surplus of Japanese yen could make a profit by moving the surplus into the United States and converting it into U.S. dollars at the prevailing spot rate. At the same time, the investor would sell immediately, the expected gains (principal plus interest earnings) in the forward market in order to avoid the uncertainty of future spot rates. On balance, the investor's "covered interest arbitrage" would yield a return that would be six percentage points higher (8 percent interest rate differential minus two percentage forward discount) than he would receive from investing the same amount in Japan.

The preceding example illustrates the theory of "interest rate parity." Simply put, other things being equal, the difference between spot and forward rates are roughly equal to the difference in the prevailing short-term interest rates between the two countries of the currencies involved. As investors move to exploit a profitable opportunity of covered interest arbitrage, the increased sales of U.S. dollars in the forward market would place downward pressure on the forward rate (the forward yen rate per U.S. dollar would appreciate), and the net purchases of spot dollars would put upward pressure on the U.S. dollar. These simultaneous movements tend to widen the discount rate of the Japanese forward rate from its spot rate. At the same time, the immediate and increased capital inflow into the United States would increase supplies of funds in the United States and lower short-term interest rates in the United States. This would reduce the interest rate differential between the United States and Japan. Theoretically, this process is repeated until there are no more lucrative opportunities for covered interest arbitrage.

Arithmetically, the interest rate parity is expressed as follows:

F = One-year forward rate of yen expressed in U.S. dollars. Selling \$1 forward yields F yen.

S = Spot rate of yen against U.S. dollar. ¥1 is converted into \$$(1/S)$.

I_j = Yen interest rate in Japan.

I_u = Dollar interest rate in the United States.

When there is interest rate parity, expected gains from ¥1 equivalent of investment in the United States at I_u interest rates are equal to those from ¥1 investment at I_j interest rates in Japan. Therefore, the following relationship has to hold between these two alternatives.

$$\text{¥1} \quad \xrightarrow{\text{Invest in the U.S.}} \quad \left(\frac{1}{S}\right)(1 + I_u) \times F$$

$$\xrightarrow{\text{Invest in Japan}} \quad (1 + I_j)$$

Accordingly, $\dfrac{F}{S}(1 + I_u) = (1 + I_j)$

and $\dfrac{F}{S} = \dfrac{(1 + I_j)}{(1 + I_u)}$

The percentage forward discount or premium is expressed as;

$$\frac{F}{S} - 1 = \frac{(1 + I_j)}{(1 + I_u)} - 1$$

$$= \frac{I_j - I_u}{1 + I_u}$$

In other words, the percentage discount or premium of the forward rate over the spot rate is approximately equal to the interest rate differential when interest rate parity prevails (only when one interest rate is zero, the difference between spot and forward rates equal to the interest rate differential). On January 20, 1982, the short-term rates of CDs, money market certificates, and Treasury Bill yields were around 10 percent per year in the United States; similar assets would have yielded about 7 percent in Japan. Under these circumstances, the forward rate of Japanese yen settled at about a 2.35 percent discount from the spot rate.

Usually, the forward rate of the currency of the lower interest country is at a discount from the spot rate expressed in the currency of the higher interest country. Figure 3-1 graphically presents the essences of interest rate parity. The vertical axis denotes interest rate differentials and the horizontal axis shows the discount or premium of the forward exchange rate in annual percentage.

Line I-I represents interest rate parity. Any point on this slope equates the interest rate differential with the discount or premium of the forward rate. Suppose that one day the forward exchange rate is found out of line with interest rate parity (Point A or B in Figure 3-1). Profit-making opportunities are now open to investors through covered interest arbitrage. At Point A (or any area below Line I-I), the capital would flow in from a foreign country. Anywhere above Line I-I, such as Point B, the capital would flow out of the country into a foreign country. These capital flows and concomitant buying and selling of foreign exchanges tend to push deviants like Point A and Point B toward Line I-I.

Line I-I is the theoretical norm. By observing the daily movements of spot and forward rates against this norm, multinational managers can easily spot any extraordinary trends of a foreign exchange rate. That is the time they should ask: What does the market know that I do not know? A theoretical understanding of the interest rate parity concept permits managers to capture the unusual and therefore alarming movements of foreign exchange rates, then, scramble for cover, if necessary.

(3) Forward Exchange Rate as Prophecy
of Future Spot Rates?

There are many who suggest we can predict future spot rates by looking at daily forward rates quoted into the future. In short, this theory says that forward rates reflect the collective and rational expectations of the market about supply and demand conditions of the

Figure 3-1. The Essences of Interest Rate Parity.

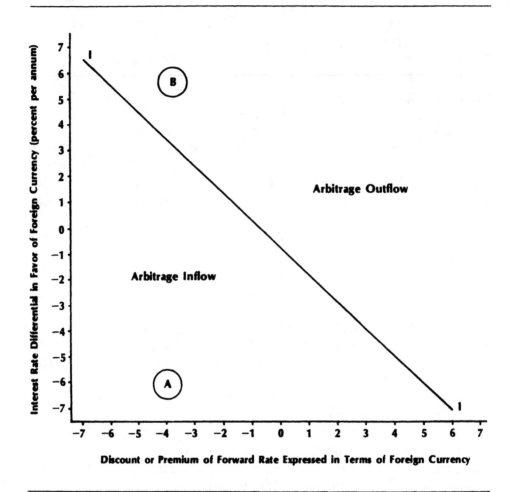

future for the currency involved. Changes in future spot rates are said to be captured by earlier changes in the forward rates.

Empirically, the jury is still out on this proposition. So far, studies (or empirical postmortem of past forward and spot rates) have shown that the forward exchange rate correctly predicted future spot rates only about 50 percent of the time. This does not mean that we should abandon our attempts at refining our understanding of the relationship between prevailing spot and forward exchange rates.

This challenge requires that we comprehend the political and economic factors that influence exchange rate movements.

(4) Exchange Rates and the National Economy

The complex relationship between exchange rates and the national economy cannot be discussed here in detail. We should, however, provide a few clues to unlocking these intricate relationships.

All nations strive for price stability, high employment, economic growth, and a favorable balance of payments. Unfortunately, more and more countries are finding it impossible to attain all of these conflicting goals at the same time. The government juggles its limited tools of monetary and fiscal policies to try to focus on one or two of these goals at a time. For example, from 1980 to 1982 the United States was suffering from stagflation and a strengthening dollar compared with other currencies. The tight monetary policy to restrict the growth of money supply produced a high interest rate, which in turn dampened the economic activities and strengthened the dollar value against foreign currencies. Strong dollars dampened U.S. exports and increased further the unemployment rate.

In the United States, such monetary policy tools as manipulation of interest rates and the money supply are politically more palatable than fiscal policies (i.e., adjustments in government spending, tax policies, and exports–imports). Monetary policy can be implemented through the decisions of the Federal Reserve Board. Fiscal policy, on the other hand, requires endless bargaining in Congress and between Congress and the Executive Branch. Even the court is called in to clean up legal and political ambiguities of the compromised packages of Congress. As a result, monetary policy is often overused.

Given the relative importance of the international sector to the economy, changes in the exchange rate immediately influence domestic prices. Changes in the exchange rate alter the relative profitability of various industries as well as the cost of products and services to industrial customers and consumers. Depreciation of a currency is likely to result in an increase in the costs of imports; currency appreciation has the opposite effect. The impact of exchange rate fluctuations on the balance of trade of an economy depends very much on world demand conditions for exports and on the nation's demand for imports (we will come back to this topic in Chapter 5).

In order to fight inflation, a country may increase its discount interest rates (the loan rate the central bank charges its member banks), which would increase prevailing interest rates in the market.

The intended goal is to dampen economic activities and to restrain the general demand level of the economy. The government hopes that the inflationary gap between general demand and the supply capacity of the economy will be eliminated. When the national policymakers are faced with unionized workers resisting wage reductions and oligopolistic firms pyramiding their target profit margins on top of cost increases, it is doubtful that by applying higher interest rates the cost-push inflationary pressures can be broken. The immediate effect would be more likely to feed inflation as increased financial costs of businesses are passed on in the form of higher prices. Higher interest rates are likely to strengthen the currency against foreign currencies. However, the strengthened currency may well increase export prices, resulting in lower exports. At the same time, imports are likely to grow, because they become relatively cheaper. All told, the balance of trade is likely to worsen. Under these circumstances the government faces some negative effects of monetary policy on the goals of price stability, full employment, and favorable balance of payments.

Unless it is cushioned by depreciation of the exchange rate or by an increase in economic productivity, inflation tends to weaken the cost competitiveness of exports in international markets. All in all, such economic fundamentals as domestic prices, production, employment, interest rates, balance of payments, and exchange rates interact with predictable regularity. International business managers can learn to predict short- and long-term interactions of key fundamentals if they grasp how national economies hang in balance with the rest of the world.

5. "OFFSHORE" MONEY MARKETS

(1) Eurodollar (Credit) Markets
Once any domestic currency is accepted "as is" for deposit outside its nation, the "offshore" money market is created outside the jurisdiction of the government or central bank of the nation of that currency.

In terms of physical volume of transactions and in terms of acceptability by banks outside the country, deposits denominated in the U.S. dollar are by far the largest. Geographically, banks in London, the Bahamas, the Netherlands Antilles, the Cayman Islands, continental Europe, and Singapore accept deposits in the U.S. dollar, London being the center of such actions. Banks that accept the U.S. dollar (or another foreign currency) denominated deposits wish to make profits by lending them out. "Eurodollar' markets refers to the market of short-term lendings (within a year) from Eurobanks to other banks (wholesale loans) and to well-known multinational firms. The medium-term credit (over one year and up to fifteen or twenty years) that Eurobanks extend to other banks and corporations are called "Eurocredit" transactions. In substance, Eurocredit and Eurodollar transactions are often used interchangeably only because the medium-term credit extensions in the Eurocurrency market have come to dominate the transactions.

In contrast, "Eurobond" market refers to the offshore bond market that deals in bonds denominated in foreign currencies outside the nations of those currencies. International syndicates of investment and merchant bankers are the intermediaries of the Eurobond market; commercial banks are the major intermediaries of the Eurocredit market.

Controversies still exist with regard to the details of the origins and transactions of Eurocredit markets. However, the following T-account will illustrate the creation of the Eurodollar market:

Step 1: A holder of U.S. dollar denominated demand deposits with the U.S. bank deposited his funds with a Eurobank.

U.S. Banking System		Eurobank	
	−DD (original deposits)	+ Cash $	+ E$ (new deposit)
	+DD (Eurobank)		

Step 2: The Eurobank lends out its cash holding of the U.S. dollars (Euro-loan).

U.S. Banking System		Eurobank	
	−DD (Eurobank)	−Cash $	
	+DD (Borrower of Euro-loan)	+Euro-loan	
Net Effect No Change	No Change	+Euro- loan	+ E$

One should notice that when netted out, the above transactions do not affect the domestic assets and liabilities of the U.S. commercial banking system as a whole. They have not declined in size. Within the Eurobank system, however, the newly created deposit (bank's liability) of Eurodollars is offset by a concomitant increase in the loan (bank's assets). When nations other than the United States borrow from the Euromarket and convert the funds into domestic currencies, the net effect is the same as straightforward borrowings from foreign countries.

(2) Asiadollar Market

The Asiadollar market was cultivated by the Bank of America toward the end of the 1960s. In 1982 its size was estimated to be around 110 billion dollars. It functioned as a submarket of the Eurodollar market whose size in 1982 was estimated to be around 1,500 billion dollars.

As the supply of lendable funds in the United States tightened in the mid-1960s, and as the supply of Eurodollars simultaneously became tighter because of the sudden increase in borrowings by American banks, the Bank of America, based in California, made its first attempt to tap the Hong Kong market. The British Administration of Hong Kong, however, would not exempt its nonresident depositors from a 15 percent withholding tax on interest earnings. The Bank of America then turned to Prime Minister Lee of Singapore, who agreed to exempt nonresident depositors from a 40 percent withholding tax on interest earnings. Thus, in 1969, the Asiadollar market was born, with the opening of Bank of America's branch in Singapore, which accepted dollar denominated deposits from nonresidents in multiples of $25,000 (as opposed to $100,000 in Eurodollar deposits). Almost immediately, five competitors of the Bank of America—First National City Bank of New York, Chase Manhattan, First National of Chicago, Continental Bank (Chicago), and American Express International—rushed into Singapore. Seven banks from Europe followed suit. One Thai bank and one Russian bank also opened shop in Singapore in order to tap Asiadollars.

Seeing that the Asiadollar market was being preempted mainly by American and European banks, the Bank of Tokyo and Mitsui Bank—two Japanese banks that had been expanding their branch networks in Southeast Asia in pursuit of expanding Japanese trade transactions—persuaded the Japanese Ministry of Finance in 1970 to permit offshore branches in Singapore. Other Japanese banks later opened offices there as lookout posts in the Asiadollar market.

By January 1974 when the Voluntary Foreign Credit Restraint Program (VFCR) was lifted, many American banks, large and small, had become entrenched in the international activities in direct competition with the large multinational banks based in the United States, Europe, and Japan. By participating actively in interbank loan markets (wholesale banking), and by forming international consortia

64

banks in order to share risks and pool resources, many multinational banks of various nationalities interlocked their economic and political interests.

(3) Recent Developments in the Offshore Money Markets

As late as in 1975, the combined size of the Eurocredit and Asia-credit markets were estimated to be about 300 billion dollars. With the OPEC oil money being recycled to the offshore money markets, both credit markets mushroomed during the balance of the 1970s. The Soviet Union and Eastern European countries became active borrowers of the offshore markets. Without any single central banking and political authority to administer the transactions, the offshore markets guaranteed the anonymity of the borrowers. Also, the lack of any single political sovereignty over the offshore markets reduced the political risks of either having deposits and other assets frozen or having borrowing transactions barred suddenly for political reasons. The interest rates of the offshore markets were tied to the London Interbank Borrowing Offering (LIBO) rates. Since many central banks exempted the offshore deposits of their member banks from the mandatory reserve requirements, Eurodollar and Asiadollar banks were able to utilize all the deposits and found eager borrowers among many fund-starved less developed countries.

However, from early 1980, when the Iranian Revolution fundamentally changed the political risks associated with the oil money, the OPEC depositors began to prefer the United States money markets, which are backed by the political strength of the leading sovereign country. Furthermore, the spread of the deepening economic recessions from the United States to the rest of the world, partly fueled by the high interest rates of the United States, hit hardest the economies of the debt-ridden countries in Latin America and other developing areas. In addition, the internal strife in Poland in 1981 and subsequent chilling relationships between the East and West undermined the Asiacredit and Eurocredit banks' confidence in their once active customers. The upshot of all these developments were drastic reductions in the offshore markets' lendings to the less developed nations and East European bloc countries. This in turn precipitated the international financial crisis by driving Poland, Brazil, Mexico, Argentina, Chile, and other debt-ridden nations to de facto insolvency. However, the United States initiatives of arranging the refinancing schemes of these debt-ridden nations were further refinements of the de facto collaborations among the central banks of the industrialized nations that had evolved since the mid-1970s.

As the risks and resources of banks based in various countries became more and more interrelated, the central banks of industrialized nations, including the Federal Reserve Board of the United States, found themselves forced to coordinate their monetary and foreign exchange policies. In the summer of 1974, the dramatic bankruptcies of Bankhaus I.D. Herstatt (West Germany) and Franklin National Bank (U.S.), both of which suffered heavy losses in speculating on Deutsche marks, shook the Eurocredit market and international consortia banks. The central banks of the key industrialized nations met in London and agreed privately on a ruling that respective central banks would be responsible for the losses, if incurred by international consortia banks, on a pro rata basis to the ownership of respective nationality banks. At the same time, central banks tightened their supervisions of foreign exchange positions and the foreign loans of their member banks.

All told, during the balance of the 1980s, we will see far more cautious lendings by Asiacredit and Eurocredit banks. And central banks of the offshore money centers will be closely overseeing foreign lendings by their member banks. However, there is no denying that both credit markets have already grown too large to be scuttled or ignored. Although they will not grow in the 1980s as rapidly as they did in the 1970s, they will continue to grow at a steady rate of about 5 to 8 percent a year—about the same rate as the steady-state growth rate of the total world trade volume.

Geographically, the relative importance of the Asiacredit markets will grow as the Pacific Basin area becomes the fastest growth areas in the 1980s and beyond. In order to redirect the efforts of American banks away from Latin America to Pacific Basin areas, American banks located in California may well choose to compete with Singapore and Tokyo as the money centers of the Asiacredit markets. And the United States will emerge as the leading force in the Pacific Basin economic and political sphere.

6. U.S. GOVERNMENT REGULATIONS AND INTERNATIONAL BANKING

(1) World Money Markets and American Banks

In the United States, banking is the most regulated of all industries. Over the years the federal government, through the regulatory authority of the Federal Reserve Board, has evolved three basic objectives of banking regulation. They are: (1) to safeguard depositors' assets by close supervision of banking activities; (2) to prevent undue concentration of banking power by limiting the geographical coverage of any given bank to regional markets; and (3) to separate banking activities from other commerce by preventing banks from owning shares in manufacturing, commercial, transportation, and communication firms. In 1933 the Glass–Steagall Act separated commercial banking from investment banking. These principles are now being put to test by the internationalization of American banks.

Paradoxical as it may sound, the recent growth in international activities by American commercial banks is due in large part to the federal restrictions placed on capital outflows, as well as to such restrictive monetary policies as placing tight ceilings on the interest paid on deposits and holding down the supply of money. First, the VFCR, introduced early in 1965 as a voluntary measure and made mandatory in 1968, severely restricted American banks' ability to lend to foreign and American multinational firms through their offices in the United States. At about this time, American manufacturing firms were accelerating their investment abroad and needed vast amounts of capital. When these firms turned to Eurocredit markets and foreign banks to meet these needs, American banks, fearful of losing their clients, began to open branches in London.

Later, the so-called Regulation K, whereby the Federal Reserve Board imposed a ceiling on the interest rates paid by banks, was coupled with the increase in reserve requirements. Large American banks based in New York began to lure individual and corporate deposits, originally placed with banks in other major cities, away to their London branches by paying higher interest rates than Regulation K permitted in the United States. Rather than see their deposits (sources of loanable funds) drained by the London branches of New York-based banks, other regional banks also opened London offices. As the money supply became tighter in the United States, those American banks with captive branches inside the Eurodollar market brought loanable funds back into the United States from the Eurodollar market.

The international activities of American banks were thus precipitated by the federal government's restrictive actions. During this period, a familiar political game developed in the United States. By 1969, small and medium-sized banks in the United States had begun lobbying with Congress and the Executive Branch, demanding rulings to permit their rather inexpensive offshore financing from such nearby spots as the Bahamas and the Cayman Islands. Both the Bahamas and the Cayman Islands vigorously solicited offshore banking from these banks by providing various tax exemptions and relaxed disclosure requirements. Once the Federal Reserve Board began, early in

1969, to permit "shell branches" of American banks in Nassau, Bahamas, offshore banking—outside U.S. jurisdiction but catering to U.S. needs—flourished.

At this juncture, leading American banks needed to develop a new offshore market, possibly located outside the reach of smaller competitors, but in the heart of a substantial pool of funds. The Asia-dollar market was thus created.

The international networks of American commercial banks have greatly expanded since the mid-1960s. Medium-sized regional banks also groped their way into the international activity of "recycling petrodollars."

At the end of 1964, eleven American banks operated a total of 181 foreign branches. By the end of 1974, the number of American banks operating abroad had reached 125 and they operated 732 foreign branches. In addition, by the end of 1974, the thirty largest American banks owned 640 foreign subsidiaries outright, with majority interests in 317 joint ventures and minority interests in another 274. The activities of these foreign direct investments ranged from various finance companies to such nonfinance businesses as data processing firms, premise holding companies, and venture capital investments.

From 1969 to 1974, for both banking and nonbanking operations abroad, these thirty largest banks revealed a distinct preference for wholly owned subsidiaries. This is perhaps because the increased interlockings of American banks' worldwide operations required closer management control. Minority equity positions in joint ventures, undertaken earlier perhaps to provide speed of entry as well as sharings of operational risks oriented to local markets became, from 1969 to 1974, significantly less important in the total make-up of American banks' profiles abroad. Such observations lead one to speculate that as is the case with manufacturing firms, the ownership patterns of the overseas ventures of American banks are related to the specific strategic moves of parent banks.

From the mid-1970s to 1983, multinational activities of American banks have further expanded. The passage of the Export Trading Company Act of 1982, which permits banks equity holding in exporting trading companies—a further relaxation of the Glass-Steagall Act—will accelerate multinationalizations of the American banking community.

(2) Foreign Banks in the United States

Since the end of the 1960s, Japanese and European manufacturers have stepped up their investments in the United States. In order to provide financial services for these client firms, Japanese and European banks have entered the United States in increasing numbers. By mid-1982, it was estimated that over 250 foreign banks were operating in the United States through over 250 branches, about 160 agencies, over 120 affiliates and subsidiaries, and over 150 representative offices. In spring 1982, foreign banks in the U.S. were still expanding. Not only have their business volume and the scope of their activities in New York and California more than quadrupled since mid-1973, but they have also opened new branches and offices in the Midwest, New England Southeast regions, Hawaii, Oregon, and the Southwest. By threading through the branches, offices, and affiliates of banks scattered throughout the United States, foreign banks were creating quasi-nationwide branching operations, much to the irritation of American banks.

In addition to meeting their original objective of servicing the needs of manufacturing firms entering the United States, foreign banks quickly solicited the deposits of American manufacturers and other businesses in the United States, in exchange for financial credits and other services to American manufacturing subsidiaries abroad. After the energy crisis of 1973 and the resultant recovery of the U.S. dollar, foreign banks began to participate in the New York Federal Funds Market by lending, on a day-to-day basis, their surplus dollars to American banks, which are required to maintain reserve deposits with the Federal Reserve System. As the oil-producing countries deposited their surplus petrodollars with banks in the United States, foreign banks used their outposts there to obtain dollar funds for financial needs elsewhere.

In addition to these activities, an increasing number of foreign banks, which are not covered by the Glass–Steagall Act, were underwriting securities and trading in them. In 1976, both the expansion of foreign banks in the United States and the international expansion of American banks were posing the following problems to the regulatory framework of American commercial and investment banks.

Complaints by Regional Banks: Regional banks wanted the Federal Reserve Board to forbid foreign banks to deal directly with American manufacturing and commercial firms. They also wanted the Federal Reserve Board to restrict or limit large American banks in developing de facto national networks of nonbanking financial services through holding companies.

Extraterritorial Application of the Glass–Steagall Act: American banks argued that foreign commercial and investment banks should also be covered by the Glass–Steagall Act. On the other hand, small commercial and investment banks of the United States wanted the U.S. government to apply the Glass–Steagall Act extraterritorially to large American commercial and investment banks engaged in activities outside the United States that were forbidden within the United States.

In 1978, the United States enacted the International Banking Act. Simply put, the act brought foreign banks in the United States under the direct control of the Federal Reserve Board and at the same time expanded the board's authority to enforce the monetary policies. The act consists of six major provisions: (1) federal licensing of the branches and agencies of foreign banks as an alternative to state chartering, (2) mandatory insurance for the deposits of foreign branches engaged in retail banking (the extension of the Federal Deposit Insurance Corporation coverage to foreign banks), (3) reserve requirements on the branches and agencies of foreign banks, (4) limited interstate branching activities by foreign banks, (5) extended prohibitions against involvement in commercial and other nonbanking activities to foreign banks (the application of the Glass–Steagall Act to foreign banks), and (6) authority for the Federal Reserve Board and the various regional Federal Reserve Banks to examine branches and agencies of foreign banks.

In short, the United States moved a step closer to the nationwide branch banking activities for American banks and at the same time reigned in the foreign banks under the tighter control of the Federal Reserve Board.

7. THE FUTURE OF INTERNATIONAL BANKING

With the increased sophistication of financial officers of manufacturing and trading firms and with the increased interlocking of economic and political relationships among large American, European, and Japanese banks, the international competition among multinational banks will be intensified. Innovative deals and services, that a given bank, security trader, or trading firm introduces to the world market will immediately be imitated by competitors. Manufacturing firms and other clients will try to obtain the best possible deals by playing one bank off against another, and both commercial banks and security houses will enter fields that have thus far been handled exclusively by merchant banks (mainly British). Indeed, many observers predict that the days of the merchant bank are numbered and that leading merchant banks will link themselves up with commercial banks and security houses. Will this kind of international consortium be viable? Or for that matter, will international consortia remain stable institutions?

In 1973 the largest security house in Japan, Nomura Securities Co., established a three-way joint venture, Trident, with Barclays Bank International Ltd. (a wholly owned subsidiary of Barclays Bank, U.K.) and Merrill Lynch International Inc. (a wholly owned subsidiary of Merrill Lynch, U.S.). The ownership of Trident was split equally among the three parent firms. According to Yukio Aida, Executive Vice President of Nomura, Trident's objective was to "engage in merchant banking and related financial services in Hong Kong, Asia and the Pacific Basin." In summer 1976, Trident's banking services included: (1) extending short-, medium-, and long-term loans in all convertible currencies; (2) managing syndicated bank credits for major project finances; (3) discounting bills of exchange and other negotiable instruments; (4) engaging in import–export finance; (5) dealing in the foreign exchange business; and (6) accepting deposit accounts and certificates of deposit. Trident also listed corporate financial services: (1) underwriting and distributing public issues of debt and equity securities in international and selected local capital markets; (2) privately placing debt and equity securities with international institutions; (3) financing venture capital; (4) providing financial and investment advisory services; (5) providing general financial planning services; (6) acting as the intermediary for mergers and acquisitions of firms; (7) identifying, evaluating, and negotiating joint venture opportunities for client firms; and (8) providing investment management services.

In other words, Trident was to take on the traditional merchant banking firms operating in the Pacific Basin communities by combining the financial and personnel resources of one commercial bank and two security houses. Trident boasted that with its three parent firms, it had immediate access to more than 5,000 offices and outlets all over the world. By summer 1975 Trident was already registering operational profits. In the financial industry, the product of which not only is internationally mobile through the instantaneous transfer of multicurrency funds by cable but renders itself subject to immediate imitation by competitors, the last competitive edge appears to be the marketing muscle that firms can muster worldwide. The merchant banks that have thus far thrived mainly on "ideas and business contacts" see their strength being eroded by commercial banks and security houses.

Outside the United States, American banks have actively expanded those nonbanking activities that are forbidden within the United

States. Banks own and operate a cargo airline, warehouses, shipping firms, retail stores, manufacturing plants, and other enterprises through subsidiaries and affiliates. Many people argue that American banks should be permitted to own nonbank businesses in order to compete with foreign banks. It remains to be seen whether the overseas nonbank subsidiaries and affiliates of American banks will establish direct business dealings with similar nonbank activities in the United States.

8. BALANCE OF PAYMENTS: TRANSACTIONAL ACCOUNTS AND ADJUSTMENT PROCESSES

The way in which a nation balances its economic transactions with the rest of the world affects not only the exchange rate but also national economic conditions. The balance of payments of the nation periodically summarize these economic transactions. Innumerable diverse transactions between individual and institutional residents of a nation and the rest of the world are estimated from various sources (e.g., custom clearance records, questionnaires completed by banks and corporations, airline traffic records, etc.).

Unlike domestic sales, the risks of collecting accounts receivable for foreign sales (exports) are inseparably tied to such country-specific risks as the convertibility of the currencies involved and to the future spot rate movements of these currencies. Country risk analysis begins with reading the balance of payments statistics.

(1) Compiling Balance of Payments Statistics

There are as yet no centralized or standardized bookkeeping formats and procedures by which nations record the economic transactions of their residents with the rest of the world. In theory, however, every international transaction for a given nation is recorded according to the same double entry bookkeeping rule used to journalize economic transactions of firms and individuals (see Chapter 2). For example, if the United States exported $100 worth of machine tools to Israel and imported $100 worth of oranges as payment in kind (a case of barter trade), the export would be entered into the account called merchandise export and the import into the account or merchandise import.

By combining exports and imports, we can create one account and call it "merchandise trade." This account is subdivided into two parts, namely, the left-hand side (called debit) and the right-hand side (called credit). The words "debit" and "credit" have meaning only as a shorthand way of designating each bookkeeping entry as either left-hand side or right-hand side of the respective accounts. According to the accounting conventions used in North America, Japan, most European countries, and an increasing number of developing nations, merchandise exports are entered on the right-hand side (credit) of the merchandise trade account just as the sales of goods and services by a private firm are recorded in the right-hand (credit) of the account called "sales" or "revenue" of the firm. Merchandise imports are entered on the left-hand side (debit) of the account called "merchandise trade" (exactly the opposite of the exports).

Each nation is free to choose whether it uses f.o.b. (free on board) or c.i.f. (cost, insurance, and freight) valuations of its exports and imports. The United States has traditionally applied f.o.b. or f.a.b. (free alongside board) valuations to both her exports and imports; most other nations adopt f.o.b. valuations for exports and c.i.f. valuations for imports.

When the United States records her imports at f.a.b. value, where in the balance of payments accounts are the freight and insurance costs entered? This depends on how the payments are made. The balance of payments keeps track only of a given nation's economic transactions with the rest of the world. Therefore, if the American importer of Israeli apparel paid for the freight and insurance costs in United States dollars to American freighter and insurance firms located in the United States, this transaction would not enter the balance of payments accounts of the United States. It is just the same as a domestic transaction—as, for example, when you purchase reference books in U.S. dollars in New York. Accordingly, we need to keep track of who does what, where and in what currency.

According to accounting conventions, an increase in national assets is always a debit entry, and an increase in national liabilities is a credit entry. This is why both outflows of foreign direct investment and portfolio investment (capital outflows) as well as increases in official reserves and gold (akin to the cash account of a private firm) all carry a debit (−) sign.

Likewise, when an American importer pays for foreign goods with a check to be drawn in dollars from an American bank in the United States, the foreigner's claims on the United States increase. Accordingly, the import transaction will be recorded as one debit entry in the U.S. merchandise trade account and one credit entry in the foreign private claims on the U.S. (short-term) account as reported by American banks. Similar entries would be made for a firm that incurred monetary liabilities (outsider's claims on the firm).

73

To be able to intelligently decipher balance of payments statistics we must be familiar with the nature of typical transactions in each account. The following two hypothetical examples should further clarify the intricacies of the balance of payments accounts.

Example 1: Michelin (France) exports $100,000 worth (f.o.b. Marseille) of radial tires to Sears Roebuck, U.S.A. and uses its entire proceeds to pay for a plant site in the United States. Sears Roebuck pays for the imports and the freight and insurance costs to American shipping firms with checks drawn on Chase Manhattan Bank in New York.

U.S. Balance of Payments Entries

Action	Debit (-)	Credit (+)
1. Michelin's exports and Sears Roebuck's payments	a. Merchandise trade (f.o.b.) $100,000	b. Foreign private claims on the U.S. (short-term capital) $100,000
2. Michelin's purchase of plant site	c. Foreign private claims on the U.S. (short-term capital) $100,000	d. Foreign private direct investment $100,000
3. Net effect	U.S. merchandise trade -$100,000	Inflow of French investment +$100,000

In the above example, entry 1b is offset by entry 2c, leaving the net effect of "U.S. merchandise trade" for the debit entry and "Inflow of French investment" (foreign direct investment in the U.S.). In reality, this interim transaction cannot possibly be linked to any specific import or foreign direct investment. Accordingly, one might go straight to the way the net effect is recorded in the above example.

Example 2: Maia Kelly in New York sends a personal check for $1,000 to be drawn on Bank of Tokyo Trust, New York, to her aging uncle in England. The uncle cashes the check in London at Manufacturer's Hanover.

U.S. Balance of Payment	Debit (-)	Credit (+)
Private remittances	$1,000	
U.S. liabilities (short-term) reported by U.S. banks		$1,000

In real life, the credit entry transaction is likely to be reported by American banks, but the debit entry transaction may be missed by the information-gathering network. In that case, it ends up in the catchall category of "errors and omissions" or "statistical discrepancy." Private remittances comprise a substantial portion of total foreign exchange earnings for such countries as Israel, Italy, Turkey, Greece, Korea, Spain, Mexico, and the People's Republic of China. These countries have laborers working abroad or many generous relatives and friends overseas who remit money home.

The balance of payments generally consists of the following nine groups of accounts shown in Table 3-1. Depending upon the informational needs of a country, these accounts are subdivided further. The United States publishes the most finely subdivided accounts, each transaction being classified into seventy-five accounts. The accounts are mostly self-explanatory. The U.S. balance of payments can be found in the *Survey of Current Business*, which is published monthly by the Department of Commerce. *International Financial Statistics*, published monthly by the IMF, carries summaries of balance of payments of member nations together with standard macroeconomic data.

Table 3-1. Balance of Payments Accounts.

(1) Merchandise (Exports and Imports)
Balance of (1): Balance of Trade (Deficit or Surplus)   (2) Services (Transportation, Travel, Tourism, etc.)   (3) Unilateral Transfer Payments (Remittances and Aids)   (4) Royalties, Fees, Dividends, and Interests
Balance of (1) through (4): Current Account (Deficit or Surplus)   (5) Long-term Capital—Foreign Direct Investment   (6) Long-term Capital—Foreign Portfolio Investment   and Long-term Loans
Balance of (1) through (6): Basic Balance (Deficit or Surplus)   (7) Short-term Capital   (8) Errors and Omissions (Statistical Discrepancy)
Balance of (1) through (8): Overall Balance (Deficit or Surplus)   (9) Official Reserves (Key Foreign Currencies, Gold and SDRs)

Note: Surplus or deficit of balance of payment is computed by combining the accounts shown above each line.

(2) Deciphering the Balance of Payments
Statistics: Fund Flow Analysis

Balance of payments statistics can best be viewed as "uses" and "sources" of funds of one nation's transactions with the rest of the world. Since the balance of payments statistics are compiled by the double entry bookkeeping method, it always balances. When all the estimates of each item (account) of the statistics do not balance the total debit entries with the total credit entries, we have to balance them by throwing in a plug figure called "statistical discrepancies" or "errors and omissions." Why, then, do we hear of the "deficits" or "surpluses" of the U.S. balance of payments?

When we read the profit and loss (P/L) statement and balance sheet (B/S) of a given firm, we quickly look at a few items of the financial statements. For example, with the P/L statement, we check the gross profit margin, the ratio of costs of goods sold to sales, and net profit figures. We even check fixed costs and expenses. We go through these exercises in order to get an idea of the general economic health of the firm, just as medical doctors quickly check patients' temperature, pulse, and blood pressure before more elaborate tests. We do the same with the balance of payments of a given country by taking a certain group of items out of the balance of payments statistics to check how these groups of items have fared.

This quick check up shows us how each country is financing its external account (transactions with the rest of the world). For example, the excess of imports over exports is defined as a "trade deficit" (the opposite is a "trade surplus"). Contrary to popular myth, this deficit is not necessarily bad. It only means that the excess of imports over exports has to be financed (filled in) by the remaining items of the balance of payments combined.

A deficit or surplus in the balance of payments is simply made by separating (drawing a line under) one group of accounts from the remainder. The deficits or surpluses of all the items above the line would have to be offset by the sum of the items below the line. Naturally, this line can be placed anywhere you like. Both the international politics and the history of this line drawing make interesting reading. For example, almost a decade ago, when increasing gold outflows from the United States caused foreign governments to cash in their dollar holdings for gold, the United States came up with the new definition called "official balance (liquidity)" that for a few years after 1968 miraculously reduced the U.S. "deficits" as defined by the new official balance. In the mid-1970s when the floating exchange rate system and increased foreign investments and trade by multinational firms dominated the world scene, the United States proposed to drop the definition of "basic balance."

When a firm's sales (a country's exports of goods and services) of merchandize and services fall short of its purchases (a country's imports of goods and services) of merchandise and services, the company must borrow funds from financial institutions, individuals, or trade to pay for the excess purchases. Likewise, if a given nation incurs a current account deficit, it must either borrow short- or long-term funds from abroad or use up (reduce) its official reserves of foreign exchange and gold or both.

Accordingly, we should first check to see how each nation balanced its external transactions for a given year. Second, by making a temporal comparison of how each nation has been balancing its external transactions, we must pinpoint a general trend in the intertemporal movements of major items in the nation's balance of payments. Third, we should then make our own judgments about economic and political feasibilities of the nation's ability to carry on business as usual. Foreign demand for the country's exports as well as the country's supply capacity for merchandise and services in demand must be checked. Can imports be contained? Are inflows of foreign direct investment on the rise? Can the nation borrow abroad from private and government sources? Is the level of official reserves plus a line of credit extended by the IMF adequate to meet the deficits of accounts of goods, services, and capital? These are the standard questions for which answers must be sought.

We must also carefully monitor movements in the errors and omissions account (statistical discrepancy). When all the accounts are estimated from different sources, their total cannot possibly match the offsetting increases or decreases in the official reserves and gold account—the nation's cash account kept by the government. These statistical discrepancies are recorded in errors and omissions. In reality, this catchall account is the depository of unrecorded border trade, illicit trade (smuggling and drug traffic), and most likely unrecorded short-term capital movements (capital flight and inflow). Empirically, the errors and omissions account tends to move in the same way as short-term capital accounts, and shows volatile change depending upon the political and economic condition of the nation.

Lately, exchange rates appear to be sensitive to the deficits and surpluses of the current account. With the increases in foreign direct and portfolio investment by industrialized nations, the current account, which captures royalty fees, dividends, and interest moved around by multinational firms, seems to influence the demand and supply conditions of the foreign currency involved.

Table 3–2. Japan's Balance of Payments, 1980 (in millions of U.S. dollars).

Merchandise	
Exports	126,736
Imports	124,611
Services	–11,343
Transfers	– 1,528
Long-term capital	2,394
Short-term capital	3,071
Errors and omissions	– 3,115
Official reserves	8,396

In Table 3–2 Japan's balance of payments of 1980 are summarized.

Let us evaluate how Japan financed her diverse transactions with the rest of the world.

Step 1: Check the balance of the merchandise trade to see whether foreign exchange earnings (sources) from exports exceeded foreign exchange outlays (uses):

Sources (exports)	+ $126,736
Uses (imports)	– $124,611
Net earnings	+ 2,125

Step 2: Check the current account balance to see whether the net earnings (or net outlays) from the merchandise trade sector offset services and transfers needs of the country:

Net earnings from trade	+ $ 2,125 (sources)
Net outlays of services	– $11,343 (uses)
Net outlays of transfers	– $ 1,528 (uses)
Net outlays	–$10,746

Step 3: Check the long-term capital accounts (foreign direct investments and portfolio investments) to see how the net outlays of the current accounts were offset by net increases in the inflows of the long-term capital transactions:

Net outlays of current accounts	– $10,746
Net inflows of long-term capital	+ $ 2,394
Remaining shortfalls	– $ 8,352

Step 4: Check how the net shortfalls (or gains) above are offset by the net transactions of two short-term capital accounts, namely, net short-term capital inflows (+ $3,071) and net "capital" outflows through Errors & Omissions (– $3,115):

Remaining shortfalls	– $8,352
Net inflows of short-term capital	+ $3,071
Net outflows of errors & omissions	– $3,115
Net overall balance	– $8,396

How did Japan finance the net overall shortfalls of $8,396 (debit entry sign denoting the shortfalls) for 1980? Of course, Japan had no choice but to delve into her cash reserve called official reserves to pay for the net overall shortfalls. This is why the 1980 balance of payments of Japan showed the net credit entry (remember a reduction of cash reserves) of her official reserves.

9. CORRECTING BALANCE OF PAYMENTS IMBALANCES

When the nation's balance of payments registers chronic deficits or surpluses, there are economic and political forces at work to right these imbalances. Under the floating exchange rate system, automatic changes in the exchange rate tend to correct the imbalances by affecting both the amount and direction of the international flow of goods, services, and capital of the nation. Under the fixed exchange rate system, the nation revalues or devalues its exchange rate with the hope that the new exchange value will do the trick. Imbalances in the balance of payments are also corrected by two built-in and automatic adjustment mechanisms of the economy and by government policies. These adjustments alter the economic factors that are responsible for continuing imbalances in the balance of payments.

There are two types of automatic adjustment mechanisms; one works through the price adjustment process, the other through the income adjustment process of the economy. The price mechanism produces changes in domestic prices and interest rates. Persistent deficits occur when capital flows from the deficit country to the surplus country. These capital outflows contract the money supply in the deficit country and expand it in the surplus country. Tightening the money supply increases interest rates in the deficit country. Inflating the money supply in the surplus country lowers interest rates. These widening interest rate differentials tend to reverse capital flows from surplus to deficit countries.

Recurring current account deficits are a signal that demand for the goods and services of the deficit country is declining while demand in the surplus country is increasing. As the surplus country approaches capacity production, the prices of its goods and services rise. Conversely, the prices of the products of the deficit country are held down by weakening demand at home. Higher prices for exports in the surplus country tend to reduce its exports to the deficit country. Relatively lower prices of the deficit country's products tend to boost its exports. How successful these adjustments in the relative price movements of the deficit and surplus countries will depend upon how sensitive changes in the quantities of goods demanded are to changes in their prices (the economist's definition of the price elasticity of demand). We will come back to this topic in Chapter 5.

To summarize, it has been postulated that a price adjustment will work when the sum of two deficit and surplus countries' relative price elasticity of demand for imports exceeds one (the Marshall-Lerner condition). When the supply capabilities of the two countries are limited (the price elasticity of supply is very low and there is a long waiting period to increase supplies of goods and services in demand), the price adjustment tends to work even if the Marshall-Lerner condition does not hold.

The income adjustment mechanism involves the effect of fluctuating income on imports and the influence of movements in interest rates on the production level of the economy. The surplus country's national income rises with increased exports. With each incremental rise in income, there is also an increase in imports because the portion of income spent on imports (the marginal propensity to import) is positive. Growing imports in the surplus country help the deficit country to reduce its deficit in its balance of trade. Rising interest rates in the deficit country reduce the production level and capital investment in new productive capacities of the economy, which in turn decreases the national income and subsequently its imports.

To ensure that the automatic adjustment mechanism will work effectively, the government intervenes in the national and international capital and commodity markets. When monetary and fiscal policies are not strong enough to dislodge the institutional and economic bottlenecks of the automatic adjustment mechanism, the government also intercedes in international markets. Erection of import barriers, restrictions on capital outflow, promotion of exports and of portfolio and foreign direct investment are all intended to resolve the structural imbalances in the balance of payments and to address the basic economic problems that caused them.

By becoming aware of the ways in which the nation tries to make adjustments in the balance of payments, multinational managers should be able to predict when and how a nation resorts to specific intervention in domestic and international markets. Naturally, different policies affect different industries and change the profile of economic and political risks in international business.

10. INTERNATIONAL CORPORATE FINANCE

Here, we will present the standard ways to approach financial decisions involving hedging the risks of foreign exchange transaction exposure. If a manager has accounts receivable or payable denominated in a foreign currency, foreign exchange rate fluctuations automatically change the real value and cost of such accounts. Consider the following example:

American Electronics Lab (AEL) of New York expected delivery of 30,000 new pocket calculators in 180 days from Imai Electronics, Japan. Imai demanded payment in yen, c.o.d., at the unit price of ¥4,250, f.o.b. Yokohama, Japan. On January 7, 1981, the spot rate of Japanese yen was ¥199.20 to $1.00 and the 180-day forward rate was ¥192.05. The Japanese interest rate for short-term time deposits and certificates of deposit in January 1981, was 10 percent per year. AEL knew that the U.S. rate was 18 percent a year and that the Japanese yen appreciated from ¥242 in September 1980 to 199.20 in January 1981.

Of course, AEL can choose to do nothing until the actual time of payment in 180 days. Although the firm can use the U.S. dollar equivalent of its payment obligation for the next 180 days, it may well expose itself to the risk of further appreciation of Japanese yen, which would make the costs of 30,000 calculators much higher than expected. A 10 percent appreciation of the Japanese yen would easily increase AEL's costs by about $6,000.

AEL wants to protect itself and to fix the U.S. dollar costs of the imports for sales and profit planning. There is a way that will permit AEL to hedge against the financial risks associated with foreign exchange rate movements. Just as the purchase of life insurance does not prevent a policyholder from dying, the hedging operation does not preclude the occurrence of a disaster. If one happens, however, "hedging insurance" would limit the financial costs of coping with it. Consider the following alternatives for AEL:

Alternative 1: AEL buys Japanese yen immediately through the spot market and deposits this amount in 180-day money certificates in Japan at 10 percent per annum (p.a.). In 180 days, principal and interest combined will be equal to ¥127,500,000 (¥4,250 × 30,000).

Alternative 2: AEL buys Japanese yen to the tune of ¥127,500, 000 in the 180-day forward market and chooses to use the dollar fund for the working capital needs of the firm (¥127,750,000 ÷ 192.05).

AEL will choose the alternative that gives the lowest cost for the imports expressed in today's dollar. We can compute the solution as follows. Please note that today's cost of Alternative 1 is arrived at by discounting ¥127,500,000 by 5 percent (one-half of the expected interest earning for one year at 10 percent p.a.). Likewise, Alternative 2 reduces the U.S. dollar fund promised for delivery in 180 days by the expected benefits from using or investing the fund in the United States for next 180 days (the opportunity cost of the fund).

$$[Y/(1 + 0.05)] \div 199.20 = A \qquad (3\text{-}1)$$

Choice between $

$$(Y/192.05) - A \times i/2 \qquad (3\text{-}2)$$

Where,

Y = the amount of yen fund to be paid to Imai; and

i = the opportunity cost of AEL's dollar fund.

By equating Equation (3-1) with Equation (3-2), we can solve the simultaneous equations for the unknown, i, the break even value of the opportunity cost of AEL's dollar fund. At the break even value of i, AEL would be indifferent between Alternatives 1 and 2. When the value of i exceeds 17.8 percent (approximately the same as the prevailing interest rate in the U.S.), AEL would choose Alternative 2. When the value of i is less than the prevailing interest rate in the U.S., the firm should choose Alternative 1.

How is AEL's opportunity cost, i, obtained? It depends on the marginal (incremental) rate of return on AEL's investment in its own woking capital. If the firm can make more than the prevailing interest rate by using the fund internally to support increased sales and manufacturing activities, AEL should hedge in the forward market. If not, it should hedge through the spot market and the riskless investment of the fund in Japan.

How does one estimate the incremental rate of return on the firm's working capital investment? The detailed exposition should be left to a basic course in corporate finance. For a quick review, multinational managers should return to the functional definition of working capital. In order to approximate the average working capital invested in the firm, accountants merely compute the difference between current assets and current liabilities. Functionally, however, managers should be able to estimate how much additional investment in working capital will be needed to support planned sales increases.

Suppose that AEL cannot cut the average collection period of accounts receivable below thirty days and the average level of inventory below forty days of sales.[1] Suppose further that AEL cannot stretch its average days of settling accounts payable beyond the past record of thirty-seven days. This means that it will take AEL seventy days (average days of inventory and collection of accounts receivable) to collect cash from the time when they bought imports (purchases added to inventory).

Luckily, this financing time is cushioned by an average thirty-seven days that AEL takes to pay its suppliers. AEL will have to finance the remaining thirty-three days by dipping into its cash reserve, borrowing short term and long term, and ploughing more funds into equity (capital and retained earnings). The capital that finances the thirty-three-day waiting period is called working capital. In order to support growing sales, AEL will have to increase the level of its working capital that will remain invested in the firm. Incremental net profits associated with incremental sales should be divided by incremental working capital needs to obtain the incremental rate of return on the working capital investment. In short, a firm like AEL is most likely to have an opportunity cost, i, that exceeds the prevailing interest rate. Under these circumstances, the firm's rule of thumb is to routinely hedge through the forward exchange market.

Like the Peterson Company discussed in Chapter 2, AEL widened its profit opportunities by tying itself to the design and production resources of Imai. AEL's import strategy more than compensates for its lack of similar manufacturing capability. However, this expanded business opportunity also exposed the firm to manageable but greater financial risks associated with the fluctuating values of Japanese yen against U.S. dollars. Accordingly, AEL must now strengthen its internal financial managers by including someone well versed in international corporate finance.

---

1. From the firm's balance sheet and profit and loss statement of the most recent year, the outstanding level of accounts receivable (AR) and the annual sales can be obtained. Then, the formula $\frac{AR}{Sales} \times 365$, will give the average days of collection of accounts receivable. The same computational procedure applies to inventory and accounts payable.

4 INTERNATIONAL TRADE
Government Policies and
Business Strategies

Never before in our history have so many technological innovations in transportation and communication brought international trade activities so readily within the grasp of so many firms, large and small. And yet, many businesses still view international trade, particularly exports, as too risky and baffling an endeavor to attempt. Of late, this risk perception seems to have been enhanced by rising and uncertain energy costs which are changing the fundamental economics of worldwide transportation networks. Many firms say their business at home is full of uncertainties and that they can do without the additional risks inherent in international trade. But are they really sparing themselves the uncertainties of international trade if they choose to bury their heads like proverbial ostriches in their home market?

In 1980, Weiss Appliance Co., a medium-sized midwestern manufacturing firm was trying to survive in the powerfully competitive standard electric household appliance market. The company managers suddenly came to the realization that its past indifference to international trade might in fact have jeopardized its competitive strength at home. In the past, every time the firm introduced new products in the United States, it received purchase feelers from abroad. But they always dwindled as time passed. Orders from Europe and Japan disappeared more quickly than those from Latin America and other newly industrialized nations. Requests from developing countries always lasted longer. This puzzled Weiss because

U.S. trade statistics showed persistently strong exports of electrical household appliances to Latin America. Recently, Weiss noticed that more and more of its distributors were stocking up on toasters, electric irons, compact dishwashers, washing machines, clothing dryers, and even electric ovens imported from Japan, Korea, Taiwan, and Singapore. Weiss was being forced to cut its price to compete with imports and to concentrate its marketing efforts on new product lines such as microwave ovens, air conditioners, and fully automatic dishwashers, dryers, and washing machines.

Table 4–1 summarizes the export trends of major industrialized countries from 1958 to 1979. Export growth rates from 1958 to 1979 varied markedly from over 3,500 percent for Japan to about 1,000 percent for the United Kingdom and the United States. Table 4–2 shows the major exports of Japan by product groups from 1963 to 1979 and illustrates how dynamically the export composites of a country like Japan changed in a relatively short time. All told, the over thirty-five fold increases in Japan's exports from 1958 to 1979 reflect the successful and continuous readjustments of the nation's industrial structures.

When world markets are increasingly linked with one another, defensive marketing strategies of survival should motivate manufacturing firms to engage in both imports and exports. In particular, an export orientation keeps companies alert to new technological, marketing, and managerial innovations that are developing in every corner of the world. Just as it has always been important for firms to monitor the behavior of their competitors in the home market, it will become increasingly necessary for companies to keep track of foreign competitors' behavior. And, of course, exports provide increased sales and profits.

To recognize opportunities for profit in the seemingly chaotic circles of international trade, multinational managers must improve their conceptual grasp of dynamic but systematic forces underlying international trade. Over the centuries, scholars, politicians, and traders have sought general laws of international trade as policy guides.

Varieties of commodities today are traded internationally, ranging from food items, mineral ores, oil, and timber to industrial machinery and consumer appliances. After World War II, the ideological commitment of leading nations to the principle of free trade as proclaimed by the General Agreements on Tariffs and Trade (GATT) and the International Monetary Fund (IMF) has helped expand international trade. The distinct rise of many multinational firms of diverse nationalities will add a new dimension to the international flow of various commodities. Today, over one-fourth of the international stream of manufactured goods is estimated to be made up of

Table 4–1. Export Trends of Major Countries, 1958–1979 (in millions of U.S. dollars, f.o.b. value).

	Japan	U.S.	U.K.	West Germany	France	Italy	OPEC Nations
1958	2,877	17,755	9,099	9,220	5,380	2,577	—
1963	5,452	22,427	12,220	14,628	8,199	5,054	—
1968	12,972	34,092	15,460	24,888	12,903	10,186	13,394
1973	36,930	70,859	31,032	67,563	36,659	22,223	38,962
1974	55,536	97,908	39,396	89,368	46,255	30,469	118,587
1975	55,753	107,592	44,523	90,176	53,118	34,816	109,690
1976	67,225	115,156	46,696	102,162	57,162	37,261	132,810
1977	80,495	121,150	58,205	118,091	64,997	45,305	145,840
1978	97,543	143,575	71,705	142,453	79,378	56,068	141,430
1979	103,032	181,640	91,016	171,887	100,691	72,232	206,910

Source: Bank of Japan, *Comparative International Statistics* (Tokyo: Bank of Japan, 1970, 1975, and 1980).

Table 4-2. Major Exports of Japan, 1963-1979 (in millions of U.S. dollars, f.o.b. value).

	1963	1968	1973	1978	1979
Foodstuffs	289	432	841	1,047	1,207
Textiles	1,247	1,977	3,279	4,870	4,908
Chemicals	315	805	2,147	5,102	6,100
Nonmetalic minerals	212	329	572	1,379	1,547
Metals	944	2,347	6,821	16,042	18,379
Iron and steel	702	1,712	5,304	11,855	14,113
Machinery	1,688	5,656	20,365	62,510	63,183
TVs and radios	230	688	1,851	3,954	3,780
Motor vehicles	135	713	3,682	15,531	17,021
Motorcycles	55	176	855	1,887	1,925
Vessels	340	1,084	3,819	7,172	3,869
Scientific/optical	149	372	970	3,448	3,861
Other	757	1,426	2,905	6,593	7,708
Total	5,452	12,972	36,930	97,543	103,032

Source: Japan Tariff Association, *Trade of Japan*, for each year.

cross-haulings between subsidiaries of the same firms. As shown in Table 4-2, export composites of trading nations are also always changing. What would be a relevant theory of international trade that could explain these dynamic patterns?

1. INTERNATIONAL TRADE THEORIES

There are today a number of international trade theories, all of which claim to offer distilled wisdom about what determines the patterns of trade among nations. None of them has proved to be the ultimate general theory applicable to all traded goods at all times. Since they are supposedly extracted from the real world of international trade, they reflect the changing realities of international trade. Since the benefits of international trade are perceived differently by various nations at distinct stages of economic development, one theory that may be promoted as most orthodox for some nations may well be considered unforgivable heresy to others.

(1) Availability Theorem
The availability theorem, set forth by Professor I.B. Kravis in the 1950s, applied to a range of commodities and manufactured goods

Table 4-3. Degree of Self-Sufficiency of Five Industrialized Nations for Major Commodities, 1978.

	Japan (%)	U.S. (%)	U.K. (%)	West Germany (%)	France (%)
Bauxite	0.0	33.5	0.0	0.0	271.3
Nickel	0.0	7.1	0.0	0.0	0.0
Oil	0.2	62.3	54.4	5.0	2.3
Iron ore	0.6	69.6	21.3	3.6	60.4
Tin	2.0	0.0	20.1	0.0	0.0
Copper	5.9	62.0	0.1	0.1	0.2
Natural gas	17.4	95.5	92.2	37.7	29.4
Lead	21.4	38.7	0.5	10.6	15.4
Coal	24.8	107.9[a]	100.1	109.8	48.7
Lumber	33.6	91.3	26.2	83.2	89.8

a. The figure exceeding 100 percent denotes net export position.
Source: Ministry of International Trade and Industry (MITI), *White Paper on International Trade* (Tokyo: MITI, 1980).

and appeared to explain the basic trade patterns for least processed natural resources including crude oil, lumber, and mineral ore. These commodities move from where they are indigenous and plentiful to where they are scarce. Table 4-3 deals with major commodities and shows the degree of self-sufficiency (the percentage ratio of home-supplied products against total domestic consumption) for Japan, the United States, the United Kingdom, France, and West Germany. To fill their needs, these industrialized nations import quantities of various commodities annually from the developing nations.

Naturally, the economics of availability-based movements of raw materials depends very much on the prevailing prices of these materials in the world market and on their exploration and subsequent production costs. Exploration and production costs are determined by such intrinsic raw material characteristics as ore grade, sulphur content, recycling capability, and the relative accessibility of reserves. For example, development of oil in the North Sea and in Alaska was economically infeasible before OPEC (Organization of Petroleum Exporting Countries) pulled the crude oil price up past $15 to $20 per barrel. In 1981, when the price of crude oil in the world market was surpassing $35 per barrel, new projects of coal liquification and shale oil developments in Canada, the United States, and Australia were undertaken.

Trade patterns for grain, marine products, fruit, dairy products, meat, and other agricultural and fishery products are also explained mainly by the availability hypothesis. However, they follow the patterns predicted by the theorem of relative availability. In theory, Canada could grow bananas and other tropical products in elaborate hothouses. Given today's rising energy costs, however, it is not yet economical for Canada to begin production of tropical crops.

Politics may distort the trading patterns of agricultural products. Farmers all over the world are politically entrenched. Few politicians or government policymakers dare invite their disapproval. For example, the average production cost per 100 kilogram of beef in 1976–77 varied from about $272 in Japan to about $74 in the United States, $62 in Australia, and $59 in New Zealand. Economics alone dictate that Japan should import beef from New Zealand, Australia, and the United States. In reality, however, the politics of beef in all four nations pitted one country against the other. The United States government wanted Japan to buy hotel-grade quality beef from the United States while it helped the U.S. cattle breeders shut out imports from Australia and New Zealand. Threatened by U.S. retaliation against Japanese exports of manufactured goods to the United States, Japan grudgingly agreed to increase import quotas of beef from the United States, Australia, and New Zealand.

The theory of absolute and relative availability suggests a further question: Why don't the nations that possess natural resources and foodstuffs process them on-site and export processed products? Why does Indonesia, for example, export her crude oil to nearby Singapore and import refined petroleum products from Singapore? Why is it economical to dig up and ship bulky, heavy dirt like iron ore to foreign countries thousands of miles away and to buy back finished iron and steel products? Will the OPEC nations achieve their goal of developing their own petrochemical industries? Here we have touched on the central portion of international trade theory: the determination of trade patterns of manufactured goods.

(2) Comparative Advantage Theorem
(Ricardian and Heckscher–Ohlin Theorems)

The availability theorem conceptually upholds the absolute advantage theorem: if Country A commands absolute advantage in production of commodity *a* over Country B, which also needs commodity *a*, and if Country B commands absolute advantage in production of commodity *b*, which Country A also needs, Country A exports *a* to Country B and Country B exports *b* to Country A. Intuitively, politicians and traders of the mercantile era believed there was no need to import products available from indigenous suppliers (the extreme case of absolute advantage theorem).

With the advent of the Industrial Revolution, the economic fundamentals of international trade underwent considerable change. The world suddenly saw the rise of various manufacturing industries, beginning with the United Kingdom. The political and economic interests of these rising industries soon came in conflict with the wishes of the landed gentry.

By the 1830s, a vocal class of industrialists arose to challenge the British trade policies predicated on the mercantilist view of the world. This challenge was introduced in the British parliamentary debates by English economist David Ricardo. Ricardo was a wealthy merchant and member of Parliament who represented an industrial constituency. At that time, national debate was raging over the "Corn Law." This law protected English grains from cheap, continental (mainly French) grains. The landed gentry desired to have it continued, but the industrialists, who wished to keep their wage payments low, favored the reduction in price of such staples as bread and flour by importing cheaper grains. This situation clearly called for a new way of evaluating the impact of international trade upon the overall economic health of the United Kingdom.

Ricardo enlarged upon the thesis of his predecessor, Torrence, and argued inside and outside parliament for the repeal of the Corn Law on the strength of what later came to be known as the comparative advantage theorem of international trade. With numerical examples, he illustrated the trade policy implications of the new theorem for England: even if the United Kingdom commanded absolute advantage in both woolen products and wine vis-à-vis Portugal, both nations would be economically better off if the United Kingdom and Portugal specialized in woolen products and wine respectively and exchanged surplus products. In other words, compared with Portugal, the United Kingdom was far more efficient in the production of woolen products (producing greater amounts of woolen products per one unit of such production inputs as labor) than in the production of wine. Likewise, Portugal was relatively more efficient in the production of wine than of woolen products. When England and Portugal specialized in woolen products and wine respectively, the total amounts of the two products available for consumption by the two countries could be greater than the combined production of the two products if each nation produced both products and traded no products between them. This is the essence of the revolutionary message that the comparative advantage theorem conveyed.

Suppose that England and Portugal possess six units and fourteen units, respectively, of labor. For one ton of woolen products, England uses two units of labor while Portugal uses eight units. For one gallon of wine, England uses four units of labor while Portugal uses six units. England clearly commands absolute advantage in the production of both woolen products and wine because she is more efficient than Portugal in the uses of labor for both. This pretrade situation is summarized in Table 4-4.

Now, England and Portugal specialize in the production of woolen products and wine (the case of complete specialization). Compared with England, Portugal is less inefficient in the use of labor for wine. Each nation exports its surplus in exchange for what it does not produce at home. The posttrade situation is summarized in Table 4-5. For an illustrative purpose, Table 4-5 depicts the extreme case of complete specialization in respective products between the two countries. In the posttrade situation, the international exchange rate between wool and wine would fall somewhere between the pretrade English rate, 3 tons of wool for 1.5 gallons of wine, and the pretrade Portuguese rate, 1.75 tons of wool for 2.3 gallons of wine. In the posttrade situation, the exact international exchange rate (the terms of trade) for wool in terms of wine or vice versa is determined by the demand conditions of the respective products that are prevailing in the world market.

The two countries have between themselves more of both goods for their combined consumption. England can still consume one ton

Table 4-4. Pretrade Situations in England and Portugal.

	England		Portugal		
	Production	Consumption	Production	Consumption	Total Production
Wool	1 ton	1 ton	1 ton	1 ton	1 + 1 = 2 tons
Wine	1 gallon	1 gallon	1 gallon	1 gallon	1 + 1 = 2 gallons

Table 4-5. Posttrade Situations in England and Portugal.

	England			Portugal			
	Production	Consumption	Trade	Production	Consumption	Trade	Total
Wool	3 tons	1 ton	2 tons	0 ton	2 tons	−2 tons[a]	3 tons
Wine	0 gallons	1.3 gallons	−1.3 gallons[a]	2.3 gallons	1 gallon	1.3 gallons	2.3 gallons

a. The negative sign denotes import.

91

of woolen products, or even more if her demand for wine remains the same, and export another in exchange for up to 1.3 gallons of wine. The exchange ratio between woolen products and wine in the posttrade situation of England is the ratio of 2 to 1.3 as opposed to the ratio of 2 to 1 in the pretrade situations. In England more wine becomes available at a cheaper price expressed in terms of woolen products. In Portugal, more woolen products become available at a cheaper price expressed in wine. Thus, the two nations are economically better off in the posttrade situation than in the pretrade situation.

It was not the logical persuasiveness of the comparative advantage theorem, however, but the subsequent rise in the political strength of the bourgeoisie, that gave the new trade theory both its theoretical and its pragmatic popularity. At the apex of industrial strength, England could afford to advocate free international trade and to preach to the world the policy implications of the comparative advantage theorem.

Ricardo's theory is based on the labor theory of value. The value of any product is determined only by the labor content of the product. Labor is the only variable factor of production. Land, the other factor, is merely treated as fixed and given. The amount of labor that is applied to the land determines the value of the product that comes from the land.

However, as the process of industrialization advanced, the labor theory of value became outmoded as people recognized another important factor of production: capital. Economists recognized labor and capital as the two factors of production and reformulated their implicit production function to define the cause–effect relationships between products and their variable factors of production. Early in the twentieth century, the comparative advantage theorem was expanded by two Swedish economists, Heckscher and Ohlin. They restructured the comparative advantage theorem until it became what is now known as the factor proportion theorem. The factor proportion theorem said that capital-abundant nations command the comparative advantage of capital-intensive products in international trade, while labor-abundant nations command export competitiveness in labor-intensive products.

The Hecksher–Ohlin version of the comparative advantage theorem still remains sacred for many economists who believe that the structure of logic is more important than the substance and relevancy of logic. This is why standard textbooks on international economics today present only the comparative advantage theorem. In reality, however, the dynamic patterns of international trade of manufactured goods often differ significantly from the patterns predicted by the comparative advantage theorem.

(3) Limitations of Comparative
Advantage Theorem

Readers should realize that Prussia, a developing country during Ricardo's era, did not think the comparative advantage theory applied to her. In Prussia, the "Historical School" (List et al.) developed the theory of the historical development stage of a nation. List argued that it was imperative for Prussia to protect her "infant industries" in order to catch up industrially with England.

The question that was raised by the Historical School still haunts us today. Suppose, as in the case of England and Portugal cited above, that Portugal did not wish to be locked in as the producer-supplier of wine and wanted to develop some time in the future as efficient a wool industry as that of England. The comparative advantage theory that was developed by Ricardo and later expanded by Heckscher and Ohlin did not deal with the dynamic question of growth of industry or persistent change in the industrial structure of the trading nation over a period of time.

As the technological gap that once existed between the United States and the rest of the industrialized countries began to narrow from the 1950s to the 1960s, the trading patterns of a wide range of newer and more technology-intensive manufactured goods were running counter to those patterns that the comparative advantage theorem would have predicted.

In the early 1950s, Harvard Professor Wassily Leontief was the first economist to econometrically demonstrate such an anomaly of international trade. His findings that American exporting industries were more labor intensive than American importing industries were dubbed by the diehard economists as the "Leontief Paradox." It was termed a paradox because the comparative advantage theorem would have predicted that a capital-abundant country like the United States would be exporting capital-intensive products and that American exporting industries would therefore be more capital intensive than American importing industries. On the whole, many economists were still too enchanted by the neat logic of the comparative advantage theorum to accept a new theory.

However, some researchers did take Leontief's findings seriously. From the mid-1960s onward, individually and sometimes collectively, these researchers systematically examined the unconventional hypotheses of international trade that Williams, Kravis, and Linder earlier suggested. What was wrong, then, with the comparative advantage theorem?

The comparative advantage theorem is built upon the following assumptions concerning the world of international trade:

- There is no difference in technological levels between trading nations;

- The relevant technology is universally available to trading nations;

- Consumer taste varies little from one trading nation to the next;

- Trading nations each enjoy full employment of such available production inputs as capital and labor;

- Trading nations possess perfect information concerning the markets of the traded goods;

- Relevant information flows freely from one trading nation to the next; and

- It is the supply (production) condition of the products, not their demand (market) condition, that determines the pattern of international trade.

Indeed, when Ricardo introduced the comparative advantage theorem into the Corn Law debates of the British Parliament, he was immediately attacked by the opposition for his unrealistic assumptions about the business world. One opposition member was particularly perceptive and entertaining. He called Ricardo's theory relevant perhaps only to "the man who was suddenly planted on a different planet where no ignorance, no restriction of trade, no taxes, and no individual rivalry existed."[1] Yet Ricardo's interest group won, and the United Kingdom came to dominate in the international trade arena. This is not to say, however, that Ricardo fabricated the comparative advantage theorem in order to advance his political interest. As a perceptive economist, Ricardo realized that with the advent of the Industrial Revolution, the mercantilist view of international trade had long outlived its utility for the United Kingdom.

The semblance of the comparative advantage theorem may explain today's trading patterns of very low-technology-intensive products. Plywood, canvas shoes, plastic sandals, transistor radios, and nails are good examples of such standard manufactured goods. When production processes are also standardized to narrow the gap of physical output per manhour (labor productivity), the production cost dif-

1. William Smart, *Economic Annals of the 19th Century*, published during 1801–1820, London, p. 733.

ferences of these standard products among the trading nations may be determined mainly by differences in wage levels and exchange rates. Even somewhat lower labor productivity may be offset by much lower wages and by undervalued currencies. In this scenario, low-wage countries tend to become exporters of standard manufactured goods. We will return to this proposition in the next section.

With the rise of multinational firms and with technological achievements expanding the horizons of industrialism, the need arose to search for a new in:ernational trade theory to fit the changing realities of the trading world. Another theory of international trade and investment activities is the product life cycle theory, which deals with the dynamic changes in international trade patterns over a period of time.

(4) Product Life Cycle (PLC) and International Trade

Studies by Williams, Posner, Hirsh, Hufbauer, Vernon, Wells, Stobaugh, Y. Tsurumi, H. Tsurumi, and Tsurumi and Tsurumi, have refined the product life cycle theory of international trade and investment.[2] They are sometimes called neotechnologists because they have built and tested their theories based on the following new assumptions.

- Information with regard to products, production processes, and markets is not possessed equally by prospective manufacturers at home or abroad and is often restricted from flowing freely across national boundaries;

---

2. Williams, J.H. "The Theory of International Trade Reconsidered," reprinted as Chapter 2 in his *Postwar Monetary Plans and Other Essays*, (Oxford: Basis Blackwell, 1947); S. Burnstam-Linder, *An Essay on Trade and Transformation* (New York: John Wiley and Sons, 1961); M.V. Posner, "International Trade and Technical Changes," *Oxford Economic Papers* 13 (October 1961): 323-341; S. Hirsch, *Location of Industry and International Competitiveness* (unpublished doctoral thesis, Harvard Business School, 1965); G.C. Hufbauer, *Synthetic Materials and the Theory of International Trade* (Cambridge, Mass.: Harvard University Press, 1966); R. Vernon, "International Investment and International Trade in the Product Cycle," *Quarterly Journal of Economics* LXXX (May 1966): 190-207; L. Wells, *Production Innovation and Direction of Trade* (unpublished doctoral thesis, Harvard Business School, 1966); R. Stobaugh, *The Product Life Cycle, U.S. Exports and International Investment* (unpublished doctoral thesis, Harvard Business School, 1968); Y. Tsurumi, *Technology Transfer and Foreign Trade: The Case of Japan, 1950-1966* (unpublished doctoral thesis, Harvard Business School, 1968); Y. Tsurumi, "Japanese Multinational Firms," *Journal of World Trade Law* 7 (January/February 1973): 74-90; H. Tsurumi, "A Bayesian Test of the Product Life Cycle Hypothesis Applied to Japanese Crude Steel Production," *Journal of Econometrics*, no. 4 (1976): 371-392; and H. Tsurumi and Y. Tsurumi, "A Bayesian Test of the Product Life Cycle Hypothesis as Applied to the U.S. Demand for Color-TV Sets," *International Economic Review* 21, no. 3 (October 1980): 583-597.

- Not only the attained level of technological capability of manufacturing industries, but also the direction and speed of change in technological competence, vary both in kind and degree from one nation to another;

- Consumers' and industrial users' tastes not only vary from one country to the next but also change over a period of time along predictable lines;

- Product characteristics in a given market change over a period of time as the product goes through a life cycle consisting of introduction, growth, maturation, and decline; and

- Such competitive forces as monopolies of export products, both imagined and real product differentiation, and static and dynamic scales of economy of production and marketing activities determine the trade patterns of manufactured goods.

Furthermore, the PLC theory of international trade combines supply side analysis (a firm's ability to produce) with demand side analysis (the impact of market characteristics on a supplier's strategies). As compared with the two factors of production—capital and labor—of the Heckscher–Ohlin theorem, the PLC proponents invariably deal with four distinct determinants of a firm's output, namely, capital, labor, technology, and marketing expertise.

Table 4-6 presents the growth trend of labor productivity (output per manhour) from 1960 to 1979 for six industrialized nations. Table 4-7 compares the interindustry differences in the growth of labor productivity among three leading industrialized countries from 1960 to 1978. From Table 4-6 and Table 4-7, we observe that the growth of labor productivity varies from one industry to the next (unbalanced growth) and from one country to the next.

Table 4-6. Labor Productivity Growth in Manufacturing Industries, 1960-1979.

	1979 (1960 = 100)
Japan	465
Italy	280
Germany	270
France	250
U.S.	190
U.K.	180

Source: Ministry of International Trade and Industry (MITI), *White Paper on International Trade* (Tokyo: MITI, 1980).

Table 4-7. Interindustry Differences in Annual Average Rate of Growth of Labor Productivity for Three Industrialized Nations, 1960-1978.

	Japan (%)	West Germany (%)	U.S. (%)
Total manufacturing	8.2	5.5	3.4
Electric machinery	11.0	6.5	4.6
Precision machinery	10.6	4.2	–
Chemicals	10.4	7.5	5.5
Iron and steel	9.7	4.2	2.5
General machinery	9.7	2.8	2.9
Transportation machinery	9.6	3.9	2.4
Pulp and paper	7.9	5.3	3.7
Textiles	7.8	6.8	3.9
Foodstuffs	3.1	5.3	3.8
Clothing	1.6	4.2	2.3

Source: Same as Table 4-6.

In Table 4-1 we observed the differences in growth exports for various countries from 1958 to 1979. Are these distinctions explained by variations in the labor productivity growth? To demonstrate the statistical correlation analysis that economists and managers use to test their hypotheses (distilled hunches) we will apply the simplest tool; Spearman's rank correlation. Table 4-6 and Table 4-1 are synthesized in Table 4-8.

Spearman's rank correlation coefficient is given by the formula:

$$R^{rank} = 1 - \frac{6 \Sigma d^2}{N(N^2 - 1)} = 1 - \frac{6 \times 2}{6 \times 35} = +0.942$$

where

d = the difference in rank between paired items, and

N = the number of the paired observations.

Simple as it is, this rank correlation analysis shows that the export growth of a nation is positively related to its labor productivity growth. Is this relationship spurious? The correlation test does not tell us anything about the cause–effect relationships between tested variables. The causality of these relationships can only be inferred from a proven theory. However, the results of Spearman's rank correlation test positively conformed to the pattern predicted by the PLC theory of international trade.

97

Table 4-8. Descending Order of Ranking of Export Growth and Labor Productivity Growth for Six Nations, 1960-1979.

Country	Export Growth 1958-1979 (A)	Labor Productivity Growth 1960-1979 (B)	Difference in Rank (A) - (B)
Japan	1	1	0
Italy	2	2	0
France	3	4	-1
W. Germany	4	3	+1
U.S.	5	5	0
U.K.	6	6	0

(5) The PLC Theory of International Trade

During the last quarter of a century, the United States produced a vast array of product innovations to meet such domestic market characteristics as mass market, high income, high wage cost, and consumer orientation to convenience. Throughout the world there are groups of consumers and industrial users who demand these American innovations and immediately import them from the United states. As these products lose their novelty in the American market and join the ranks of standard and mature products, the United States not only loses its export markets but also increasingly begins to import old and new products that were originally developed in the United States. This occurs because foreign manufacturers have substituted their own products in their home market for the "new products" from the United States and have come to export those goods to the United States.

In other words, new products developed to meet the needs of one market, say the United States, spread internationally just as new products from an innovative firm subsequently spread domestically. How fast imitators, both at home and abroad, can copy the innovator depends mainly on their technological and financial competence. How strongly they become motivated to imitate depends on the extent to which the new products pose a threat to the market position of their existing products. Successful imitation by other nations, of course, presupposes that the technology required to produce the specific product is transferred to the imitating nation.

Today, even though they are still scarce, empirical studies suggest that the agents of technology transfer are products, persons, and documents (designs, blueprints, data, etc.). Above all, the manufactured products that embody new technology often serve as the trans-

98

fer agents. Even when newly developed product-related technologies are patented by the inventor, the proven fact that some specific product has been successfully manufactured somewhere else will encourage and aid the follower firms to accomplish the same results. The uncertainties inherent in product development are now substantially reduced by the successful examples of innovators.

Needless to say, the development of new products is not the monopoly of American industry. When other industrialized nations, which generally still have lower wages than the United States, develop new products and attain technological advances, their exportation of such products tends to survive international competition for a considerable period of time. They not only possess technological leads over other nations, including the United States, but they can also compete favorably with other countries in terms of production costs even when these products become standard in the world market.

Even when their wages are rising rapidly, countries like Japan and West Germany often set up production on a large scale to supply expanding home markets and traditional export markets. This economy of scale in production often provides Japan and West Germany with additional production cost advantages vis-à-vis the United States.

Meanwhile, in the United States market, the product in question continues to mature, and purchasers become increasingly conscious of the prices of these mature products. In the terminology of the economist, the price elasticity of demand for such products is becoming greater while the income elasticity of demand for the same product rapidly declines. By this time, manufacturing technology for the products is spreading throughout the world. Such semi-industrialized nations as Israel, Ireland, Taiwan, Korea, Singapore, and Mexico may have gained the necessary production technology and begun exporting these same products to the United States, Europe, and Japan.

The preceding accounts capture the gist of the changes in export competitiveness among diverse nations with varying degrees of technological competence. Throughout the life cycle of a given new product, the world trade market goes through the phases of the monopolistic suppliers' market (few innovators) to oligopolistic competition (a few more imitators), and finally to competition among many producers (many more imitators). In the last phase of competition among many producers, some semblance of the trade world envisaged by the comparative advantage theorists is likely to emerge. The PLC model of international trade points to the process by which relevant technology is transferred from one country to the other.

(6) The PLC and the Concept of Barrier to Entry

During the innovation stage, a new product or product idea emerges from a firm's research and development laboratory, goes though pilot production, and is launched into the market. The research and development and pilot production are likely to be both costly and time consuming to the firm but produce highly specialized knowledge. The company that makes the investment to develop a new product is not likely to share this knowledge. Therefore, any other firm that seeks to develop a similar product has to make a comparable investment to generate its own knowledge. There is always the risk that the new product, once launched into the market, might never be able to generate enough revenue to recover the original investment.

At the innovation stage there are barriers to entry for new firms that might develop and sell the product. Any firm that makes the investment is afforded some protection from competition by these barriers to entry. The new product itself, by virtue of its newness, is differentiated from other products on the market. It may perform a function that no other product performs. It may also perform a function more satisfactorily than other products. In all likelihood, only a small number of firms—perhaps only one—will initially choose to develop and market the new product. Therefore, in the innovation stage, barriers to entry are high, the number of sellers low, and the product highly differentiated.

If the market accepts the product, the product enters the market growth stage of the product life cycle. Inventive firms will strive to improve the product while simultaneously learning how to produce it more cheaply. This has the effect of causing the barriers to entry to become even higher. Offsetting this, however, are several factors. First, the initial risk that the market might not accept the product has been substantially lessened or removed entirely. New firms wishing to develop the knowledge needed to produce the product themselves can do so at less peril. Second, as the product is improved, new entrants may be able to copy the improved product and bypass some steps in the development of the product that the initiating firms went through. The barrier to entry, based on development of specialized knowledge required to produce the product, may also fall. Over time, the reduced risk and increasing ease of copying the product will cause the net barrier to entry to fall.

The inventor firms, by virtue of their initial quasi-monopoly position in the market for the new product, can initially extract a rent from the sales of the product. (We define "rent" as profit in excess of some "normal" return to capital.) This rent, in turn, enhances the attractiveness of participating in the market for the new product. As barriers to entry fall, new firms enter the market. As this new entry occurs, rents will be driven down, and profits will gradually be reduced to competitive levels.

Generally, as more and more firms offer a closely substitutable product, product differentiation diminishes. However, one or more companies, which may or may not be the original innovators, may create a buyers' preference for a particular brand or trade name through advertising. If any firm succeeds in doing this, it creates artificial product differentiation, based on trade name, which in itself constitutes a barrier to entry. The firm with the successful trade name is able to create a "mini-monopoly" and possibly earn rent from sales of the branded product.

As more time passes, the product enters the mature product phase of the life cycle. Companies selling the product may succeed in locating all the potential buyers of the product. Hence, initial sales to consumers who never purchased it before fades away. Further sales of the product must be replacement sales to buyers who have already purchased it but have consumed it or worn it out. As a consequence, the rate of growth in demand for the product is likely to decline.

In the mature product stages, barriers to entry can either be high or low, depending upon the importance of consumer brand preference and upon the economies of manufacturing scale. If no firm is able to create a preference for a particular brand name and economies of scale are not significant, the barriers to entry are low and the industry becomes competitive. The textile industry is an example of a mature industry that fits this case. If consumer brand preference is important, as is the case in the cigarette industry, or if economy of scale is important, as is the case of most mature, vertically integrated industries such as oil, steel, copper, and aluminum, barriers to entry are much higher and the industry structure becomes oligopolistic.

Often, as a product passes from the market growth stage into the mature product stage, scale economies or brand preferences result in an industry "shakeout"—a reduction in the number of sellers in the industry. The firms that develop scale economies or brand preferences are able to force other firms out of business. For example, shakeouts are apparently occurring today in the color television and automobile industries. Sometimes, the original inventors of the product are among those firms forced to leave the industry. In the aircraft, automobile, and computer industries, for example, many of the pioneering firms are no longer operating.

2. BUSINESS POLICY IMPLICATIONS OF THE PLC THEORY

The PLC model provides business and government with a conceptual scheme for answering the question: Who produces what, where, and most efficiently, over a period of time?

Unlike the comparative advantage theorem, the PLC model incorporates marketing considerations into its theoretical structure. For example, as a product becomes mature and standard, the concomitant increase in the price elasticity of demand alerts businesses to pay more attention to the physical coverage of the market and the logistics of physical distribution as well as the attainment of the lowest cost production. The purchase decisions of potential customers are now significantly influenced by even small differences in price and shopping convenience.

In fact, as a product becomes standard in a given market, the mass merchandising abilities of its manufacturer become a crucial competitive factor, and the location of production facilities can now be separated geographically from the markets. With the standardization of product specifications, there is less need for the constant interaction between markets and production facilities required in the stages of introduction and early growth. With mature products, worldwide procurement capabilities may become crucial for manufacturing firms.

Conversely, if an American manufacturer begins to lose its American market position to European and Japanese producers, the viable defensive responses are essentially twofold. It can upgrade major product lines to more innovative products and sell sales engineering skills and customer services through missionary sales efforts, or it can overhaul and automate its production in the United States to obtain economy of scale. Furthermore, the manufacturer can have its U.S. plants concentrate on more unusual technology-intensive products and procure standard products from overseas suppliers. The innovator firm can sell its maturing technology to foreign firms through technical licensing agreements (technology exports).

These specific strategies are not mutually exclusive. Businesses should recognize the persistent but predictable changes in market demand characteristics of their products as they pass through the stages of the product life cycle. For example, consumer demand continues to shift as buyers become accustomed to products. The markets become finely segmented as newer uses of similar products spread. As consumers begin to pay increasing attention to the function of the product, their preference for the functional reliability or product quality increases. As mass production and mass marketing determine the success of companies in maturing markets, their ability to mass produce products without debasing the product quality are likely to determine the winners in the market.

3. RIDING THE PLC UPSTREAM

If you are the leading innovators, your strategy should be to ride the international product cycle downstream. If you are an imitator in a developing nation, your plan should be to ride the international product cycle upstream. For example, in the household electric and electronic markets, imitators may first concentrate on replacing imports of transistor radios from the United States with their own products. Then they begin to export them to other follower nations nearby and eventually back to the United States. Once imitators establish international distribution channels linking the United States with their country and other follower and developing nations, they can leapfrog their foreign competitors and first introduce their own new products in the United States. At the same time they can expand their home plant capacities to meet the increases in the same new products at home. Indeed, the success of Japan's export-led industrial growth during the postwar era owed much to Japanese firms' conscious efforts to absorb foreign technology, improve on it, and then develop their own marketing abilities for channeling newly acquired products first to neighboring Asian nations and later to the United States and Europe. This refinement of the PLC theory was first made by Y. Tsurumi [1968 and 1973] and more rigorously by H. Tsurumi [1976] and Tsurumi and Tsurumi [1980].[3]

Today, such newly industrializing nations as Korea, Hong Kong, Singapore, and Taiwan have successfully followed the strategy of riding the international product cycle upstream as Japanese firms did from the 1950s to the 1960s. They show a willingness to make a major shift in a product line of a domestic plant long before the domestic market is ready for an innovative product. The People's Republic of China, Mexico, Peru, Ireland, Greece, Brazil, and other nations are now also attempting to accelerate the pace of their industrialization by riding the international product cycle upstream. Of course, the key to the success of this plan is the international trans-

3. See the works cited in footnote 2 of this chapter.

fer of product- and production process-related technology. We will return to this theme in Chapter 13.

In the case of Japan, it was found that the rapidly changing profile of manufactured exports (Table 4–2) was positively and significantly explained by Japanese industries' increasing R&D efforts and international marketing techniques.) After all, growing labor productivity is a proxy for both increasing national technological competence and ever expanding capital investments in newer and better production facilities. The stimulus for technological innovation comes mainly from the close interaction of companies with their markets. This is why developing nations with exportable raw materials cannot easily establish manufacturing industries to process them. Only when production know-how and commodities marketing are standardized can on-site processing become economically feasible.

4. MICRO-INTERNATIONAL ECONOMICS: THE BUSINESS STRATEGY OF A FIRM

Multinational managers must be able to bring such macroeconomic analytical tools as the PLC theory of international trade, the balance of payments adjustment process, and foreign exchange determination to bear upon the pressing problems of their own firm. Familiarity with macroeconomic analysis can help managers to firmly grasp the changing fundamentals of the macroeconomy and to identify the potentially adverse impact on their own firm. Once these problems are identified they can be solved.

Successful solutions to anticipated problems require that the firm alter its traditional behavior. From pricing to product distribution, a wide range of marketing issues will have to be examined and changed. The firm has to seize upon its perceived strength or strengths—such as the loyalty of its employees—and technological competence to effect necessary changes. As market competition increases at home and abroad, the firm will have to acquire the manufacturing skill to cut production costs and at the same time maintain (or increase) product quality.

Early in the 1970s, once they chose to sell subcompact cars in the United States, the Big Three auto makers (General Motors, Ford, and Chrysler) chose respectively three different ways to obtain the products. The automobile had long been a standard feature of American life, and about one-fourth of the purchasers of new cars were already attracted to the price, operational economy, and performance of Japanese and European cars. Around 1957, the United States automotive industry shifted from "net exporter" to "net importer." If it were not for the United States–Canada Automotive Trade Agreement that accelerated after 1968 — American automakers' duty-free cross-hauls of automotive products between the two countries — American exports of cars would have not increased as drastically as they did after 1968. Inside the United States, by the early 1970s, Japan captured over 3 percent of the entire import market of cars and dislodged West Germany from the position of the leading exporter to the United States.

Over the years, Toyota, Nissan (Datsun), Volvo, Volkswagen, Renault, and other foreign automakers had successfully built up their own sales and service networks in the United States and Canada in direct competition with General Motors, Ford, and Chrysler. The Big Three automakers had concentrated on large cars and ignored the market of subcompact cars. One of their executives was quoted as having stated: "Mini cars produce mini profits." By the early 1970s, however, foreign subcompact cars had carved out too large a market for the Big Three to ignore.

With nationwide dealer networks and established brand images, the Big Three knew that they had only to develop captive sources of supplies of subcompact cars at a price competitive with foreign imports. The options were essentially threefold: (1) to find a foreign producer of desired cars, (2) to produce in the United States hybrid cars by importing necessary parts and engines of subcompact cars, and (3) to build in the United States an automated plant permitting a long production run of a single model for maximum production efficiency. The critical factor for success in each move varied from one option to the next. The first option required mainly the firm's ability to import foreign cars on a long-term purchase contract. The second option required the firm to coordinate production schedules and designs between its American plants and overseas suppliers (most likely, subsidiaries). But the firm could depend on the production efficiency of its foreign suppliers. The third option depended critically on American workers' attitude and their resultant production efficiency. The required capital investment was the smallest for the first option and the largest for the third.

The Big Three appeared intuitively aware of the dynamics of automobile trade as predicted by the PLC model Chrysler, which had the smallest financial and managerial resources vis-à-vis Ford and General Motors, chose to import Colt subcompacts from Mitsubishi Automobile in Japan (in which Chrysler held a minority interest) and distribute them under the brand name of Dodge Colt through the existing Chrysler sales networks. Ford chose to import engines and transmissions from its European subsidiaries and have them assembled into bodies produced in the United States. General Motors committed a vast amount of capital to its highly automated new assembly plant in Lordstown, Ohio. The long production run of the plant was expected to provide such a large scale of production efficiency that even with the high wage costs, the labor cost content of the Vega model would be kept competitive with the Japanese and European imports.

The workers of the Lordstown plant, however, sabotaged production. This labor strife initially denied General Motors of the expected production efficiency (and resultant low-cost production of Vega). When the plant workers discovered that the increased production efficiency meant not only speedups on the assembly work pace but continued layoffs of "surplus" workers, they stopped cooperating with the plant manager.

An understanding of the PLC model made General Motors realize that the success of Vega depended on an uninterrupted operation of the Lordstown plant. The firm had grown all the more vulnerable to worker response to production efficiency. But the Lordstown plant continued with the old management-labor practice of achieving production efficiency at the expense of the worker job security. In fact, a new strategy of fighting foreign imports of compact cars required that General Motors change its attitude toward rank and file employees.

Then, the oil crises of 1973-74 and 1979 hit the United States. The U.S. demand for cars had been shifting in preference of more and more well made and fuel efficient compact and subcompact cars. The oil crises simply precipitated this shift of U.S. demand, and General Motors, Ford, and Chrysler were all caught unprepared by that shift.

When all manufacturing and marketing attempts to recapture subcompact car markets from Japanese imports failed, and when the U.S. economy plunged into the drawn-out stagation from 1979 to 1983, the United Auto Workers (UAW) and the American auto manufacturers turned to political defensive measures. Together, they lobbied successfully both Congress and the Executive Branch to obtain in 1981 the "voluntary export restraint" (import quota) of Japanese cars from Japan. The Japanese imports were to be restricted to 1.68 million units a year or 17.5 percent of the U.S. market demand. In order to overcome such trade barriers, Honda, Nissan, and Toyota commenced their assembly operations of passenger cars and light trucks in the United States. In February, 1983, General Motors and Toyota announced a joint production venture of subcompact cars in the former General Motors' plant in Fremont, California.

Meanwhile, General Motors, Ford, and Chrysler increased their procurements of subcompact cars from their affiliated firms in Japan.

In your analysis of the case, make sure that you develop your own views of the immediate future of the strength of the Deutch mark to the dollar on the basis of the attached balance of payments and other macroeconomic statistics. Please suggest the immediate methods of hedging the short-term financial risks associated with the DM-dollar relations. How is this DM-dollar situation likely to affect the firm's competitive position in North America against the Italian competitor?

CASE 2:
BAYERISCHE WURST–MACHINE GmbH

Mr. Hans Sachs is the president of Bayerische Wurst-Machine (BW) GmbH, a company located in Munich, West Germany. Its chief product is sausage machines, the unit price of which is DM 10,000 (approximately $2,500 f.o.b. BW). Bayerische Wurst is a relatively small company with annual sales of about DM 40 million expected for 1969. However, about 65 percent of its sales are export sales to the United States and Canada. The remaining sales came from customers and exporting firms located in Germany. Mr. Sachs believed that about one-third of "domestic sales" ended up eventually in France, Italy, the United Kingdom, and Scandinavia. BW has about 200 employees, most of whom are highly skilled craftsmen. For a variety of cultural and legal reasons, it would be very difficult for BW to discharge employees. For BW this constraint is even stronger because of the long years of loyal service given by its employees and their willingness to work through arduous overtime schedules during boom periods.

Having grown up in the postwar era, Mr. Sachs is accustomed to thinking of the U.S. dollar as a strong currency and has accordingly required that all of his export sales be made on the basis of confirmed, irrevocable (sixty-day) letters of credit denominated in U.S. dollars. From Mr. Sachs' point of view, this requirement eliminated all risks arising from his export sales. He knew that BW would get paid. All the domestic sales were made in DM denominated credit (thirty days f.o.b. BW).

Because it manufactured a specialized product, the company had traditionally enjoyed a dominant position in its export markets. These markets have been relatively stable and free from seasonal fluctuations. It sold its machines only to American and Canadian distributors who agreed not to handle the products of competitors. The distributors were asked to add at least 6 percent markup on f.o.b. BW price, but were free to make its own pricing decisions. The transportation costs, which ran, on the average, 5 percent of f.o.b. BW price, were passed onto final purchasers of the BW machine. Distributors and purchasers had to make their own financial arrangements to obtain necessary letters of credit.

In the last year, however, the U.S. market had become more competitive. Italian exporters were moving into the U.S. and Canadian markets with comparable machines and were shipping them to distributors on consignment. These exporters were, then, selling their machines on ninety-day credit (D/P or D/A arrangement). Their U.S. distributors were immediately paid 5 percent sales commission on their customers' acceptances of shipments. Sachs' exclusive distributors began to complain that his credit policy was too strict and suggested that he would have to start extending credit soon to maintain his market share. Besides, it was reported that the list price of the Italian machines was about 15 percent less than the list price of BW machines. Sach's distributors warned him that the local, small-scale processors who used to buy his machines were losing out to larger, more tightly run operations that bought in volume and demanded more generous terms. Sachs believed that the superior quality and reliability of his products would continue to sell them, but his new competitors made him very cost conscious and very reluctant to raise his prices.

Sachs had recently switched banks and he was now taking his banking business to the Munich branch of the United Bank of Los Angeles, a newcomer to the German scene. The Bayerische Wurst account was handled for United by Harry Beckmesser, a U.S. national who speaks German fluently. Although he had no experience in banking, Beckmesser was hired by United because he had very good contacts in Bavaria and could use them to bring new accounts to United. So far Beckmesser had brought United a lot of new business.

On September 15, 1969, Sachs attended a party given by United for its Bavarian clients and friends. Sachs was having a fine time listening to Beckmesser's imitations of various political figures when he saw his old friend Walther von Stoltzing. Stoltzing was a manager of a large manufacturing firm and had a reputation as a very sophisticated type. Sachs greeted Stoltzing and engaged him in a short conversation. Both were pleased with how well their firms were doing, but Stoltzing commented at the end of their talk that he found the currency situation troubling. Sachs asked what Stoltzing meant, but Stoltzing replied "Ask your banker!" and went on his way. Unnerved by this comment, Sachs arranged to have Beckmesser visit him the following week.

When Beckmesser came to see Sachs, Sachs told him the story and explained that about 65 percent of his accounts receivable (comprising all of his export sales) were covered by confirmed, irrevocable letters of credit in U.S. dollars. His total accounts receivable amounted to DM 7 million. Beckmesser assured Sachs that he would be paid and that there was no cause for concern. He promised to think over Sachs' question and contact him soon. "These Germans," thought Beckmesser as he drove home, "they always have to have something to worry about!"

That evening as Beckmesser read his newspaper, he noticed in New York the ninety-day (forward) U.S. dollar to Deutsche mark rate (U.S. dollar per DM) was 2 percent premium over the spot rate. In another article he read that the short-term interest rate in Germany was now 0.5 percent lower than that in New York. The same article mentioned that the West German balance of payments statistics estimated for the third quarter would be released in the next few days.

Exhibit 4-1. Bayerische Wurst GmbH Income Statements (in thousands of DM).

		1967		1968
Net sales		32,400		36,000
Costs of goods sold		23,328		27,123
Direct and indirect labor	11,664		14,220	
Factory overhead[a]	6,998		7,215	
Raw materials	4,666		5,688	
Gross profit		9,072		8,877
Sales and administrative expenses		3,240		3,480
R&D expenses		1,620		1,520
Interest changes and miscellaneous		750		880
Profit before tax from operations		3,462		**2,997**
Dividends and interest income		327		585
Profit before tax		3,789		3,462
Income tax (@ 48%)		1,819		1,662
Profit after tax		1,970		1,920

a. Depreciation expenses constituted approximately 60 percent of total factory overhead.

Exhibit 4-2. Bayerische Wurst GmbH Balance Sheets (as of the end of the year, in thousands of DM).

	1967	1968
Cash	2,850	2,915
Marketable securities	3,568	5,890
Accounts receivable	5,184	5,460
Inventory	5,832	6,081
Plant and equipment	7,328	7,421
Total assets	24,762	27,767
Accounts payable	3,968	4,872
Bank loans (short-term)	2,100	2,235
Unpaid taxes	455	417
Long-term loan	2,756	3,260
Paid-in capital	3,500	3,500
Retained earnings	11,983	13,483
Total liabilities and capital	24,762	27,767

Exhibit 4-3. Exchange Rate Quotations and Discount Rate of Central
Banks (end of month).

		Exchange Rate (DM per US$)		Central Bank Rates	
		Spot	90-day Forward	U.S.	Germany
1968	January	4.004	3.980	4.50%	3.00%
	February	4.004	3.982	4.50	3.00
	March	3.981	3.952	5.00	3.00
	April	3.988	3.983	5.50	3.00
	May	3.983	3.948	5.50	3.00
	June	3.995	3.960	5.50	3.00
	July	4.019	3.988	5.50	3.00
	August	3.972	3.948	5.25	3.00
	September	3.976	3.955	5.25	3.00
	October	3.976	3.954	5.25	3.00
	November	3.988	3.960	5.25	3.00
	December	4.000	3.958	5.50	3.00
1969	January	4.010	3.968	5.50	3.00
	February	4.022	3.989	5.50	3.00
	March	4.024	3.984	5.50	3.00
	April	3.973	3.921	6.00	4.00
	May	4.002	3.935	6.00	4.00
	June	4.003	3.947	6.00	5.00
	July	4.004	3.962	5.50	5.00
	August	3.978	3.923	5.25	5.00

Exhibit 4-4. Balance of Payments Statistics of West Germany
(in millions of DM).

	1966	1967	1968	1Q'69[a]	2Q'69[b]
Trade balance	1,878	4,166	4,485	718	901
Services to foreign troops	1,224	1,310	1,299	305	341
Other services	-1,394	-1,401	-1,230	-352	-302
Transfers (private)	-863	-780	-793	-221	-222
Transfers (government)	-718	-829	-1,035	-187	-235
Private capital	912	-831	-2,406	-1,280	-500
Official capital	-685	-336	-86	-88	6
Short-term bank deposits	-144	-1,206	614	-1,180	90
Net errors and omissions	141	4	855	482	1,815
Official reserves	-351	-97	-1,703	1,803	-1,894

a. First quarter of 1969.

b. Second quarter of 1969.

Source: *International Financial Statistics*, I.M.F. Washington, D.C., for appropriate years.

5 PRICE AND INCOME ELASTICITIES OF DEMAND AND INTERNATIONAL MARKETING

From October to December 1980, spiraling interest rates in the United States increased the cost of durable consumer goods such as passenger cars, which are usually bought in eighteen- to thirty-six-month installments. Higher prices dampened the volume of cars sold by automobile dealers. Chrysler, which banked its survival on sales of its newly designed K-car subcompact series, was desperate. Unexpectedly, the firm announced it would give a price cut equivalent of incremental percentage point differences over and above 12 percent. The intended goal of this effective price reduction was to increase Chrysler's sales at the expense of its competitors. Furthermore, if potential customers who had been scared away earlier by soaring interest costs were lured back to purchase Chrysler models rather than postponing planned replacements of their existing cars, this price cut by a contender in the American automobile market could also mean that total cars sold in the United States might increase.

At the same time, Chrysler and Ford and the United Auto Workers lobbied the U.S. International Trade Commission to impose restrictive quotas on imports of Japanese subcompacts. Instead of demanding tariff increases, which would merely boost the unit price of imported cars, the quotas would restrict the absolute number of cars that could be imported to the United States. Advocates of this import quota were implying that American consumers' demand for Japanese subcompacts was not sensitive to their prices. Even when prices of Japanese imports were pushed up by increased tariffs,

American consumers' preference for such nonprice qualities as fuel efficiency (long-term reduction in operating costs), product reliability, styling, workmanship, and relative riding comfort outweighed their negative reaction to the price increases of the Japanese imports. Besides, the disposable income of American consumers was also rising to nullify any adverse effect of the price increase.

In fact, it was estimated econometrically in 1978 that approximately a 25 percent increase in tariffs on Japanese imports in general could easily be offset by a 5 percent rise in the disposable income of American consumers. This explained why, in 1978, the rapidly appreciating yen did not reduce Japan's widening trade surplus with the United States.

In Chapter 4, we postulated that as a product goes through its life cycle from introduction and growth to the maturing stage in the market, the price elasticity of demand increases and the income elasticity of demand declines. Dynamic changes in market demand characteristics can be captured by these key concepts in market analysis. Multinational managers must master these analytical tools and their application to international marketing problems.

What are price and income elasticities of demand and how are they measured? In what follows, we will present all that multinational managers need to know concerning these two concepts. Their usefulness for marketing decisions should be self-explanatory.

1. APPLICATION OF PRICE AND INCOME ELASTICITIES OF DEMAND

From 1976 to 1977, the price of coffee quadrupled, irritating American consumers. In coffee-producing countries, however, higher coffee prices improved the balance of payments and benefits of these higher coffee prices trickled down to the impoverished farmers and coffee plantation workers. American consumers were involuntarily giving economic aid to people in developing Latin American countries. The *New York Times*, on February 23, 1977, reported from Mexico:

> The high prices being paid for coffee in American supermarkets are beginning to benefit the impoverished farmers of the Indian village high in the Mexican Sierra, five hours by donkey from the nearest road. . . .
>
> The increase in world coffee prices in the last year together with the devaluation of the Mexican peso in August has meant that, in terms of local currency, the small producers are earning six or seven times more than, say, three years ago.

Higher coffee prices will reduce the quantity of coffee demanded, assuming consumers' income, taste, and other factors influencing coffee demands do not change. But even if the quantity demanded is smaller, revenue may not decline; it may very well increase. Revenue, R, is equivalent to the price, p, times quantity, q:

$$R = pq \ .$$

Consequently, whether revenue goes up or down due to increasing coffee prices depends on how much the quantity demanded, q, will decrease. The price elasticity of demand is a concept that predicts what will happen to revenue as the price goes up or down.

2. DEFINITION AND INTERPRETATION OF THE PRICE ELASTICITY OF DEMAND

The price elasticity of demand, E, is defined as

$$E \ = \ - \ \frac{\% \text{ change in quantity demanded}}{\% \text{ change in price}} \tag{5-1}$$

Elasticity is nothing but a ratio of two given ratios. Generally speaking, except for the case of inferior goods whose demand declines as their consumers' income increases, products' prices and their quantity demanded more in opposite directions. This is why E carries a negative sign. The meaning of price elasticity will become clearer if we rearrange Equation (5-1) as follows:

$$\% \text{ change in quantity demanded } = -E \times \% \text{ change in price.} \tag{5-2}$$

Using Equation (5-2) we can ask, "If the price of coffee doubles (i.e., increases by 100%), how much will the quantity demanded be reduced?" If we have information on the magnitude of price elasticity, E, then we can answer this question. One study estimated the price elasticity of coffee to be about 0.2.[1] If we take this estimate, the answer will be

$$\% \text{ change in coffee demand } = -0.2 \times 100 = -20\%$$

Therefore, if the coffee price doubles, coffee demand declines by only 20 percent.

If doubling the price leads only to a 20 percent reduction in demanded, then revenue (quantity times price), should go up—the

1. G. Adams and J. Behrman, Econometric Models of *World Agricultural Commodity Markets* (Cambridge, Mass.: Ballinger Publishing Company, 1975).

smaller the price elasticity of demand, the larger the increase in revenue caused by a price hike. For example, if $E = 0$, then quantity demanded would not change even if the price changed, and a higher price would directly push total revenue up.

We can easily establish an algebraic relationship between price elasticity and changing revenue. Let us begin with Equation (5-1).

$$E = - \frac{\% \text{ change in quantity demanded}}{\% \text{ change in price}}$$

and restate it as

$$E = - \frac{\dfrac{\Delta q_t}{q_{t-1}} \times 100}{\dfrac{\Delta p_t}{p_{t-1}} \times 100} = - \frac{\Delta q_t}{q_{t-1}} \cdot \frac{p_{t-1}}{\Delta p_t} = - \frac{\Delta q_t}{\Delta p_t} \cdot \frac{p_{t-1}}{q_{t-1}} \quad (5\text{-}3)$$

where

Δq_t = change in quantity demanded, say, for coffee at time t measured in pounds of coffee: $\Delta q_t = q_t - q_{t-1}$;

q_t = quantity of coffee demanded at time t, in pounds;

Δp_t = change in price at time t, measured in cents; and

p_t = price of coffee at time t, in cents.

The revenue at time t, R_t, is given by

$$R_t = p_t q_t$$

and its increment, ΔR_t, is given by

$$\Delta R_t = R_t - R_{t-1} = p_t q_t - p_{t-1} q_{t-1} \quad (5\text{-}4)$$

Since $p_t = p_{t-1} + \Delta p_t$, and $q_t = q_{t-1} + \Delta q_t$, Equation (5-4) becomes

$$\Delta R_t = (p_{t-1} + \Delta p_t)(q_{t-1} + \Delta q_t) - p_{t-1} q_{t-1}$$

$$= \Delta p_t q_{t-1} + \Delta q_t p_{t-1} + \Delta p_t \Delta q_t$$

$$= \Delta p_t q_{t-1} \left(1 + \frac{\Delta q_t}{\Delta p_t} \cdot \frac{p_{t-1}}{q_{t-1}}\right) + \Delta p_t \Delta q_t$$

$$= \Delta p_t q_{t-1} (1 - E) + \Delta p_t \Delta q_t \quad , \quad (5\text{-}5)$$

since

$$E = - \frac{\Delta q_t}{\Delta p_t} \cdot \frac{p_{t-1}}{q_{t-1}} \quad .$$

If a change in price, Δp_t, and/or the resulting change in quantity demanded, Δq_t, are small, we may neglect the term $\Delta p_t \, \Delta q_t$ and Equation (5-5) becomes:

$$\Delta R_t = \Delta p_t \, q_{t-1} \, (1-E) \tag{5-6}$$

for a small change in p_t and/or q_t.

Equation (5-6) establishes a relationship between change in revenue, ΔR_t, and a change in prices, Δp_t. The results are reviewed in Table 5-1.

In summary, we observe from Equation (5-6) that price and revenue change in the same direction if the price elasticity is less than 1 (i.e., *inelastic*: $0 < E < 1$). They move in opposite directions if the price elasticity is greater than 1 (i.e., *elastic*: $E > 1$). For unitary elasticity ($E = 1$), revenue stays unchanged as prices move.

If we divide both sides of Equation (5-6) by revenue,

$$R_{t-1} = p_{t-1} \, q_{t-1}$$

and multiply by 100, we have

$$\frac{\Delta R_t}{R_{t-1}} \times 100 = \frac{\Delta p_t}{p_{t-1}} \times 100 \, (1-E) \tag{5-7}$$

or

$$\left(\begin{array}{c} \% \text{ change in} \\ \text{revenue} \end{array} \right) = \left(\begin{array}{c} \% \text{ change in} \\ \text{price} \end{array} \right) \times \begin{array}{c} (1 - \text{price elasticity} \\ \text{of demand}) \end{array}$$

for a small change in p_t and/or q_t.

Table 5-1. The Relationship between Changes in Revenue and Prices.

Elasticities E	Prices p	Revenue R = pq
$0 < E < 1$ (inelastic)	up down	up down
$E = 1$ (unitary)	up down	no change no change
$E > 1$ (elastic)	up down	down up

116

To illustrate Equation (5–7), suppose that the price elasticity of coffee is 0.2. Then doubling the coffee price leads to an 80 percent increase in revenue.[2]

$$\begin{array}{c} \% \text{ change in} \\ \text{revenue} \end{array} = 100\% \, (1 - 0.2) = 80\%.$$

Once the price elasticity of demand is understood, we should focus our attention on some of the assumptions underlying the basic concept.

(1) Elasticity is Derived Under a Ceteris Paribus Condition

The definition of price elasticity in Equation (5–1) is based on the assumption that, except for price, all variables that influence quantity demanded remain unchanged.

Quantity demanded, q, is composed of many variables. If, for example, we write the demand function for coffee, the dependent variable, q, would be determined by many independent variables listed in the parentheses.

$$q = f(p, p_t, p_m, p_s, Y, F, S, A, T \ldots) \tag{5-9}$$

where

q = coffee demand in pounds;

p = price of coffee in cents;

p_t = price of tea in cents;

p_m = price of milk in cents;

p_s = price of sugar in cents;

Y = household income;

F = family size;

S = sex composition of the household;

A = age composition of the household; and

T = taste of the household.

---

2. Actually, a 100 percent increase in price is not a "small" change in p_t. So we should not neglect the $\Delta p_t \, \Delta q_t$ term in Equation (5–5) by $R_{t-1} = p_{t-1} q_{t-1}$, we have

$$\frac{\Delta R_t}{R_{t-1}} = \frac{\Delta p_t}{p_{t-1}} \, (1 - E) + \frac{\Delta p_t}{p_{t-1}} \, \frac{\Delta q_t}{q_{t-1}} \tag{5-8}$$

$$= \frac{\Delta p_t}{p_t} \, (1 - E) + \left(\frac{\Delta p_t}{p_{t-1}}\right)^2 (-E).$$

In this analysis of price elasticity of demand, we assume that p_t, p_m, p_s, Y, F, S, A, and T all remain unchanged. The statement that says: "Given a price elasticity of demand of 0.2, a 100 percent increase in coffee prices will reduce the quantity demanded by 20 percent and increase revenue by 80 percent (or, more precisely, by 60 percent)" should hold true only when all the other variables (p_t, p_m, p_s, Y, F, S, A, T ...) remain unchanged.

In the real world, of course, everything changes, so some argue that the price elasticity of demand should be defined allowing for that fact. In order to do so, however, we must know precisely *how* everything changes. In the case of coffee, we have to know how a rise in coffee prices will affect p_t, p_m, p_s, Y, and T, which is often impossible to discover. Consequently, it is better to apply price elasticity of demand to a situation, assuming that other things remain constant but recognizing that this assumption may not always be true. So, for example: If other variables remain the same, an increase of 100 percent in the coffee price will lead to a 20 percent decrease in quantity demanded and a 60 percent increase in revenue.

(2) Price Elasticity is a Point Concept

It is not the slope of the demand curve. Often price elasticity of demand is confused with the slope of the demand curve because economics instructors tend to draw a flatter curve to represent a price-elastic demand curve and a steeper curve to indicate a price-inelastic demand curve. This pedagogical overdramatization is very graphic, but is incorrect. Price elasticity of demand is defined as a point on the demand curve. It may vary at each point on the demand curve even if the slope is the same. To illustrate this point, assume that the demand curve is represented by the following linear equation involving q and p.

$$q = 12 - 2p$$

or   (5-10)

$$p = 6 - \frac{1}{2} q$$

Given that $E = 0.2$ and $\Delta p_t / p_{t-1} = 1$ (i.e., 100%), we have $\Delta p_t / q_{t-1} = -0.2$. Using Equation (5-8), we see that the resulting change in revenue is shown by

$$\frac{\Delta R_t}{R_{t-1}} = 1 \times (1 - 0.2) + 1 \times (-0.2) = 0.6$$

or 60 percent rather than 80 percent. For a case in which Δp_t is large, we should use Equation (5-8) rather than (5-7).

Figure 5-1. Different Price Elasticities on the Same Line.

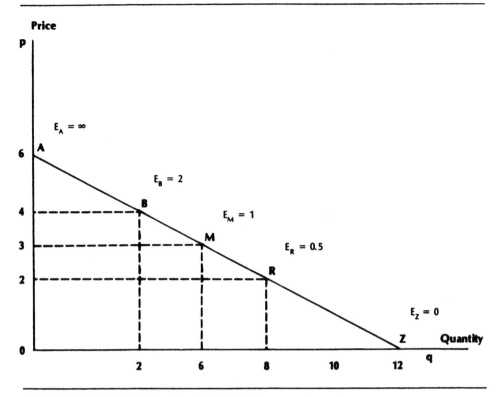

Note: Price elasticities vary at each point on the curve.

Figure 5-1 shows the demand curve (5-10) in a (q, p) plane with price, p, on the vertical axis and quantity, q, on the horizontal axis.[3]
Then price elasticity at each point on Figure 5-1 is given by

$$E_A = - \frac{\Delta q_A}{\Delta p_A} \cdot \frac{p_A}{q_A} \qquad E_Z = - \frac{\Delta q_Z}{\Delta p_Z} \cdot \frac{p_Z}{q_Z}$$

A small change in price and quantity at each point, $\Delta q_A / \Delta p_A$, is given by the slope of the curve, -2, which is the same for all points on the curve:

$$\frac{\Delta q_A}{\Delta p_A} = \frac{\Delta q_B}{\Delta p_B} = \frac{\Delta q_M}{\Delta p_M} = \frac{\Delta q_R}{\Delta p_R} = \frac{\Delta q_Z}{\Delta p_Z} = -2$$

3. Students who have taken economics in the Anglo-Saxon tradition are accustomed to a diagram showing price on the vertical axis. This is due to Alfred Marshall, who believed that quantity influences price (in other worlds, price adjusts to the quantity supplied and demanded rather than quantity adjusting to prices). In the continental (e.g., Swiss and French) tradition quantity, q, is always on the vertical axis.

But price elasticities of demand are different:

$$E_A = -(-2)\frac{6}{0} = \infty \; ; \; E_B = -(-2)\frac{4}{4} = 2 \; ;$$

$$E_M = -(-2)\frac{3}{6} = 1 \; ; \; E_R = -(-2)\frac{2}{8} = 0.5, \text{ and}$$

$$E_Z = -(-2)\frac{0}{10} = 0 \; .$$

As a matter of fact, the price elasticities of demand at any point between A and M are greater than one, while those at any point between M and Z are less than one.[4]

Price elasticity of demand is given as the slope times the ratio of price to quantity at each point on the curve, A point M:

$$E_M = -(\text{slope at M}) \times \frac{\text{price at M}}{\text{quantity at M}} \; .$$

The slope at M is given as the first derivative evaluated at M:

$$\frac{dq}{dp} = \lim_{\Delta \to 0} \frac{\Delta q}{\Delta p}$$

The elasticity at M is most precisely defined as:

$$E_M = -\left(\frac{dq}{dp}\right)_M \frac{p_M}{q_M} \tag{5-11}$$

where $(\frac{dq}{dp})_M$ indicates the first derivative evaluated at M.

Functions with Constant Elasticities: Although the price elasticity is defined at each point on the demand curve, there is a family of functions that produce the same elasticity value at *all points* of a function. Figure 5-2 reveals some special cases.

4. This is easy to prove since the price elasticity of demand

$$E = -(-2)\frac{p}{q} = 2\frac{6 - q/2}{q} = 2\left(\frac{6}{q} - \frac{1}{2}\right)$$

is a monotonically decreasing function of q, and at $q = 6, E = 1$.

At point A, $E_A = -(-2) 6/0$ may be defined to be indeterminate, but more logically we may define 6/0 to be ∞, since it is viewed as:

$$E_A = \lim_{q \to 0} -(-2)(6/q - 1/2) = \infty \; .$$

Figure 5-2. Special Cases of Functions with Constant Price Elasticities of Demand.

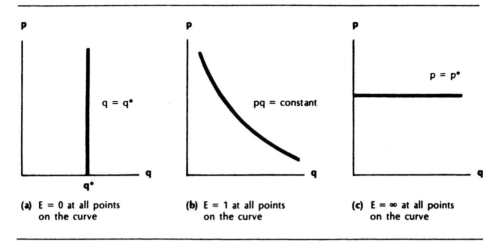

(a) E = 0 at all points
    on the curve

(b) E = 1 at all points
    on the curve

(c) E = ∞ at all points
    on the curve

It is easy to show that a "log-linear" demand function produces a constant elasticity, but the converse is also true. To demonstrate this, suppose a demand function is given by

$$q = 50\,p^{-\alpha} \tag{5-12}$$

or

$$\log q = \log 50 - \alpha \log p.$$

Parameter, α, becomes the price elasticity of demand for curve (5-12) at all points on the curve. If we differentiate Equation (5-12) totally, we have the following:

$$\frac{1}{q}\,dq = -\alpha\,\frac{1}{p}\,dp$$

or rearranging the term, we find:

$$\frac{dq}{dp}\,\frac{p}{q} = -\alpha\ . \tag{5-13}$$

Comparing the above equation with (5-11), we see

$$E = -\frac{dq}{dp}\,\frac{p}{q} = \alpha\ .$$

In Equation (5-12), if we put $\alpha = 0$, we show Case (a) of Figure 5-2:

$$\alpha = 0 \quad q = 50p^{-0} = 50,\ \text{with}\ q^* = 50\ .$$

121

If we put $\alpha = 1$, Case (b) of Figure 5–2 appears:

$$\alpha = 1, \quad q = 50p^{-1}, \quad \text{or} \quad pq = 50 = \text{constant}.$$

If we put $\alpha \to \infty$, we have Case (c) of Figure 5–2:

$$\log p = \frac{1}{\alpha} \log 50 - \frac{1}{\alpha} \log q \to 0 \quad \text{as} \quad \alpha \to \infty$$

or $\quad p \to 1 \quad$ as $\quad \alpha \to \infty$

or more generally,

$$p = \text{constant} \quad \text{when} \quad \alpha = \infty \ .$$

Accordingly, we have shown that log-linear demand functions exhibit constant elasticities.[5]

3. STATISTICAL ESTIMATIONS OF ELASTICITIES

There are various ways of computing the price elasticity of demand for a commodity. At present the most popular method is to begin by directly estimating a demand function.

Let us illustrate how to estimate price elasticities and income elasticities with an example—the demand for gasoline. First, we designate which demand function to evaluate.

$$q_t = \alpha + \beta p_t / p_{c,t} + \gamma Y_t + \delta q_{t-1} \tag{5-14}$$

where

q_t = gasoline consumption per car at time t, measured in gallons;

p_t = gasoline price at time t, in cents;

$p_{c,t}$ = consumer price index at time t;

Y_t = per capita income at time t, in thousands of dollars.

---

5. To show the converse, that is, that constant elasticities give rise to log-linear demand functions, we integrate Equation (5–13)

$$\int \frac{1}{q} \, dq = -\alpha \int \frac{1}{p} \, dp$$

to yield

$$\log q = \text{constant} - \alpha \log p \ .$$

Equation (5-14) reveals that gasoline consumption per car, q_t, is determined by the gasoline price relative to other consumer prices, $p_t/p_{c,t}$ and by per capita income, Y_t. Gasoline consumption in the previous period, q_{t-1} is also often included in demand equations to capture the habit effect of consumers. For a constant elasticity estimate, we may specify a log-linear demand function

$$\log q_t = \alpha + \beta \log p_t/p_{c,t} + \gamma \log Y_t + \delta \log q_{t-1} \; . \qquad (5\text{-}15)$$

Once a demand equation is determined, data on q_t, p_t, $p_{c,t}$, and Y_t are collected for any specified time period. Then we can estimate the parameters $(\alpha, \beta, \gamma, \delta)$ in Equations (5-14) or (5-15) by some appropriate method. The most commonly used method is the least-squares procedure of regression analysis.

For example, eighty monthly observations in the United States, for the period from January 1970 to December 1976, provide estimates for the parameters in Equation (5-15) as:

$$\log q_t = -0.662 - 0.325 \log p_t/p_{c,t} + 0.212 \log Y_t + 0.102 \log q_{t-1} \; .$$

$$(5\text{-}16)$$

Since Equation (5-16) is log-linear, price elasticity of demand is given by the parameter of $\log p_t/p_{c,t}$, 0.325. Similarly, income elasticity of demand is given by the parameter of $\log Y_t$, 0.212.[6]

If the equation is specified by (5-14), the estimate of price elasticity of demand is given by

$$-(\text{estimate of } \beta) \times \frac{p}{q} \; .$$

As values for (q, p), it is customary to use sample averages of p_t and q_t, $\overline{p}$ and $\overline{q}$. Therefore, we have:

$$\begin{array}{c}\text{Price elasticity of demand} \\ \text{at sample means}\end{array} = -(\text{estimate of } \beta) \times \frac{\overline{p}}{\overline{q}} \; .$$

(1) Price and Income Elasticities of Demand
for Gasoline in the United States
Houthakker and Verleger estimated the price and income elasticities of gasoline consumption for each year between 1949 and 1971 using cross-sectional data. Each state is represented as one

---

6. For a definition of income elasticity, go to the end of this chapter. In quantitative studies, it is customary to present statistics along with parameter estimates, but they are excluded in Equation (5-16) to avoid confusion.

Table 5-2. Price and Income Elasticities of Demand for Gasoline in the U.S., 1949-1971.

Year	Price Elasticity		Income Elasticity	
	Short-run	Long-run[a]	Short-run	Long-run[a]
1949	-0.659	-1.153	0.484	0.848
1950	-0.611	-1.070	0.483	0.846
1951	-0.545	-0.954	0.460	0.800
1952	-0.517	-0.906	0.447	0.783
1953	-0.511	-0.896	0.440	0.770
1954	-0.501	-0.878	0.428	0.750
1955	-0.476	-0.834	0.428	0.750
1956	-0.469	-0.822	0.429	0.751
1957	-0.465	-0.815	0.425	0.744
1958	-0.439	-0.768	0.421	0.738
1959	-0.425	-0.744	0.419	0.734
1960	-0.427	-0.748	0.419	0.734
1961	-0.419	-0.733	0.424	0.743
1962	-0.416	-0.729	0.416	0.729
1963	-0.390	-0.683	0.434	0.760
1964	-0.375	-0.656	0.445	0.779
1965	-0.369	-0.646	0.458	0.802
1966	-0.359	-0.629	0.463	0.811
1967	-0.352	-0.617	0.465	0.816
1968	-0.331	-0.574	0.454	0.804
1969	-0.314	-0.551	0.449	0.787
1970	-0.291	-0.520	0.448	0.784
1971	-0.282	-0.495	0.448	0.785

a. Long-run elasticities are defined at the end of this chapter. It is customary to present the price elasticity of demand with negative (-) sign. This is because an increase in price is assumed to decrease quantity demanded.

Source: H.S. Houthakker and P.K. Verleger, Jr., "The Demand for Gasoline: A Mixed Cross-sectional and Time Series Analysis," (Report to the Energy Policy Project, May 1, 1973).

sample unit. Thus, for each year, there are fifty observations. Their estimates of price and income elasticities are given in Table 5-2.

Table 5-2 shows that price elasticities for gasoline consumption declined for the years from 1949 to 1971, while income elasticities stayed more or less unchanged. The estimates of price and income elasticities of gasoline demand from the monthly time series data given in Equation (5-16) are 0.325 and 0.212, respectively. They are fairly close to the approximations obtained by Houthakker and Verleger using cross-sectional data. There are many other valuations for price and income elasticities of U.S. gasoline consumption and these recent estimates show price elasticities from 0.08 to 0.4 and income elasticities from 0.2 to 1.0.

4. INCOME ELASTICITY OF DEMAND

So far we have focused our attention on the price elasticity of demand. Income elasticity of demand can be easily defined as

$$\text{Income elasticity of demand} = \frac{\% \text{ change in quantity demanded}}{\% \text{ change in income}} \tag{5-17}$$

High income elasticity for a commodity indicates that as income grows, the demand for that commodity increases even faster. Often, high-growth industries have commodities the income elasticities of which are greater than one. It is difficult to establish an algebraic relationship between revenue and income.

If income elasticity of demand is defined as in Equation (5-17), elasticity may be seen as nothing but a ratio of percentage changes. Any elasticity can be defined as long as the explanation is operationally meaningful. The supply elasticity of price and the price elasticity of supply are often mentioned with respect to a substitutable good (i.e., cross price elasticity of demand). For example, a cross price elasticity of coffee with respect to tea is broken down as

$$\text{Cross price elasticity of coffee with respect to tea} = \frac{\% \text{ change in coffee demand}}{\% \text{ change in price of tea}}$$

The reason an elasticity is defined as the ratio of percentage changes is that it does not vary with unit changes. If an elasticity were to be defined as a ratio of absolute changes, as follows:

$$\frac{\text{Change in quantity demanded}}{\text{Change in price}} = \frac{\Delta q}{\Delta p}$$

then a change in units, say, from cents to dollars or from ounces to pounds, will change the value of an elasticity.

Cross price elasticities of demand can be defined for both complementary and substitute product relationships. Demand for sugar may go up as coffee prices go down. In general, when there are many product substitutes, the price elasticity of demand for these items tends to be high (greater than one), and vice versa. If there were ample supplies of non-oil-based energy and many products that could be used as chemical feedstocks instead of petrochemicals the unilateral OPEC price increases on crude oil would have brought disaster to the OPEC nations. They would have priced themselves out of the market. In reality, there are very few substitutes that can

125

replace oil in all of its uses. As a result, the OPEC nations have been singularly successful in boosting their prices.

Generally speaking, as some products become necessities, the price elasticity of demand for such products tends to be inelastic, or less than one. For example, in the case of the American standard of living during the post–World War II era, as depicted in Table 5–2, price elasticities of demand for gasoline consumption declined annually and substantially from 1946 to 1971.

Observers of the American scene during this period would agree that sprawling suburbs were created because of the increasing reliance of Americans on their own cars as their foremost mode of transportation. As public transportation systems decayed and as more and more families chose to live in suburbia their reliance on passenger cars increased. Gasoline soon became one of the basic necessities of American living. This change in the American lifestyle is reflected in the declining price elasticities of demand for gasoline in the United States from 1946 to 1971.

5. LONG-TERM PRICE AND INCOME ELASTICITIES OF DEMAND

Referring to the impact of coffee price increases and the devaluation of the Mexican peso, the article quoted in the beginning of this chapter described how the short-run price elasticity of American demand for Mexican coffee was less than one and the international price of coffee was quoted in U.S. dollars. Under these circumstances, the position of poor Mexican peasants and Mexico's balance of trade would improve a great deal. Mexican coffee export revenues would rise because the percentage reduction in quantity of Mexican coffee demanded by Americans was easily offset by large price increases.

However, if the sharp upswing in coffee prices was sustained, consumers would be likely to switch to coffee substitutes. There would always be quick profit-seeking coffee processors who would substitute cheaper products, like chicory and other additives, for coffee grounds. On May 30, 1977, *Time* magazine reported as follows:

> With the cost of brown gold hovering above $4 per pound, and sales beginning to fall off, producers are hustling a variety of substitutes, additives and extenders to take the sting out of coffee prices. General Foods, the biggest U.S. coffee roaster (Maxwell House, Yuban, Sanka) is test marketing a new brand called Mellow Roast, that is a combination of coffee and other ingredients—46% wheat, bran and molasses in the instant. Mellow Roast ads not only stress low price (about $2.90 for 8 oz. of instant) but also maintain that additives yield "a delicious coffee taste without the bitterness" of the real

126

thing. Nestle's entry in the field, which goes by the tongue-twisting name of Sun Rise Instant Coffee Mellowed with Chicory, is aimed at the younger generation raised on sweet cola drinks. . . .

Proctor & Gamble's entry in the cheaper-java derby, Folger's Flaked Coffee ($2.99 for a 13 oz. can), has no extenders but still yields 20% more brewed coffee per pot than ordinary ground varieties. The secret: the coffee is shaved into tiny flakes to increase the surface area that comes in contact with the hot water. . . .

As implied in the quotation from *Time*, the substitution of cheaper products for higher priced merchandise along with technological innovations that improve the use value of the more expensive items tend to increase the long-run price elasticity of demand for the higher priced product. Both price and income elasticities of demand change over time. In the long run, more and more substitutes will be put on the market, and over time, user taste is likely to change irreversibly. Accordingly, we can expect that long-run price elasticities of demand will surpass the short-run price elasticities of demand.

We cannot say anything definite about the relationship between short-run and long-run income elasticities of demand except in the case of inferior products. If there were two products, each fulfilling the same functional purpose but one being higher priced than the other, and one were considered inferior, the long-run income elasticity of demand for the superior product would rise and that of the inferior product would fall as the general income level of the nation increased. A classic case is the demand for potatoes and bread. Potatoes were considered inferior to bread. Therefore, as the general income level of the nation rose, more and more people switched from potatoes to bread. However, when the rising income level of people in the United States permitted them to eat out more often, the demand for potatoes began to increase. This time, potatoes were consumed as french fries and other side dishes. At any rate, it is imperative to be alert to changes in consumer habits that are induced by fluctuations in the level of prices and income.

In Table 5-2, long-run price (or income) elasticities are presented. Long-run elasticity is usually calculated as follows: Given the log-linear demand function, we will have

$$\log q_t = \alpha + \beta \log p_t + \gamma \log Y_t + \delta \log q_{t-1} \ . \qquad (5\text{-}18)$$

We may define the long run to be the steady state in which q_t does not change, that is, $q_t = q_{t-1} = \ldots = q^*$. Then substituting q^* into Equation (5-18), we will have

$$\log q^* = \alpha + \beta \log p_t + \gamma \log Y_t + \delta \log q^* \qquad (5\text{-}19)$$

127

or

$$(1 - \delta) \log q^* = \alpha + \beta \log p_t + \gamma \log Y_t \ .$$

By dividing both sides of the equation by $(1 - \delta)$

$$\log q^* = \frac{\alpha}{1 - \delta} + \frac{\beta}{1 - \delta} \log p_t + \frac{\gamma}{1 - \delta} \log Y_t \ . \qquad (5\text{-}20)$$

Therefore, long-run price elasticity is given by $-\dfrac{\beta}{1 - \delta}$ and the long-run income elasticity by $\dfrac{\gamma}{1 - \delta}$. In Table 5-2, we have short-run and long-run elasticities for 1970, as follows:

Price Elasticities		Income Elasticities	
Short Run	*Long Run*	*Short Run*	*Long Run*
-0.282	-0.495	0.448	0.785

From these numbers, we will find the values of β, γ, and δ, by solving the following simultaneous equations.

$$\begin{cases} \beta = -0.282 \quad \text{Short Run Price Elasticity} \\ \gamma = 0.448 \quad \text{Short Run Income Elasticity} \\ \dfrac{\beta}{1 - \delta} = -0.495 \quad \text{Long Run Price Elasticity} \\ \dfrac{\gamma}{1 - \delta} = 0.785 \quad \text{Long Run Income Elasticity} \end{cases} \qquad (5\text{-}21)$$

Therefore, $\beta = -0.282$, $\gamma = 0.448$, $\delta = 0.430$.

6. INTERNATIONAL MARKETING IMPLICATIONS

Multinational managers must always realize that the price and income elasticities of demand for their products are always determined by specific markets. The product that has a high price elasticity of demand in one country market may well possess a high income elasticity of demand in another place. Local markets, of course, reflect all the cultural, economic, and political fundamentals of the nations involved. We will deal with these issues in the next chapter. However, multinational managers will find it essential to understand how price and income elasticities of demand for their products are changing in their own home markets and to delineate changing economic and social trends that cause discernible shifts in price and income elasticities of demand. In order to analyze the potential acceptance of their products in foreign markets, multinational managers should examine the underlying social, cultural, economic, and political forces that determine price and income elasticities of demand for their products in foreign markets. Valid responses to various products in foreign markets can be reasonably predicted if the impact of social, cultural, economic, and political factors are included in calculations of market demand.

In any consideration of price and income elasticities of demand for products it is important to distinguish the creation of primary (new) demand that is induced by lower prices from the shift of demand from a higher priced product to a lower priced product (demand switching). Throughout this chapter, we focused on changes in primary demand that are induced by price and income elasticities of demand. When its $600 per car cash rebate took sales away from its competitors, Chrysler benefited only from demand switching. Its success is likely to be short-lived as competitors retaliate through price cutting and other measures. When United Airlines' super-saver fares encouraged travelers to fly instead of driving, their fare reduction created primary demand for air travel. When competing airlines join in price cutting, they may collectively create a large primary demand for air travel as a whole. People may be persuaded to travel more frequently than before the fare reduction. Business travelers may take their families along too because of the reduced fares.

Accordingly, managers following the international market should be able to estimate the net effects of price cutting strategies or non-price promotional activities on their units of sales in different national markets. Other marketing programs will have to be adjusted to expand primary demand or capture as much product switching as possible. Potential counter moves by the competitors determine how effective the strategies are going to be. Hence, the cardinal rule of marketing: preempt the competitors.

6 FOREIGN MARKET ANALYSIS

Except for the product life cycle (PLC) theory (see Chapter 4), most international trade theories do not account for the impact that individual manufacturers' marketing agility and export orientation have on trading patterns among nations. In particular, mere differences in production costs of durable and nondurable consumer goods of various nations rarely explain why one country appears adept at exporting diverse goods while others remain inactive exporters. In drawing business and national policy implications from international trade theories it is important to be aware of how individual company decisionmakers can be encouraged to develop and maintain their commitment to export marketing. Consider the following episodes.

Encouraged by its success in Japan, Heublein, Inc., the owner of Kentucky Fried Chicken Co. (KFC), opened KFC chains in Hong Kong in 1974. The firm adopted the Chinese name for KFC, added to its menu the spring roll—a time honored Chinese dish—and waited for Hong Kong Chinese to flock to their stores. But the Chinese did not respond, and KFC left after losing over $2 million.

Tupperware, a subsidiary of Dart & Kraft, Inc., which had successfully sold plastic housewares and food storage containers in the United States, recognized what it thought was an opportunity in Japan, where the number of households owning refrigerators was increasing rapidly from 1971 to 1973. Tupperware wanted to transplant its unique direct sales method of the "home party" overseas.

At a home party gathering, which housewives agree to host for their neighbors, Tupperware sales personnel demonstrate Tupperware products and try to get orders. The attempt in Japan turned out to be a dismal failure.

In the mid-1960s, in the United States, Matsushita Electric of Japan discovered that the firm's familiar brand name in Japan, "National," had long been used by an obscure New England manufacturer. While Matsushita was advertising its products in the United States under the name "Panasonic," the firm finally purchased the brand name "National" from the New England manufacturer only to learn that by then American consumers had become familiar with "Panasonic" and did not respond favorably to "National." So Matsushita returned to its "Panasonic" brand name for its products sold in the United States.

In 1979, Sony introduced its new stereo cassette player which enabled listeners to walk about while listening to tape through light but highly sensitive earphones. The product was introduced in Japan as "Walkman" and as "Soundabout" in the United States. The product was an instant hit both in Japan and the United States. About a year later, the marketing group of Sony (Japan) directed Sony (America) to use the "Walkman" brand. Not only were the advertising dollars already spent for "Soundabout" wasted, but the name "Walkman" had a strong ring of Japanized English. Besides, some feminist consumers reacted negatively to "Walkman" as smacking of male chauvinism. However, this minor fiasco was offset by the rising popularity of their innovative product.

These four episodes are examples of how marketing managers can fail because of their ethnocentricity. Often, we have no choice but to extrapolate from our own experience to make some sense out of the uncertainties of unknown foreign markets. However, those extrapolations sometimes cause otherwise successful marketing attempts to backfire.

1. REPACKAGING MARKETING MIX

The essence of any marketing program is to generate sales. In order to sell products and services, sellers have to produce an internally consistent configuration combining certain marketing factors. This is called the marketing mix, and it is a package of such decision variables as: (1) price; (2) product quality and feature; (3) brand name; (4) packaging; (5) advertising theme and choice of advertising media; (6) selection of distribution channels, delivery logistics, and warehousing; and (7) uses of sales and customer service personnel.

131

No doubt, the art of arriving at an appropriate marketing mix is far more difficult for consumer products than for industrial products. In the case of industrial products, utilizing sales personnel (personal selling) is relatively more important than it is for consumer products. Personnel selling industrial products must understand how the manufacturing operations of their potential customers are set up and how their customers plan to beat market competition. With an awareness of the needs of its potential customers, industrial marketing personnel can adjust incremental differences in the three variables that determine sales of industrial products, namely, price, product quality, and reliable product delivery. Unlike general consumers, industrial customers are highly sensitive even to slight differences in these three variables.

Hamada, a Japanese manufacturer of industrial machinery and printing equipment, has succeeded in Japan by emphasizing customer services and aggressive direct sales. Potential customers are invited to the firm's golf and recreational facilities, which happen to have on the side the exhibits and demonstrations of the firm's products. Once Hamada sells its products, it provides customers with ready repair and maintenance services, for Japanese customers are notorious for their impatience with slow and unreliable services. Hamada's meteoric success in the United States owes much to the firm's complete adaptation of its Japanese marketing method to the United States. When the customers located on the East Coast telephone Hamada's office in Los Angeles just before the closing time of 5 P.M. eastern standard time, Hamada immediately dispatches its trained service personnel to catch the red eye special (10 P.M. pacific standard time flight out of Los Angeles), which permits the service personnel to visit the customers' plants the next morning before 9 A.M. Hamada's American competitors often take a few days to two weeks to dispatch their service personnel. That was the industry's standard before Hamada changed it. Hamada purchased a golf course near Los Angeles in 1980 so that its aggressive invitational sales promotion could be stepped up.

Since industrial product users must adapt their own products to the dynamic changes in technology and the economic conditions of their businesses, they demand that their suppliers stay abreast of market fluctuations that require adjustments in price, product quality, and delivery schedules. After all, industrial products eventually end up, one way or another, in consumer markets, which are subject to the unpredictable whimsy of consumer tastes and needs.

Today, industrial products account for about 50 percent of the international sales of manufactured goods. Their relative importance to international trade and investment is not expected to wane in the future. However, marketing skills can best be sharpened by the consumer marketing experience, which requires marketing managers to handle a large number of variables in the marketing mix. The transfer of marketing experience from consumer products to industrial products seems easier than the other way around.

For the purpose of this chapter, we will mainly handle consumer marketing problems as the more general case of the two. However, we caution readers not to assume that the transition from consumer oriented marketing to industrial oriented marketing is either automatic or simple. The transition sometimes requires that managers become newly sensitized to foreign cultures in order to understand the idiosyncracies of their industrial customers' overall needs and finances and also to build a new corporate culture conducive to industrial marketing.

In addition, the art of international marketing involves redesigning the marketing mix to fit the social, cultural, and economic conditions of foreign markets. It calls upon managers to exercise a much greater degree of awareness of the influence of foreign culture and economic conditions on all the variables of the marketing mix. The cultural sensitivity that international marketing managers develop from dealing with consumer marketing problems in foreign markets can be transferred to the industrial marketing setting.

Appropriate repackaging of the marketing mix requires managers to consider at least the following points for each variable:

(1) Product Planning

Marketing management begins and ends with product planning. Managers must always watch for changes in their customers' needs and reshape their products to fit such variances. If this sounds like simple common sense, one might ask why it is, then, that one firm after another fails to follow this dictum. Many firms fail in product planning because they have developed internal resistance to change. To adapt products to volatile market conditions, firms have to maintain effective and flexible internal communication and cooperation across such functional areas as marketing, sales, R&D, finances, and production. However, without constant observation, each functional area is likely to evolve into its own bureaucratic fiefdom that resists any new ideas suggested by groups outside their own. To pursue international marketing opportunities, product planning must involve all key opinion leaders from various functional areas. This lateral communication across functional lines and the ability of managers and employees to become tuned to the demands of their international customers are crucial to the company's success in international product planning.

Multinational managers must decide whether or not their established products are marketable abroad. The PLC theory of international trade can help managers position their products in foreign markets on the basis of innovative characteristics as seen by their intended users. An awareness of just how the firm's products are viewed abroad is an important part of product planning. Managers must be familiar with foreigners' stereotypes about the home country and its products so they are equipped to recognize favorable opportunities and areas of resistance to products by targeted foreign customers. Sometimes stereotypes can be exploited to successfully reposition products in foreign markets.

Kentucky Fried Chicken, for example, was introduced to Japan as "fashionable fast food" from the United States and was aimed at urban upper middle class families. This was done because the Japanese public generally had a favorable stereotyped image of the United States as the source of new, youthful, and fashionable products. The Japanese urban upper middle class not only acts as an opinion leader for new products in Japan but also is most favorably predisposed to the products and lifestyles of the United States and Europe. As a point in fact, Benihana of Tokyo, a swashbuckling steak grill restaurant in the United States, is advertised as Benihana of New York in Japan.

In short, the relative advantage of the product and its compatibility with the intended market segment must be clearly identified. If the company is a follower rather than the innovator, then all that has to be done is to carefully study how the leader, whether it is a foreign firm or one from the same country, has established itself in the market.

By now, the label "Made in Japan" has earned the reputation of meaning good quality. A message like "Another Quality Product from Japan" could enhance a company's ability to position its new product as an innovation in foreign markets. On the other hand, if the country has not earned such a favorable reputation, a manager can still position his or her products in the market at the appropriate stage of the product life cycle on the basis of price and product appeal. What is important here is for the manager to aim at the best quality product image within the market segment of his or her initial choice (relative to the price of the product). Once established, this image can be transferred to the next generation of new products aimed at the next stage in the product life cycle.

(2) Price

Even when the firm is not selling directly to the ultimate users, a manager should start pricing the product, beginning with the retail pricing decision. Middlemen's distribution margins and discounts can then be computed. There are two schools of thought concerning product pricing in foreign markets. The first school advocates charging what the local traffic will bear; the second promotes worldwide uniform pricing mainly to avoid the problem of smuggling (contraband trade) or possible legal charges of dumping or price gouging.

Dumping is suspected when the wholesale price of a product at home is higher than the comparable wholesale export price of the same product in foreign markets. This wholesale-to-wholesale comparison is the rule of thumb. If a dumping charge is filed against a company in the United States or elsewhere, it is up to the firm to prove its innocence to the investigating body. The investigative body would demand to see the company's detailed and even confidential cost data.

The problem of contraband trade, which disrupts a firm's planned demarcation of market territories, cannot be eliminated if the company is selling very valuable products the price and value-added per pound (physical size) of which are too large to be ignored by privateers. Cosmetics, pharmaceuticals, watches, portable household appliances, and other products that are internationally advertised are vulnerable to contraband trade. In the case of pharmaceuticals, which might be sold to government-controlled medical insurance bodies, as is done in England, too wide a price differential for the same product from one country to the next would invite charges of price gouging from the country paying the higher price. Hoffmann La Roche of Switzerland ran into this kind of problem with the English government and the antitrust body of the European Economic Community. Worldwide uniform pricing would have saved the company from this litigation. For other products, local price differentials are recommended.

Product positioning, competitors' moves, and price and income elasticities of demand for the company's products in foreign markets should help the manager determine basic pricing policy just as would similar considerations in the home market. As these characteristics of the company's target foreign market changes, pricing policies must be adjusted. What managers must be wary of are the effects of fluctuating foreign exchange rates upon the prices of the firm's products in foreign markets. When the home currency is appreciating vis-à-vis the currency of the key export market, managers would have to continue increasing their price quoted in foreign currency just to avoid dumping charges. When the home currency depreciates, the company could be triggering preemptive pricing strategy prematurely.

(3) Brand

Ethnocentric zeal tends to force many firms to use their brand names either in the original or in their foreign language translations. Since names are linguistic products, they are likely to be very culture bound. What may sound phonetically pleasant and elegant in one language may sound harsh, irrelevant, or even obscene in another. Pan American Airlines built a private lounge inside the airport of a Latin American country and called it the "Rendezvous Lounge." Very few came to use it because the word "rendezvous" sounded like a Spanish word meaning a place for lovemaking. A Japanese soft drink called "Calpis" sounded too close to an English term for bovine urine.

These comical episodes remind us to be completely open-minded about naming or renaming products in foreign markets. Better yet, a company plans to sell its product abroad, the original name chosen should be phonetically multilingual. Some firms go so far as to give themselves new names that sound better in multicultural settings, as did Toyo Tsushin Kogyo and ESSO, which were renamed, respectively, SONY and EXXON.

It is imperative for companies to register their brand names in every conceivable foreign country regardless of their uses there. Just as in the case of industrial patents, the legal registration of corporate names and brand names is often handled by each country. There are many countries that are not signatories to the Paris Convention of Patents and Industrial Property Rights (originally established in 1883) and other regional treaties designed to protect patents, trademarks, and copyrights. In 1973, a leading manufacturer of male toiletries in Japan discovered that their trademark, Tancho, was registered in Indonesia by Indonesian individuals as their own brand name. Tancho was forced to fight a costly legal and political battle to win back the right to use the Tancho brand name. Similar calamities occur all over the globe.

(4) Packaging and Labels

Optimal packaging size depends upon a number of factors including the frequency of product purchases by targeted customers and the price those customers are willing to pay without much resistance. There are additional factors to consider—preserving product quality and discouraging piracy and unlawful doctoring or imitation of the product. For example, medicine bottles, jars, and cans are vulnerable to unlawful repackaging and doctoring by bootleggers. For such products, metal and plastic tubes, laminated film, and other types of packaging should be considered. Otherwise, packaging and labels are universally applicable. The economics of unit sales price and packaging costs can be the determining factors of choice of packaging and labels for overseas consumption.

(5) Advertising Theme and Choice of Advertising Media

This variable is the most culture bound of all the elements of the marketing mix. Advertising themes and messages depend not only upon direct expressions but also on metaphor and analogy, word association, simile, and body language including gestures and facial expressions. Even the choice of particular actors and actresses is significant. They are all specific to local culture and language. Even so, many multinational firms merely replicate the advertising theme and media choices that were successful in the home market of the parent firm. Thus, messages like "Put a Tiger in Your Tank," and "Have a Coke and a Smile" are translated into many languages and echo over multimedia channels worldwide.

These firms are hoping to achieve a worldwide uniformity of product and corporate image through repetition of the same message everywhere. They want to avoid any possible conflict of messages and product images that diverse themes could bring. Unless their uniform message runs against religious, cultural, or social taboos, it will be aired and printed in foreign markets.

This approach tends to ignore the effectiveness of changing the emphasis of advertising themes to achieve product positioning that differs from one country to the next. During the introductory stage of a product, the advertising theme must provide an educational, instructional, and informational message. Once the product is positioned at the growth stage, the advertising theme may well emphasize product appeal to the opinion leaders of targeted markets. When the product finally enters the mature stage of the product cycle, advertising should become more competitive and switch to a mass appeal.

Both American and Japanese firms tend to overemphasize the pull strategy of sales promotion by trying to draw consumers to their products through mass media advertising. This approach was chosen because American and Japanese companies have grown accustomed to the tendency of housewives in their home markets to base their buying habits on advertised messages rather than on their own product examinations or the recommendations of shopkeepers. In Europe, particularly in France, housewives and other consumers tend to listen to their friends or the recommendations of retailers more than do their American counterparts. In developing countries where the illiteracy rate is substantial, radio and television messages have a prestigious advertising image. These forms are supplemented by billboard and poster advertisements. However, shopkeepers' recommendations are often more effective than mass advertisements in developing countries, perhaps because retailers command some authority and economic strength as creditors to the masses in developing nations.

In developing countries, multinational firms should recognize the political cost of visible mass advertising. Although consumer products need mass distribution, and mass distribution depends on mass advertising, mass advertising may give the mistaken impression that foreign firms are monopolizing the local market. As a result, mounting frustration by groups such as university students and the unemployed is likely to be vent on those multinational firms whose mass advertising has put them in the spotlight.

Furthermore, developing nations often fault multinational firms for misleading the masses with mass advertising that encourages adopting social economic behavior considered undesirable by host governments. Baby food advertising that encouraged mothers in developing countries to stop breast-feeding is a classic example of such unwelcome advertising. Consequently, more and more developing nations have begun to enforce their own regulation of advertising.

(6) Distribution

Some products can be most effectively promoted through the chains of distributors to final users. Even when firms choose to emphasize the pull strategy for sales promotion, they have to distribute their products physically through layers of distributors or through their own direct sales force. When the income level of consumers is low and consumers' earnings are not stabilized, the tendency to purchase varieties of products frequently but in small quantities increases. When many small neighborhood stores dominate shopping areas of the nation, there tend to be many layers of wholesalers and distributors servicing the credit risks, warehousing needs, and delivery requirements of small retailers. Multilayers of distributors tend to lengthen the time required for the collection of accounts receivable extended by the manufacturers to distributors.

Multistructured distributorships also carry with them complex social and economic obligations from manufacturers to wholesalers and eventually to retailers. In order to manage these distribution channels, therefore, a multinational manager must deal with the needs of the distributors on the one hand and its retailers on the other.

(7) Sales and Service Personnel

Sales and service personnel are critically important to industrial marketing and are also important to consumer marketing. Except for complete and exclusive direct sales to consumers, the sales and service personnel in consumer and industrial marketing have to do business with distributors, warehouses, and other intermediaries. If a company sells directly to consumers (door-to-door sales by sales personnel, for example, or direct ownership of retail stores), it will be completely dependent on its sales personnel for building customer loyalty and for gathering vital marketing information. In addition, sales personnel will have to be trained to help collect the firm's accounts receivable from distributors and retailers.

How the sales force is paid depends partially on the social customs of the nation and also on the firm's incentives policy. A combination of sales commissions and salaries is used in many countries. In Japan and Korea, the salaried status of sales personnel is widely adopted when the sales function is seen as an integral part of a worker's apprenticeship within the firm. When sales is distinctly separate from other corporate functions in terms of promotions, sales personnel are treated as sales specialists and are paid on a commission basis. Therefore, in Japan those sales personnel who are paid on a commission basis are commonly life insurance salesmen, door-to-door cosmetics salesmen, and sales help specializing in mass consumer products and services.

2. MARKET RESEARCH AND TEST MARKETING

There is often semantic as well as conceptual confusion concerning the terms "market research" and "test marketing." Market research refers to a wide array of research methods and findings that are designed to explore what prospective customers' reactions are to any one of the contemplated elements of the marketing mix. Test marketing pertains to the actual market test of the selected marketing mix in a specific test market area before the product is offered to other markets. It is hoped that the results of such a test would help the seller to perfect the marketing mix before the product is formally introduced to the targeted market.

(1) Five W's and Three H's

To repackage the marketing mix for foreign markets, international managers should ask themselves the following five w's and three h's:

who, what, why, when, where, how, how often, and how many. When these managers are evaluating the feasibility of introducing established products in the home market to foreign markets, they should first analyze the marketing success of their products in the home market in terms of the five w's and three h's as follows:

Who are the consumers? Who makes the purchasing decision? And who actually uses the product? Social, economic, and cultural profiles of consumers (users) and purchasers should be clearly drawn. For example, it has been found that imported car buyers in the United States are more highly educated, more oriented to urban ways of life, and more skeptical of television advertisements than is the general public.

What do users buy? What are they looking for in the product? Those who purchase cosmetics are said to be buying the fantasy of becoming beautiful and are satisfying the need to appear proper and attractive. Average buyers of household appliances do not wish to be bothered with frequent repairs, so they are concerned with convenience and reliability. We all buy products and services to satisfy some need. If a country commands a mystique or favorable image in foreign markets, purchasers of a product from that place may be trying to partially fulfill a desire to visit that country or to understand that culture. These questions delve into the deeper psychology of consumers.

Why do consumers buy a certain product? This inquiry combines the investigation of the consumer psychology with an understanding of his or her social behavior. Do buyers purchase certain things just to keep up with the social trends of the group they associate themselves with most strongly? What is their reference group then?

When do consumers buy the product? How often do they buy it? The seasonality of consumption patterns as well as the frequency of such purchases are important factors to discover.

How do consumers learn about the product? Who is the opinion leader, market leader, and source of authoritative recommendation? Recommendation by word of mouth is said to be the most persuasive form of advertising and endorsement in most cultures. How can a sales organization encourage word-of-mouth endorsements?

Where do they buy the product? Can this location be changed? The answers to these questions are critical in helping to decide on the appropriate distribution strategies and sales promotion. The importance of storefront displays (point-of-purchase advertisements) and storefront demonstrations will be determined by the answers to these questions and the question "How do consumers learn about the product?"

How do they buy it? Do they buy it on credit? Is the installment purchase plan socially and economically acceptable to the buyers? Can installment payments be collected? If customers are buying the proudct on credit with private charge accounts at nearby stores, then the emphasis should be on retailer discounts to persuade store owners to push the product even at the expense of mass advertising plans.

How many potential customers are there? The focus of the first seven questions was on building a profile of the consumer, particularly his or her buying psychology. Once consumers have been analyzed they should be counted. Head counting is not only geographical but economic analysis. Once pockets of potential consumer concentrations have been identified, they must be covered with a market-by-market approach.

For a start, the income distribution of the nation reveals the general or skewed scattering of potential customers. While the middle-income class tends to have similar consumption patterns from one nation to the next, there may not be a large middle-income class in the targeted foreign country.

The art of obtaining the answers to these five w's and three h's is an important skill for global-minded managers. Where appropriate, indigenous and foreign competitors' successes and failures can also be studied, especially if they are analyzed in light of how their marketing mix packages fit with the answers to the questions discussed above. Market research should be limited to finding out the replies to those questions that cannot be fully answered merely by studying the present social, economic, and cultural conditions of the market and competitors' actions there.

International managers can improve their market analysis skills if they apply the following check list approach. First, managers should examine existing product market interactions in their own home market. They may consider how differences in socioeconomic variables may change their answers to the five w's and three h's in the target foreign market. This comparative approach provides managers with systematic exercises and the necessary self-discipline to succeed in foreign markets. The art of foreign market analysis can also be applied to domestic markets.

(2) A Check List of Socioeconomic Variables in Foreign Markets

When compared with similar data from the home market, the following macroeconomic data and demographic information from foreign markets should improve an evaluation of intended foreign markets by revealing the market size and degree of receptivity to the products. Income distribution data, in particular, should suggest whether or not to position products as luxury items or as mass consumer items.

Population. (annual growth rate, age distribution by sex, urban-rural density, and average family size): Together with the income data, this demographic information should help a manager decide how much market coverage to give the products in foreign markets.

Gross National Product (real growth rate, per capita income, industrial and employment composites): The relative economic size of the overall market is positively correlated to the comparative size of the real GNP. For example, although the People's Republic of China has a population of one billion, its estimated GNP puts the relative size of its economy in the same ranking as Brazil. However, if the company's products are food and other daily necessities, the GNP of populous developing nations tend to underestimate the potential size of the mass market by 25 percent or so.

Income Distribution (employment patterns, wage levels, and average calorie intake of daily diets): The breadth of the targeted market segments can be calculated from this data. When a large, extended family system prevails, many individual family members may pool their meager earnings to buy a limited number of consumer appliances. This information has to be interpreted in the light of demographic data and socioeconomic data listed below.

Surface Transportation Conditions: Not only is this information vital for planning the physical distributional logistics in foreign markets but, more importantly, it will help determine the general radius of commuting of consumers.

Male and Female Roles: Actual purchasers and purchasing decisionmakers vary from one product to the next. The division of tasks is strongly related to the socially dominant notions of male and female roles for housekeeping, childbearing, income generating, and general shopping.

Dominant Social Values: Popular attitudes toward frugality, convenience, foreign products and customs, fashion, upward social mobility, and private property determine foreign consumers' responses to foreign products and advertising themes.

Folklore and Religious Taboos: Dominant themes in folklore and religious taboos indicate the prevailing values of a foreign society. How receptive foreign consumers will be to products and advertising themes will probably depend upon how congruent product positioning and promotional sales themes are to accepted social values.

Population Diversity: Regional rivalry, tribal factionalism, provincial pride, and other local differences influence whether or not one dominant standard advertising theme should be used for the nation as a whole. For example, in a homogeneous country like Japan, most of the population conforms to whatever is in vogue in Tokyo.

Number of Retail Stores and Customary Retail and Wholesale Markups: This information is useful for planning distribution strategies. Storekeepers' attitudes toward large sales volume with small unit markups would indicate what kind of dealer services will be needed.

General Literacy Rate, Media Consumption Habits, Relative Cost of Media (TV sets, radio, printed matter): All of these factors influence a company's decision of where to advertise its products. When this information is combined with prevailing folklore and social taboos, opinion leaders and innovators will be easily identified.

Sometimes the answers to the above check list are difficult to obtain. In particular, developing countries have not yet set up their own internal administrative apparatus to collect, summarize, and report relevant data. Even trade statistics from these nations are scanty and unreliable. The United States and Japan, however, publish extensive trade data. The United Nations, the European Economic Community (EEC), and the General Agreement on Tariffs and Trade (GATT) regularly publish trade information on various world markets. Since the imports and exports of developing nations are likely to be captured by their trade with leading developed nations like the United States, Japan, and the EEC, global-minded managers can compile trade statistics for those products on the basis of the trade data of the industrialized nations.

143

The following are some useful periodicals containing trade statistics in English that are readily available from public agencies:

The United Nations (Statistical Office) publishes the *Yearbook of International Trade Statistics*, Statistical Paper Series D, on commodity trade for each member nation. However, these data are published by only up to the three-digit product categories of the Standard International Trade Statistics (SITS), which are too rough to be useful in scanning potential foreign markets but can give an overview of general trading patterns. *The Statistical Yearbook* provides general macroeconomic data for member nations. The International Monetary Fund publishes monthly *International Financial Statistics*, a list of macroeconomic data and balance of payment statistics for more than 100 nations.

The most helpful trade statistics are published by the U.S. Department of Commerce, and they are available to any subscriber for nominal annual fees. The Commerce Department also publishes the *Index to International Business Publications*, a list of all the publications of the department, particularly for use by international business managers. *U.S. Commodity Exports by Country*, Foreign Trade Report, FT410, a monthly published by the Bureau of the Census, contains a record of all U.S. commodity shipments to foreign countries by dollar value and quantity. Similar data for U.S. imports are also printed if potential foreign supply sources of particular products are needed. GATT publishes *Compendium of Sources, Basic Commodity Statistics*, and *International Trade Statistics*.

All these statistics are useful to gain a broad overview of world markets. This market scanning should be supplemented by an analysis of the exportability of the company's products. The best way to do this is to organize intensive on-site field research in targeted foreign markets *after* the preliminary studies of these markets are completed.

3. ENTRY FORMATS IN FOREIGN MARKETS

If a company wishes to export its products to foreign markets without allotting excessive personnel or capital resources to the development of overseas sales subsidiaries and distribution channels, then a combination of the following three approaches should be used. The key to this approach is to find suitable foreign import agents. The unplanned selection of import agents can prove to be a costly mistake.

(1) Need for Planning

Keeping the PLC model of international trade in mind, a manager must decide how far reaching the company's involvement in foreign markets should be. As the first product loses its appeal in foreign markets, marketing and sales efforts should be increased to keep the firm's position competitive in terms of pricing, advertising, distributor relations, and sales management. At the same time, the manager may be forced to bring new products into the market to provide a renewal pull for the old ones. Although this plan of action is straightforward, many firms select their import agents without evaluating their flexibility in coping with the changing needs of the marketing environment.

(2) Export Managers

At minimum, a company needs one full-time export manager who is knowledgeable about business details focuses on the social, economic, and political structures of the foreign countries involved. This export manager would travel frequently to foreign markets serving as the company's "eyes and ears" to pick up the slightest changes in foreign market conditions. At the same time, this manager must monitor, cajole, and motivate foreign distributors and import agents.

The export manager has to be backed up at home by a competent staff that can handle the routine details of physically transporting products on time and also stay in touch with regulations, export assistance, and legislation that the home government provides to stimulate exports. Even if the company chooses to subcontract to outside trading firms and export brokers to perform the functions usually carried out by export managers, an internal staff must be developed that will keep a close watch on these outside subcontractors.

(3) Import Agents

Foreign import agents can be chosen from foreign trading firms, foreign retailers and wholesalers, foreign manufacturers, and sales subsidiaries of foreign investors. These agents should be selected mainly for their product and market compatibility with the firm's products. Their own technical, manufacturing, and marketing capabilities will have to be considered together with their own market coverage.

When negotiating import agent agreements one should assume that any relationship with them is bound to be unstable. Accordingly, these import agency contracts should require a periodic review of the company's specific relationships with them. If a manager wants to stay in touch with foreign market developments, he or she will have to have considerable input into the key marketing decisions concerning the company's products.

3. Up until the economic depression of 1981–83, the skin care, make-up, fragrance, and other cosmetic markets were believed in the United States to be recession free. However, from 1981 to 1983, cosmetic markets of the United States suffered a general sales decline. Competition for market shares and sales was intensified by well-established American firms. True to the tradition of "pull" strategy supremacy, these American firms were intensifying their direct advertising campaigns to consumers. But Shiseido, the leading cosmetic firm of Japan, which entered the U.S. market about ten years earlier, was deliberately emphasizing the "push" strategy by spending most of its marketing efforts and budgets for counseling and training retail sales ladies of leading department stores throughout the United States. Judging from Shiseido's success, the Japanese style of push strategy worked well in the United States. Why?

4. Analyze the attached care, *Fried Chicken in Japan*. In addition to answering the study guide questions at the end of the case, identify clearly how the U.S.–Japan joint venture successfully repositioned its products in the Japanese market and how the marketing mixes of the American experience were adapted to the socio-economic conditions of Japan.

CASE 3:
FRIED CHICKEN IN JAPAN

In the summer of 1975, Yamashita, managing director of Kentucky Fried Chicken (Japan), KFCJ, had just reached his mid-30s, an unusually young age for such a responsible position in a seniority-conscious country like Japan. Total sales of KFCJ were expected to pass 6 billion yen (U.S. $20 million) for the fiscal year 1975, almost a 100 percent growth in sales from the previous fiscal year. Reflecting upon the past five years, which Yamashita had devoted to establishing KFCJ's toehold in the growing "fast food" market in Japan, he felt relieved that KFCJ's past trial-and-error approaches to the Japanese market had imbedded in him a sense of confidence as well as an aspiration for new challenges in the years to come. Challenges indeed were there for him to seek.

The fast food market, which is merely a portion of the total "eating-out and catering service" industry in Japan had come by 1975 to attract new foreign and

Japanese entrants. From the United States, MacDonalds, Burger Chef, A&W, Dairy Queen, Dunkin' Donuts, Mr. Donuts, Pizza Hut, Golden Pioneer, and an assortment of ice-cream chains had already followed KFC into Japan. Like KFC, these U.S.-based fast food firms had invariably chosen a joint venture or straight licensing agreement with Japanese firms. In the years to come, not only would other U.S.-based fast food firms specializing in fried chicken enter the Japanese markets, but the existing ones might well attempt to add fried chicken to their product lines. In addition, Japanese restaurants and food companies as well as assortments of textile, mining, and chemical firms, were already entering into growing fast food markets in Japan as their traditional lines of business continued to decline.

The intensifying market competition was challenging, and Yamashita knew that the task of maintaining and building employee morale would become crucial for its future success. Perhaps because of KFCJ's affiliation with Mitsubishi Corporation, a leading trading firm in Japan, and perhaps because of KFCJ's product image as "modern, American, and Stylish," KFCJ had been able to attract many young, ambitious, and entrepreneurial employees. The rapid spread of KFCJ's stores to major cities had enabled the firm to place these young and ambitious employees in challenging and growing situations. From 1974 to 1975 alone, KFCJ added 30 new stores, bringing the total to 130. About one-half of these stores were run directly by KFCJ; franchises had never constituted more than one-half of KFCJ stores. Yamashita knew, however, that in the years to come, KFCJ's growth tempo would continue, but not as spectacularly as in the past. Would KFCJ be able to satisfy the career aspirations of store manager candidates and other hard-working young employees who had been drawn to the growth potentials of KFCJ? With a spread of fast food chains, centralized operations like central kitchen and depot systems were feared as reducing store operators from "chefs" to "waiter and assemblers." Perhaps because of demoralizing effects of such modern fast food service systems on young employees, labor unions appeared, spreading from one large restaurant chain to the next.

The growth of KFCJ also brought the problem of procuring an increasing supply of such necessary ingredients as chicken, vegetable oil, flour, and assortments of fresh food items. Japan, which possessed about 110 million people in 1975, was already importing over 30 percent of all her food and animal feed requirements combined. As more and more countries came to fear a worldwide food and feed shortage, the Japanese government was looking into the whole question of procuring food and feed items worldwide. The Japanese dietary habit changed drastically from 1950 to 1975. By 1975, on the average, the Japanese daily intake of protein had almost doubled to about 80 grams, about 43 percent of which came from animal protein including dairy products and fish. But fish and shellfish accounted for less than one-half of the Japanese intake of animal protein.

Meanwhile, especially since the early 1960s, broiler farms in Japan had rapidly increased in number, and by 1975 their rapid production had come to surpass the demand. While this overproduction appeared to be temporary, the broiler farmers were already organizing the drive to "regulate" the total supply of broilers in their favor. From 1965 to 1975, the total number of broiler farms declined from about 20,000 to 13,000. By 1974, over 40 percent of all broilers were supplied by about 700 farms, each of which at the time was supplying over 100,000 broilers to markets. A sign of further concentration among broiler farms was seen in 1975.

Exhibit 1 shows the broiler production and consumption levels in Japan. The Japanese government was expected to be drawn into the rescue operations of prefectures and farmers' associations that had already exhausted their financial means of keeping stockpile "surplus" broiler meats or of continuing to guarantee broiler farmers the "minimum floor price" for their broilers. The increasing importation of frozen broilers might well become a "political" focal point in the "chicken debate" to come. Even without the organizing attempts of broiler farmers, the Ministry of Agriculture and Forestry, the Ministry of Welfare and Health, and the Ministry of International Trade and Industry were all closely watching the growing fast food market to see which ministry should be put in charge of administering the industry.

How Fried Chicken Flew to Japan

Mitsubishi Corporation, a leading trading firm, was in the mid-1960s the leading Japanese importer (and domestic distributor) of animal and chicken feeds, corn, and milo. With a rapid increase in the living standard of the Japanese population, their consumption of animal protein, eggs, beef, pork, and chicken was also increasing. Since the production lead-time of chicken was shorter than that of other animal meats, and the raising of broilers was technically the easiest, Mitsubishi Corporation took the initiative in starting large-scale broiler farms in Japan, at first mainly as the captive customers of Mitsubishi's corn and milo feeds. In order to find captive markets for their increased chicken feed businesses, the trading firm continued to open broiler farms around the major cities in Japan. Originally, over three-quarters of all broiler breeds were imported from the United States, and the remainder from Canada, the United Kingdom, and Europe. The indigenous breeds were improved through crossbreeding with imported breeds.

Mitsubishi's broiler farms continued to increase the supply of broilers so much that by around 1967, the trading firm was saddled with surplus broiler meats. One logical way out of this problem was to create an expanding and new demand for broilers.

At that time supermarket chains such as Seiyu and Jasco were expanding their networks in Tokyo and other major cities. Since the boning of broilers required cumbersome handling and was an extremely costly operation (the weight ratio of bone to meat being the greatest for chicken than for steer and hog), the supermarkets tried to sell their chicken packaged without boning. While this package offered chicken at a much lower price than filleted chicken, the Japanese housewives had long considered good chicken to be "boned" and did not purchase chicken packages sold "bone, stock, and barrel."

The Tokyo headquarters of Mitsubishi then cabled its Chicago office to get suggestions for new ways of increasing chicken consumption in Japan. They requested in effect, that their Chicago office "identify the largest broiler consuming firm in the United States." The man who received this request was Aso, in his early forties. Aso had long been familiar with American food chains and supermarkets, having sold to them in the past an assortment of canned foods and other food-related items. Being stationed in Chicago, the center of agribusiness in the United States, Aso had watched from around 1965 the opening of Kentucky Fried Chicken franchises in the Midwest. Aso's intuitive reply was: the greatest single user of broilers in the United States must be Kentucky Fried Chicken. Aso's children had long been converted to Colonel Sanders' fried chicken, and Aso himself had found it "sporty" to munch on.

In order to confirm his hunch, Aso went to a Chicken Farmers' Convention in Kansas City in 1967. There, he witnessed Colonel Sanders receive a standing ovation from the chicken farmers. Being convinced of the wisdom of bringing Kentucky Fried Chicken (KFC) to Japan, Aso went immediately to Nashville and implored KFC to come to Japan. KFC's reception was, Aso recalled, worse than his worst expectation. The firm was totally preoccupied with expanding in the United States. Besides, as Aso did not know then, an American with Japanese ancestry had obtained KFC's franchise for Japan in 1962 and his initial entry proved to be a total disaster and a discouraging experience for KFC. No individual KFC manager was receptive to international expansion.

Undaunted, Aso kept sending feelers to KFC, even after he returned to Japan in 1968. The year 1969 saw a faint change in KFC's attitude against going international. At that time, KFC was exhausting its expansion possibilities in the United States and was turning its attention to Canada. In addition, KFC's corporate counsel, who was subsequently fired by KFC's owner and president, appeared unusually international-minded and was urging KFC to accept Aso's offer.

Having persuaded KFC to form a joint venture with Mitsubishi, Aso needed to convince the top management of Mitsubishi Corporation that they ought to get involved in the "fried chicken" business. The initial response of the board members was overwhelmingly skeptical. "You imagine that our Mitsubishi is going to run a restaurant?" "You dare call this quaint taste a marketable meal?" "No Japanese would buy it."

Aso's replies were in essence that "KFC is not a conventional restaurant but a modern manufacturing plant." "The younger generation of the Japanese will like KFC-flavored fried chicken." "KFC will use lots of our broilers." "Increase in broiler sales means increase in our feed sales." Thus, Kentucky Fried Chicken (Japan) was born early in 1970, 50 percent owned by Mitsubishi and 50 percent by KFC (U.S.A.). KFCJ was to pay KFC (U.S.A.) a royalty of 4 percent of total sales and 10% of franchise royalties revenue. The initial capitalization of KFCJ was 70 million yen (US$200,000). And more important, Aso secured from the top echelon of Mitsubishi Corporation two basic rules concerning the operation of KFCJ, namely, (1) not to treat KFCJ as a dumping ground for Mitsubishi's retiring managers and employees; and (2) not to obligate KFCJ to buy broilers, equipment, and other necessary materials exclusively from Mitsubishi.

150

KFCJ's Early Marketing Experience

Just after KFCJ was established, EXPO'70 was opened in Osaka, an industrial and commercial center. This international event was expected to attract over 30 million visitors, including thousands from abroad. The United States sent "Moon Stone" to its gigantic exhibition hall and she was already the talk of the town before EXPO opened.

Near the United States Pavillion stood the "Kentucky Fried Chicken" store with all the authentic appearance and decorum of the "finger lickin' good" store found in the United States. This EXPO store was opened and managed by KFC (U.S.A.), assisted and closely watched by KFCJ personnel including Aso and Yamashita.

From the outset until EXPO'70 closed, the popularity of the KFC booth kept rising among the visitors. All the necessary ingredients of KFC items were procured in Japan. A slight change in menu was made along the way when mashed potatoes were abandoned in favor of French fries. Soft drinks and ice cream were added to the menu. Likewise, cole slaw was down-played as few Japanese indicated a preference for it. In sum, KFC in EXPO'70 proved to be resounding success.

Immediately after EXPO'70, KFC (U.S.A.) suggested to KFCJ that in order to exploit the success of EXPO'70 in Osaka, two or three test stores be opened in the Osaka area. These KFCJ test stores were to be located in the newly emerging shopping centers in or near suburban housing developments, whose residents were predominately the families of white collar employees and lower to middle management. The test store was to be in a free-standing building, occupying 4,400 square feet and was to cater to take-out orders. In short, a typical KFC store found in the suburbs of the United States was to be transplanted, practically as is, to the Osaka area.

Yamashita and Aso had a hunch that the Tokyo area, not Osaka, should be the first test place. They thought that KFCJ should capitalize on the stylish image of "fashionable fast foods" fresh from the United States. As with any other "fashion products," Tokyo should be the starting point. Historically, new fashions and new ways of life have spread invariably from Tokyo to other areas, not the other way around. The Japanese staff of KFCJ and Mitsubishi also had intuitive skepticism about the size of the proposed store, KFC's overemphasis on take-out service, and the specific store location (in shopping areas near new housing developments). But they decided to go along with KFC's proposal simply because "too much revision of the KFC know-how and manuals from the outset was feared to destroy the original KFC know-how." According to Aso, "there will be ample time later, to fiddle with KFC (and American) know-how, once we know how to pick and choose."

During eighteen months of test operations, two of the three initial KFCJ stores in the Osaka area never registered sales above calculated break even points and were subsequently closed. The remaining store barely stayed above the break even point. Each store's sales (production) capacity was 15 million yen per month. But actual monthly sales hovered around 2 million yen. During the first nine months of operation, KFCJ ran up accumulated accounting losses of over 220 million yen ($600,000). In short, the test stores were less than a resounding success. Middlefield, who was sent in 1970 by KFC (U.S.A.) to manage KFCJ, recalled in 1975, "We wanted to make mistakes during the initial test period, in Osaka, not in Tokyo, so that the Tokyo market would be left undamaged."

"KFC" Comes to Tokyo

The Osaka experience demonstrated a need for radical change in KFC's "marketing approach" à la American if KFCJ was to succeed. Aso, Yamashita, Middlefield, and Takagi (who was Aso's assistant on the KFCJ project inside Mitsubishi) debated the necessary adaptations of the KFC know-how to the Japanese market. They agreed upon the following premises that the KFCJ should use to promote Kentucky Fried Chicken:

1. Product to be promoted as "new fashion" from the United States;
2. The Japanese children and youth, ranging from kindergarten to university ages, to be the principal target customers, along with housewives in their late 20s and early 30s;
3. The family background of the target customers to be the upper middle and upper class of corporate executives and professionals who have gone abroad or are capable of going abroad;
4. With a slight sign of success of test stores, KFCJ's direct-owned stores to be increased in number as rapidly as possible;
5. Price and product appeal to be competitive with an eat-out or home-delivered meat meal popular with Japanese customers.

In order to adapt the KFC product and marketing package to the market attributes mentioned above, KFCJ came up with the following marketing and product package. The experience of the first three test stores in the Osaka area was amply woven into the renewed "marketing package" to be tested in the Tokyo market:

1. *Brand*: "Kentucky Fried Chicken" to be spelled out both in Japanes phonetics (Katakana) and English.
2. *Price*: Most popular three-piece tray to be competitive with a popular Japanese meat dish, *katsudon* (sirloin pork cutlet placed over spiced rice).
3. *Location of test stores*: Near key stations of the Toyoko Commuter Line stretching from Shibuya, a southwest leisure center of Tokyo, through the southwest suburban area of Tokyo, to Yokohama where upper middle class and high-income families reside. Residents within a radius of 2 kilometers from the store to be considered "potential customers" of the store.
4. *Store size*: Standard size to be reduced to 66 square meters (about 2,100 square feet) from 132 square meters (about 4,400 square feet) specified in the KFC manual so that rent and other maintenance expenses be reduced.
5. *Store space*: Tenant store in the existing building.
6. *Advertisement and sales promotion*: Leafletting all the houses within market coverage of each store. Promote "KFC Booth" to the "Bazzar," "Rummage Sales," "Picnic," "Athletic Meeting," and "Excursion Tour" of PTAs,

schools, and kindergartens within the market coverage of each test store. These direct promotional campaigns to be supplemented with spot commercials on TV and radio between 2 P.M. and 4 P.M. when school children come home and desire afternoon snacks.

7. *Store function*: Eat-on-premises to be promoted as well as take-out services.
8. *Store decoration*: Red and white striped appearance to be maintained, together with Colonel Sanders' "real-size statue in front of the store.
9. *Menu*: Luxurious looking menu to be printed in color matching store decoration.

In particular, these marketing and product approaches were considered necessary because the cost of TV commercials in Japan were about three times as great as in the United States and because store rents and key money deposits were also two to three times as great in Japan. Costs of various ingredients were just about the same as those in the United States. In order to make maximum use of limited space, the cooking and kitchen equipment were also reduced in size and redesigned to be arranged vertically with much of the equipment being used for multiple purposes. All key equipment was to be leased rather than purchased outright. In this way, the initial cash outlays were kept to a minimum and each store was expected to "pay as it goes." The Food Processing Equipment Division of Mitsubishi Corporation, to which Takagi formally belonged, became the key leasor of the kitchen equipment. The breakeven sales level of the new standard store of KFCJ was reduced to about 3.5 million yen ($12,000) per month.

The promotion of eat-on-premises was considered absolutely necessary in order to draw potential customers. The idea was to promote the KFCJ store as a "fashionable place to eat in," which also provides take-out services. The ratio of eat-on-premises sales to take-out sales was expected to vary from 70 percent for a downtown store to 40 percent for a store in a residential area. In addition to six stores in the Tokyo area, one test store was opened inside the fashionable shopping arcade called "Toa Road" in Kobe further west of Osaka. Unlike the Osaka area, the Kobe area has traditionally attracted the residences of upper middle class and professional families and has formed the "Toyoko Line Resident" of the west. In particular, the shopping arcade "Toa Road" is frequented by the housewives and children of the upper middle class.

When the seven test stores showed a sign of success, twelve new stores were opened early in 1972. All of them were under the direct management of KFCJ and were located along the Toyoko Line and the Odakyu Line to the north of the Toyoko Line. A number of residential areas along the Odakyu Line possessed many similar socioeconomic attributes of the Toyoko Line.

The overall break even number of KFCJ stores in 1972 was estimated to be around twenty-five. Thus, KFCJ wanted to accelerate the momentum of expanding the store networks. From mid-1971 to 1972, the Japanese economy plunged into the "borrowers' market" in capital and loan markets. This "extraordinary liquidity" of the financial institutions, as the Japanese called it, was mainly brought about by the combination of increased export sales and the leveling off of the capital investment needs of Japanese manufacturing firms.

Manufacturing firms were trying to repay their past debts to banks and other financial institutions, and financial institutions were scurrying around in search of potential borrowers. As a result, banks relaxed their past reluctance to lend funds to "entertainment and restaurant" businesses. Being associated with Mitsubishi Corporation, the KFCJ found it easy to borrow money from the financial community.

Meanwhile, toward the end of 1971, KFC (U.S.A.) was acquired by Heubline Co., Hartford, Connecticut, and the 50 percent ownership of KFCJ was transferred to Heubline. Recognizing a need for increasing the number of KFCJ stores in the Tokyo and Osaka–Kohe area, Aso persuaded Heubline to agree to increasing the paid-in equity base of KFCJ from $200,000 to $2 million. Armed with increased equity funds as well as additional borrowed funds, KFCJ rented "whatever appropriate store spaces" were available in target market areas. During 1972, altogether sixty new stores were opened under the management of KFCJ. In December alone, fourteen new stores were opened. This time, KFCJ also ventured to downtowns and other "leisure centers" in the Tokyo and Osaka areas, catering to both eat-on-premises and take-out customers.

During 1973, KFC continued to open new stores and at the same time called for KFCJ franchises in remote areas of Japan. Starting with nominating franchises in Hokkaido (northernmost island) and the Sanin area (southwest facing Japan Sea) in 1973, KFCJ added new franchises in 1974 in Kyushu (southernmost areas). The areas were selected primarily on the basis of the trend of per capita income of each prefecture as well as on the basis of the urban population in regional cities. Learning from the success of Coca-Cola in Japan, KFCJ carefully selected the franchises. The franchises were also established and leading regional firms. The franchise fee was 4 percent of total sales.

When the year 1974 ended, KFCJ had 122 stores which were evenly divided between the direct management of KFCJ and the franchises. Meanwhile, Mitsubishi Corporation renegotiated successfully with Heubline for a reduction of the royalty fee from the initial 4 percent to 3 percent of sales of KFCJ. Also maintained that KFCJ needed to plough as much profit as possible into expanding store networks and that KFCJ was totally operated and managed by the Japanese portion of KFCJ including Mitsubishi. As a result, by the end of 1973, KFCJ began to register an annual profit. With the continued growth of sales and profits, it was expected that by the beginning of 1976, even accumulated accounting losses would be totally cleared. In 1974, on the average, each store was producing profits corresponding to about 13 to 20 percent of sales.

The Fast Food Market in Japan

In 1975 there were about 450,000 stores and restaurants throughout Japan engaged in one form or other of retailing meals, snacks, alcoholic, and nonalcoholic beverages for eat-on-premises and take-out customers. The bulk of these operations were a single store operated by members of the owner family. While these stores tended to feature one of three menus, "Japanese food," "Chinese food," and "Western food," there were many menus that consisted of the stores' own combinations of these three categories. These small, family-owned single stores had long existed in Japan. In their operational format and behavior, how-

154

ever, these stores were to the fast-growing chain restaurants of the food service industry what small craftsmen's workshops were in the past to the growing sector of the modern manufacturing firm.

As the Japanese economy grew, especially from the early 1960s, not only individuals' disposable income but also leisure time increased. The five-day work week and paid holidays were spreading from one firm to the next. Furthermore, young work forces and student populations, both male and female, emerged as the big spenders on fashions, sporting goods, entertainment, traveling, and eating out. These spenders thronged to the large cities as the urbanization of the Japanese populace progressed. Fashions of the American youth culture, such as hair style, attire, and taste for music were quickly being taken up by young consumers in Japan.

Around 1965, the total annual sales of "eating out" and "catering services" was estimated to be less than 1,000 billion yen ($2.7 billion). Most people associated eating out with such special occasions as weddings, company-sponsored outings, athletic meetings, and other recreational events of schools and family gatherings. From the mid-1960s, the "eating and drinking out" market began to grow at an exponential rate. Generally, the Americanization of the Japanese drinking taste progressed, as was witnessed by the rapid growth of Coca-Cola sales after 1965. In 1975, the eating out and catering services market was in total passing 4,000 billion yen per year. And the market was growing at an annual rate of over 10 percent. The growing fast food market alone was estimated to pass 30 billion yen in 1975.

For instance, in 1963, the average monthly expenditure on eating out was about 1,000 yen per household. In 1971, the same expenditure was over 2,700 yen. The monthly expenditure per household for eating out in 1963 was twice as large for Tokyo as the national average. This trend remained the same in 1971. From 1963 to 1971 other large cities like Osaka, Nagoya, Yokohama, and Kobe moved much closer to Tokyo in terms of respective city household's monthly expenditure on eating out. Figure 6-1 schematically shows the trend of a household's monthly expenditure for eating out purposes from 1963 to 1971 by respective prefectures.

From the early 1960s to the early 1970s, the amount of eating out consumers' one-time expenditure on a meal or snack also increased from 200 yen to 600 yen. This rate of increase was significantly greater than the general rate of inflation during the period. As consumers' "one-time expenditure—the amount eating out consumers were financially and psychologically prepared to spend— increased from 200 yen to 600 yen consumers' preference for specific items also changed. While income elasticity of demand for such conventionally popular items as Japanese and Chinese noodle dishes remained low (less than the unity), income elasticity of demand for more prestigious dishes such as *sushi* (raw fish fillet with rice), coffee shop items, "Western foods," bar and beer-hall items registered large value (significantly greater than the unity)—indicating that the eating and drinking out markets of westernized or "traditional but prestigious" Japanese dishes expanded far more quickly than conventionally popular dishes.

KFC's entry into Japan simply coincided with the time when Japanese urban consumers were about to embrace the idea of eating and drinking out and were

Figure 6-1. Monthly "Eating out Expenditure" per Household.

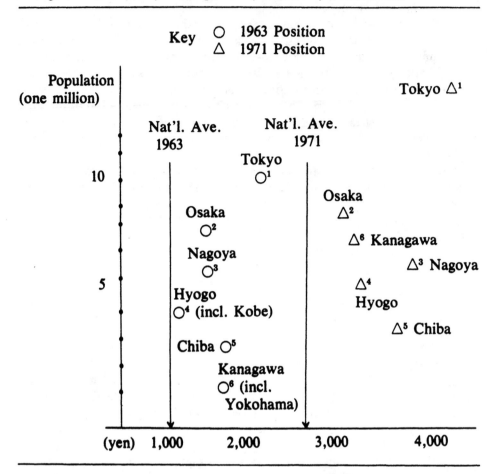

about to loosen their purse strings upon fashionable fast food items. In retro-
spect, the initial growth phase of KFCJ could not have better coincided with the
Japanese economy. After the oil crisis hit Japan in October 1973, the financial
markets again became "lenders' markets." As money became tighter, even blue-
chip manufacturing firms found it difficult to borrow much from the financial
communities. Fledgling fast food and entertainment firms were literally squeezed
out of the capital and loan markets.

Economics of the KFCJ Operations

Exhibits 4 and 5 show the financial statements of KFCJ for the fiscal year
1974 ending on May 31, 1974. Overall costs of goods sold were about 50 percent of the total sales of stores under the direct management of KFCJ. About
80 percent of these costs were ingredients and raw materials purchased from outside suppliers. Mitsubishi Corporation supplied about one-half of KFCJ's total
purchases.

To open a store with approximately 3,000 square feet of rented space, the key-money deposit in 1975 was about 10 million yen ($32,000). In addition, about 15 million yen were needed to make improvements on leased space and equipment. Each KFCJ store was urged to aim at 13 to 20 percent as the minimum profit after costs of goods sold and various expenses. The KFCJ stores began first with four to five regular storekeepers, but the number of regular KFCJ employees was reduced on the average in May 1973 to 2.7 per store. It was left to each store manager to hire part-time and nonregular helpers depending on the sales fluctuations by day and by month. Store hours were ordinarily from 11:00 A.M. till 9:00 P.M. seven days a week. However, a store manager could petition the KFCJ headquarters to lengthen his store hours. Some stores were open until midnight.

From 1972 to 1975, KFCJ experienced a very low rate of employee turnover (about 10 percent for the first three years). After a three-month training period, a regular store employee was promoted to assistant store manager. Some high-performing assistant managers, after six months in that position, were promoted to store manager. The minimum salary of the store manager in 1975 was about 130,000 yen ($440) per month approximately twice that of assistant store managers. In addition, according to the Japanese salary system, regular employees were paid about a six-month salary equivalent of bonus per year. Promotion was determined on the basis of written and field tests on KFCJ's operational manual plus superiors' evaluations of employees' working attitudes. Annually, five or six employees were selected to go on a month-long study tour abroad (mainly in the United States) at KFCJ's expense.

A store manager was evaluated on the basis of his store's sales and profit records. All stores under the direct management of KFCJ were ranked monthly according to actual sales and profits (their growth rate and actual amounts), containment of costs, and expenses against the targeted members. This ranking was published in the KFCJ monthly newsletter distributed to all KFCJ personnel. Supervisors, each of whom oversaw eight to ten stores, were asked to help store managers improve their performance. If store managers' performance was not improved in six months, they were demoted and sent back to work within the store.

Accordingly, aggressive and imaginative store managers improvised various ways to increase their sales and profits. For example, one store happened to be located right across from a television station in Tokyo. Every afternoon, there appeared a long queue of visitors to live filmings of popular programs. The store manager walked up and down the queue and sold ice cream and soft drinks. Another manager in Tokyo noticed that the second floor of one store was being used as the storage space for the KFCJ store downstairs. He persuaded Yamashita to open a restaurant and bar on the second floor instead of the storage space. This new establishment was to cater to two different groups of customers: daytime, to young office girls and college coeds, and at night, to young male customers and their dates. The menu was changed twice a day according to the target customers. At night a female singer and a guitarist provided live music. This store proved to be a hit, and a KFCJ decided to institute discount services in this store to the KFCJ employees as a fringe benefit for them. Soon, many young KFC employees were seen frequenting this store with their dates. The store manager of this special restaurant was rotated among KFCJ store managers so that he could enjoy a change of air from selling KFC items.

Another employee suggested to Yamashita that surplus chicken drumsticks could be smoked and vacuum packed. Intrigued by this suggestion, Yamashita sent this young graduate in agricultural chemistry from Hokkaido University to the laboratory of his alma mater, together with 200,000 yen. Three months later, he came back with the perfected methods of smoking and vacuum-packing chicken. This new product was sold in the store as a delicacy. The KFCJ store managers pushed smoked chicken to other restaurants and bars in the neighborhoods of their stores. In the summer 1975 smoked chicken was contributing sales and profits to KFCJ stores.

Each store was also selling fried drumsticks by piece as well as a mini-pack of one fried drumstick and a child's portion of french fries. These items were popular with children. Coleslaw, potato salad, home roll-breads, and french fries were sold in addition to milk shakes, ice cream, coffee, cola, and orange juice. Some downtown stores in Tokyo were in, summer 1975, selling bottled wines to take-out customers.

Private Thoughts of Yamashita and Middlefield
In summer 1975, Yamashita recounted his experience with KFCJ as follows:

> Right now, our first problem is how to reduce the interest payments. The required compensating balances on the borrowed funds bring the effective rate of interest to about 13 percent a year. . . . We have a tough time in explaining this Japanese peculiarity to Heubline. . . . Ever since Heubline took over KFC (U.S.A.), Heubline has placed us on strict Heubline's reporting and control system. They want tons of information on the Japanese market. This is all right. But their emphasis on ROI per store and per whatever does not take into consideration the "human side" of KFCJ operations. . . .
>
> For example, in order to maintain and cultivate the comradeship among our employees, we often sit down on the floor almost half-naked after store hours and pass drinks among us. We rap about many things and keep encouraging one another. I doubt Heubline would understand the precious need for such things as this. . . .
>
> Japanese consumers' taste for fast foods is rapidly broadening. In order to maintain and expand our market share, we will have to keep broadening our menu. . . . Up until six months ago, Heubline kept telling us to think only chicken. Mitsubishi is no problem. They recognize a need for exploiting changes in Japanese consumers' taste. . . .
>
> Last year, Heubline took KFC to Hong Kong. It changed KFC to a Chinese name and added spring rolls to its menu . . . I thought that the venture was totally misconceived. I understand that Heubline spent about $2 million and retreated from Hong Kong. No two markets look alike. . . .
>
> Naturally, I have enjoyed my work with KFCJ. . . . I came to KFCJ in order to sell posters and other paper products from my former employers, a printing firm. They asked me to join the firm. I am glad that I did.

Middlefield, the sole American (or foreigner) in KFCJ reminisced in summer, 1975:

> I was fascinated by Japan when I commanded an all-Japanese crew transport ship during my active duty in the Korean War. . . . They saved my face by covering up my mistakes. And I wanted to come back to Japan. . . .

158

I joined IBM as a salesman but I did not have any hope of being sent to Japan. I worked for IBM for about sixteen years. Then I was sent to Nashville. I happened to live next door to the owner and president to KFC (U.S.A.). . . . As far as he was concerned, I was the "Japan expert." . . . When he asked me to go to Japan in 1970, I did not hesitate to take the job. . . . I decided to visit Europe on my way to Japan. In Greece, one day when I was sightseeing, I ran into a Japanese executive. I told him that I was on my way to KFCJ. . . . He asked me to look up Yamashita of his printing company because his firm would be interested in doing business with KFCJ. . . . Being fluent in English and bright, Yamashita would be a nice person for me to know, anyhow, he said.

I don't recall in which books and articles I read on doing business in Japan. But I recalled, then, that a Japanese and foreign joint venture often failed because the Japanese partner used it as the dumping ground for his own reject employees. So I thought that if Yamashita was a good person, I would cultivate personal friendship with him and would ask him to join KFCJ. I was going to demand that Mitsubishi respect KFCJ's own Japanese personnel. . . . As it turned out, Mitsubishi was thinking along the same line. . . .

Yamashita showed me around Tokyo and showed me how Japanese eat-on-premises fast foods were sold and served. . . . Eventually, I convinced Yamashita to join KFCJ. . . .

When Heubline bought KFC (U.S.A.), I was scared of being fired. Unlike Japanese firms, American firms have a habit of firing managers associated with the previous firm just acquired. . . . As it turned out, I was one of the few who survived. . . . When Heubline people came to Japan, Mitsubishi people went out of their way to tell them that I was doing a good job. . . . Mitsubishi people even assured me that if and when Heubline fired me, they would find a job for me. . . .

In order to get free but good publicity for KFCJ I made it a rule to appear on radio and television shows featuring "peculiar" foreigners in Japan. . . . We got lots of free publicity this way. And it was useful when we were starting up our business. Television air time costs a lot more here than in the States. . . .

When we asked in 1972 Heubline to increase the equity base of KFCJ, I pointed it out to them that the Japanese yen was going to be revalued again. . . . Heubline paid its increased share before the yen became 15 to 17 percent dearer vis-à-vis the U.S. dollar. . . .

I am hoping that American businesses will recognize the positive correlation between market share and profit. Japanese businesses have intuitively known this and have attempted to expand sales and market share. . . . Growth is in essence a deferred profit for a firm. . . .

American marketing techniques and manuals have to be adapted to Japanese situations. . . . Compare MacDonalds' success with Burger Chef's failure. . . . Both of them came later than us. MacDonalds watched us closely and duplicated our own adaptations. . . . Burger Chef insisted on and continued with mechanical application of its American manuals in Japan. . . . Burger Chef had to sell its business back to its Japanese partner. . . .

I understand that the American fast food chains are now moving back to downtown and eat-on-premises markets. Perhaps Heubline could use the operational know-how of KFCJ.

Exhibit 6-1. Production and Consumption of Chicken 1960-1973.

Year	Chicken Production (ton)			Consumption	
	Broiler	Other Chicken	Total	Per Household	Per Capita
1960	17,496	57,154	74,650	1,566g	382g
1965	89,253	115,087	204,340	4,699	1,108
1970	353,913	136,162	490,075	8,655	2,715
1971	400,689	139,276	539,965	8,799	2,222
1972	482,154	140,074	622,228	9,582	2,420
1973	546,050	140,283	686,333	10,233	2,617

Source: The Ministry of Agriculture and Forestry, Tokyo, 1975.

Exhibit 6-2. Projection of Production and Consumption of Meats and Eggs in Japan 1972-1985 (in thousands of tons except for per capita consumption).

	Consumption		Production		Per Capita Consumption	
	1972	1985	1972	1985	1972	1985
Total Meats	2,147	3,193	1,730	2,747	14.2 (kg)	18.6 (kg)
Beef	367	625	290	508.	2.4	3.6
Pork	883	1,335	793	1,325	5.6	7.5
Chicken	668	915	640	914	4.7	5.7
Eggs	1,848	2,206	1,811	2,205	14.6	15.0

Source: The Ministry of Agriculture and Forestry, Tokyo, 1975.

Exhibit 6-3. Balance Sheet of the Kentucky Fried Chicken (Japan) as of May 31, 1974 (in thousands of yen).

Current Assets		**Current Liabilities**	
Cash	549,422	Notes payable	30,125
Accounts receivable	32,114	Accounts payable	134,313
Inventory	61,925	Short-term debts	1,161,396
Prepaid expenses	120,993	Reserve for employees'	
Loan	31,719	bonus	50,539
Fixed Assets		**Long-term Liabilities**	
Land	262,641	Long-term debts	493,630
Buildings	18,202		
Improvements on leased		**Capital**	
equipments	337,640	Paid-in capital	600,000
Equipment and machinery	102,185	Earned surpluses	71,085
Automobiles and trucks	3,637		
Prepaid construction	26,100		
Invisible Assets			
Leased property rights	120,946		
Long-term prepaid			
.expenses	74,188		
Investments	599,932		
Deferred Assets			
Royalties	55,469		
Issuing expenses of			
new stock	1,805		
	2,398,918		2,398,918

Source: Corporation Annual Report.

Exhibit 6-4. Profit and Loss Statement of the Kentucky Fried Chicken (Japan) From June 1, 1973 till May 31, 1974 (in thousands of yen).

Sales	¥ 2,101,996	
Franchise royalties	84,544	¥ 2,186,540
Costs of goods sold	1,081,062	
Sales and administrative expenses including payments[a]	1,003,430	2,084,492
Gross profits		102,048
Interests earned	11,922	
Other nonsales profits	5,603	17,525
Interest expenses	100,472	
Other expenses	2,124	102,596
Profit before tax		¥ 16,977

a. Including depreciation expenses of 35,682,000 yen.
Source: Corporation Annual Report.

STUDY GUIDE QUESTIONS

1. Describe the causes of KFCJ's success in Japan in up to two words. Entry timing? Any other description?

2. Why is KFCJ's emphasizing the direct ownership of its stores? How did KFCJ exploit such socioeconomic factors in Japan as changes in income level, social opinion leaders and the like?

3. Check the economics of the joint venture arrangement. How much has Heubline made in a year? How much has Mitsubishi made in a year (assume that for a commission Mitsubishi charges 3 percent of sales of whatever raw materials it sells to the KFCJ and that Mitsubishi makes 10 percent per annum on equipment and premises leased to KFCJ)? Has each parent firm made roughly equal amounts?

4. Will this joint venture be stable? Could KFCJ have entered the fast food market of Japan alone? If you were Heubline what would you do to interlock your economic interest with that of Mitsubishi?

5. Why did Heubline fail in its entry into Hong Kong? What is the unique strength of KFC that permits multinational spread? Product? Brand? Management? Finance?

4. Managing Distributors and Industrial Customers

Although many foreign firms have failed in their attempts to introduce products in Japan, some American firms have successfully penetrated the Japanese markets. This author contends that their success depended on understanding the consumer and industrial marketing systems in Japan, and that the skill gained by American managers in managing Japanese systems will aid them in surviving in U.S. markets. This chapter describes the Japanese distribution and production systems and includes case studies that illustrate how some American firms have adapted to Japan's marketing environment.

From 1981 to 1982, as Japan's trade surplus with the U.S. reached the all-time high of about $18 billion per year, there arose ever louder demands in the U.S. for "equal market access" or "reciprocity" between the two countries. Among the trade barriers identified was the Japanese distribution system. Over time, American managers and business scholars have characterized the distribution channels in Japan as archaic, inefficient, and impenetrable. Some of them have even called the Japanese distribution system a conspiracy against foreign goods.

In reality, however, there are many American firms that have already successfully penetrated Japanese markets. Although Pepsi Cola failed, Coca-Cola has succeeded in garnering about 80 percent of the Japanese cola market. Although General Foods had a long but unrewarding experience, Nestle's instant coffee became the number one selling brand in Japan. Even American fast food chains, encouraged by the outstanding successes of Kentucky Fried Chicken and McDonald's, have been quick to establish their market positions in Japan.

What then separates the successes from the failures? This article attempts to answer this question by examining Japan's distribution system and comparing it to that of the United States. Case studies are included to illustrate how American businesses can improve their ability to penetrate Japanese markets by understanding the consumer and industrial marketing systems in Japan.

The Logic of Japanese Distribution Systems

Every socioeconomic system has a logical basis and the Japanese distribution systems are no exception. It would serve no purpose to impose a distribution system like that in the U.S. on a foreign country like Japan. In fact, outside Canada and the U.S., local distribution systems tend to resemble Japanese systems more than American ones, particularly in the developing countries. American exporters have failed where their Japanese counterparts have succeeded in parts of Asia, Latin America, the Middle East, and Africa. This failure can be traced to American managers' reluctance to adapt to marketing systems that differ from those found in the U.S., Canada, and Europe. Once American marketing managers become familiar with Japanese systems, they will find it easier to manage equally complex, multipart distribution systems throughout the world.

Multilayered Distribution Channels

The number of wholesalers and retailers in Japan has not changed much during the last decade. There are about 250 thousand wholesalers and 1.5 million retailers for a Japanese population of approximately 110 million. This is nearly twice the number of wholesalers and retailers found in the U.S., even though the U.S. covers a much larger geographic area and has a population twice that of Japan. More importantly, over 60 percent of Japanese wholesalers have fewer than nine employees and over 70 percent of retailers have fewer than four staff members. In the U.S., combined sales of wholesalers in 1981 were about the same as combined retail sales, whereas in Japan combined sales of wholesalers were roughly four times as large as those of retailers.

Multiple layers characterize Japanese distribution channels of mass-consumed food items, packaged goods, drugs, toiletries, utensils, and small item appliances. Between manufacturers and retailers, there are often three, four, and sometimes five layers of wholesalers and subwholesalers, with each retailer and wholesaler covering limited pockets in regional or product markets. These multilayered distribution channels have evolved as the most economical and efficient means of serving a market environment that has long been characterized by relatively small per capita income, crowded living quarters, and heavy reliance by consumers on public transportation and on-foot travel.

Because of this environment, Japanese consumers tend to make frequent purchases of mass consumption items in small quantities. Food-related items, for example, are usually purchased daily; lack of home storage space and small disposable incomes make such frequent purchases necessary to satisfy consumers' daily needs. In addition, consumers' extensive reliance on travel by foot makes them dependent on widely scattered small neighborhood retailers. Because these small retailers are too financially and managerially weak to carry large inventories, they become dependent on frequent deliveries, extended working capital loans, sales supports, and other services provided by manufacturers and wholesalers.

These cultural characteristics alone make it economically efficient for many manufacturers and foreign exporters to Japan to rely on the existing layers of wholesale and subwholesale systems. However, distribution channels such as those found in Japan have additional functions that make utilizing the channels more efficient than attempting to sell directly to consumers or retailers.

Delivery, Sales Calls, and Point-of-Purchase Advertisements

A manufacturer can reduce significantly the number of sales calls required by using many levels of wholesalers rather than by selling directly to retailers scattered throughout the country. For example, suppose there are n manufacturers and r retailers ($n, r \geqslant$ 3). If the manufacturers make one call per retail store, then $n \times r$ contacts would be needed. Therefore, to meet the daily or weekly needs of neighborhood stores, the direct sales method of distribution would require an astronomical number of delivery and other logistical supports; the resulting cost would be prohibitive to most small- or medium-sized manufacturers, as well as to some large manufacturers. If, alternatively, a national wholesaler were to service these firms by making one call per retailer and one call per wholesaler, the number of calls would instead be $n + r$. Adding this one layer in the distribution system drastically reduces the total number of logistic support calls necessary to satisfy manufacturers and retailers.

With careful use of additional layers of wholesalers, manufacturers may benefit not only from the reduction in sales calls but also from the wholesalers' specializations. Specifically, with wholesalers specializing in servicing particular product groups of certain geographic sections of the national market, manufacturers can expect their products to receive greater attention. Cumbersome as it may appear, the multilayer system of wholesalers that has evolved in Japan—particularly for daily use consumption items—has actually helped many small- to medium-sized manufacturers market their products nationally at a fraction of the cost of direct sales.

Collection of Accounts Receivable, Working Capital Financing, and Market Information Feedback

The multilayered distribution system facilitates a form of trade finance, which is beneficial to manufacturers, wholesalers, and retailers. Small, financially weak retailers demand that their wholesalers finance not only their working capital needs but also often their capital investments, such as store expansion. Even in the case of neighborhood stores where consumers make daily cash purchases, retailers often have 100 to 120 days to pay their wholesalers. At the other end of the distribution system, manufacturers, by using common wholesalers, share the cost of helping their retailers and wholesalers finance working capital. These wholesalers in turn spread similar costs to other wholesalers down through the distribution line.

Manufacturers also benefit from this relationship by receiving credit risk screenings from their wholesalers for downstream subwholesalers and retailers. In addition, once such invisible channels of capital supply and credit checking are in place, these same

165

channels can be manipulated by manufacturers and wholesalers to collect needed information about market trends and competitors' moves. As more financially and managerially powerful manufacturers and large wholesalers become involved in a system—for example, by underwriting such economic and social programs as employee training and recreation for small manufacturers and retailers—the links among these three groups are completed.

Continuity of Contractual Relationships

For too long Japanese and foreign researchers alike have believed mistakenly that Japanese innately love harmony (*wa*) and that this somehow explains the apparent reluctance of Japanese manufacturers, wholesalers, and retailers to switch suppliers. This attitude, the researchers claim, is due to attempts by the Japanese to harmonize interpersonal relationships and to avoid interpersonal conflict. In reality, Japanese interpersonal and interfirm relationships are just as conflict-ridden as those of Americans. However, Japanese often choose a different method of resolving their problems.

Unlike the U.S., where only written contracts are considered enforceable and where verbal gentlemen's agreements are frequently broken, verbal and psychological contracts in Japan—as in any other traditional society—are considered to be as binding as written contracts. The promise behind a handshake in Japan can be broken only at great peril. Japanese society imposes social sanctions against those individuals and firms that renege on contracts which tend to be more swift, efficient, and unforgiving than any court penalties. This is not because the Japanese people are more honorable than Americans, but rather because contracts between two individuals or firms in Japan are always assumed to be continuous. Any specific conflict that arises in a contractual relationship is resolved so as to maintain the essential continuity of the relationship. Therefore, instead of utilizing the court system, the Japanese prefer to resolve problems through compromise, reconciliation, and often third-party arbitration. Because the parties to the contract assume that their business relationship will continue, they try to split the difference and vow to work better together in the future.

This assumed continuity of contractual relationships carries real cash value in Japan. It provides effective insurance against the uncertain outcome of contractual relationships and is an effective substitute for formal court proceedings. Accordingly, Japanese firms are reluctant to switch suppliers and customers because the continuity of business relationships carries higher cash value than the discounts and other economic benefits offered by new suppliers and customers.

Consumer Product Marketing

American "Demand Management"

For American marketing and sales managers schooled in the U.S. system of cut-and-dried relationships with wholesalers and retailers, the primary marketing task is what I call "demand management" (popularly called "pull strategy"). Backed by large advertising budgets, a marketing manager often must concentrate on getting customers to switch to his or her product. Cents-off coupons and other promotional gimmicks are used heavily to entice customers away from competing products. Product development is usually the task of some other department such as research and development; marketing managers are given a final product and told to promote it.

To marketing managers in the U.S., the control of final demand through price and advertisement manipulation is the challenging task, and management of wholesalers and retailers is secondary. Most marketing managers assume that as a product progresses through its life cycle, its demand characteristics change from that of a specialty item to that of a commodity item, whereupon consumers become extremely sensitive to prices. This consumer behavior affects wholesalers' and retailers' decisions to carry different product brands. These intermediaries respond to slight differences between brands in turnover and return on sales by selling their shelf space to those manufacturers whose products are "pulled" by consumers. Each sales contract is considered separately from the next.

Japanese "Supply Management"

In contrast, one of the most difficult tasks facing Japanese marketing managers is the management of sales forces and distribution channels, sometimes called "supply management" (or "push strategy"). The price manipulation that is characteristic of U.S. consumer product marketing is not a tactic used frequently in Japan. Unlike marketing and sales managers in the U.S., the Japanese believe that as a product goes through its life cycle, its demand characteristics continue to be those of a specialty item; therefore, consumers remain sensitive to product quality rather than to price. In addition, within the multilayered distribution systems it is preferable to avoid multiple price changes because they could lead to massive confusion.

Prices to consumers are controlled through the techniques of supply management. To guard against the possibility that any intermediaries might multiply their handling commissions and thus price the product out of the market, marketing managers in manufacturing firms carefully control the amount of supplies throughout the distribution system. By preventing the system from becoming overloaded with the product, the risk of price dumping by cash-starved wholesalers and retailers is reduced. Manufacturers also judiciously use rebates and other hidden economic rewards in an attempt to hold their final prices constant and to maintain control of otherwise unruly, independent wholesalers and retailers who might be bid away by the competition. Underlying this marketing process are the close personal relationships of marketing managers and their intermediaries which provide insurance for all parties concerned.

Even in Japan, however, the power relationships between manufacturers and wholesalers and between wholesalers and retailers are slowly but steadily changing. National chains, such as Daiei, Ito Yokado, and Seiyu Stores, and many of their regional competitors that mass merchandise food items, dry goods, drug items, and toiletries have not only destroyed many individual, small neighborhood grocers, butchers, and dry goods stores but have encouraged many manufacturers to deal directly with these retail chains. In fact, by 1982 these mass merchandisers had cornered about 20 percent of total retail sales in Japan. Partly as a defensive measure, many national and regional wholesalers have also increased their own wholesaler-retailer groups in order to play one manufacturer off against another. Furthermore, with the rise of mass consumer markets, large manufacturing firms have weeded out many weaker wholesalers and retailers from their support systems and consolidated their own direct control over a select number of intermediaries. In the 1980s these realignments of the distribution channels are likely to become more widespread.

When SmithKline & French (SK&F) of the U.S. decided to introduce its proprietary drug Contac 600 into the Japanese market in 1966, Henry Wendt, the first general manager of SK&F (Japan) and present chief executive officer of SK&F, and his Japanese colleagues set out to manage the distribution system. Today, Yoshio Masuda, general manager of SK&F (Overseas) says: The Japanese distribution channels are not as discrete as you would find in the U.S. The distribution channel is not readily available for your instant use.... (It) is something the marketer must establish and grow up with together...." Sensing the trend of concentration among wholesalers, SK&F (Japan) carefully selected thirty-five regional wholesalers covering all forty-seven Japanese prefectures as its first-tier wholesaler representatives. This was a gamble at that time because Japanese competitors were routinely dealing with about one thousand or more wholesalers.

During the next decade, while Japanese competitors were realigning their channels of distribution by reducing the number of wholesaler relationships to about 150 per firm, SK&F concentrated on linking up its thirty-five regional wholesalers with about half of the fifty thousand retail drug outlets throughout Japan. As a new entrant to the market, Masuda admits now: "SK&F did not have to bother about tradition and long accumulation of mutual obligations in dealing with wholesalers." SK&F's associations with its select prestigious, regional wholesalers facilitated efforts to plant its product image and information in the minds of consumers and succeeded in getting the product on the shelves of drug retail outlets.

In order to service such a delicate, organic entity as Japanese distribution channels, SK&F's sales representatives make daily contacts with wholesalers and key retail outlets. Most representatives live in the same cities as the wholesalers; they attend the morning gatherings of the wholesalers' sales forces and participate in the wholesalers' regular recreational events and evening parties. They also make regular calls to retail outlets and become closely acquainted with these store owners. In addition, SK&F's executives and president frequently call on wholesalers and cultivate close personal ties with the wholesaler executives. These visits by high-level executives of the manufacturing firm confirm vividly the importance they attach to special relationships with their wholesaler customers.

By 1982 SK&F had mastered the knack of managing Japanese distribution channels. The success of Nestle in Japan is a similar story.

Not all firms, however, have enjoyed profitable experiences in Japan. For example, the disappointing performance of Nestle's competitor, General Foods, reveals the firm's attempt to transplant its American "pull-supremacy" tactics to Japan; a few years ago, General Foods finally decided to join forces with Ajinomoto, a leading food processor in Japan.

Industrial Product Marketing

Nowhere is the importance of manufacturers becoming a vital part of the organic supplier-customer relationships more vividly illustrated than in industrial product marketing in Japan. Here again, the failure of American firms reveals the fundamental weakness of American manufacturing systems, now often plagued by product defects and low productivity.

In the U.S., industrial marketing managers try to make quick deals with the purchasing managers of their industrial customers by juggling three product variables: price, delivery, and quality. All of these variables are treated as economic tradeoffs. Since delivery and quality are often set at the level of the "adequate industry standard," price becomes the single most important haggling point between supplier and purchasing agent. Inside the typical factory, the quality control manager, purchasing manager, and production manager rarely consult with one another about the plant's problems, namely defective products, low productivity, and supply problems. Each has his own turf to manage. Quality control is functionally separate from the production process. The actions of the production manager, foreman, and plant manager drive workers to pay attention only to the number of products they are expected to complete each hour, according to work standards set by industrial engineers. At the end of the production line are quality control inspectors who are supposed to check the quality of finished and semifinished products according to the "acceptable quality level" (AQL) set some time ago by industrial engineers.

Japanese Manufacturing Systems

During the last thirty years, Japanese factories, both large and small, have developed their own manufacturing systems. These systems often challenge the conventional wisdom of industrial engineering, manufacturing operations, and operations research as taught in the U.S. Suppliers have to strive for "zero-defect" quality and frequent (often daily or twice a day) delivery schedules set by customer plants. Before suppliers are accepted, purchasing managers and quality control managers of customer plants carefully check the suppliers' production processes to evaluate whether the suppliers are capable of meeting their rigid standards. Supply prices are often set by customer plants or negotiated between supplier and customer to ensure that the prices are sufficient to permit suppliers to maintain the required product quality and delivery service. If necessary, technical, and sometimes financial assistance is provided by customers to suppliers for the improvement of their production processes.

Suppliers are often expected to provide additional services, such as absorbing surplus manpower and early retirees from their customer plants. In return, these customers guarantee exclusive purchases at prices favorable to the suppliers.

Through these interactions, a relationship develops between supplier and customer that can impede foreign manufacturer entry into a Japanese market. This has been the case with government monopolies, such as the National Telegraph and Telephone Corporation (NTT) and Japan National Railways (JNR), which control independent suppliers by demanding that suppliers be ever ready to meet their economic, technical, and social needs. The bond between government monopolies and their suppliers, based mainly on economic rationale, transcends the arm's-length transaction. Therefore, in the past foreign exporters found it almost impossible to sell their products to NTT and JNR, even for prices better than those offered by Japanese competitors. The JNR regarded the apparent price advantages of foreign exporters as insufficient to offset nonprice benefits received from suppliers within Japan.

Production Management. The Japanese "just-in-time system" (*kanban* system) of factory production scheduling allows suppliers to satisfy customers' requirements for frequent and strict delivery schedules. The production schedule is changed frequently to meet market demands, and this adjustment has to be made with practically no work-in-process or supply inventories. In order to provide the just-in-time deliveries, suppliers often build their warehouses just outside major customers' factories, and they strive to synchronize their production schedules with those of the major customers.

To permit suppliers to meet the rigorous delivery and quality schedules that are often subject to change, buyer-plants inform their suppliers of their long-term production plans and product developments. Furthermore, buyer-plants make long-term purchase commitments to suppliers so that suppliers can invest confidently large sums of money in the improvement of their production facilities and in the training of rank-and-file workers. If possible, all of these production plans are used to develop level annual production schedules for each shift. Changes in the number of production shifts and overtime employed, as well as the flexibility of production runs, are used to cushion cyclical demand fluctuations.

The differences between this system and that in the U.S. are clear. For example, the average production run of a typical compact car factory in Japan is two days, as compared to an average time of ten days in the U.S. The average time needed to change dies in a typical compact car factory is four to six hours in the U.S., while the same procedure takes just five minutes in Japan.

The just-in-time system can also lead to substantial operational savings from reduced inventory. For example, in 1981 the ratio of total inventories to sales for General Motors was 17 percent, while in the same year Toyota's ratio was merely 1.5 percent. The production systems at these two firms were significantly different. One difference was the number of suppliers used: GM had over 3,000 independent suppliers, while Toyota worked with about 300 "related" suppliers. Most of these related suppliers were legally independent firms that had been incorporated into the support system trained and organized by Toyota. Now in 1982 GM says that it practices the Japanese system of just-in-time (*kanban*) delivery from its suppliers. In reality, however, the General Motors method is to cut production costs solely at its suppliers' expense. This is a far cry from the Japanese system of mutual support relationships between customers and suppliers.

Quality Control and Quality Improvement. In general, the American manufacturing system tries to "inspect" quality into products while the Japanese manufacturing system builds quality into its products. The responsibility for quality control of supplies is often shifted to suppliers. As in any other Japanese factory, quality control is integrated into the production process. Quality and productivity are not treated as tradeoff variables; instead, quality is assumed to determine productivity.

The superiority of this system over the standard American system was underscored by the experience of Matsushita (Panasonic) in the U.S. after it took over Motorola's Quasar factory in 1974. From 1974 to 1980 the same factory with the same managers and employees cut product reject rates from 63 percent to 2 percent and reduced annual warranty expenses from about $16 million to less than $1 million. At the same time, the value added per worker nearly doubled. This drastic improvement in both quality and productivity was mainly due to three major changes in the factory's management and supply system. First, three hundred of Quasar's six hundred nonproduction workers were reassigned to direct production jobs, cutting drastically the number of quality inspectors from seven per twenty-five workers to fewer than one per twenty-five workers. Second, machine-paced assembly line conveyors were replaced by man-paced tray-and-roller stands; in this way, each worker could take as much time as necessary to complete the assigned task with singular attention to product quality. Third, the purchase of major components was switched from American suppliers to Matsushita's suppliers in Japan. The most likely sources of product defects were "designed out" by these Japanese suppliers who had intimate knowledge of Matsushita's production systems. In order to support this worker-oriented manufacturing system, Matsushita managers helped the American managers assume as their primary task the training and assistance of rank-and-file employees.

The Japanese quest for zero-defect products is not a finicky pastime as many American engineers and managers would have one believe. Through cumulative trial-and-error experiments, many Japanese firms have found it wrong to apply binomial or other probability distribution functions to simulate the probability of randomly having any single work station build a defect into the whole product. For one thing, one worker's probability of building a defect into the work-in-process is not independent of another worker's similar probability. Accordingly, if the factory as a whole aims at, say, a 98 percent "reliability rate" for its total production, each production station cannot possibly be given 2 percent as the "allowable margin of error." Instead, each work station must aim at zero defect performance. Mathematically speaking, if 2 percent is the allowable defect rate for the entire production process, then 2 percent divided by n is the maximum allowable defect rate for each of the n total work stations in the factory. Since n is often a very large number in a modern factory, the maximum allowable rate of defect for each station is extremely small. Giving each work station a 2 percent acceptable quality level is likely to produce as much as 20 to 31 percent product defects for the factory as a whole.

Incentives to improve product quality are also built into the Japanese manufacturing system. Buyer-plants are entitled to quality improvements, and they demand scheduled price reductions from suppliers. In this way, suppliers are pressured to improve product quality and to cut production costs as they ride down the fabled experience curve. Price increases are rarely permitted unless suppliers vastly improve products or develop new products that help buyer-plants cut their production costs or improve product quality. No one has ever heard of an acceptable quality level or "adequate industry standard."

The difference between quality considerations in the typical U.S. and Japanese production systems is well illustrated by the following example. One large U.S. firm opened its wholly owned manufacturing subsidiary in Japan over twenty years ago. The technological superiority of a certain industrial chemical product permitted the firm to become the leading supplier to the largest Japanese can manufacturer, Toyo Seikan. As expected, Japanese competitors entered the market and gradually eroded the American firm's market, first by price cutting and then by providing better delivery services. Still the superiority of the American firm's product helped the company maintain its leading position in the market during the next decade.

As Japanese competitors closed the technological gap with the American firm during the 1970s, the American firm let slip its hold over its leading industrial customer. In the U.S., the American firm said the adequate industry standard was one product defect per fifty thousand units. The Japanese customer kept demanding better and better product standards, however, and the Japanese competitors met the rising product standard by achieving one product defect per five million units. In order to avoid hindering Toyo Seikan's continuous production of large volumes of a variety of cans, its suppliers were expected to work together with Toyo Seikan's technical staff to eliminate product defects. Unfortunately, the American firm's urgent, repeated requests to its research and development laboratory in the U.S. for improvements in product quality, as well as for greater details of product-specific technology, were often met with total disbelief. The U.S. parent firm could not appreciate the importance of its Japanese subsidiary becoming, as it were, an integral part of the supplier support system of the leading customer. In 1982 this firm is still trying to regain its lost market share in Japan.

Corporate Culture. It has taken the Japanese manufacturers over twenty years to build their production systems. Contrary to popular belief, the Japanese manufacturing system and its supportive corporate culture is a distinctly post–World War II phenomenon. In a sense, they are far more modern and contemporary than their American counterparts. Quality control circles and other forms of workers' participation in the improvement of product and production processes have evolved only after drastic changes in management's attitude toward manufacturing systems and rank-and-file employees. For this culture to be feasible, the workers and managers of customer and supplier plants must learn to work together to form support systems.

American Industrial Marketing in Japan

In the 1980s American firms will have a much greater chance to supply industrial materials, semifinished goods, equipment, and chemicals to Japanese customers. However, their success will largely depend on their mastery of managing close supplier-customer relationships. American firms' mere marketing presence will not be sufficient to win a share of the Japanese market. The degree of supply assurance and product tailoring that Japanese industrial customers demand make local production necessary.

Conclusion

Today, the Japanese market is very much open to foreign businesses as long as they learn to behave like their Japanese competitors. American firms can take advantage of this opportunity. More importantly, even if American firms do not actually operate in Japan, they would find it useful to monitor the behavior of their Japanese and foreign competitors there. The experience of surviving the competitive consumer and industrial markets in Japan can provide an additional competitive edge even in U.S. markets. The knowledge of Japanese marketing practices, in addition to those in America, can help in the management of distribution channel systems. In such a competitive market as the U.S., this additional marketing tool would prove extremely useful. For industrial marketing purposes, the knowledge of supplier-customer behaviors in Japan would also help American firms to solidify their relationships with American industrial customers.

This is especially true in the 1980s, when numerous American industrial customers will be adopting many forms of productivity and quality improvements that have long been part of standard manufacturing practices in Japan.

For the first time in its history, the U.S. faces the job of managing economic growth with an increasing scarcity of capital, raw materials, energy, managerial skill, technology, and market opportunities. Japanese firms have been forced for over a century to cope with such scarcity in an increasingly interdependent world. Japanese marketing systems are indeed shaped by Japanese firms' efforts to manage their growth given the scarcity of resources. As a result, American firms will find contemporary lessons in mastering the ways to survive well in the Japanese market.

5. Honda in America: A Gamble That Paid Off

In 1983, the Harley-Davidson Corporation in Milwaukee, Wisconsin, won from the U.S. government long-sought political protection that raised import duties tenfold on Japanese heavy motorcycles. Behind the demise of Harley-Davidson in the American motorcycle market remains the 20-year success story of Japanese motorcycles in the American market. The story of Japanese motorcycles in the U.S. involves a successful, tenacious void-filling market strategy pursued by Honda, Kawasaki, Suzuki, and Yamaha. The market leader, Honda, in particular, had relentlessly cultivated new American demand for Japanese motorcycles.

Honda's Gamble in the U.S.

Back in 1959 few people, either Japanese or American, ever imagined that in less than ten years, Honda and other Japanese motorcycles would dominate the world market, including the United States market. For Honda, it was a risky venture to enter the U.S. market, but it had little alternative if it wanted to remain competitive in world motorcycle markets.

As the Japanese economy entered a period of accelerated growth early in the 1960s, the Japanese market for motorcycles as a major means of primary transportation began to level off. In turn, the demand for four-wheel motor vehicles and light trucks began to soar. The motorcycle market in Japan had entered the maturing phase. Honda had to find a growth market for its motorcycles. The question was, where? The United States was the only logical choice. For some time, Honda had been exporting its lightweight motorcycles. To publicize the durability and performance of its lightweight motorcycles, Honda for some time had been entering its machines in the international motorcycle race on the Isle of Man (Britain) and had become the habitual winner in the less-than-100cc-size engine class. Through its exposure to motorcycle races in Europe,

Honda's management became aware of a predictable shift in the nature of the market demand for motorcycles, depending on the general income level of the country markets.

A Country-to-Country Difference in the Product Life Cycle

What Honda's management came to understand at first was that there seemed to be a country-to-country difference in the time lag for the different uses of motorcycles. Uses of motorcycles are closely related to the nation's economic level. When a nation's income level is relatively low, as it was in Japan during the 1950s, the primary use for motorcycles is as a lower-cost means of basic transportation than cars. As rising income led motorcycle users to switch to cars, the primary use of motorcycles declined. At the same time, secondary uses increased. These uses were mainly recreational, but motorcycles were also being used for short-distance commuting by students and younger professional groups. In this secondary phase of motorcycle use, cyclists look to motorcycles not as lower-cost substitutes for cars but as a desirable means of transportation and recreation. Motorcycles afford greater freedom of movement than four-wheel cars.

Figure 11.1 shows schematically the primary and secondary use patterns for motorcycles in Japan and the U.S. The vertical axis represents the diffusion of products in a given country market as measured by ownership as a percentage of population. The dotted line, C_p, is a ceiling for the primary use of motorcycles. C_p's value varies with the country, depending on its geographical and socioeconomic composition. However, in the case of motorcycles, the value of C_p is usually between 2.5 percent and 5.0 percent ownership rate for the population. More importantly, the secondary use phase often pushes the demand for motorcycles well beyond the ceiling set for the primary use of motorcycles. Due to the higher per capita income level in the U.S. in 1959, compared to Japan, the secondary use phase for motorcycles in the U.S. was already in the latent formative stage. It was at this time that the primary use cycle for motorcycles in Japan began to decline.

For Honda to survive in Japan alone, it would have had to retrench its production and sales of motorcycles for some time until the advent of the secondary use phase, some time in the future. Honda's alternative was to reposition its motorcycles in a secondary use market such as the United States. By the time Japan entered the secondary use phase, Honda would be ready for it. Honda gambled on its venture in the U.S. In 1959, both Honda and Yamaha (a leading competitor of Honda) entered the U.S. market.

The U.S. Market

Around 1960, annual sales of motorcycles in the U.S. were less than 20,000 units. The overwhelming majority of motorcycles sold in the U.S. were heavyweight models with engine sizes of 500cc or larger. The market was dominated by Harley-Davidson (an American company), BMW (a German company), and the British company, Triumph. In addition to the military police force, American motorcycle buyers were young males who tried to show off their macho life styles. Although most motorcycle riders were decent citizens, the public image of motorcycle riders was of ruffians wearing

175

Figure 11.1

Primary and Secondary Use Patterns for Motorcycles
(Japan and the United States)

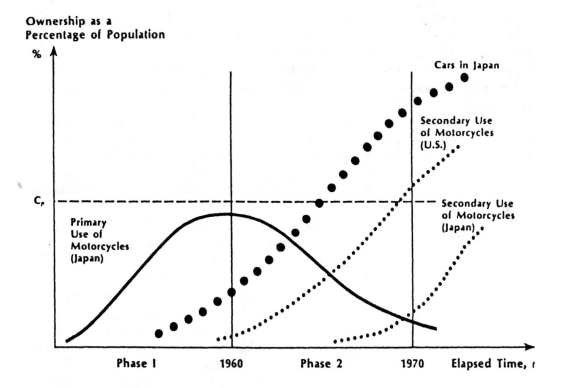

black leather jackets, sporting tattoos and chain belts. Infamous motorcycle gangs with names like "Hell's Angels" and "Satan's Slaves" contributed to the unsavory image of motorcyclists. In 1953, the Hollywood movie *The Wild Ones* featured Marlon Brando leading a motorcycle gang that terrorized small American towns and rode around on 650cc Triumphs. The image of rowdy motorcycle riders stuck in the American public's mind.

Heavyweight motorcycles required a rider with considerable muscle, strength, driving skill, and a daredevil spirit. Accordingly, around 1960, American motorcyclists were almost exclusively males with a mechanical flair who loved tinkering with and maintaining their machines. In other words, the motorcycle was definitely for the fun-loving, mechanically-minded jock—not for amateurs who did not want to pay $1,000 to $1,500 for machines too heavy for them to push.

Honda's Entry Strategy

Even if Honda wanted to make frontal attacks on the market positions firmly held by American and European heavyweight machines, it did not have appropriate products. Honda's machines were lightweight models with engine sizes of less than 350cc, which suited the slim Japanese for riding on the narrow, congested roads in Japan. In fact, the bulk of Honda's products were at the smaller end of the lightweight model line, with engine sizes of 55cc to 125cc. In 1960, the American market for lightweight motorcycles was about 10,000 sales units per year, compared to over 1.5 million sales units in Japan.

Therefore, Honda's strategy of repositioning its lightweight motorcycles in the secondary use cycle of the U.S. market required the creation of totally new customers for its products. Honda gambled in its entry strategy on attracting those American consumers who had never even considered riding a motorcycle, let alone buying one. Without erasing the negative image that many American consumers had of motorcycles and motorcyclists, Honda would have no chance of success in the American market.

Product. Honda chose the smallest lightweight motorcycle, with a 55cc engine, as its entry into the American market. This model was already very popular in Japan, even with housewives and small store owners who had never ridden a motorcycle before. It had a three-speed transmission, an automatic clutch, and an electric starter. It even looked different from ordinary motorcycles and had a step-through frame for women. Its five-horsepower motor was twice as powerful as American lightweight motorcycles of comparable size, and its quality was superior to that of the lighweight models sold by Sears in America. Honda's 55cc came in bright colors and two-tones appealing to young and educated consumers, and easy-to-ride features took the fear out of motorcycling.

Price. Honda gave its 55cc model a $250 retail price, in contrast to the $1,000-$1,500 price tags given to the heavyweight models sold by Harley-Davidson and European firms.

Target Consumers. Honda's customers were college-age riders and young urban professionals who used their cycles for short-distance commuting and shopping trips. Honda chose the retail rice of $250 to make its machine affordable to its targeted buyers.

Distribution. Honda knew that it had to create a new network of Honda distributors. If it distributed the Honda model through existing motorcycle dealers, its product would be handled by those dealers who catered to existing customers who preferred medium to heavyweight machines. Besides, the kind of consumers that Honda wanted to reach would not venture near existing motorcycle dealers, where "Hell's Angels" types might be congregating. Honda decided to build its own exclusive network of distributors by teaching bicycle shops and other appliance stores how to sell and service motorcycles. Incidentally, Honda had already succeeded in building up its dealer networks in Japan, in a similar fashion.

Advertising. In addition to billboards and roadside signs, Honda chose to advertise in respectable but popular magazines like *Newsweek* and *Time,* which were widely read by Honda's target customers. Television advertising time was carefully purchased to supplement the advertising on billboards and in the printed media.

The promotional theme was "You Meet the Nicest People on a Honda." This was clearly aimed at presenting Honda motorcycles as respectable products for good

Americans. In order to capture the essence of this promotional theme, Honda's early advertisements exclusively featured a blond college coed riding her Honda machine in a red school blazer and a neat skirt. She carried her books in the side rack of her Honda, and her blonde hair streamed from the inside of her helmet.

In 1959, Honda established its fully-owned American subsidiary, Honda Motor Company of America. Honda's move was quite a contrast to American and European motorcyle firms that relied on independent distributors. Honda was determined to distribute its products directly to retail outlets through its own distribution and service company, Honda Motor Company of America. Otherwise, Honda worried that precious market information and consumer reaction would not be quickly relayed to Honda. Besides, the creation of an entirely new market segment demanded complete control over distribution and customer service operations. Honda Motor Company of America had to train its newly signed-up dealers to treat customers nicely and honestly.

Once Honda decided to create an entirely new market segment for American motorcycles, it put together an internally consistent package for the initial marketing mix. More as an act of faith, the firm ventured on the uncharted area of the American market. In order to minimize its risks as well as to maximize what it learned in the process, Honda adopted a market-by-market approach to penetrate the vast American market. It trained its eyes first on California and other West Coast markets in the United States and Canada.

Honda's Initial Successes (1960–1974)

As more and more Americans responded positively to Honda's approach, Yamaha and other Japanese motorcycle firms followed suit. Together, these firms expanded the primary demand of American consumers for easy-to-ride, lightweight motorcycles. By 1964, Honda had embarked on its program to cultivate the urban markets on the East coast from the Montreal-Toronto-Boston-New York areas-as well as in the Mideast areas.

By 1964, the U.S. motorcycle market had expanded phenomenally to the level of 200,000 sales units annually from a mere 40,000 sales units in 1962. By 1966, the market size had expanded further to 475,000 sales units a year. Japanese motorcycles, led by the Honda models, had garnered about 90 percent of the market.

Fortunately for Honda and other Japanese motorcycle firms, American and European motorcycle companies chose to ignore the expanding market segment of lightweight models. In September 1966, William H. Davidson, president of Harley-Davidson, was quoted in *Forbes* as saying

> The lightweight motorcycle is only supplemental. Back around World War I, a number of companies came out with lightweight bikes. We came out with one ourselves. We came out with another one in 1947 and it just did not go anywhere. We have seen what happens to these small sizes....

Little did they realize that Honda and other Japanese motorcycle firms were creating an entirely new market for motorcycles and filling a tremendous void left unattended by American and European firms. Instead, American and European firms hoped that

178

they would catch the newly-found American motorcyclists when they started trading up their machines from lightweights to heavyweights.

By 1974, the number of annual sales units of motorcycles in the U.S. had reached 1.3 million, with Japanese firms holding about 90 percent of the market. Harley-Davidson was the slowest to recognize this new trend in the market. British and German firms belatedly expanded their efforts to capture American cyclists who were trading up their machines to medium and heavyweight models.

Purchasing Behavior of American Motorcyclists

Because of the successful creation of a new market segment of the American motorcycle market by Honda and other Japanese firms, a large number of new cyclists had been brought into the market. As a result, by 1974, when the U.S. market began to show signs of maturing finally after a decade of rapid growth, the profiles and purchasing behavior of American motorcyclists were very much different from the days of *Hell's Angels* and *The Wild Ones*. As a group, American motorcyclists came to resemble their fellow consumers of stereo and other audio equipment, color television sets and even automobiles. Table 11.1 summarizes the age profile of American motorcyclists.

In addition, it was learned that 90 percent of motorcycle buyers were male, and about 55 percent of them were married, with above-average median incomes of $12,720 in 1974. About 43 percent were college-educated, and their median age was 25. In sum, American motorcyclists were distinctly urban middle class. How different this profile was from the prevailing image of cyclists in the 1950s as teenage troublemakers

Table 11.1

Age Profiles of American Motorcyclists, 1974

Age	Percentage of Owners	
	In This Class	Cumulative
Under 16	13	13
16–17	10	23
18–20	13	36
21–24	15	51
25–29	15	66
30–39	19	85
40–49	10	95
50 and over	4	99
No answer	1	100

Source: Gallup Survey, 1974.

and ruffians. In 1974, on average, American motorcyclists were young, male family men in their late twenties to early thirties.

With the drastic change in the personal profiles of motorcyclists, purchasing behavior also changed. Table 11.2 summarizes the major reasons for American consumers' selecting one brand as opposed to another. It was also found that over 80 percent of motorcyclists were introduced to motorcycles by family members. On average, it took eight weeks of shopping before they made a purchase. About 85 percent of consumers bought after word-of-mouth recommendations from motorcycle owners. About 83 percent of consumers used dealer visits to obtain information on motorcycles, while approximately 70 percent of them consulted motorcycle magazines. On the other hand, only about 52 percent of consumers relied on manufacturers' literature for necessary product information. Publicized competition results and actual test driving were cited as sources of influence for making final model selection by about 38 percent of customers. On average, 3.7 makes or models were considered before one was selected. Choice of brand and model was influenced by a number of factors, as shown in Table 11.2.

The data in Table 11.2 and the careful shopping behavior of American motorcyclists clearly show that potential motorcycle buyers are concerned, just as are potential buyers of any large appliance, about the product's durability and quality. How do they

Table 11.2

Factors Influencing Selection of Motorcycle Brand and Model in the U.S.

Product Attributes	Percentage of Buyers Rating Attribute as Important or Very Important for Purchase Decisions
Quality if workmanship	94.6
Availability of parts	91.6
Handling/performance	88.9
Power/acceleration	85.9
Styling/appearance	84.6
Recommendation of owners/friends	81.3
Dealers' reputation	80.4
Dealers' service	76.9
Resale value	74.8
Warranty coverage	72.1
Economy of operation	63.9
Test drive	56.3
Owned same make before	34.3

judge product quality? Visual appeal of workmanship and customer service (availability of parts) are the two most important factors that influenced purchasing decisions. How does product reputation spread? Reputation spreads by word-of-mouth and by the "authoritative" recommendations of motorcycle magazines. Dealer reputation and service are also very important. In other words, by 1974, the motorcycle had become another recreational product, like pleasure boats and sports cars.

Although all the motorcycle models were used for recreational riding, there were special products designed particularly for off-road recreational use. These off-road machines were more powerful for comparable engine size and built to withstand the rugged handling required for off-road bike riding. Some models are made to be used as both on-road and off-road machines.

Honda and other Japanese firms had extended their product lines for the U.S. market as market demand proliferated. After they initiated more and more American consumers to the lightweight and easy-to-ride models, Honda and other Japanese firms motivated them to trade up their models for easy-to-ride but more powerful motorcycles. This trading-up behavior was more pronounced for motorcycles than for automobiles or other durable appliances. For example, in 1974 one consumer survey showed that about 52 percent of first-time motorcycle buyers chose machines in the 50cc to 174cc engine size range. In particular, about three quarters of those who bought machines with engine sizes of less than 90cc as their first-time purchases chose bigger machines in their repeat purchases. Besides, brand switching among different makes became a rule. Only one third of the customers remained with their old brands.

Honda and other Japanese motorcycle firms relied on their product extensions, heavy advertising, and dealer support to satisfy the youthful consumer of motorcycles in the U.S. In fact, from the mid-1960s to the mid-1970s, the postwar "baby-boom" population of the U.S. entered the market. Table 11.3 shows that Honda and other Japanese firms were shifting their product focus from on-road machines to off-road models between 1968 and 1975. They made such product shifts to satisfy changing consumer needs.

Between 1968 and 1974, the market composition changed significantly. In 1968, about 41 percent of motorcycles sold were models of the under-125cc class. In 1974, this segment of the market constituted only 19 percent of sales. Instead, the medium to heavy models of the over-350cc class made up over 53 percent of the products sold. To remain competitive, Honda and other Japanese firms shifted their product and marketing focus from lightweights to medium and heavyweights. Japanese firms came to supply motorcycles from the 55cc class all the way up to the 749cc class. In 1974, Japanese firms were poised to enter the top end of the heavyweight market semgent, the 750cc class.

Changing Market Demand Beyond 1974

From 1960 to 1974, the percentage of the American population owning at least one motorcycle rose sharply from 0.3 percent to 2.3 percent. During this time period, Honda and Japanese motorcycle firms combined garnered nearly 90 percent of the market. However, the American market was entering the maturing stage rapidly past

Table 11.3

Number of Models Offered by Usage Category in the U.S. Market in 1968 and in 1975

	On-Road	Combination	Off-Road
Honda—1975	7	13	6
1968	20	1	—
Yamaha—1975	9	5	15
1968	18	4	—
Kawasaki—1975	9	7	7
1968	10	3	2
Suzuki—1975	7	9	8
1968	3	1	—
Harley-Davidson—1975	6	4	1
1968	9	1	—
Triumph—1975	15	1	1
1968	14	6	—
BMW—1975	4		
1968	3		

Source: Motocycle Appraisal Guide, April–July 1975.

the mid-1970s. In addition to the accelerated trend of trading up to heavier machines among existing owners, a slower growth in the primary demand for motorcycles was forecast for the remainder of the 1970s and beyond. This was due to a combination of factors. First of all, the motorcycle age group of 15-24 years was dwindling rapidly. The postwar baby-boom group was moving into something else and relinquishing its involvement with motorcycles. Secondly, the anti-noise and air pollution requirements, as well as the ecological protection of off-road areas, were increasingly restricting the use of motorcycles for recreational and transportational uses.

To persuade women and older people to use motorcycles, Honda and other Japanese firms intensified their new advertising campaigns but met with little success. Accordingly, after the mid-1970s, the annual growth of the American motorcycle market was estimated to be at around 3 percent. Reflecting the trading-up trend of existing motorcyclists, however, the growth of the market for heavier machines with engine sizes of over 750cc was estimated at around 6 percent annually. At this juncture, Honda and other Japanese firms had no choice but to shift their marketing emphasis from void filling to a frontal attack on the market positions long held by Harley-Davidson, BMW, and Triumph.

In Europe, similar market developments occurred. By the mid-1970s, in each country except Italy, which limited the import of Japanese motorcycles, Japanese makes combined captured about 75 percent of the market. The success of Honda and other Japanese firms was achieved in the same way as in the U.S. They used their "void-filling strategy" to create a market segment of lightweight machines and followed consumers' trading-up habits aggressively.

The Sources of Honda's Competitive Strength

For its successes in the U.S. and Europe, Honda owed much to its intensive research and development and to superb manufacturing productivity. For example, Honda had on its staff 1,300 R & D personnel, seven to ten times as many as its American and European competitors. Honda translated its R & D superiority into an ability to introduce newer and newer models as world markets changed. In the two years from 1974 to 1975, Honda introduced 26 different models, including its 1,000cc heavyweight model, to the American and European markets. From the conception of a new product idea to the actual delivery to the market, it took Honda only 18 months. Furthermore, Honda had a number of new designs and models in its laboratories so that it would be ready to manufacture them as the market developed.

The R & D capability of Honda would have been wasted if it had not been backed by Honda's equally superior manufacturing capability. Unlike the labor-intensive production systems of its American and European competitors, which were suited to small-scale production, Honda had built capital-intensive, automated production systems. Honda's manufacturing policy was an integral part of its worldwide marketing strategy. Productivity and quality became distinctive elements of Honda's business strategy. Honda managed its R & D activities with a view to balancing product engineering, improvements in production processes, and marketing efforts.

Rather than designing its production processes within the constraints of the machines and equipment available from outside suppliers, Honda designed and made machines that were tailored to its production needs. Honda's automated production processes, which utilized its own special-purpose machines, required a large production volume to be economical.

Unlike Honda, its American and British competitors were locked into labor-intensive, rigid production processes that did not permit any large-scale production. Triumph and Harley-Davidson could not hope to build more flexible, capital-intensive manufacturing systems. Without such flexible manufacturing systems, these firms could not hope to generate a large sales volume by keeping up with the dynamically shifting demand conditions of their markets. For example, Triumph invested £1,300 of net fixed assets (mainly machinery) per employee to produce £4,200 of value added per employee annually. On the other hand, Honda used £5,000 of net fixed assets per employee and generated £18,000 of value added per employee per year.

As a result, each Honda and other Japanese company factory was operating by 1975 at an annual production level of 500,000 units to 2 million units, while each Triumph, BMW, and Harley-Davidson factory was operating at an annual production level of 11,000 units to 40,000 units. Honda's annual production per employee was on average over 250 units, while Harley-Davidson, BMW, and Triumph were recording a meager 10 units to 20 units of production per employee annually. The resultant differences in productivity between Honda and its American and European competitors gave Honda a commanding lead in supplying newer products expeditiously to worldwide customers.

Supported by ever-improving manufacturing experience and dynamic economy of scale, Honda and other Japanese motorcycle firms utilized (experience curve effects) forward pricing moves to their fullest pricing advantage. Their products were priced at an extremely competitive level from the outset, and held steady. This pricing move not only made their products better values for customers than American and European models, but more importantly, avoided dealers' confusion over frequently changing prices. The reliability of quoted prices served to enhance the image of reliability of Honda and other Japanese models in the American and European markets.

Distribution Channels

By the mid-1970s, there were about 10,000 dealers for motorcycles and their accessories in the U.S., with about 80 percent of them exclusively franchised by manufacturers. From 1961 to 1974, Honda had increased its exclusive dealers in the U.S. from 125 to 1,974. Yamaha, Suzuki, and Kawasaki, other Japanese manufacturers, also had come to hold over 1,000 dealers each. Meanwhile, American and European manufacturers were holding less than 500 dealers each.

Although motorcycle dealers in the U.S. were generally small businesses, the dealers for Honda and other Japanese manufacturers were larger than the dealers for Harley-Davidson, BMW, and Triumph. Japanese motorcycle dealers became financially more powerful because of their larger sales volumes of Japanese models. Their financial strength in turn permitted them to build up their customer service and to provide necessary maintenance service for their customers. As a result, more and more customers were attracted to Japanese motorcycle dealers. The reinforcing cycle renews itself.

Honda's New Promotional Theme

In 1980, Honda adopted a new promotional theme: "Follow the Leader." All around the United States, billboards and other advertisements featured a male racer riding a powerful heavyweight machine under the banner "Follow the Leader." In 1961, Honda spent about $150,000 for advertisements, but increased its ad budget to over $8 million in 1974.

In addition to TV spots, radio spots, and outdoor billboards, Honda emphasized motorcycle magazines as its major print media advertisement. Furthermore, regional advertising and sales promotions were extensively carried out in cooperation with dealers. However, because of Honda's larger sales volume, its advertising and sales promotion expenses per motorcycle sold were less than one fifth of the expenses incurred by Harley-Davidson in the U.S. Harley-Davidson was forced to increase its advertising budget from about $75,000 in 1961 to over $1.7 million in 1974.

The Decline of Harley-Davidson

The defensive measures of Harley-Davidson were singularly predicated upon the premise that newer motorcyclists initiated to motorcyle riding by Honda and other Japanese firms would trade their machines up to well-known, real medium to heavyweights made by Harley-Davidson. From the mid-1960s to the mid-1970s Harley-Davidson waited for American motorcyclists to finally discover the American makes by Harley-Davidson.

By the mid-1970s, it became apparent that American motorcyclists were trading their Japanese makes up for other Japanese models. Meanwhile, the annual sales of Harley-Davidson were reduced by 30 percent to 40 percent as Honda and other Japanese firms made inroads into the medium to heavyweight model segments of the market. At this juncture, Harley-Davidson ran to the U.S. International Trade Commission for political protection against Japanese imports. Harley-Davidson's market share was reduced to a mere 4 percent in 1966 and to a mere 2 percent in 1974.

What went wrong with the wait-and-see defensive measure of the one-time market leader, Harley-Davidson? Harley-Davidson's management did not realize that it was facing a group of American consumers entirely different from the traditional users of Harley-Davidson's machines. These new American motorcyclists were brought into the market by Honda and other Japanese firms, convinced that they were different from the traditional Hell's Angels who sported heavy Harley-Davidson machines. Furthermore, these first-time riders often went back to dealers from the same Japanese manufacturer or to dealers from other Japanese manufacturers when they wanted to trade up their machines. Since over 70 percent of the motorcycle dealers in the U.S. belonged to Japanese manufacturers, American motorcyclists had a greater chance of encountering any one of the dealers for Japanese motorcycles. Unlike financially hard-pressed dealers from Harley-Davidson, the dealers for Honda and other Japanese firms were capable of offering better customer service.

Besides, first-time cyclists became satisfied with the easy-to-ride features of Honda and other Japanese models. Even when they traded up their machines, they still sought the familiar easy-to-ride features of Honda and other Japanese models. Their satisfaction with the workmanship and reliability of Honda and other Japanese motorcycles predisposed them to look for other Japanese motorcyles when they shopped around for more powerful machines. Versatile product development and manufacturing operations of Honda and other Japanese firms permitted them to move a step ahead of the dynamic shifts in market demand.

Conclusion

The successful story of Honda and other Japanese motorcycles in the U.S. and elsewhere provides a textbook illustration of their void-filling strategy. Only when they had completely outflanked their American and European competitors did Honda and other Japanese manufacturers launch successful frontal atacks on the market leaders.

Similar strategies have been successfully used in the U.S. and elsewhere by Japanese manufacturers of electronic appliances, small copiers, typewriters, automobiles, and machine tools. However, unlike Harley-Davidson, American market leaders in electronic appliances and office equipment, for instance, have been making concentrated efforts to link their product development and manufacturing with their marketing activities the same way their Japanese competitors did. Japanese manufacturers often suffer from one competitive disadvantage compared to American market leaders: their distribution networks tend to be weaker than those of their American competitors.

As market competition intensifies, the future success of Japanese firms in the U.S. depends on their building capable sales organizations with American personnel who will manage their dealer networks. When the competitive edges between Japanese and American firms are equalized in the areas of product development and manufacturing versatility, the remaining areas of managing sales forces and dealer networks will become the deciding factor for success.

7 FOREIGN DIRECT INVESTMENT

1. INTRODUCTION

In 1981, as climbing energy prices continued to raise transportation costs for air and ocean freight, Japanese, American, and European electronics firms were forced to choose between increasing the production volume of their manufacturing subsidiaries in East Asia and Southeast Asia and automating and expanding production plants in the United States, Europe, and Japan. Their problems were compounded by the specter of chronic political instability that seemed to plague countries like Korea, the Philippines, and Indonesia, all of which hosted many offshore production facilities for multinational manufacturing firms.

Meanwhile, in the U.S. color television market, from 1980 to 1981, high-quality products were produced in the United States by Japanese firms, and many American products were manufactured by U.S. firms in Taiwan and Mexico and shipped back to the United States. This reversal of the manufacturing location of Japanese and American products seemed to refute the claims of American producers that television sets cannot be produced economically in a high-wage country like the United States. It also added to the examples of successful foreign direct investment in the United States.

Foreign direct investment – firms of one nationality operating manufacturing and service companies in another country – is, of course, not new. What distinguishes foreign investments of the post-

World War II era from those made prior to World War II is the sheer number and diversity of such undertakings by firms from all over the world. There are also marked differences in the ways each group of multinational parent-subsidiaries coordinates complex activities at home and abroad. During the post–World War II period, the contraction of international communication and travel distances facilitated the multinational expansion of many firms.

The history of multinational operations for some U.S. companies goes back to the nineteenth century. By 1900, such companies as Colt Industries, Singer Sewing Machine, Standard Oil, International Harvester, General Electric, United Fruit Company, and perhaps a dozen more firms were already multinational corporations, each with operations in several countries. By the mid-1920s there were as many as three or four dozen U.S. companies that could be described as multinational. The majority of these either were in petroleum or were engaged in some facet of metalworking or metal product fabrication. A number of food, drug, and chemical companies also began to venture abroad during this period.

During the 1930s and 1940s, owing in part to the Great Depression and World War II, there was generally a contraction in the multinational activities of U.S.-based firms. Some multinational firms gave up or sold their foreign subsidiaries altogether. This cutback was also partly the result of a system of international cartels that came into existence in a great many industries from the mid-1920s through the beginning of World War II. These cartels, many of which included U.S. firms, often specifically prohibited firms of one nationality from participating directly in some other national market. During the 1940s and early 1950s, the involvement of U.S. firms in these cartels was in many instances found to be in violation of the antitrust laws, for the U.S. government had done little to stop or restrain U.S. companies from entering international cartel agreements during the 1920s and 1930s.

A major expansion of the international activities of U.S. firms begun in the late 1940s has continued into the 1980s. The rate of expansion of U.S. foreign direct investment increased noticeably from the end of the Korean War in 1953 to the middle to late 1960s, when it began to level out and then decline. The rate of expansion of foreign direct investment of U.S. firms continued to decrease from the middle to late 1960s to the middle 1970s, although the absolute magnitude of U.S. foreign direct investment increased steadily.

By and large, the non-U.S.-based multinational corporation is a new phenomenon. Relatively few of these companies existed prior to the middle 1960s, although some of them have had long histories of multinational operations. A list of such firms would include the British–Dutch firms Royal Dutch/Shell and Unilever, several British firms such as I.C.I. and Courtalds, Canadian firms such as International Nickel and ALCAN, Ltd., the Dutch firm Philips, the Belgian firm Union Minier, the Swiss firms Nestle, Ciba–Geigy, Hoffmann-La Roche, and several others. A number of German firms might have had long multinational histories if their foreign direct investments had not been seized in 1914 and again in the 1940s.

The fully grown multinational firm pools resources such as capital, managerial skill, and technology from its parent and subsidiaries throughout the world to achieve the organization's common goals. Multinational firms have often been accused of working to maximize their own returns even at the expense of labor, local firms, consumers, and other groups. This widespread negative public image of multinationals places them at odds with the economic and political goals of their own government and those of foreign host governments.

Contrary to popular belief, multinational firms are not restricted to large private firms in non-Socialist, developed nations. Russian oil corporations behave in much the same way as EXXON, Mobil, Shell, and other private multinational oil companies. Russian banks participate in Singapore's Asia-dollar market just as Citibank, Bank of Tokyo, and other private banks of capitalist countries do. India, Korea, Argentina, Brazil, Mexico, and other newly industrializing and developing nations have produced some of their own multinational firms. And a number of state-owned enterprises, most notably in Italy, are also engaged in multinational activities. In Japan, direct foreign investment was spearheaded by small to medium-sized firms. Only toward the end of the 1960s, did large Japanese companies begin to become multinational.

As of the early 1980s, however, most of the foreign direct investment in the world is thought to be owned by a relatively small number of companies, probably no more than 500 to 600 in all. Each of these firms operates in more than one nation. These large multinationals appear to control an increasing volume of manufactured products that are ostensibly traded on the world market. In actuality, this activity is merely the cross-hauling of goods between companies that are connected to the multinationals. Accordingly, the terms "multinational firm," "transnational corporation," or "multinational enterprise," came to mean a large firm with extensive international operations.

2. FOREIGN DIRECT INVESTMENT VERSUS FOREIGN PORTFOLIO INVESTMENT

Conceptually, these two forms of foreign investment should be approached differently since they respond to different economic and political stimuli, have dissimilar effects on national economies, and appear to be motivated by different factors.

Simply defined, if a citizen of one country makes an investment in another country with the intention of actively managing the physical assets and organization acquired or created as a result of the investment, the investment is commonly termed a foreign direct investment. If, by contrast, the investor intends only to hold the foreign investment in anticipation of financial gain and does not intend to manage the investment, it is termed a foreign portfolio investment or simply a portfolio investment. For example, if a U.S.-based corporation were to establish and manage a European subsidiary that manufactured a product that the corporation had previously exported to Europe, the subsidiary would be considered a foreign direct investment. If, on the other hand, a citizen and resident of Great Britain were to buy several hundred shares of common stock of a major U.S. corporation, this would be a foreign portfolio investment. Generally, when a citizen of one nation holds a high enough percentage of the common equity of a corporation or other commercial entity of another nation to be able to potentially control that corporation, the holding is regarded as a foreign direct investment. This is true regardless of whether or not control is actually exercised. What percentage of common equity constitutes a potentially controlling interest depends upon the size and inclinations of the shareholders and the distribution of shares among them. An individual who holds 50 percent or more of a corporation's common equity, for example, certainly has a controlling interest. If the stock of the corporation is widely held, an individual may be able to exercise effective control even if he or she holds a much smaller percentage. Somewhat arbitrarily, the United States Internal Revenue Service has determined that a U.S. citizen "directly controls" a foreign corporation if the citizen holds 25 percent or more of the corporation's common equity.

Since foreign portfolio investment is behaviorally and functionally the same as domestic portfolio investment, the focus of this chapter will be on foreign direct investment. As stated above, foreign direct investment is distinguished from foreign portfolio investment by the investor's intent and ability to control and manage physical assets abroad. Legal ownership per se is not a requirement of foreign direct investment. Foreign direct investment usually takes one of the following forms or a combination thereof.

Management Contract: This arrangement is common among international hotel chains and other service operations. For example, if Holiday Inn of America were to enter into a management contract with a foreign business, the American hotel would assume the managerial responsibility for hotels in foreign countries. They receive prenegotiated fees for a predetermined length of time. The foreign business is entitled to use the internationally known brand name "Holiday Inn" and the referral booking services of international travelers handled by the Holiday Inn chain.

When manufacturing firms export plants, the export contracts often carry management contracts in which exporting firms agree to manage the plants and train foreign purchasers to operate the plants for a predetermined duration. The management contract allows for no or only nominal ownership of foreign business.

Joint Venture: When two or more investors jointly own physical assets, the investment is called a "joint venture." As in the case of fully owned foreign investments, a joint venture can be started from scratch by the investing parties or by one party acquiring partial ownership in an existing overseas company. Since the majority owner must hold more than 50 percent of the equity in a joint venture to retain legal control of the operations, investors classify joint ventures as majority-owned or minority-owned. When more than three investors jointly own foreign operations, the operations are often called an international "consortium." Consortia are very common in large-scale natural resource development projects and in international banking operations.

Fully Owned Subsidiary: When one foreign investor owns more than 95 percent of a foreign subsidiary, it is considered "fully owned." Ownership patterns seem to be closely tied to the specific characteristics of firms (e.g. high technology firm).

Licensing Agreement: The three forms of foreign investment outlined above often carry licensing agreements between foreign investors and foreign subsidiaries. Licensing agreements often permit licensors of specific technology and brand names to obtain a nominal ownership (e.g. 5 percent) of the equity of foreign licensees. Licensing agreements for the purpose of obtaining access to specific technology are called technical licensing agreements, the most common form of licensing. Technical licensing agreements are the most widespread means of exporting technology and are usually negotiated for a definite period of time. Licensors are paid lump sum fees (the initial payment) plus royalty fees computed on the sales value or sales volume (physical units of sales) of the products incorporating the licensed technology. Royalties generally range from 2 to 4 percent of sales value and rarely exceed 5 percent of sales. Technical licensing agreements usually designate where the licensed products and technologies may be sold. The agreements are either "exclusive" or "nonexclusive." An exclusive license means that only the licensee can use the licensed technology in particular markets. When two firms exchange new technologies, the arrangement is called "cross-licensing"—paying for technology with technology.

3. RECORDS OF FOREIGN DIRECT INVESTMENTS

As shown in Table 7–1, since 1960, firms based in the United States, the United Kingdom, continental Europe, and Japan stepped up their manufacturing operations outside their own borders. As of the end of 1980, I estimated that the total physical assets owned overseas by multinational firms reached about 310 billion dollars worth of book value for manufacturing, natural resource development, and commercial activities. The United States remained the unquestioned leader in this field with about 200 billion dollars of direct investment abroad. The United Kingdom, West Germany, and Japan followed the United States, each with about 23 to 30 billion dollars of direct investments.

Table 7–2 summarizes the foreign direct investment position of major industrialized nations for the years 1967, 1971, and 1977. While the United States maintained its leading position, West Germany and Japan showed the most marked rates of increase from 1967 to 1977. This disparity in the amount expended as foreign direct investment by industrialized nations offers an important clue to some of the causes of foreign direct investment which will be discussed in the next section of this chapter.

Table 7–3 shows the U.S. foreign direct investment position for a variety of industries in developed and less developed nations. The contrast of the foreign direct investment positions of different industrialized nations is very distinct. The United States has allotted about two-thirds of its total book value of foreign direct investment in

Table 7-1. Number of Foreign Manufacturing Subsidiaries Established or Acquired by a Sample of U.S.-, U.K.-, Continental European-, and Japanese-based Enterprises, 1914-1970.

| Period | Nationality of Parent Firms | | | |
	U.S.	U.K.	Continental Europe	Japan
Pre–1914	122	60	167	0
1914–1919	71	27	51	0
1920–1929	299	118	249	1
1930–1938	315	99	112	3
1939–1945	172	34	44	40
1946–1952	386	202	129	2
1953–1955	283	55	117	5
1956–1958	439	94	131	14
1959–1961	901	333	232	93
1962–1964	959	319	229	160
1965–1967	889	459	532	235
1968–1970	N.A.[b]	729	1,030	532

a. These data are for a sample of 187 large U.S.-based multinational firms, 47 large U.K.-based multinational firms, 88 large continental European-based multinational firms, and 75 large Japanese-based multinational firms (including trading companies).

b. Not available.

Sources: Data of U.S.-, U.K.-, and continental European-based manufacturing subsidiaries were compiled from the *Harvard University Multinational Enterprise Data Book* (Cambridge, Mass.: Harvard University Press, 1969). Japanese data were compiled from *Kigyobetsu Kaigai Toshi* (Tokyo: Keizai Chosa Kyokai, 1972).

developed countries. Although geographical spreads of foreign investment positions of other industrialized nations are not shown here, observers of the expansion of foreign investments would agree that European investments are more equally divided between developed and developing areas than U.S. investments. Japan's foreign direct investment positions in Asia and Latin America in 1980 still outweighed similar investments in Europe and the United States. However, since the end of the 1970s, Japan's investments in developed nations, most notably the United States, have shown the fastest growth.

Moreover, this geographical disparity was most pronounced for foreign investments made by manufacturing firms. By 1980, the majority of Japanese manufacturing subsidiaries were still found in Asia, Latin America, and other developing nations, although Japanese manufacturers had been stepping up their plant openings in the United States and Europe since the latter half of the 1970s. Manufacturing subsidiaries owned by firms based in such developing

Table 7-2. Foreign Direct Investment Position of Selected Nations, 1967, 1971, and 1977 (in billions of U.S. dollars).

	1967	1971	1977
U.S.	59.5	87.0	148.8 (7.9% of GNP)
U.K.	17.5	24.0	26.5 (10.8)
France	6.0	9.5	11.9 (3.4)
West Germany	3.1	7.3	22.5 (4.3)
Switzerland	4.3	6.8	18.6 (31.8)
Canada	3.8	5.9	11.1 (5.8)
Japan	1.4	4.4	21.3 (3.1)
Netherlands	2.2	3.5	9.8 (11.1)
Sweden	1.5	3.4	5.0 (6.7)
Belgium–Luxembourg	2.0	3.4	3.6 (5.4)
Italy	2.1	3.2	2.9 (1.7)
Others	4.8	7.3	14.1 (N.A.)

Source: United Nations, *Multinational Corporation in World Development* (MITI), Ministry of International Trade and Industry (MITI), *White Paper on International Trade* (Tokyo: MITI, 1979).

nations as Korea, Singapore, Brazil, India, and Argentina were invariably located in neighboring states whose industrial activities were generally less developed.

Table 7-3 also shows that a relatively large proportion of U.S. foreign direct investment is concentrated in relatively few industries—the petroleum industry in particular. Manufacturers with foreign investments are dominated by the following industries: chemicals, pharmaceuticals, automobiles, food processing, electronics, electrical and nonelectrical machinery, and nonferrous metals and rubber. U.S. foreign direct investment is notably distinguished by the absence of participation of the following industries: steel, tobacco, textile and apparel, printing, furniture, and aircraft. This difference in the propensity to invest abroad by various industries also offers an important key to the factors that motivate firms to go multinational beyond simple export and import activities.

The foreign direct investment position of nations in the United States for the year 1979 is presented in Table 7-4. Contrary to the popular belief that OPEC nations have been buying up the United States and that Japan was the leading investor, Europe and Canada still held the bulk of foreign assets in the United States. The visibility of Japanese investments was caused by their fast growth in just two years from 1977 to 1979.

During the same period, another trend in overseas investment was the tendency by many industries to cross invest in one another's

Table 7-3. U.S. Foreign Direct Investment Position at Yearend, 1979 (in billions of U.S. dollars).

Area		Developed Countries					Less Developed Countries (LDCs)			
Industry	Total	Canada	Europe	Japan	Oceania and South Africa	Total Developed	Latin America and Caribbean	Asia	Africa and Middle East	Total LDCs
All Industries	192.6	41.0	81.4	5.7	9.8	137.9	36.8	7.8	3.2	47.8
Mining and smelting	7.2	3.1	N	0	1.6	4.7	1.6	0.2	0.7	2.5
Petroleum	41.5	9.1	18.5	2.1	2.1	31.8	4.6	2.1	3.0	9.7
Manufacturing	83.6	19.2	41.2	2.7	4.2	67.3	14.2	1.4	0.7	16.3
Food Products	7.2	1.7	3.3	0.2	0.6	5.8	1.2	0.1	0.1	1.4
Chemicals	19.0	3.2	9.8	0.7	0.9	14.6	3.6	0.7	0.1	4.4
Metals	4.6	1.3	2.0	N	0.2	3.5	1.0	0.1	N	1.1
Machinery	23.7	3.8	13.5	1.1	1.0	19.6	4.0	N	N	4.1
Transportation Equipment	11.6	3.8	5.3	N	0.5	9.6	1.5	0.3	0.2	2.0
Others	17.5	5.4	7.2	0.7	0.9	14.2	2.9	0.2	0.2	3.3
Transportation, communication and utilities	3.6	1.1	0.2	N	N	1.3	2.0	0.1	0.2	2.3
Trade	20.7	2.7	10.4	0.7	1.1	14.9	3.7	1.2	1.1	5.8
Finance and insurance	27.5	4.6	8.0	0.2	0.4	13.2	11.2	2.0	1.1	14.3
Other	8.5	1.2	3.1	N	0.2	4.5	2.2	1.5	0.3	4.0

Note: N denotes negligible amount. The figures are rounded to the next million dollar.
Source: U.S. Department of Commerce, Survey of Current Business (August 1980).

Table 7-4. Foreign Investment in the United States at Yearend, 1979 (in millions of U.S. dollars).

Canada	6,974
Europe	35,999
United Kingdom	9,39i
France	2,214
Germany	5,004
Italy	212
Netherlands	12,462
Switzerland	3,290
Others	3,516
Japan	3,441
Latin America	4,878
Middle East	474
Others	494
Total	52,260

Source: U.S. Department of Commerce, *Survey of Current Business* (August 1980).

home markets. Firms from all over the world were inclined to invest in their same industry in another country. This phenomenon was apparent in Europe and the United States in the petroleum and aluminum industries. Recently, cross investment has spread to American and European companies in the automotive tire and automobile industries. Japanese firms in the tire and automobile industries also joined. Consumer electronics firms have been participating in cross investment for some time between the United States and Europe as well as between the United States and Japan. Cross investment by large corporations of diverse nationalities in oligopolistic industries throughout the world can be explained as a special case of the general theory of foreign direct investment.

A number of studies of U.S.-based multinational firms indicate that something like 200 U.S. corporations account for the bulk of U.S. foreign direct investment. A 1971 study by Raymond Vernon identified 187 U.S. manufacturing and petroleum companies as "multinational" in the sense that each of these companies in 1967· or before had owned manufacturing or mining subsidiaries located in six or more countries other than the United States. Each of these 187 corporations was among *Fortune* magazine's 500 largest U.S. corporations in 1967. On average, the 187 multinationals were larger in terms of sales, assets, and employees than the average *Fortune* corporation. The 187 multinationals, on average, were more diversified and spent more money as a percent of sales on research and development and advertising than the average Fortune 500 corporation. The 187 multinational corporations accounted for nearly 40 percent of sales of all U.S. manufacturing and petroleum companies and over 45 percent of total assets. Vernon also noted that the 187 corporations tended to operate in oligopolistic industries.

Vernon's data demonstrated that most of the manufacturing subsidiaries of the 187 multinationals produced merchandise locally for local sale. Relatively few of these subsidiaries manufactured products primarily for export to the United States, although there are many "offshore" subsidiaries—those that exist primarily to export to the United States—in some industries, especially electronics. Within the European Economic Community (EEC) there is a substantial amount of cross-hauling by the 187 multinational corporations. Cross-hauling involves the manufacture of a product in one country for sale in another; it is also practiced outside the EEC, but not to any great extent.

An important finding of the 1971 study was that the 187 multinationals generally had extensive research and development activities. Their expenditures on R&D as a percentage of sales were substantially higher than those of the other Fortune 500 companies. In most cases, when any of the firms became multinational, they were usually technological innovators in their industries. United States automobile companies, for example, extended their operations overseas in the late 1920s and 1930s, when they were pioneers in mass production techniques. U.S. electronics firms became multinational during the late 1950s and 1960s. Information about foreign industry market shares held by U.S. multinational corporations is somewhat sketchy. A 1968 study by Hufbauer and Adler for the U.S. Treasury Department indicated that while U.S. multinational corporations did not account for a particularly large percentage of all firms' total sales in any foreign country in the world except Canada, these corporations did have a particularly strong position in more technologically advanced sectors of the economies of many nations. In Canada, for example, where U.S. firms play a more dominant role than in any other foreign country, subsidiaries of U.S.-controlled firms accounted for 50 percent of the sales of locally produced chemicals, 72 percent of rubber products sales, 100 percent of nonelectrical machinery sales, and 100 percent of automobile sales in 1964. In Latin America, in the same year, subsidiaries of U.S. firms produced 28 percent of the sales of locally produced chemicals, 58 percent of rubber products, and about 23 percent of all other products. In Europe, subsidiaries of U.S.-controlled firms took up 6 percent of locally produced chemicals, 13 percent of rubber products, 9 percent of electrical machinery, and 13 percent of transport equipment. In highly advanced industries such as computers and telecommunications, U.S. firms have accounted for perhaps more than half of the total world industry outside the United States.

A United Nations study of market shares held by U.S. multinational corporations in foreign countries in 1973 did not indicate any radically different findings. In the 1970s as well as in the 1960s, the overall share of non-U.S. markets held by U.S. multinationals was not huge, but U.S. firms continued to hold a disproportionately large position in the advanced sectors of foreign economies.

As noted previously, Japanese direct investment abroad was spearheaded by small to medium-sized manufacturing firms during the 1960s. Until the mid-1970s these firms, traditionally specializing in labor-intensive rather than technology-intensive products, ventured out of Japan into neighboring developing countries in Asia. Large Japanese companies took over their role of leading Japanese investments abroad in the mid-70s. In Korea, by the mid-1970s, Japanese investors came to own 63 percent of the hotel business, 55 percent of industrial machinery, 41 percent of construction, 40 percent of textiles, 32 percent of clay, glass, and cement, 24 percent of electric and electronics products (all standard parts and products), 23 percent of fisheries, 23 percent of water and sewage supplies, 20 percent of the automobile industry, 16 percent of transportation and warehouses, 16 percent of chemicals, and 14 percent of electric power utilities.

The profile of U.S. and Japanese foreign investment was strikingly different. American foreign investment was dominated by technology-intensive industries; Japanese foreign investment was not. Only after the mid-1970s did large Japanese companies at the forefront of technological innovation produce a new phase of Japanese investments. This new phase involved an increase in Japanese investments in North America and Europe and a consolidation of Japanese investments in Asia and Latin America. This apparent difference in the thrust of U.S. and Japanese foreign investments can be explained by the general theory of foreign direct investment.

4. THEORIES OF FOREIGN DIRECT INVESTMENT

International trade theories are developed to generalize the factors that determine the patterns of trade among nations. Theories of foreign direct investment are proposed to consolidate the causes of the patterns of foreign direct investment. Compared with international trade theories, however, the focus of foreign direct investment theories is more on microeconomics of firms since they aim at explaining the investment behavior of firms rather than countries.

If the world economy conformed to the classical microeconomic model of perfect competition, foreign direct investment would not take place at all. In a world of perfect competition, producers and sellers of given products would be so numerous and their market share so small that the actions of any one participant would not influence the market as a whole. Product differentiation would never take place. Market information and manufacturing know-how would be equally shared among all sellers. Total product demand would be unaffected by any seller's actions, nor would product supply be influenced by demand. No seller acting alone could change the prevailing market price at any time.

Any business that tried to initiate international operations would incur the transportation and management costs and risks of operating across national boundaries. In any perfectly competitive market, foreign investors would be at a disadvantage relative to indigenous firms that had no additional costs of operating in their countries. The higher costs of operating overseas would eventually drive foreign investors out of the market. Therefore, in the world that approximates perfect competitive market conditions, there would be no foreign direct investment.

In reality, we see the proliferation of foreign direct investment by companies from many nations. Foreign direct investment is, in effect, the product of imperfect market competition. What types of market flaws produce foreign direct investment and how are they likely to evolve through time? For foreign investors to survive in unfamiliar overseas business environments they must have inherent management, marketing, and manufacturing skills that are strong enough to offset the business handicaps of foreign markets. What may be the unique strength of a firm today can fade as more and more competitors, both domestic and foreign, acquire similar attributes. Some foreign direct investment may be further advanced by firms seeking to prolong their advantageous position by adding new markets and sources of products abroad that have not been captured by competitors.

(1) Oligopolistic Structure—The Hymer Theory

In 1960, Stephen Hymer postulated in his MIT doctoral dissertation that foreign direct investment occurred most prominently in those industries with oligopolistic structures. He also demonstrated that the traditional theory of international capital movement—the flow of capital from areas in the world where returns on capital are low to areas where they are higher—does not explain the appearance of foreign direct investment. According to Hymer's theory, the stark differences in the foreign direct investment positions of various industries reflected the diversity of industrial oligopolistic structures.

In Hymer's view an investing firm's strengths must lie in production economies of scale allowing it to operate more efficiently than a smaller company or in that particular expertise which would enable it to offer for sale the differentiated products demanded by customers throughout the world.

The industries in which a limited number of firms with superior product knowledge or manufacturing economies of scale dominate are oligopolistic. Companies that possess these advantages can capture market share from those firms that do not. If economies of scale were unbounded so that an ever increasing yearly production volume would result in decreasing costs, the industry would probably evolve into a monopoly. If superior proprietary knowledge were so great as to enable a firm to produce a superior or preferred product nonstop, the industry might also become monopolistic. In actuality, there usually are limits to production volumes beyond which economies of scale cease to be significant. Over time a company's superior proprietary knowledge can be learned by other competing firms. Even if the expertise is protected by a patent, the patent will eventually expire. Therefore, rarely in any industry does an enduring monopoly come about.

Once manufacturing economies of scale and specific expertise for effective product differentiation are singled out as essential attributes, we have progressed in our search for the causes of differences in interindustry and interfirm propensities toward foreign investment. In refining Hymer's theory of foreign direct investment, we should add that manufacturing economy of scale is achieved not only from large-scale operation, which Hymer emphasizes, but also from the company's cumulative learning and manufacturing experience. The importance of a firm's cumulative learning and experience was postulated by Kenneth Arrow in his learning-by-doing model (dynamic economy of scale) and has been popularized by the Boston Consulting Group's adoption of the "experience curve" as a strategic planning paradigm.

(2) The Experience Curve as a Planning Tool
For a variety of manufacturing operations, we can empirically observe the so-called experience or learning curve effect on produc-

tivity. The crudest form of the experience curve effect shows that the amount of work required to produce one unit of merchandise tends to decline by about 20 percent each time production volumes are doubled. Similar experience curve effects are seen in complex modern factories. Each time the cumulative units of production are doubled, average production costs tend to decline by 20 to 30 percent. In this sense, manufacturing economy of scale is a function of cumulative production units.

Suppose that Factory A and Factory B have identical production capacities. Factory A has been operating for twice as long as Factory B, so Factory A's cumulative production units (manufacturing experience) is twice that of Factory B. Under these circumstances, it is anticipated that the average production costs for Factory A will be about 20 to 30 percent lower than for Factory B.

If economy of scale were determined solely by the factory size (the length of the production run), all that a competitor must do to catch up would be to replicate the size of the leading firm's plant or build an even larger factory. However, when true economy of scale is dynamically determined by the cumulative amount of manufacturing experience, then a competitor will have difficulty overtaking the leading firm.

The unique competitive strength of a manufacturing firm, therefore, is likely to be determined by its market share. The larger the market share, the greater the firm's cost advantage and profitability. Once a company achieves a dominant position in the global market, then its unique advantage commands undisputed longevity. To prevent competitors from undercutting marketing strength, a firm only has to cut its prices periodically just before its competitors undercut their prices. Behind successful preemptive pricing strategy lies the experience curve effect of a company that has attained the commanding position in the market.

Japanese motorcycle firms—notably, Honda, Suzuki, Yamaha, and Kawasaki—were the first to exploit their experience curves to dominate the worldwide markets of light-weight motorcycles. And, as the preference of American and European motorcyclists leaned toward medium- to heavy-weight models, the Japanese firms successfully drove English and American producers of medium- and heavy-weight motorcycles out of world markets. Their successes have led them to build motorcycle factories all over the world so they can hold on to their market shares. Japanese manufacturers of compact color television sets and other electronic consumer appliances and Japanese producers of compact and lower priced photocopiers also appear to be exploiting their experience curves, establishing themselves in compact model markets and later moving into and overtaking American and European competitors in larger model markets.

(3) Corporate Culture as a Scale Factor

The successful pursuit of market share maximization requires a long-range view of the profitability of a firm. Rather than maximizing short-term and immediate profits, firms would invest time, managerial attention, and funds in developing new products and production processes and in opening up world markets for the firm's products. Managers and employees would have to be trained to stay abreast of market and technological innovations. Furthermore, a corporation can only reap the benefits of the experience curve effect if it maintains the loyalty and cooperation of its office and factory workers. Job security, which produces the lowest possible employee turnover, is a necessary condition to gaining the maximum benefits of experience curve effects.

A company must be able to turn out mass quantities of new products of impeccable quality and to develop new merchandise that will match the dynamic shifts in world market demand. A firm can only accomplish this if it cultivates organizational flexibility to permit the free exchange of information and ideas across various functional areas including R&D, manufacturing, and marketing.

For example, when General Motors Corporation was turning out Vegas of questionable workmanship and quality at its newest Laudstown plant at 75 cars per hour, Honda's factory in Japan, which was of similar size, was easily producing high quality subcompacts at 100 to 110 cars per hour. Both factories were equally automated and equipped with new machines. The difference in productivity, let alone quality, was attributed to the contrast in corporate culture— including management philosophy and ability. Formal organizational structure as seen in an organizational chart was not a major factor. We will return to this topic in Chapter 11.

(4) The Product Life Cycle Theory
of Foreign Direct Investment

The theory of foreign direct investment involving oligopolistic structure leaves one major question unanswered: Why should a manufacturing firm with a unique advantage choose to exploit that advantage through foreign direct investment rather than domestic manufacturing and exporting? Many studies involving the foreign trade and direct investment of multinationals based in the United States, Europe, and Japan show that their foreign direct investment is often preceded by exports of the same product by the firm to the same foreign market. There seems to be a logical sequence between international trade and international investment.

Furthermore, we need a new theory to clarify the timing and factors that trigger foreign direct investment by oligopolistic firms. This new theory must explain how many firms exploit their proficiency in product differentiation for international investment.

The product life cycle (PLC) theory of foreign direct investment, which was developed by Raymond Vernon and his colleagues at the Harvard Business School in the mid- to late 1960s, is a blending of the Hymer theory of foreign direct investment with product life cycle models initially developed by marketing scholars at graduate business schools. The PLC theory's explanation of international trade was discussed in Chapter 4. This theory tries to explain foreign direct investment by firms whose advantage is based on product technology. The advantage of product differentiation is superior technical knowledge. To be commercially useful, superior knowledge must be incorporated in a differentiated product. The PLC theory also clarifies why historically the vast majority of foreign direct investment has been carried out by U.S.-based firms. We will discuss each of these in turn.

The PLC theory states that when a new product is first created and marketed, it is more likely to be sold only in the home country. The costs and risks would be too great to justify attempting to sell the product in a foreign country. Thus, in the innovation stage, all production and sales occur in just one country.

If the marketplace accepts the new product and its sales grow to the extent that it reaches the market growth stage, then foreign demand for the product will probably develop. Initially, firms usually choose to export it rather than manufacture it in foreign countries. This is because demand in any foreign nation is likely to be too small at the outset to warrant overseas manufacture; also, continual changes in the product and the manufacturing process necessitate frequent communication within the seller's organization. This communication would be costly to achieve if manufacturing were conducted at geographically widespread locations.

Over time, however, foreign demand for the product is likely to grow. In certain foreign nations, as the product enters the market growth stage locally, demand may reach high enough levels to support local manufacturing plants of minimumly adequate efficiency. Furthermore, as barriers to entry based on market risk and technical knowledge fall, it is possible that local firms in these nations will attempt to enter the market. In order to encourage local manufacturing, the government may create tariffs or other barriers to trade to discourage imports.

At this point, the exporting firm must make a decision. It may give up the foreign market to local firms, possibly granting them licenses to patents of the product for a fee and thereby gaining some continuing reward for past efforts. The exporting firm may choose, alternatively, to create a subsidiary to manufacture the product within the foreign country and thus become a local manufacturer. The exporting firm's decision is a function of the magnitude of the perceived advantage it holds over potential new entrants to the foreign market. If the perceived advantage is slight, the firm will probably choose to license, but if the perceived advantage is substantial, direct investment is the more likely alternative.

If direct investment is chosen, the multinational firm faces the disadvantage of the increased costs and risks of conducting business over a large distance. If the multinational firm cannot sustain some offsetting advantage—maintenance of a continuing technological lead over local competitors, establishment of a brand preference, or creation of economies of scale—its foreign operations may cease to be profitable. This is most likely to happen when the product reaches the mature product stage. If this does happen, the firm is likely to withdraw from the foreign market.

Vernon[1] uses the PLC theory to explain the preponderance of U.S. direct investment. He suggests that beginning sometime around the turn of the century in the United States, a set of stimuli motivated U.S.-based firms to innovate and begin production of manufactured products that appealed to high-income consumers or were labor saving. These stimuli included the large size of the domestic U.S. market, the relatively high per capita income of the U.S. consumer, and a relative scarcity of artisan labor. According to the PLC concept, in many foreign markets, especially those in Western Europe in the post–World War II period, as per capita income grew, a demand arose for consumer and labor-saving products similar to those pioneered in the United States. U.S. firms were able to supply much of this demand through exports. In doing so at the outset, U.S. firms possessed an advantage over European competitors based on knowledge of the technology required to produce these products. Over time, however, European firms learned to produce those products that the U.S. firms had been exporting. In order to defend their

1. In his book, *Sovereignty at Bay: The Multinational Spread of U.S. Enterprises* (New York: Basic Books, 1971).

established markets in Western Europe from the threat of local competitors, the U.S. firms established manufacturing facilities within the European market.

Empirical tests of the product cycle hypothesis indicate that it can adequately explain certain types of U.S. direct investment in Western Europe during the post–World War II period. The product cycle cannot, however, explain all U.S. direct investment in Europe during that period, nor can it by itself account for the European direct investment in the United States that occurred at an increasing rate during the 1960s and 1970s.

Y. Tsurumi[2] applied the PLC theory to explain the emerging patterns of foreign direct investment by Japanese firms. Japanese foreign direct investments were led by small to medium-sized firms exporting standard and least-technology-intensive products to Asia and other places since Asian host countries had adopted import substitution of light and standard manufactured goods. The Japanese were very vulnerable to such measures to shut out imports. To meet this challenge, during the 1960s and 1970s, Japanese manufacturing subsidiaries were set up mainly in the developing nations of Asia and Latin America. Beginning in the mid-1970s, however, large Japanese firms that had already established themselves in the world oligopolistic markets in direct competition with American and European firms were pulled into manufacturing operations in American and European markets. Similar to their Asian and Latin American experience, Japanese investments in North America and Europe also often sprang from the attempts of host countries to restrict Japanese imports. However, a closer investigation of Japanese investments abroad in both developing and developed nations produced a new dimension to the PLC theory of foreign direct investment.

(5) Market Competition: A Motivator of Foreign Direct Investment

As a product matures in a given market, the price elasticity of demand for such a product increases markedly. At this juncture the firm must find ways of lowering production costs. Since the production processes are already standardized to permit absorption by less industrially sophisticated nations, the sales people are likely to take their standardized production processes abroad to lower wage countries and import the same product manufactured by their overseas subsidiaries. This is called an offshore production arrangement.

2. In his article "Japanese Multinational Firms," *Journal of World Trade Law* (February 1973): 74–90.

Foreign investors still have superior experience and knowledge of their own markets back home. Indigenous firms, located in low-wage countries cannot export their standard products to the United States, Europe, and Japan to compete with American, European, and Japanese firms that still maintain marketing superiority over them.

Foreign investors invariably choose to tightly control their offshore manufacturing subsidiaries because more market competition at home requires that they lower production costs and improve product delivery schedules and product reliability. This market competition leads many firms to set up their own manufacturing subsidiaries abroad rather than import the same products from independent foreign suppliers.

While some large American consumer electronics firms and semiconductor producers often set up their own manufacturing operations in low-wage countries, Japanese firms and some American corporations chose to fight the increasing price competition in Japan and the United States by automating their production processes. This capital-intensive solution to tougher price competition permitted these firms to continue operating in high-wage countries. Automated processes also often reduced product defects. Japanese firms that have developed production processes suitable to high-wage countries like the United States set up their own production bases in the United States and Europe beginning in the 1970s.

Furthermore, U.S. markets are so complex that they cannot easily be touched by exporting from distant supply bases outside the country. In particular, a wide range of industrial products and complex consumer products requiring sales engineering, customer service, and prompt delivery can best be supplied from bases located in the same country as the customers. One of the early Japanese manufacturing subsidiaries in the United States, for example, was the zipper factory operated by Yoshida, KK. In order to satisfy the demands of apparel and shoemakers for frequent changes in size, color, and other product combinations, Yoshida, KK moved its final cutting, assembling, and packaging operations to the United States.

(6) Follow-the-Leader and Exchange-of-Hostage Moves

We have already noted that defense of export markets often motivates foreign direct investment. In reality, when one firm sets up overseas subsidiaries, its domestic competitors often follow suit immediately. Followers often choose the same area of the same country as the leading firm. This follow-the-leader phenomenon had long been observed in natural resource industries such as oil, copper, bauxite, and tropical timber. Of late, this phenomenon has been increasingly observed among oligopolistic firms in diverse manufacturing sectors.

Two theories of foreign direct investment based on oligopolistic behavior have been advanced—one by Knickerbocker[3] and another by Graham.[4] There are several international industries in which a large number of multinational firms operate. The number of multinational firms in these industries is sufficiently large, in fact, to make one question whether they could all possess an edge that would make their multinational operations feasible.

Knickerbocker noted that in certain industries there is a tendency for U.S.-based firms to follow each other into major non-U.S. markets within a relatively short time. Knickerbocker reasoned that this follow-the-leader behavior must be explained by oligopolistic imitation. Scholars of oligopoly behavior have noted that in order to maintain stability within an oligopoly, oligopolists must collectively ensure that no one firm in the industry momentarily gains the upper hand over its competitors. If one firm were to gain an advantage, it could use that advantage to better its position relative to other firms. If other firms, in an attempt to defend themselves, were to retaliate, industry warfare could break out.

Warfare in this sense usually refers to price warfare. Formal economic theory tells us that in an oligopoly the equilibrium price generally is indeterminate unless the patterns of behavior within the oligopoly and the cost function of each oligopolist are known. If oligopolists act collusively, a monopoly price can be achieved which maximizes joint industry profits. This is called "shared monopoly." However, if oligopolists have differing cost functions, the monopoly price does not maximize the profits of all firms individually. This price can be maintained only if some oligopolists are willing to forgo some of their own profits in the interest of maximizing industry welfare.

Overt collusion is not only illegal in most developed nations but, more importantly, is unstable even if large firms agree on the equalization of their competitive terms. Instead, these firms imitate one another so that no firm is likely to be caught unaware or unprepared for a sudden move by another firm. This campaign by oligopolists to equalize their competitive standing with other firms in the same industry produces the follow-the-leader phenomenon of foreign

3. F.T. Knickerbocker, *Oligopolistic Reaction and Multinational Enterprise* (Cambridge, Mass.: Harvard University Press, 1974).

4. E.M. Graham, *Oligopolistic Imitation and European Direct Investment in the U.S.*, Unpublished doctoral thesis, Harvard Business School, 1974.

direct investment. Y. Tsurumi[5] showed that the oligopolies' imitative behavior accounted for much of the expansion by competing Japanese synthetic fiber firms and electronic and electric appliance producers. Even among the American, Japanese, and European banks, this behavior has been commonly observed.

When one firm beats the others to a national market, the others not only follow suit but try to beat this leader to the other remaining markets. Among a few large firms vying for the industrial leadership position, follow-the-leader behavior can be observed with the rotation of the leadership position from one national market to the next.

Graham noted that in certain industries, European multinationals tend to make direct investments in the United States after U.S. multinationals have already made direct investments in Europe. These industries were in most cases the same ones that Knickerbocker showed reflected follow-the-leader behavior. The reason suggested by Graham for this cross investment is that European firms attempt to imitate their U.S. competitors by exposing themselves to the same opportunities as these competitors. In this case, the European firms must enter the home markets and not the foreign markets of U.S. firms. Such a strategy of cross investment by European firms would undermine the possibility of price cutting by U.S. firms in the European market to gain market share while maintaining price stability in the United States. If European firms were to enter the U.S. market, they could retaliate against such price cutting in Europe by cutting prices themselves in the United States. By investing in the United States, European firms would set up an "exchange-of-hostage" situation. Aggressive tactics in one market could be met with a counterattack in the other market.

Knickerbocker and Graham found that measures of follow-the-leader and cross investment patterns are in each industry positively related to measures of industry concentration. This gives indirect evidence that both observed phenomena are a result of oligopolistic behavior. Both authors also were able to cite individual cases where oligopolistic imitation was cited by company officials as the major reason for an investment. The available data suggest that many of the industries in which U.S.-based firms have been active in foreign investment are the same industries in which non-U.S. firms have most heavily invested in the United States. Examples of industries in which such cross investment occurs are food processing, industrial chemicals, pharmaceuticals, petroleum, tires, aluminum and, increasingly, motor vehicles and high technology microelectronics.

5. Y. Tsurumi, *The Japanese are Coming: A Multinational Interaction of Firms and Politics* (Cambridge, Mass.: Ballinger Publishing Company, 1976).

Exactly why cross investment should take place is not a well-resolved issue. The exchange-of-hostage hypothesis is a possible answer, for it can at least partially explain a number of major cases of direct foreign investment in the United States—for example, the entrance of the Royal Dutch/Shell group in 1910, which resulted in the creation of the U.S. Shell Oil Company; the acquisition of Howe Sound Company by Pechiney, the French aluminum firm, in 1963; and possibly the recent investment in the United States by large German chemical companies. The exchange-of-hostage theory, however, is an explanation that is largely limited to U.S. investment by major non-U.S. firms in highly oligopolistic industries. Certainly not all direct investment in the United States fits this category.

Reasons cited in the press or by the investing companies themselves for foreign direct investment in the United States should be considered. One such reason is exposure to the stimulus of the U.S. market. Here the reasoning is that the U.S. market has unique characteristics that stimulate technical innovation. A foreign firm might seek exposure to this market in order to be on the leading edge of innovation. This would make sense if the foreign firm were to have U.S.-based competitors in its home market. According to public statements by Olivetti's management, that company's 1959 acquisition of the U.S. Underwood Company was motivated by Olivetti's need to remain technologically abreast of its major competitors in the office equipment industry, most notably IBM. The entrance of the German minicomputer firm Nixdorf A.G. into the U.S. market was, according to the company's own statements, similarly motivated. The exchange-of-hostage hypothesis and the "exposure to the stimulus of the U.S. market" hypothesis are intellectually similar. Both hypotheses indicate essentially defensive reasons for foreign direct investment in the United States. U.S. investment is made not for immediate profits per se, but to defend the home market from the ability of U.S. firms to initiate price warfare or the introduction of new technologies by U.S.-based firms.

Many foreign firms, upon investing in the United States, have announced as their prime motivation a need to participate in the world's largest market or words to that effect. Students should realize that this alone is not a satisfactory explanation for entrance into the United States. (The first question students should ask is "What took you so long? After all, the United States has been the world's largest market since the end of the nineteenth century.") To operate internationally, a company must either have some advantage that enables it to overcome the intrinsic disadvantages of international operations or it must be acting out of defensive considerations.

For many foreign firms operating in the United States, a differentiated product developed in the home market may constitute an advantage. Such may be the case for European and Japanese automotive manufacturers such as Volvo, Volkswagen, and Honda, all of which in the 1970s moved to manufacture their products in the United States. Although the exact reason cited by both Volkswagen and Volvo for their entrance was that it was more economical to manufacture in the United States than to continue to export from Sweden and Germany, few persons would question that the American market's acceptance of European automobiles, which were differentiated from the U.S. manufacturers' products, was a prerequisite for the investment decision. As has been noted by a number of scholars, introduction of a differentiated product into the United States by a non-U.S. firm suggests a product cycle model similar to the Vernon model with the flows reversed.

In 1970, Michelin, the leading European tire manufacturer, first came to the North American market via Canada, where the automotive tire market was dominated by the same American tire firms pressuring Michelin in Europe. Michelin was already exporting radial tires to the United States through the private brand, Atlas, sold by Sears Roebuck. Michelin's move was also timed when its production capactiy in Europe was already bursting at the seams. It needed to add production capacity, and North America was the place to do it. When American tire firms lobbied the U.S. Congress and the Executive Branch to block Michelin's tire exports to the United States from Canada, Michelin simply moved up the planned date it would open its tire factory in the United States.

Likewise, in the chemicals, electronics, industrial machinery, and automobile industries, American firms' investment in Japan was often spurred when these firms faced increasing Japanese imports in the United States and Asia. Obviously, the growing size of the Japanese market provided additional economic incentive to be inside the market. But these firms invariably chose direct investment rather than mere exports to Japan. Direct investment gave the investors greater latitude to penetrate the market as well as to signal potential retaliation to Japanese competitors.

(7) A Firm's Vertical Integrated Structure as a Determinant of Foreign Direct Investment

A vertical integration of a firm's operation from the raw materials to their final products have long been observed among such natural resource industries as oil, copper, aluminum, timber, and rubber. This structural characteristic is closely related to the oligopolistic and imperfect market competitions of these products worldwide.

In industries like steel and synthetic fiber, however, large Japanese firms that have built up de facto vertical integration through industrial groupings (see Chapter 1) are found to have actively initiated the foreign direct investments abroad in their downstream products such as galvanized iron sheets, textile weaving, and even apparel. And yet, their equally large American and British competitors are often found to have produced far fewer foreign direct investments.

As the governments of developing nations increasingly expanded their strategies of import substitution from the end of the 1960s to include intermediate products, say, from apparel making to cloth printing and dyeing operations, leading synthetic fiber firms of Japan, Toray, Teijin, and Kanebo took the initiative in organizing overseas manufacturing operations for their own manufacturing groups. In contrast, such leading manufacturers of synthetic fiber as DuPont of the United States and ICI of the United Kingdom had, on the whole, remained independent suppliers of raw materials to equally independent yarn manufacturers. Yarn manufacturers in turn sell their products to independent weavers, who in turn sell their products to independent apparel makers. Consequently, DuPont and ICI were isolated from the stimuli for overseas investments arising from the import substitution strategies of the developing nations.

(8) Other Theories of Foreign Direct Investment

There are financial economists who extend the analogy of portfolio investment to foreign direct investment. Another group of financial economists argue that the exchange rate risk arising from capital market imperfections triggers foreign direct investment. In reality, these financial economists' theories are based on the fallacy of composition. What appeared to be plausible after investments were made was advanced as the prior cause of foreign direct investment.

Aliber[6] postulates that liquid asset holders are willing to pay some sort of premium to be able to hold these assets in one currency rather than another. Logically, the premium would be attached to the stronger currency. There is an a priori expectation that this currency will appreciate in the long run. If the premium is reflected in the effective interest rate differential between the two countries so that the differential is equal to the premium plus the expected rate of the appreciation of the stronger currency, the investor with the stronger currency is thought to have a lower cost of capital and a lower discount rate than the investor in the weaker currency. Since capital markets cannot differentiate between the income flows from

6. R. Aliber, "A Theory of Direct Foreign Investment," in C.P. Kindleberger, ed., *The International Corporation* (Cambridge, Mass.: MIT Press, 1970).

a stronger currency area and income flows from a weaker currency area, the net present value of an income stream from a weaker currency area would be greater for an investor in the stronger currency area. As a result, investment opportunities in the weaker currency area that are unattractive to local investors might become attractive to foreign investors from a stronger currency area. If this were the case, direct investment capital might flow from strong currency areas to weaker ones.

Levy and Sarrat,[7] on the other hand, argue that national firms become multinational to extend to their investors the option of holding claims on foreign income streams in their investment portfolios. This option is not available to ordinary investors except through the services of such financial intermediaries as multinational firms. By holding foreign assets, multinationals can construct something akin to a portfolio of securities, which has more optimal risk-return characteristics than one containing only assets located in one nation.

These financial economists' theories are not well supported by empirical data, and their logical flaws are too many to list. First, even if you accept the proposition that the firms in the stronger currency areas have lower cost of capital (and lower discount rate) than firms in the weaker currency areas, how can you be sure that firms in the stronger currency area possess requisite technological and managerial capabilities to succeed in the weaker currency area (foreign market)? After all, a subsidiary is different from financial securities (bonds, shares, and bank deposits) that can be purchased in capital markets rather freely. Empirically, Aliber's line of reasoning is contrary to the trends of the mid- to late 1960s, when the U.S. dollar was overvalued with respect to major European currencies. During this period, the rate of U.S. direct investment in Europe was at unprecedentedly high levels and greatly exceeded the rate of European direct investment in the United States. From the mid-1970s to the early 1980s, American investments in Japan were rising strongly although the Japanese yen was appreciating markedly against the U.S. dollar.

The portfolio theory of direct investment does not hold up when we note that U.S.-based firms diversify within the U.S. economy across various industries more often than across national boundaries within the same industry. There is no guarantee that the advantages of international diversification, if any, more than offset the additional costs and risks of operating businesses across national boundaries.

7. H. Levy and M. Sarrat, "International Diversification in Investment Portfolios," *American Economic Review* (1970).

Despite popular platitudes of business managers, they hardly have the best interests of many investors at heart. No business manager would feel compelled to go multinational merely because foreign direct investment might permit investors to indirectly hold income-generating assets abroad.

Financial and investment decisions are two different things. Investment decisions are mainly determined by strategies in the marketplace. Once firms screen various strategic options, including foreign direct investment, they turn to the problems of how to finance the implementation of such strategies.

8 DECISION PROCESSES OF INTERNATIONAL INVESTMENT

Chapters 2 and 3 provided a basic introduction to foreign exchange markets and the balance of payments areas that multinational managers should understand. In this chapter, the focus will be on their corporate skills of investment evaluation and financing. As in the case of domestic corporations, the responsibilities of international financial managers are twofold. They are: (1) to allocate limited financial resources among investment projects (the capital budgeting process), and (2) to choose the least costly method of financing new and ongoing operations.

Since the companies are operating worldwide, managers have to evaluate the additional economic and political risks inherent to international business. The volatility and uncertainty of foreign currencies—particularly foreign currency convertibility—and the changes in tax rules regarding income generated abroad all affect the economics of foreign operations.

1. EVALUATION OF FOREIGN INVESTMENT PROJECTS

Planning Horizon: As in the standard procedure for domestic investment projects, the net present value method of ranking and evaluating foreign investment projects is recommended.[1] Since any

1. Appendix 8A permits you to review this analytical method.

foreign investment requires a seven- to ten-year planning horizon, and because cash inflows are likely to begin three to four years in the future, the payback period approach will not apply. Besides, the payback period method does not help the investing firm discriminate properly between its investment projects with different patterns of cash inflows and outflows.

Hurdle Rate: Whose hurdle rate should be used—that of the foreign subsidiary or of the parent firm? The hurdle rate (or cut-off rate) is the minimumly acceptable rate of return on investment (ROI) that the investing firm wants to realize to compensate for the firm's cost of capital and the specific risks inherent in the proposed investment. In evaluating any foreign investment, the investing firm evaluates the economics of the proposed investment against alternative ROIs that the firm would be able to earn from using the same amount of investment funds elsewhere. This rate is called the "opportunity cost."

Since the opportunity cost of capital varies from one country to the next, depending on the expectation of inflation and financial risks, the weighted cost of capital of the foreign subsidiary in question should not be used as the hurdle rate. Does the fact that the foreign subsidiary has high financial leverage (a higher debt-to-equity ratio than the parent's) mean that the subsidiary will have a lower effective weighted cost of capital? In real terms, a highly debt-ridden capital structure of a subsidiary would increase the financial risks of the operations and therefore raise the opportunity cost of equity capital. The opportunity cost of the subsidiary's equity capital should be at least equal to the incremental and riskless return that the parent firm can earn elsewhere.

Repatriated Return versus Consolidated Profit: The parent firm should evaluate the foreign investment project from the viewpoint of total incremental return to the parent-subsidiary system as a whole. Some of the income generated from the investment may be captured by the parent and by the parent's other subsidiaries located outside foreign Country X where the parent is contemplating the new investment. This happens where there is an intracompany flow of goods and services. Other income from the investment may be captured first by the new subsidiary in Country X.

There are two schools of thought concerning what constitutes returns to the parent-subsidiary system as a whole. Conservative managers want to count only those cash inflows repatriated from subsidiaries to the parent. Others subscribe to the worldwide income concept (consolidated profit) since they count all cash flows regardless of where and how these flows are generated and captured within the parent-subsidiary system.

I subscribe to and recommend the worldwide income concept as the appropriate method of evaluating foreign investment projects because unrepatriated profits are ploughed back into foreign operations and consequently expand the investment position of the parent firm. Sometime in the future, this enhanced investment position would help the parent firm to generate greater cash inflows, some of which would surely be repatriated to the parent.

However, there are some foreign investment projects in developing economies and in the socialist nations—Eastern Europe, the People's Republic of China, and the Soviet Union—that carry much higher political risks of profit remittance and business operations. Under these circumstances, the repatriated returns may form a reasonable basis for economic evaluation of the profitability of the investments from the investing parent's point of view. At any rate, the two-rate of returns can always be computed—one on the basis of the consolidated return and the other on the repatriated return. If the difference between the two-rate of returns is too great, transfer pricing arrangements may be considered, which affect the size of repatriated returns.

Let us consider the World Systems, Inc. (WSI) foreign investment proposal: WSI is a U.S.-based firm that manufactures a wide range of electrical appliances. It is evaluating an eighty-twenty joint venture with an Indonesian firm to produce standard appliances for the Indonesian market. The pro forma income statement of the proposed investment is given in Table 8-1. WSI's appropriate hurdle rate for this venture was set at 20 percent (15% of the weighted cost of capital of the parent plus a 5% risk premium) which the parent firm uses for similar manufacturing operations in developing nations like Indonesia. A planning horizon of seven years was also selected. The initial investment was 30 million rupiahs, which will be divided eighty-twenty between WSI and its Indonesian partner.

By picking only those items that produce incremental returns to the WSI system, we can compile Table 8-2, which provides a basic check list identifying the incremental returns to the investing multinational firm. They are as follows:

- Legal ownership of the joint venture gives each investor a pro rata share of the projected profit of the joint venture;
- When the new subsidiary purchases goods and services from its parent and its subsidiaries in countries other than the location of

216

Table 8–1. Pro Forma Income Statement for P. T. WSI, Indonesia (in thousands of rupiahs).

	1981	1982	1983	1984	1985	1986	1987
Sales	40,000	50,000	60,000	70,000	72,000	72,000	72,000
Cost of goods sold	28,000	34,000	42,500	50,000	51,000	51,000	51,000
Local labor	5,000	7,000	12,500	15,000	15,000	15,000	15,000
Local materials	4,000	5,000	6,000	7,000	7,000	7,000	7,000
Imported materials[a]	15,000	18,000	20,000	24,000	25,000	25,000	25,000
Depreciation	4,000	4,000	4,000	4,000	4,000	4,000	4,000
Gross profits	12,000	16,000	17,500	20,000	21,000	21,000	21,000
Selling and administrative	5,000	6,000	6,500	7,000	7,100	7,100	7,100
Technical fees (4% of sales)[b]	1,600	2,000	2,400	2,800	2,880	2,880	2,880
Profits before taxes	5,400	8,000	8,600	10,200	11,020	11,020	11,020

a. All import materials are purchased from WSI (U.S.A.).
b. Technical fees of 4 percent on sales are paid by P.T. SWI to SWI (U.S.A.).

Table 8-2. Estimated Return to the SWI System (in thousands of rupiahs).

	1981	1982	1983	1984	1985	1986	1987
80% of profits before taxes	4,320	6,400	6,880	8,160	8,816	8,816	8,816
Incremental profits on exports to WSI (Indonesia), e.g. 40% of sales	6,000	7,200	8,000	9,600	10,000	10,000	10,000
Technical fees	1,600	2,000	2,400	2,800	2,880	2,880	2,880
Total returns before taxes	11,920	15,600	17,280	20,560	21,696	21,696	21,696
U.S. taxes (50%)	5,960	7,800	8,640	10,280	10,848	10,848	10,848
Net return	5,960	7,800	8,640	10,280	10,848	10,848	10,848

the new subsidiary, only incremental profits from such sales should be recorded as net incremental returns to the parent-subsidiary system;

- As in the case of intrafirm trade, technical fees are frequently used by the parent firm to "repatriate" liquid funds from the new venture to the parent;

- U.S. taxes are levied on most of these returns.

Depending on how the depreciation-related cash inflows to the subsidiary are disposed of, they may comprise a package of incremental returns to the investors. For WSI (Indonesia) we ignored this item only to capture some of the cumulative investments at the end of the seven-year planning horizon that are projected to include profits and depreciation-related cash inflows ploughed back to the subsidiary. Some firms consolidate both the profits and losses and balance sheets of their majority-owned subsidiaries abroad. Under these circumstances, the depreciation and other amortized noncash expenses of the overseas subsidiary may provide the parent with tax shields. If so, these tax shields may be added to Table 8–2 as additional incremental returns.

Table 8–3 illustrates the procedure of arriving at the total present value of the expected incremental returns to the WSI system that will be generated by P.T. WSI (Indonesia). The terminal book value of the Indonesian firm is included in the seventh year, representing the streams of further incremental returns after 1987. The net present value of the project is derived from the familiar formula.

Table 8–3. Present Value of Estimated Streams of Net Returns to the WSI System.

	Net Return	80% of Terminal Book Value		Discount Factor (@ 20%)		Present Value
1981	5,960		X	0.833	=	4,964
1982	7,800		X	0.694	=	5,413
1983	8,640		X	0.579	=	5,002
1984	10,280		X	0.482	=	4,954
1985	10,848		X	0.402	=	4,360
1986	10,848		X	0.335	=	3,634
1987	(10,848 +	22,000)	X	0.279	=	9,164

Total Present Value = 37,491

Therefore:

Net Present Value = Total Present Value – WSI's Initial Investment
= Rps 37,491 – Rps 30,000 × 0.8
= Rps 13,491

It is shown that the proposed investment in P.T. WSI (Indonesia) appears to provide greater yields than the hurdle rate of return of 20 percent per annum. This conclusion, however, must be modified. The proposed investment appears to have a higher rate of return than the hurdle rate if and only if there was no foreign exchange portion in WSI's initial investment of 24 million rupiahs. If WSI is planning to invest foreign exchange-based funds, and if WSI has alternative uses for rupiah-based funds outside Indonesia, additional analysis must be done to account for foreign exchange exposure, transaction losses, and other risks inherent in the proposed P.T. WSI (Indonesia) venture.

2. RISK SENSITIVITY ANALYSIS

The financial risks inherent in the proposed venture are schematically shown in Figure 8-1. Each risk has a range of outcomes, but we do not know even the probability of these outcomes of each risk.

Figure 8-1. The Financial Risks Inherent in a Proposed Joint Venture.

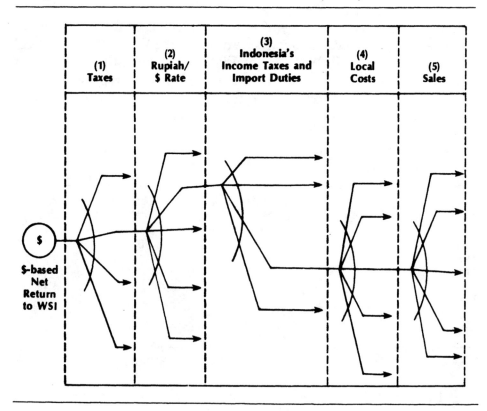

Accordingly, an evaluation of how sensitive U.S. dollar-based returns are to the key risks inherent in the new venture must be done. Without using the computer, we can conduct a systematic analysis of the risk sensitivity of the new venture. The following steps will help you pinpoint the specific vulnerable areas of the venture:.

1. Compute the ratio of net present value of return to the initial investment. For P.T. WSI (Indonesia), this ratio is 1.56 (Rps 37, 491 ÷ Rps 24,000).
2. Select one of the significant downward (unfavorable) outcomes of those five risks (e.g. 30% decline of sales). You can see how much this new assumption of projected sales level reduces the ratio of projected return to the initial investment. This is nothing but an extension of the elasticity analysis presented in Chapter 5 (sales elasticity of net present value ratio). Don't forget that changes in sales will alter the technical fee remission.
3. Repeat the same evaluative projection with a risk of 30 percent devaluation of the rupiah, for local cost overrun, and for the extent of income tax and import duty exemptions given (or not given) by the Indonesian government.

The above-mentioned procedures will help to identify how prone to risk the proposed venture is. To cushion the impact of major risks, the investing firm may want to look into the ways in which technical fees are computed and how it can shore up sales and production activities.

Neither a financial evaluation (present value method) nor risk sensitivity analysis should be used as the go or no-go gauge. All these tools are useful only when they are applied intelligently to rank more than one investment project and to quantify the extent of their exposure to plausible risks. The ultimate selection of an investment should, of course, be based on the company's strategy.

When investment projects are mainly for defensive reasons (e.g., the exchange-of-hostage defense strategy discussed in Chapter 7), the projected return table should also include the "opportunity losses" that your venture is expected to erase. For example, KAT, Inc. was the world leader in the machine tool industry. It feared increasing Japanese competition in eastern and Southeast Asia (outside Japan). The firm also believed that eventually Japanese competitors would penetrate the U.S. and European markets long held by KAT. KAT was convinced that its own physical manufacturing base inside Japan was absolutely necessary to discipline the otherwise fierce competitive behavior of Japanese firms. KAT was also sure that such a defensive investment would enable the firm to annually retain at least a $250,000 net profit after taxes linked to the firm's exports to eastern and Southeast Asia (outside Japan). Under these circumstances, KAT's projected streams of net incremental returns from its Japanese venture should include $250,000 per year in addition to the returns generated inside Japan. KAT's financial tables should capture as much of the strategic implications of the investment as possible.

3. FINANCING THE OVERSEAS SUBSIDIARY DURING PERIODS OF CURRENCY FLUCTUATION

In Chapters 3 and 4 we demonstrated how exporting firms can hedge their foreign exchange transaction exposure. When Bayerische Wurst-Machine GmbH had 4.6 million Deutche marks worth of its accounts receivable denominated in the declining U.S. dollar, the firm could have hedged against the plausible revaluation of Deutsche marks either by selling the borrowed U.S. funds in the spot market or by selling in the forward market U.S. dollars equivalent to the exposed accounts receivable. In the former case, the firm would pay back the borrowed U.S. fund as the firm collects the U.S. dollar denominated accounts receivable. Such hedging operations are routine for many multinational firms.

Let us take another example: Suppose you were negotiating a delicate joint venture agreement in Japan during the spring of 1978. All the indications pointed to the rapid appreciation of the Japanese yen from the summer to the fall of that year. A mere 10 percent appreciation of the Japanese yen would have increased considerably the U.S. dollar-based portion of your investment share. Under these circumstances, you might be under tremendous pressure to conclude the joint venture agreement as soon as possible. Sensing your uneasiness, your Japanese negotiator might try to extract final and major concessions for you. One way to feel at ease would be for you to arrange a yen-based loan commitment from Japanese and American banks or to buy the yen forward at this time.

When there are active spot and forward markets, they permit you to hedge your foreign exchange exposure risks. When there is no forward market, as in the case of developing nations' currencies, you may be still arranging the semblance of forward market transactions. This is called a "swap agreement."

The Swap Agreement: Even for the most risk prone developing country, there will always be some individual or firm whose future foreign exchange needs are likely to compliment yours. Some banks and foreign exchange traders even specialize in matching these needs privately among individuals and corporations. In essence, the swap agreement is functionally a substitution of private contracts for forward market transactions. As in the forward market, the forward rate is negotiated making a commitment between the parties regardless of how the actual spot rate turns out in the future. Consider the following example:

On January 15, 1981, your Brazilian subsidiary requested 50 million cruzeiros (Cr.) to finance an investment and working capital needs for the balance of the year. The proposed investment met both economic and strategic criteria. However, the Brazilian government appeared to be intent on continuing with a mini-devaluation scheme in which the cruzeiro would be devalued 1 to 2 percent every month or semimonthly. When it is compounded to the end of the year, the cumulative impact of the mini-devaluation would not be negligible. There was no forward market for the Brazilian cruzeiro, and the Brazilian subsidiary could not borrow locally.

Banco do Brasil in New York offered a swap agreement. You would deposit the U.S. dollar equivalent of 50 million cruzeiros at the agreed exchange rate of Cr. 50 to $1.00 with the New York Branch of Banco do Brasil. Its Sao Paulo branch would, then, make a Cr. 50 million loan to your Brazilian subsidiary at the interest rate of 20 percent per year. Your original deposit would earn no interest. At the end of 1981, when your Brazilian subsidiary pays back Cr. 50 million to the Sao Paulo branch, the New York branch will return your deposit. The interest payments in Brazil can be deducted for Brazilian corporate income tax (40%). You would also charge your Brazilian subsidiary 15 percent opportunity cost for the deposit you would have to make under the swap arrangement.

On the other hand, you can make direct loans to your Brazilian subsidiary for one year. If the cruzeiro depreciates further, the foreign exchange exposure loss would not be deductible either for Brazilian or U.S. corporate income taxes. You would simply charge your Brazilian subsidiary a 15 percent opportunity cost which is not tax deductible either for Brazilian or U.S. corporate income taxes. On January 15, 1981, the spot rate of the Brazilian cruzeiro was quoted at Cr. 64 to $1.00 in New York.

Analysis: Since neither the investment return nor the strategy would be affected by your choice of the swap agreement or direct loan, your economic decision rule would be to choose the least costly financing alternative. Schematically, the decision problem is presented in Figure 8-2.

Figure 8-2. Alternative Costs of Financing Foreign Direct Investment.

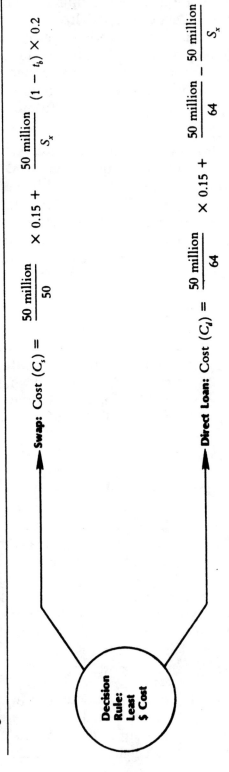

Swap: Cost $(C_s) = \dfrac{50 \text{ million}}{50} \times 0.15 + \dfrac{50 \text{ million}}{S_x} (1 - t_b) \times 0.2$

Direct Loan: Cost $(C_d) = \dfrac{50 \text{ million}}{64} \times 0.15 + \dfrac{50 \text{ million}}{64} - \dfrac{50 \text{ million}}{S_x}$

Decision
Rule:
Least
$ Cost

S_x: Future spot rate of the cruzeiro (uncertain)
t_b: Brazilian corporate income tax rate

The above alternatives are expressed by hyperbolic functions. If we plot the U.S. dollar-based cost on the vertical axis and future spot rate of the cruzeiro (S_x) on the horizontal axis, we can place the two hyperbolic functions on the (S_x, C) plane, as shown in Figure 8-3.

By solving Equation (8-1), we find that the break even exchange rate, S_x, of the cruzeiro is 75.

$$\begin{cases} C_s = 150K + \dfrac{6{,}000}{S_x} \\[3em] C_d = 898K - \dfrac{50{,}000}{S_x} \end{cases} \qquad (8\text{-}1)$$

Figure 8-3. Comparisons of Net Financing Costs of Swap and Direct Loan under Uncertainties of Future Spot Rates.

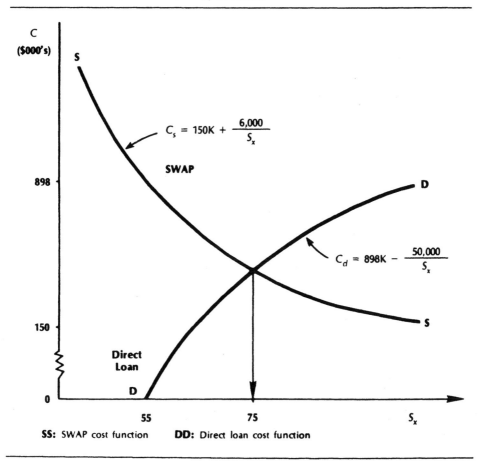

SS: SWAP cost function   DD: Direct loan cost function

As shown in Figure 8–3, if you believe that cruzeiros are likely to depreciate further beyond 75 by the end of 1981, you would choose the swap arrangement. However, if you are convinced that the year-end spot rate of cruzeiro will be less than 75 to $1.00, you would choose the direct loan. How can you tell? As we discussed in Chapters 2 and 3, we have to carefully examine the political and economic fundamentals of Brazilian society that influence the strength of the cruzeiro. On the other hand, if you estimate that by the end of 1981, the Brazilian cruzeiro will not be able to be converted to hard currencies such as the U.S. dollar, you would take advantage of the swap arrangement regardless of your views on the future spot rate of cruzeiro.

APPENDIX 8A
PRESENT VALUE ANALYSIS OF INVESTMENTS

Time Value of Money

Future Value (or Compounding): An example showing how future value is determined will make its meaning clear. By depositing $1,000 in a bank account that pays interest at 6 percent interest (with annual compounding), what can you expect to have after one year? To answer this question, the following variables must first be defined:

$$r = \text{the interest rate}$$
$$X = \text{the amount of interest earned per year}$$
$$PV = \text{present value (amount at the start of the period)}$$
$$FV_n = \text{future value (amount after } n \text{ years)}$$

Note that for a period of one year

$$FV_1 = PV + X$$
$$FV_1 = PV + PV(r)$$
$$FV_1 = PV(1+r)$$
$$FV_1 = \$1,000(1+0.06)$$
$$FV_1 = \$1,060$$

and for a period of n years the equation

$$FV_n = PV(1+r)^n$$

Table 8A-1. Future Value of $1.00 at the End of n Periods for Indicated r Values (1% through 20%).

Period	1%	2%	3%	4%	5%	6%	7%	8%
1	1.0100	1.0200	1.0300	1.0400	1.0500	1.0600	1.0700	1.0800
2	1.0201	1.0404	1.0609	1.0816	1.1025	1.1236	1.1449	1.1664
3	1.0303	1.0612	1.0927	1.1249	1.1576	1.1910	1.2250	1.2597
4	1.0406	1.0824	1.1255	1.1699	1.2155	1.2625	1.3108	1.3605
5	1.0510	1.1041	1.1593	1.2167	1.2763	1.3382	1.4026	1.4693
6	1.0615	1.1262	1.1941	1.2653	1.3401	1.4185	1.5007	1.5869
7	1.0721	1.1487	1.2299	1.3159	1.4071	1.5036	1.6058	1.7138
8	1.0829	1.1717	1.2668	1.3686	1.4775	1.5938	1.7182	1.8509
9	1.0937	1.1951	1.3048	1.4233	1.5513	1.6895	1.8385	1.9990
10	1.1046	1.2190	1.3439	1.4802	1.6289	1.7908	1.9672	2.1589
11	1.1157	1.2434	1.3842	1.5395	1.7103	1.8983	2.1049	2.3316
12	1.1268	1.2682	1.4258	1.6010	1.7959	2.0122	2.2522	2.5182
13	1.1381	1.2936	1.4685	1.6651	1.8856	2.1329	2.4098	2.7196
14	1.1495	1.3195	1.5126	1.7317	1.9799	2.2609	2.5785	2.9372
15	1.1610	1.3459	1.5580	1.8009	2.0789	2.3966	2.7590	3.1722
16	1.1726	1.3728	1.6047	1.8730	2.1829	2.5404	2.9522	3.4259
17	1.1843	1.4002	1.6528	1.9479	2.2920	2.6928	3.1588	3.7000
18	1.1961	1.4282	1.7024	2.0258	2.4066	2.8543	3.3799	3.9960
19	1.2081	1.4568	1.7535	2.1068	2.5270	3.0256	3.6165	4.3157
20	1.2202	1.4859	1.8061	2.1911	2.6533	3.2071	3.8697	4.6610
21	1.2324	1.5157	1.8603	2.2788	2.7860	3.3996	4.1406	5.0338
22	1.2447	1.5460	1.9161	2.3699	2.9253	3.6035	4.4304	5.4365
23	1.2572	1.5769	1.9736	2.4647	3.0715	3.8197	4.7405	5.8715
24	1.2697	1.6084	2.0328	2.5633	3.2251	4.0489	5.0724	6.3412
25	1.2824	1.6406	2.0938	2.6658	3.3864	4.2919	5.4274	6.8485

so that if n were seven years

$$FV_7 = \$1,000 \ (1.06)^7$$
$$FV_7 = \$1,503.63$$

Of course, n can indicate compounding in any time interval. Compounding factors, $(1 + r)^n$, may either be calculated as needed or looked up on readily available tables. Table 8A-1 summarizes future value of $1.00 at the end of n periods.

Present Value (or Discounting): Investors are often advised that an investment of a certain amount today is likely to be worth a certain amount more after some time interval. How can such estimates be compared? Let us work out an example of such a comparison. If an advisor offered an investor an investment that for $1,000 now

Table 8A-1. continued

Period	9%	10%	12%	14%	15%	16%	18%	20%
1	1.0900	1.1000	1.1200	1.1400	1.1500	1.1600	1.1800	1.2000
2	1.1881	1.2100	1.2544	1.2996	1.3225	1.3456	1.3924	1.4400
3	1.2950	1.3310	1.4049	1.4815	1.5209	1.5609	1.6430	1.7280
4	1.4116	1.4641	1.5735	1.6890	1.7490	1.8106	1.9388	2.0736
5	1.5386	1.6105	1.7623	1.9254	2.0114	2.1003	2.2878	2.4883
6	1.6771	1.7716	1.9738	2.1950	2.3131	2.4364	2.6996	2.9860
7	1.8280	1.9487	2.2107	2.5023	2.6600	2.8262	3.1855	3.5832
8	1.9926	2.1436	2.4760	2.8526	3.0590	3.2784	3.7589	4.2998
9	2.1719	2.3579	2.7731	3.2519	3.5179	3.8030	4.4355	5.1598
10	2.3674	2.5937	3.1058	3.7072	4.0456	4.4114	5.2338	6.1917
11	2.5804	2.8531	3.4785	4.2262	4.6524	5.1173	6.1759	7.4301
12	2.8127	3.1384	3.8960	4.8179	5.3502	5.9360	7.2876	8.9161
13	3.0658	3.4523	4.3635	5.4924	6.1528	6.8858	8.5994	10.699
14	3.3417	3.7975	4.8871	6.2613	7.0757	7.9875	10.147	12.829
15	3.6425	4.1772	5.4736	7.1379	8.1371	9.2655	11.973	15.407
16	3.9703	4.5950	6.1304	8.1372	9.3576	10.748	14.129	18.488
17	4.3276	5.0545	6.8660	9.2765	10.761	12.467	16.672	22.186
18	4.7171	5.5599	7.6900	10.575	12.375	14.462	19.673	26.623
19	5.1417	6.1159	8.6128	12.055	14.231	16.776	23.214	31.948
20	5.6044	6.7275	9.6463	13.743	16.366	19.640	27.393	38.337
21	6.1088	7.4002	10.803	15.667	18.821	22.574	32.323	46.005
22	6.6586	8.1403	12.100	17.861	21.644	26.186	38.142	55.206
23	7.2579	8.9543	13.552	20.361	24.891	30.376	45.007	66.247
24	7.9111	9.8497	15.178	23.212	28.625	35.236	53.108	79.496
25	8.6231	10.834	17.000	26.461	32.918	40.874	62.668	95.396

would pay \$1,503.63 after seven years or another equally risky investment that would pay \$1,593.85 after eight years, which is the better choice? Note that

$$FV_n = PV (1 + r)^n$$

so that

$$PV = \left[\frac{FV_n}{(1 + r)^n} \right]$$

or

$$PV = FV_n \left[\frac{1}{(1 + r)} \right]^n$$

Table 8A-2. Present Value of $1.00 Promised for nth Period Discounted at the Indicated Discount Rates (1% through 24%).

Period	1%	2%	3%	4%	5%	6%	7%	8%	9%
1	.9901	.9804	.9709	.9615	.9524	.9434	.9346	.9259	.9174
2	.9803	.9612	.9426	.9246	.9070	.8900	.8734	.8573	.8417
3	.9706	.9423	.9151	.8890	.8638	.8396	.8163	.7938	.7722
4	.9610	.9238	.8885	.8548	.8227	.7921	.7629	.7350	.7084
5	.9515	.9057	.8626	.8219	.7835	.7473	.7130	.6806	.6499
6	.9420	.8880	.8375	.7903	.7462	.7050	.6663	.6302	.5963
7	.9327	.8706	.8131	.7599	.7107	.6651	.6227	.5835	.5470
8	.9235	.8535	.7894	.7307	.6768	.6274	.5820	.5403	.5019
9	.9143	.8368	.7664	.7026	.6446	.5919	.5439	.5002	.4604
10	.9053	.8203	.7441	.6756	.6139	.5584	.5083	.4632	.4224
11	.8963	.8043	.7224	.6496	.5847	.5268	.4751	.4289	.3875
12	.8874	.7885	.7014	.6246	.5568	.4970	.4440	.3971	.3555
13	.8787	.7730	.6810	.6006	.5303	.4688	.4150	.3677	.3262
14	.8700	.7579	.6611	.5775	.5051	.4423	.3878	.3405	.2992
15	.8613	.7430	.6419	.5553	.4810	.4173	.3624	.3152	.2745
16	.8528	.7284	.6232	.5339	.4581	.3936	.3387	.2919	.2519
17	.8444	.7142	.6050	.5134	.4363	.3714	.3166	.2703	.2311
18	.8360	.7002	.5874	.4936	.4155	.3503	.2959	.2502	.2120
19	.8277	.6864	.5703	.4746	.3957	.3305	.2765	.2317	.1945
20	.8195	.6730	.5537	.4564	.3769	.3118	.2584	.2145	.1784
25	.7798	.6095	.4776	.3751	.2953	.2330	.1842	.1460	.1160
30	.7419	.5521	.4120	.3083	.2314	.1741	.1314	.0994	.0754

We know that in one case n is seven years and in the other eight years. If both investments are discounted by 6 percent as follows,

$$PV = FV_7 \left[\frac{1}{(1 + 0.06)} \right]^7 \qquad PV = FV_8 \left[\frac{1}{(1 + 0.06)} \right]^8$$

$$PV = \$1,503.63 \, (0.6651) \qquad PV = \$1,593.85 \, (0.6274)$$

$$PV = \$1,000 \qquad PV = \$1,000$$

We see that the present value of the two investments is the same so that our investor will be indifferent between them. Now another advisor offers an equally risky investment that promises to pay $1,838.46 in nine years on the same initial amount. Let us discount it over nine years at the same interest rate,

$$PV = FV_9 \left[\frac{1}{(1 + 0.06)} \right]^9 = \$1,838.46 \, (0.5919) = \$1,088.18.$$

229

Table 8A-2. continued

Period	10%	12%	14%	15%	16%	18%	20%	24%
1	.9091	.8929	.8772	.8696	.8621	.8475	.8333	.8065
2	.8264	.7972	.7695	.7561	.7432	.7182	.6944	.6504
3	.7513	.7118	.6750	.6575	.6407	.6086	.5787	.5245
4	.6830	.6355	.5921	.5718	.5523	.5158	.4823	.4230
5	.6209	.5674	.5194	.4972	.4761	.4371	.4019	.3411
6	.5645	.5066	.4556	.4323	.4104	.3704	.3349	.2751
7	.5132	.4523	.3996	.3759	.3538	.3139	.2791	.2218
8	.4665	.4039	.3506	.3269	.3050	.2660	.2326	.1789
9	.4241	.3606	.3075	.2843	.2630	.2255	1.938	.1443
10	.3855	.3220	.2697	.2472	.2267	.1911	.1615	.1164
11	.3505	.2875	.2366	.2149	.1954	.1619	.1346	.0938
12	.3186	.2567	.2076	.1869	.1685	.1372	.1122	.0757
13	.2879	.2292	.1821	.1625	.1452	.1163	.0935	.0610
14	.2633	.2046	.1597	.1413	.1252	.0985	.0779	.0492
15	.2394	.1827	.1401	.1229	.1079	.0835	0.649	.0397
16	.2176	.1631	.1229	.1069	.0930	.0708	.0541	.0320
17	.1978	.1456	.1078	.0929	.0802	.0600	.0451	.0258
18	.1799	.1300	.0946	.0808	.0691	.0508	.0376	.0208
19	.1635	.1161	.0829	.0703	.0596	.0431	.0313	.0168
20	.1486	.1037	.0728	.0611	.0514	.0365	.0261	.0135
25	.0923	.0588	.0378	.0204	.0245	.0160	.0105	.0046
30	.0573	.0334	.0196	.0151	.0116	.0070	.0042	.0016

Discounted at the same rate, this investment has a greater present value so it will be preferred to the others. In the example given above, any interest rate may be chosen and the present value of the third investment will always be greater than those of the first two. Note that the discounting factor is always the reciprocal of the compounding factor so that for any interest rate it is very easy to calculate one of these factors once the other factor is known. It is even easier to look up a discounting factor in a table like Table 8A-2. To understand how this table is used, let us determine the present value of a series of five annual payments of $500 each discounted at 10 percent. The computation is summarized in Table 8A-3.

Table 8A-3. The Present Value of a Series of Five Annual Payments Discounted at 10 Percent.

Year	Expected Cash Inflow (A)		Discount Factor (B)		Present Value (A × B)
1	$500	×	0.9091	=	454.55
2	500	×	0.8264	=	413.20
3	500	×	0.7513	=	375.65
4	500	×	0.6830	=	341.50
5	500	×	0.6209	=	310.45
Present value of annual payments of $500				=	1895.35

A SELECTED REFERENCE

Aharoni, Y. *The Foreign Investment Decision Process.* Cambridge, Mass.: Division of Research, Harvard Business School (distributed by Harvard University Press), 1966.

Decisionmakers' personal feelings and knowledge about specific foreign nations are important elements of foreign investment decisions. A behavioral explanation of foreign direct investment.

Kitching, J. "Winning and Losing with European Acquisitions." *Harvard Business Review* (March–April 1974).

Many American firms prefer a whole or partial acquisition of existing foreign firms as expedient ways to enter foreign markets. Success and failure of such moves are analyzed.

Kobrin, S. J. "The Assessment and Evaluation of Non-Economic Environments by American Firms." *Journal of International Business Studies* (Spring/Summer 1980).

American firms' evaluation of social and political risk factors in their foreign investment decisions.

Wilson, B. D. "The Propensity of Multinational Companies to Expand Through Acquisitions." *Journal of International Business Studies* (Spring/Summer 1980).

Firm-specific characteristics of firms prone to prefer acquisitions of foreign firms.

9 ORGANIZING MULTINATIONAL ACTIVITIES
Corporate Structure and Ownership

In the fall of 1981, the IBM headquarters in Armonk, New York finally unleashed a part of its planned reorganization of the IBM Corporation. Typical of an essentially single-product-line firm, IBM has conducted its increasing volume of business worldwide in two-tier forms. The operations inside the United States were organized along product groups such as data processing (main-frame computers) and office equipment (typewriters and photocopiers). International operations were coordinated by the IBM World Trade Corporation—a form of international division). Usually, under the IBM World Trade Corporation, country markets were grouped together into regional (world areas) subheadquarters. In each country market, productwide divisions were the general rule.

The unveiled plan of reorganization was first mainly concerned with IBM's operations inside the United States. It appeared that the firm was going to regroup the operations by such major functional differences as sales, production, finance, and research and development. In particular, it was said that the reorganization would put together sales personnel currently scattered across different product divisions. In this way, the firm hoped to eliminate the serious problem of various salespersons of different product divisions descending on the same outside customers. The confusion and conflicts among the IBM salespersons had for some time been alleged to have handicapped IBM in relation to such competitors as Digital Equipment and Data General in the burgeoning minicomputer markets. Even in the large main-frame computer markets, IBM was bracing itself for a fierce competition in the coming decades from three Japanese firms: NEC, Hitachi and, above all, Fujitsu.

With IBM's decision to enter the personal computer and small photocopier market in direct competition with American and foreign firms, it was said to be reorganizing its internal structure to better meet the needs of its customers. Customers were said to prefer dealing with one IBM salesperson who could handle all the IBM product lines rather than getting lost between organizational cracks of IBM's internal corporate bureaucracy. The new competitive marketing and product development strategy of IBM for the balance of the 1980s necessitated organizational change.

While IBM was responding to intensifying market competitions, it also faced new technological developments that had eliminated once traditional demarcations between typewriters and computers. With the spread of office automation and the development of "mechatronics," which technologically merged traditional mechanics of machine with electronics, IBM was also driven to combine manufacturing and product developments that were once separated into different product groups. In order to keep abreast with American and foreign competitors worldwide, IBM needed to make the best of both dynamic and static economies of scale of manufacturing operations.

In January 1982, when IBM won the antitrust litigation by the Justice Department to break up the firm, it further intensified its pricing and other marketing tactics to defend its market positions. On August 9, 1982, The *New York Times* noted this new IBM posture:

> The recent pricing changes are part of a larger plan by IBM to meet increasing price competition, especially from Japanese companies, which have been willing to lower prices and profits to gain market share. . . .
>
> IBM has invested heavily in automated manufacturing facilities to produce computers in large volumes and at low costs and therefore needs to sell large quantities. The recession has made it more difficult than usual, contributing to the price flexibility.

About the same time, the IBM created its wholly owned but unconsolidated subsidiary, the IBM Credit Corporation, the major and initial function of which was to remove financing problems from product and marketing managers. All the leases and purchases of IBM equipment were to be financed by the IBM Credit Corporation. This subsidiary formed a leasing partnership with Merrill Lynch, the largest security brokerage and investment banking house in the United States, in order to pass the investment tax credit savings—amounting to 15 percent of the original costs of equipment—to customers. There emerged an awesome profile of "the fighting IBM."

1. STRATEGY AND STRUCTURE

We are indebted to Alfred Chandler for his seminal work, *Strategy and Structure*, which illuminated the impact of corporate strategies upon their internal structure. Simply put, as shown in the case of IBM, in order to pursue new strategies, firms must reorganize their internal structures. In other words, when inefficiency of internal and external communication and other stresses of organization do not allow a firm to implement its new competitive strategy, it reorganizes the ways in which its human resources, information flows, and allocation of managerial resources are grouped.

Likewise, as firms add new product lines, market areas, and operations in order to grow, they are seen periodically rearranging the ways in which their different product groups, market areas, and functions internally interact. The international business activity is but one form of such diversification. Accordingly, both American and non-American firms have been observed to go through predictable paths of organizational changes as the scope of their international businesses expanded from the mere export–import phase to management of overseas subsidiaries.

With the growth of the modern forms of corporations that came with the Industrial Revolution, divisions of labor and task were further refined to carry out manufacturing and mercantile activities. As these job specializations became increasingly fragmented, there arose a greater need for timely and efficient coordinations among different and specialized jobs. The role of the manager or business administrator who spends almost all of his or her attention and time on coordinating different and specialized jobs was practically unheard of before the 1850s in England and the end of the nineteenth century in the United States and Germany. In Japan as well, the appearance of full-time management was a result of the nation's concerted efforts to industrialize from around the 1870s.

The appearance of Big Business in the United States and elsewhere is also a modern phenomenon. Documents of business histories show us that in fact many surviving large firms grew large precisely because of their abilities to restructure themselves. In order to cope with dynamic market and technological environments, these firms rearranged the ways they identified new business opportunities and internally reallocated such scarce resources as managerial skills, capital, technology, and products to their targeted goals. Rather than

234

relying on the invisible hands of outside markets, these firms used the visible hands of managerial coordinations to procure necessary resources from outside, blend them with their internally generated resources, and opportunely apply them to their targeted activities.

According to Chandler, the first modern U.S. big businesses appeared with the development of railway networks in the country. In order to move even one railroad cargo from one point to another, thousands of logistical decisions had to be made at any moment by the hundreds of people involved. The timely coordination among these job-specific decisions were also vitally important so that one train would not collide with another. In order to handle such a monumental task, two things had to happen. First, within the firm, there appeared the functional divisions of task between different levels of managerial hierarchy. The top management echelon was primarily concerned with the strategic decisionmakings that would determine the direction and scope of their firm's future growth. The middle management echelon was primarily concerned with the implementation of the strategic decisions, and an increasingly greater degree of these implementation tasks were again given further down to the lower middle echelon management. Second, the day-to-day implementation of the agreed on tasks and even tactical decisions were to be given to the managers and supervisors who were closer to the action scenes. This delegation of authority from the top management echelon to the lower management echelon and even further down to the supervisory levels was necessary to coordinate myriad specialized job-specific decisions and actions that were taking place throughout the corporate organization.

The task of job coordination requires systematic ways to gather relevant information concerning the status of the jobs being implemented and to feed such information back to managers in charge of coordinating different jobs. As a firm expands its business, the task of job coordination multiples in geometric progression. Unless some ways are found to streamline the layers of job coordination tasks, the firm would soon find itself too overburdened financially and managerially by job coordination tasks to help sustain actual operations like production, sales, and research and development.

Regardless of the types of their businesses, many firms in many nations generally learn to group first their operational activities by such distinct functions as marketing, production, and research and development. In order to help these operating units standardize such common tasks as personnel administration, accounting, and corporate finance, these support functions are likely to be grouped together as the corporate headquarter functions. Interfunctional coordination, then, will be formally handled by managers in charge of respective functional units. This is the basis of the functional structure of the firm.

The functional structure of the firm could help the firm expand rather rapidly by responding timely to opportunities and risks posed by dynamic market and technological environments. The headquarter function also expands as does the need for assisting functional unit managers to improve lateral communication and coordination between different functional units.

Just like any man-made system, however, the functional structure also outlives its usefulness as the firm expands its line of products and its markets. Diversities of product-market mixes also multiply diversities of product- and market-specific information that the firm must be able to evaluate and act upon. At this juncture, the functional structure leads managers to confuse between different functions the priorities of the product- and market-specific information that they should report quickly to the top management echelon in the corporate headquarters.

Solutions to these structural problems are usually found by many firms in their attempts to regroup their operating and support units by product or by market area depending on the diversities of product-market mixes of the firm. If the firm needs to manage the diversities arising from myriad products that have similar market interactions, the firm is likely to restructure its internal organization along the product-division structure. On the other hand, if the firm needs to manage the diversities emanating from ethnic, geographical, cultural, and other market-specific diversities, it is prone to adopt what we call the area (geographical) structure as the first divisional level units reporting to their headquarters.

2. EVOLUTION OF INTERNAL STRUCTURES

Imagine how a firm upgrades its international business over a period of time from mere trading (export and import) to foreign direct investments. In the case of American firms, we can generalize the evolutionary path of the organizational focus of international business activities of many corporations. In Chapter 7, we ascertained that American firms' patterns of international activities have followed in the main the changing trading patterns between the United States and the rest of the world. These changing trading patterns were explained by the international product life cycle of any given manufactured good. Accordingly, the life cycle of the organizational focus of the international activities of corporations also follow the organizational needs to suit different international business strategies.

(1) Export Department

Many American firms stumbled into exporting businesses when potential overseas customers made inquiries about purchasing their innovative products. At the early growth stage of the product, it usually found pockets of overseas demands similar to the early U.S. market demands. In order to handle an increasing number of export inquiries and orders, many firms simply added an export manager whose function was not much different from the order filler and expediter clerk for domestic sales businesses. However, as the export activities expanded, the firm found increasing needs for special customer services abroad, special arrangements of customs clearance and other international logistics, trade financing, and collections of accounts receivable from overseas customers. Soon, the one-person operation of the export manager was expanded to house a few persons under the new organizational unit called "export department." Then, the export department grew by increasing the lines of exporting products and the numbers of overseas customers. At the same time, the export department learned much of trade financing, credit checking of foreign customers, foreign market surveys, and arrangements of shipping and other logistical needs that the firm used to purchase from outside service oriented firms like banks, forwarders, export management companies, airlines, and shipping agents.

Inside the firm, the expanding export department represented the interests of foreign constituencies (customers) of the firm. Their requests for specific modifications of the products and expedited deliveries were transmitted by the export department to other appropriate divisions and departments of the same firm. Especially when the firm had to ration its products between domestic and foreign customers, the export department manager defended the interest of the foreign customers. Often, his or her negotiating clout was higher profitabilities of the export sales and the fact that domestic product divisions had to depend on exports from time to time to unload product surpluses caused by seasonal fluctuations at home.

As a result, the addition of the export department to the functional, product, or area structure of the firm was often adequate to handle an increasing volume of trading activities.

(2) International Division

Exporting activities lead to commencement of manufacturing operations abroad. At this juncture, the tasks of the export department would have to be expanded to evaluate appropriate foreign investment opportunities. The export department must supervise its sales and manufacturing subsidiaries abroad and must train multinational managers suitable for overseas assignments. The department must also coordinate two-way flows of products and manufacturing technologies between the parent firm and its overseas subsidiaries.

In the case of American multinational firms, the Harvard Multinational Enterprise Project group found that from the mid-1960s to the mid-1970s most American multinational firms created their own international division, often out of their former export department, when their number of overseas subsidiaries reached four. In the case of Japanese multinational firms, Tsurumi[1] found that the number four also pushed most Japanese multinational firms to create their own international divisions. Similar organizational pressures were found at work for many European multinationals, indicating that managerial coordinating tasks of mixed operations of trading and investments confront multinational firms with far greater tasks than those formerly handled by export department structures.

Figure 9-1 schematically depicts a typical structure of international division and its relationships with the rest of the parent organization. The international division structure of American firms suited their corporate dichotomous views of the world, namely, domestic and foreign. Domestic operations are separated from international operations. The international division functioned as a quasi-autonomous subunit with the organizational mandate to represent the international interest of the firm. This organizational structure permitted many American, European, and Japanese multinational firms to execute the additive and piecemeal expansions of their international trade and investments.

Inside the international division, each country market was placed under the country subsidiary, which was in turn often placed under area headquarters coordinating operations of several countries in the area. Inside each country market, a replica of the parent's functionally divided organization or product-to-product groupings was common.

However, as overseas businesses expanded further, the international division's needs for products, technologies, and managerial

---

1. Y. Tsurami, *The Japanese Are Coming: A Multinational Interaction of Firms and Politics* (Cambridge, Mass.: Ballinger Publishing Company, 1976).

Figure 9-1. International Division Structure.

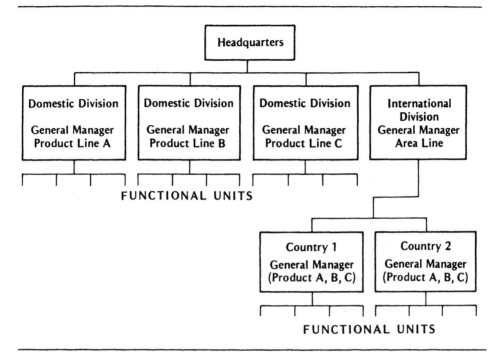

resources held by the domestic side of the business multiplied. Besides, every time the international division replaced the export with the local production, the domestic product or functional division that also used to record the export as their own incremental sales suddenly lost the business. Furthermore, the domestic side of the business functions along product and functional interests of the firm while each country market of the international division vies for maximizing its own area interest. At this juncture, there arose the worldwide problems of coordinating products and functions across various areas. As a result, in the case of many American multinational firms, the international divisional structure was short-lived. It was found by Fouraker and Stopford[2] that the international division was often broken up as its size (measured by sales) approached the smallest product or functional division of the domestic side of the business or as the sales of the international division reached around 10 percent of total sales of the firm. In the case of Japanese firms, the international divisional structure enjoyed much more enduring

2. L.E. Fouraker and J.M. Stopford, "Organizational Structure and Multinational Strategy," *Administrative Science Quarterly* (1968).

Figure 9-2. Worldwide Product Divisions.

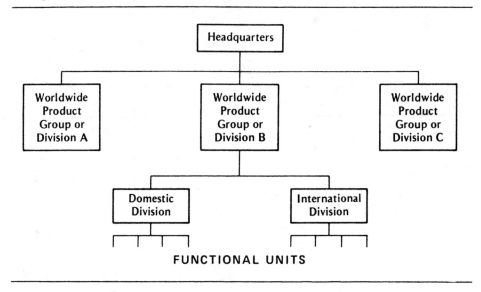

FUNCTIONAL UNITS

longevity. This difference in corporate culture will be presented in the next chapter.

(3) Worldwide Divisions

Once broken up, all the necessary tasks that used to be handled by international division structures were farmed out to product or area divisions of the parent. In other words, depending on the breadth of product lines of the firm, the next step of the multinational activities was handled either by product divisional forms or by area divisional forms.

Figure 9-2 shows schematically a typical product divisional form. This structure is common among multiproduct and multinational manufacturing firms of the United States. Since marketing and manufacturing needs of this firm vary by product group rather than by area of the world, each product division assumes all the necessary tasks of planning, coordinating, and otherwise allocating necessary resources among various domestic and overseas activities. This organizational structure permits a smooth transfer of product and its manufacturing technologies from the home market to foreign markets within the same product group.

Figure 9-3 summarizes a typical area divisional form. This structure is commonly found among manufacturing firms with a narrow range of product lines whose market characteristics are similar. Under these circumstances, the worldwide competitive strategies

240

Figure 9-3. Worldwide Area Structures.

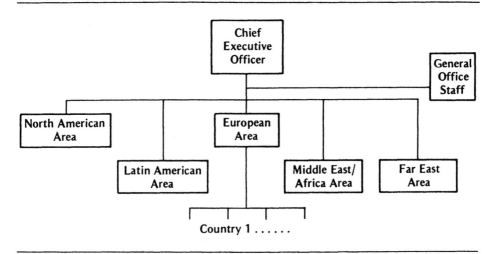

require such firms to standardize and coordinate marketing tactics area by area.

The area structures are particularly suited for the firms that have mature products being produced by standardized production technologies. The success factors of such firms in the worldwide markets are: the ability to respond to local market conditions, legal and political constraints, and country-specific idyosyncrasies of local customers. The firms must often make timely incremental product alterations to suit such local market conditions. The uniform pricing of such mature markets in the same area is also central to the success of such firms. The firms that have favored the area structures are, therefore, found among food, beverage, container, automobile, farm equipment, cosmetics, and pharmaceutical industries.

Of course, each firm has to evaluate the changing needs of its management of job specialization and job coordination between products, functions, and areas as its competitive environment changes. Depending on the country-to-country and product-to-product differences in such organizational tasks, they could easily adopt mixed structures of product and area groupings. For some products and areas, even basic functional groupings of corporate manufacturing and marketing activities may be the best.

For example, as a product evolves through its life cycle, the initial innovative thrusts of the product-specific marketing and manufacturing actions may best be handled by product structures. When the product reaches its market maturity, the marketing tactics will have to be finely tuned to local market conditions. Accordingly, the area structure will become more suitable for this kind of product.

241

3. USES OF EXPORT TRADING COMPANIES
FOR INTERNATIONAL TRADE

The enactment of the Export Trading Company (ETC) Act of 1982 signaled the long overdue orchestration of the U.S. commitment to promoting international trade for American firms, large and small. The export trading companies are intended to help small to medium-sized firms that are individually too weak financially and managerially to identify foreign markets and conclude sales abroad or to procure products and technologies from overseas.

Prior to the ETC Act, there already existed about two hundred small export management companies (EMCs) in the United States that functioned as American manufacturers' representatives for pockets of overseas markets. The average size of such EMCs is rather small, the average number of employees being twenty to twenty-five. It remains to be seen whether anyone of these EMCs will finally grow to become a large multinational export trading company as intended by the ETC Act.

Just as the inevitable organizational stresses between international and domestic divisions of American multinational firms often break up their international divisions, the business relationships between outside exporting agents, like export trading companies and EMCs on one hand and manufacturing firms on the other, tend to be unstable.

For instance, Scientific-Atlanta (SA), Inc. is a growth oriented multinational firm based in Atlanta. It was founded in 1951 by seven engineers as a spin-off business venture from the Georgia Institute of Technology. By 1977, its employee pool had grown to over 1,500 and its annual sales to about $60 million. Exports accounted for at least 25 percent of that figure and was definitely on the rise. This high technology firm in the field of electronics communication equipment grew by expanding its product lines as well as by expanding sales and manufacturing activities abroad. The evolution process of SA's exports went through three distinct stages. Its process illustrates predictable stresses between outside EMCs and manufacturing firms like SA.

First Stage, 1959–1963: In 1959, completely out of the blue, SA's president received a phone call from a representative of a French company who saw an advertisement for the module housing for electric switches placed by SA in a U.S. trade journal. SA obtained a letter of credit from the French customer through a local bank in Atlanta and shipped the order. SA had no staff with the

242

knowledge of export shipment and necessary documentation. Since the shipment lacked the necessary document for customs clearance, the airport customs personnel did not know how to classify the technical product and did not process the shipment. It was not until the irate French customer telephoned a month later that SA began to trace the shipment. SA then hired an EMC to handle the necessary shipping and customs clearance details and to generate additional exports in Europe. This EMC took the title to SA's products in Atlanta and handled all other exporting details, including the pricing of the SA products to foreign customers. SA gave this EMC a ninety-day credit for the sales and a one-year contract.

In a year or so, SA's exports reached about $150,000 out of about $2 million annual sales. At this juncture, SA began to receive an increasing number of requests for customer services and incremental changes in product specifications. It also noticed that different foreign customers were quoted different prices for the same product by the EMC. Also, the EMC refused to show SA the list of its overseas customers. As a result, SA turned to a second EMC — one that showed the same overseas marketing philosophy as SA and was willing to introduce the president of SA to important European customers in exchange for the two-year exclusive export agent contract.

The second EMC also continued to handle only SA's standard and catalogue item product lines such as module housing and other standard electronics equipment. By 1963, SA's annual exports reached about $600,000 — 10 percent of the firm's total sales. Meanwhile, as SA continued to receive diverse customer inquiries from abroad, the firm assigned one full-time sales engineer as the export manager to offer the technical services and supports to foreign customers that the EMC was technically incapable of providing. As the essential marketing and technical assistances of SA's overseas distributors and customers were increasingly handled directly by SA's export manager and his secretary, this two-person export department acquired more and more necessary knowledge of export procedures mainly through the training assistance offered by the U.S. Department of Commerce, local banks, and many handy references.

Second Stage, 1963–1972: By the time SA's contract with the second EMC was amicably terminated, SA had already internalized the necessary logistical skills of export order processing and customer services abroad. By 1969, the export department grew to a five-person team that became capable of selling all the product lines of the firm to anywhere in the world and of collecting the payments. Annual exports already passed $1 million in 1967 and continued to increase rapidly. The other accounting and billing procedures of SA as a whole were often changed to standardize such paperwork between export and domestic sales.

Third Stage, 1972 and Afterward: In 1972, SA ceased to let the single export department handle all the exports for the entire product line of the firm. The export department was broken up, and its functions were integrated into separate product divisions. Each product division had its own export manager and a support staff that was only responsible for export operations of their product division. In this way, SA expanded not only exports but overseas manufacturing operations of its wide range of product groups.

As illustrated from the history of SA's export growth, such small outside export trading firms as EMCs were very useful for small to medium-sized manufacturing firms' ready entry into export activities. However, EMCs could not stay with predictable export expansions of a high-technology-intensive firm like SA from standard catalogue items to more technically sophisticated product groups. In order to handle the latter types of products, the communication and interactions between export department (and outside EMCs) and requisite product divisions had to be carried out with the minimum impediments. At this juncture, small EMCs were often cut off by their one-time manufacturing clients.

Large export trading companies patterned after Japanese *sogoshosha* may be able to prolong the life of the export agent contracts with even high-technology-intensive manufacturing firms. This is partly because large *sogoshosha*-like organizations can continue to command export initiatives vis-à-vis their manufacturing suppliers by actively developing overseas markets and by organizing large-scale international biddings and development projects for their manufacturing clients. In addition, large export trading companies can help their manufacturing clients link up with necessary supply sources of technologies and scarce resources.

4. THE OWNERSHIP OF FOREIGN SUBSIDIARIES

(1) Patterns of The Ownership

As shown in Table 9-1, a parent's ownership of subsidiaries outside its own country varies significantly from one parent's nationality to the next. As of the beginning of 1971, U.S. parent firms in effect wholly owned over two-thirds of their foreign subsidiaries.

Table 9-1. The Ownership of Overseas Manufacturing Subsidiaries by the Nationality of Largest Parent Firms,[a] as of January 1, 1971.[b]

	Parent's Ownership of Subsidiaries					
Parent's Nationality	95% 100	94% 51	50%	49% 26	25% 5	Total
France	38%	23%	9%	18%	12%	100%
West Germany	56	22	9	10	5	100
Italy	65	13	5	12	4	100
Belgium–Luxembourg	52	21	6	10	13	100
Netherlands	65	18	7	7	2	100
Sweden	80	9	4	5	3	100
Switzerland	62	25	6	5	3	100
Canada	68	12	7	10	3	100
Japan	27	8	7	25	33	100
United Kingdom	51	15	14	11	9	100
Average of non-U.S. firms	53	18	7	12	10	100
U.S. firms	71	20		9		100

a. "Largest" parent firms are defined as those investing firms recorded in *Fortune's* list of "500 Largest Firms in the U.S." in 1967 and *Fortune's* "200 Largest non-U.S. Firms" in 1970.

b. The U.S. data are as of January 1, 1968.

Source: The Data Bank of the Multinational Enterprise Project, the Harvard Business School, 1968–1976.

On the average, European and Canadian parent firms wholly owned about one-half of their foreign subsidiaries. Moreover, Japanese parent firms demonstrated a distinct propensity to settle for minority positions in their subsidiaries abroad.

These observations raise tantalizing questions. Are the ownership differences in foreign subsidiaries by the parent nationality related to the parent's corporate culture? To the timing of entry into foreign countries? To the locations of manufacturing subsidiaries? To unique characteristics of product- and process-related technologies owned by respective parent firms? Furthermore, are the ownership differences related to parent firms' strategies (motives and performances of their direct investments)? If one is able to answer these questions, one final question arises: Are these ownership patterns likely to remain stable? For example, are not Japanese parent firms likely to seek majority ownership of their subsidiaries?

The entering Japanese firms generally commenced a limited scale of simple manufacturing in a joint venture with a local partner who had formerly been the Japanese firm's import agent. For example, I found in Indonesia that about 83 percent of the Japanese manufacturing subsidiaries operating during the first quarter of 1973 had as their local partners either former import agents or indigenous manufacturers who had formerly imported semiprocessed products from Japan. Over one-half of the Japanese manufacturing subsidiaries that were not directly related to local government-owned business had their former import agent as their local partner. Similar patterns were observed through East and Southeast Asia and Latin America.

Rather than insisting on majority ownership of a subsidiary that might fail, the Japanese parent investor often spread the risks by involving other Japanese partners and more than one local partner in the venture. The local market orientation of the Japanese manufacturing subsidiaries, which did not insist on bringing sophisticated technologies into the host countries, gave the local partner greater bargaining strength in demanding a sizable, even majority, ownership. Even when the local partners did not provide their share of capital, either in kind (plant sites, etc.) or in cash, the Japanese parent firms would still extend loans to them. In the case of Japanese investments in Indonesia, over one-third of the Japanese manufacturing subsidiaries had loaned money to their local partners—money with which the latter paid for their share of the joint venture.

Elsewhere in Asia, similar practices by Japanese investing parents were widespread and well accepted by local partners. Little did Japanese investors realize then, however, that such expedient forms of entry into host countries would later come to haunt them, starting in the mid-1970s.

(2) The Instability of Joint Ventures

As one after another Japanese multinational discovered during the latter half of the 1970s, the changes in their multinational competitive strategies strained the fragmented ownership patterns of their joint ventures abroad. As was the case of American multinational firms, the stability of foreign joint ventures Japanese multinational firms were determined by Japanese parent firms' worldwide strategies.

One of the critical strategy choices for a multinational firm is the choice between foreign product diversification and foreign product concentration. Firms that base their competitive strength on the development of new products for many different overseas end-use markets appear to have a high degree of tolerance for joint ventures. Firms that maintain a competitive strength consisting of a monopolistic control over natural resource deposits and that sell products made from that resource to many end-use markets also appear to be highly tolerant of manufacturing joint ventures with foreign partners. However, firms that constrain their foreign operations to serving a particular customer group tend to purge themselves of joint venture partners after a time.

Corporate policy decisions—not conflicts between partners—are the most frequent causes of ownership change in joint ventures. The policy decisions found to destabilize joint ventures primarily concerned centralization of the marketing function. Cost cutting production specialization decisions are also found to provoke joint venture instability. High and low R&D firms were found at both ends of the spectrum from joint-venture tolerant to joint-venture intolerant firms.

Interestingly, the above-mentioned tendencies are found widely across the U.S.-, Europe-. and Japan-based parent firms, thus suggesting that the instability of given joint ventures may well be predicted (therefore, coped with in advance) according to the strategies of market, product, and technology of parent firms. On one end of the spectrum, firms—like Coca-Cola and IBM—that are expanding the worldwide market coverage essentially with a single product line, have invariably avoided joint ventures abroad. Coca-Cola gives bottling and distribution tasks to locally owned franchises, but it tightly controls the marketing details and wholly owns the concentrate-making plants in each nation-market. The worldwide standardization of Coca-Cola products and their specific marketing actions has singularly shaped the firm's intolerance of joint ventures. In the case of IBM, the wholly owned subsidiaries are perceived as critical for the firm's standardization of worldwide marketing moves, for cross-hauling parts and finished products among the firm's subsidiaries abroad, and for safeguarding the firm's proprietary technologies.

On the other end of the spectrum, there are firms that pursue the strategies of multiproduct diversifications supported by a high degree of R&D performance. In this case, joint ventures oriented to local markets often provide the multiproduct and multidivisional parent firm with expedient entry into many national markets in a short span of time. And their diverse technological competence provides parent firms with continuing unique bargaining strength vis-à-vis joint venture partners. As the novelty of old products fades, the parent firms can continue to upgrade their technological support to joint ventures by transferring new product- and process-related technologies.

Table 9–2 shows a breakdown of the responses given by Japanese multinational firms that were asked their reasons for preferring a majoring equity ownership of their overseas subsidiaries. As pre-

Table 9-2. Reasons for Subsidiaries' Majority Ownership.

Question: *When you desire to own over 51 percent of the equity of your overseas subsidiaries, how important are the following six reasons?*

	Japanese Parent Firm's Normalized Score[a]	
Reasons	*Small to Medium-sized Firms*	*Large Firms*
a. Worldwide consistency of sales policies	1.124 (1)	1.284 (2)
b. Parent's choice of production schedules and products of overseas subsidiaries	0.830 (3)	1.447 (1)
c. Uncertainty of local customs and greater distance from Japan	0.908 (2)	−1.144 (6)
d. Avoidance of confusion of export markets	0.717 (4)	−0.781 (5)
e. Maintenance of secrecy of production processes and sales strategies	0.005 (5)	−0.331 (3)
f. Dividends from subsidiaries	−0.362 (6)	−0.494 (4)
Number of respondents	40	82

a. The numbers in parentheses indicate the descending order of the relative importance of each reason for the two groups of Japanese parent firms.

Source: Y. Tsurumi, *The Japanese Are Coming*: A Multinational Interaction of Firms and Politics (Cambridge, Mass.: Ballinger Publishing Company, 1976), p. 210.

dicted, multinational parents' strategic moves to consolidate their global activities pushed them to prefer majority-owned subsidiaries.

Table 9-3 summarizes the ranking order of the conflicts between Japanese multinational parents and their joint venture partners abroad. Again predictably, the transfer pricing considerations put obvious strains on the relationships between Japanese parents and their foreign business partners. American and European multinational firms have reported similar problems.

(3) The Intended Benefits of Joint Ventures

The results of my own questionnaire survey among Japanese parent firms clarified the intended benefits of Japanese investors regarding their joint ventures abroad. The relevant question and responding firms' answers regarding their joint venture partners are reproduced in Table 9-4.

Table 9-3. Conflicts with Foreign Partners.

Question: *Of the requests that you received from the foreign partners of your joint ventures abroad, and of the conflicts that you encountered from your foreign partners, how serious and frequent were the following ten sources of conflicts?*

Conflicts of Interest	Means of Indicated Score[a]
1. Transfer prices of parts and semi-processed materials shipped from Japanese parent to joint ventures.	4.08
2. Timing and extent of expansion of equity of joint ventures.	3.18
3. Transfer prices of products produced by joint ventures and shipped to Japanese parent.	3.03
4. Dividend policy.	2.97
5. Quantity of products produced by joint ventures.	2.92
6. Selection of products to be produced by joint ventures.	2.90
7. Specifications of quality of products produced by joint ventures.	2.85
8. Demarcation of export markets of joint ventures and direct shipments of exports from joint ventures.	2.69
9. Uses of trademarks and brand names.	2.49
10. Budget of sales promotions of joint ventures.	1.73

a. The scoring scale is from "6" (most frequent and serious) to "0" (least serious).
Source: Same as for Table 9-2, but p. 212.

The degree of importance that responding firms placed on each contribution expected from their local partner varied little with the size of the parent firm. The most common expectation Japanese firms had of their local partners—general management skills—can be summarized as the ability of local partners to supply sales personnel and knowledge of local customs, manners, and political situations. It should be added that this ranking order also varies little from one industry group to another.

Compared with large firms, small to medium-sized firms expected a great deal more from their local partners in terms of the latter's ability to supply capital, sales personnel, and necessary input materials that were available locally. Large firms counted more significantly on their local partners' ability to distribute additional goods imported from Japan; they also placed relatively greater importance than the smaller firms on their partners' knowledge of local customs, manners, and political situations.

Table 9-4. Expected Contributions of Foreign Partners.

	Japanese Parent Firms Normalized Score[a]	
Expected Contributions from Local Partner	Small to Medium-sized Firms	Large Firms
a. General managers and general management skills	1.129 (1)	0.930 (1)
b. Capital funds	0.054 (5)	−0.514 (5)
c. Ability to supply sales personnel	0.679 (2)	0.250 (3)
d. Ability to distribute local imports from Japan	−0.367 (6)	−0.098 (4)
e. Speed of entry	−1.611 (7)	−0.735 (7)
f. Knowledge of local customs and political situations	0.373 (3)	0.584 (2)
g. Ability to procure necessary raw and input materials locally	0.222 (4)	−0.515 (5)
Number of respondents	40	82

a. The numbers in parentheses indicate the descending order of the relative importance of each contribution expected from local partners.

Source: Same as for Table 9-2, but p. 205.

In-depth interviews with the responding firms indicated that large firms of Japan were more politically sensitive about their public visibility in the host countries than were small to medium-sized firms. This reflected the political and economic realities of fall 1972 in Japan and abroad (the date of the questionnaire survey), when Japanese mass media and government agencies like the Ministry of International Trade and Industry (MITI) were sounding increasingly alarmed over the "behaviors of Japanese investors abroad." In the midst of such an atmosphere in Japan, large firms were not only already more politically vulnerable than smaller ones but were also more concerned about the possibility that the mishandling of sensitive matters anywhere abroad in the course of their more abundant overseas expansion could cause them political damage that might tarnish their worldwide image.

The expectations of Japanese investors concerning their local partners' contributions do not differ greatly from those of American investors except on one point. Stopford and Wells found that American investors mentioned "speed of entry" as the second most important contribution expected from the local partners of their joint ventures. Local partners' "general knowledge of local economy, politics and customs" was the most important contribution that American firms expected from their joint venture partners.

In contrast, neither small to medium-sized firms nor large firms of Japan rated "speed of entry" (where a joint venture is the entry condition for local sales of products involved) significantly high. Further interviews with randomly selected respondents revealed that Japanese firms, large or small, perceived the joint venture with local partners as a vehicle for sharing political and economic risks. This meant that even when joint ventures were not mandatory for entry into a host country, Japanese investors nonetheless actively chose them as their initial entry format.

5. CONCLUSION

One important skill of multinational managers is to pinpoint the organizational constraint when they contemplate new worldwide strategies. In reality, however, every corporate bureaucracy soon develops its resistance to organizational change. Accordingly, organizational stresses are likely to be bottled up inside firms, only to surface and engulf the entire corporation caught in a grave crisis. If managers remain aware of the organizational stresses of their firm, they can at least seize on the crisis atmosphere to overhaul long overdue changes in the internal structures of their firm.

The organizational change can be used by the alert management to alter the corporate culture. For example, in the case of Scientific–Atlanta (SA) that we saw that in 1972 the firm broke up its export department and held each product division responsible for its own export activities. This move was mainly caused by the firm's new president, who wanted to eliminate the firm's traditional way of treating its domestic market as if separated from the world market.

Without a concomitant change in the firm's internal culture that was mainly oriented to the U.S. market, no amount of organizational change would have made SA internationally competitive. And the organizational change was the powerful body language that the new president wanted to inculcate in his firm.

A SELECTED REFERENCE

Strategy and Structure of Corporations

The following seminal works are essential readings for serious managers and scholars:

Chandler, A.D., Jr. *Strategy and Structure.* Cambridge, Mass.: MIT Press, 1962).

10 MANAGEMENT CONTROL OF MULTINATIONAL FIRMS

The fact that international divisional structures of many American multinational firms were often broken up and absorbed by product or area structures was closely associated with the corporate culture of these multinational firms. Their corporate culture was in turn shaped by the ways in which the headquarters utilized the profit center forms of international management control of worldwide activities. Each division was treated as the profit center even if its operation was intertwined with other divisions and functions. When each division chiefs were spurred to compete with each other for the promotion and other recognitions of their respective divisions' successes, domestic product and area divisions often coalesced to divide the businesses of their rival international divisions.

This interdivisional rivalry was often complicated by the biases that crept into the financial reporting of economic performances of overseas subsidiaries exposed to different political and economic risks from those of their parent domestic operations. These inevitable biases in the international reporting and management information flows were caused by the ways in which economic performances expressed in one foreign currency were translated into consolidated financial reports expressed in the currency unit of the parent's nation.

As soon as a company increases its involvement in international activities from the stage of pursuing export–import opportunities to that of operating foreign marketing and manufacturing units as well, it faces business transactions carried out in diverse currency units. Furthermore, the movement of goods and services among its own operational units across national boundaries complicates transfer pricing decisions. Not only does the strength of local currencies vary from country to country, but also such trade barriers as tariffs and quotas as well as national differences in tax structures affect transfer pricing decisions.

When profits (and losses) expressed in one unit of currency are translated into the financial statements expressed in another unit of currency, they often incur "translation profits (and losses)," depending on the degree of changes in the relative value of the two currencies. Multinational managers need stay alert to see whether the operations of their subsidiaries, and in particular intersubsidiary transactions, involving these currencies are causing actual economic leakage out of their multinational system.

For example, as shown in the case of Chesebrough-Ponds Uruguay at the end of this chapter, the firm's translation method from Uruguay's currency to U.S. dollars distorts actual performance of its branch in Uruguay. What appears to be a huge "economic leakage (loss)" is nothing but a visionary distortion. On the other hand, in buying products and services from a Swiss subsidiary, when the Swiss franc continues to appreciate vis-à-vis other currencies, the actual payments to factors of productions procured in Switzerland and the tax payments to the Swiss authorities constitute actual economic leakage from the multinational system. In order to plug such leakage, management might revise the transfer pricing formulas for intersubsidiary transactions. All told, the reporting and control of multinational firms requires general managers and controllers well versed in the intricacies of international transfer pricing practices and reporting in multiunit currencies.

1. INTERNATIONAL REPORTING

In Chapter 2, a fully grown multinational corporation was defined as a corporate entity that operates marketing and manufacturing units in more than one country on the basis of common strategies and a common pool of such crucial resources as management skills, technology, and capital. In order to implement such common strategies, corporate resources must be optimally allocated to enable marketing and manufacturing units throughout the world to carry out their assigned activities.

The optimal allocation of corporate resources requires some form of management control system designed to allocate corporate resources efficiently and to keep track of how well corporate strategies are implemented by the operational units. Accounting information can be useful if it is properly compiled and used to fulfill the following three functions of management control systems:

1. To communicate what each operational unit (e.g., division manager, area manager, country manager) is assigned as its own task;
2. To motivate the managers to accomplish the assigned tasks; and
3. To evaluate the actual performance of the managers to see if the assigned tasks are carried out as well as to see if assigned tasks need any future revisions.

It should be noted that the definition of management control offered above is concerned with what the management control *ought* to be. When you are concerned with the performance measurement of the reporting managers, this normative supposition leads one to consider built-in biases that different forms of translation of foreign financial records may contain. Such translated accounting information is used for management control purposes by the multinational corporation.

2. TRANSLATION EXPOSURE

In Chapter 4, we saw that the Bayeriche–Wurst Company was alarmed by the appreciating Deutsche mark which threatened the mark-based value of the firm's accounts receivable denominated in U.S. dollars. The same foreign exchange loss could be incurred when converting repatriated foreign earnings into the appreciating currency and repaying foreign loans denominated in the appreciating currency. The opposite is also true when a foreign currency appreciates and increases the monetary value of foreign cash inflows converted into the depreciating currency unit. This is called a foreign exchange "transaction gain (loss)."

On the other hand, when you need to consolidate the financial statements of foreign subsidiaries into the financial statements of the parent firm, you would have to translate financial statements denominated in foreign currency units into statements denominated in the parent firm's currency. This is done even if you do not plan to physically move financial assets and liabilities from subsidiaries to your parent firm and vice versa. Depending on which exchange rates you choose to translate each item of your financial statements, you could incur paper losses (gains) called "translation loss (gain)."

There are three different translation methods, although some variants of these methods are undoubtedly in use today. These methods are called (1) the current asset method, (2) the financial asset method (monetary–nonmonetary method), and (3) the net asset method (all current method). These methods are distinguished from one another in that each recommends its own way to apply either the currently prevalent foreign exchange rate or the historical foreign exchange rate to each item of the balance sheet. The profit and loss statement of the foreign subsidiary is always translated at the current exchange rate.

Current Asset Method: This method applies a current exchange rate to current assets and current liabilities but a historical exchange rate to noncurrent assets (most notably, fixed assets) and to noncurrent liabilities (most notably, long-term debts). One variant of this method is called the modified current asset method because it applies a current exchange rate to noncurrent liabilities and a historical exchange rate for the noncurrent physical assets.

Financial Asset Method (Monetary–Nonmonetary Method): This method is designed to convey the up-to-date value of financial assets in particular. It applies a current exchange rate to current monetary assets like cash and accounts receivable and to current and noncurrent liabilities, but it uses an historical exchange rate for inventory and noncurrent physical assets.

In 1975, the Financial Accounting Standard Board (FASB) of the United States issued its Opinion #8, requiring that U.S.-based multinationals uniformly adopt the monetary–nonmonetary method. This method requires firms to translate all monetary assets and liabilities at the current exchange rate quoted on the closing date of the balance sheet. Other assets and liabilities are to be translated at the historical exchange rate. In addition, FASB #8 mandated that firms report foreign exchange gains and losses on a quarterly basis. No reserves to smooth out such gains and losses are allowed.

Net Asset Method (All Current Method): This method purports to record the up-to-date value of net assets. It applies only the current exchange rate to all items of the balance sheet.

After adjusting to FASB #8 for over five years, American firms registered serious complaints with the board about the mandatory use of the monetary–nonmonetary method. For one thing, quarterly reports of foreign exchange losses and gains made multinational firms' performance appear far more volatile than its reality. Besides, the FASB #8 ruling often forced multinational managers to behave against the long-term interest of their foreign operations. In 1981, by dint of the FASB #52 ruling, the board recommended that the net asset method must be used by American firms for income tax returns and other external reporting needs. Unlike the FASB #8 ruling, however, all the foreign exchange gains and losses were to be directly charged to the retained earnings of the balance sheet.

Table 10–1 provides computational examples under the three different translation methods. Under the current asset method, the amount of exposure (to fluctuations of foreign exchange rates) is estimated usually by the difference between current assets and current liabilities. When the parent firm uses the financial asset method of translation, however, the amount of exposure is the difference between cash plus accounts receivable on one hand and current liabilities plus long-term debts on the other. Under the net asset method of translation, the amount of exposure is the difference between total assets on one hand and current liabilities plus long-term debts on the other.

Table 10–1. Translations of Balance Sheet Items under the Three Translation Methods (current spot rate of Ps. 2/$1 and historical spot rate of Ps. 1/$1).

	Local Currency Unit	Current Asset Method	Financial Asset Method	Net Asset Method
Assets				
Cash	Ps. 100	$ 50	$ 50	$ 50
Accounts receivable	300	150	150	150
Inventory	200	100	200	100
Net fixed assets	300	300	300	150
Total	Ps. 900	$600	$700	$450
Liabilities and Owner's Equity				
Current liabilities	Ps. 200	$100	$100	$100
Long-term debts	200	200	100	100
Capital and retained earnings[a]	500	300	500	250
Total	Ps. 900	$600	$700	$450

a. Since total assets must be equal to total liabilities plus owner's equity, the owner's equity (capital plus retained earnings) is used as the plug factor to balance the balance sheet and to absorb the translation losses.

3. INFORMATIONAL DISTORTIONS AND TAX TREATMENT OF FOREIGN EXCHANGE LOSSES

The reader may be concerned whether or not a particular translation method tends to motivate a *homo economicus* manager to do a certain thing. Such built-in biases of foreign managers' reactions inherent in each translation method stem from the fact that the level of prices and the strength of currency of a foreign nation vis-à-vis the parent nation are often moving in one of the following nine possible directions:

Permutation: (3 × 3 = 9)			
Foreign Currency		*Price Level*	
Situation A:	Appreciating (the extreme form is a unilateral revaluation)	Situation a:	Rising
Situation B:	Stable	Situation b:	Stable
Situation C:	Depreciating (the extreme form is a unilateral devaluation).	Situation c:	Declining

All told, the most likely situation that the parent company in a country like the United States faces vis-à-vis developing nations would be that not only are the currencies of the foreign countries depreciating relative to the U.S. dollar, but also the price levels of the foreign countries are rising faster. Under these circumstances, what would be the attitude of the foreign manager if he or she were indeed made responsible for the *translated* profit of his operation? Might not he be likely to act one way under one translation and another under the other translation method?

In Table 10-2 actions that the foreign manager might prefer under the above circumstances toward each item of the balance sheet are summarized by each translation method. It is assumed that the manager of the foreign operation is made responsible for the net translated profit in terms of U.S. dollars after the resultant foreign exchange loss or price adjustment loss is deducted from the translated profit. It will be a good exercise if the student convinces himself of the manager's preference under eight other possible circumstances (like appreciating currency with falling price, etc.). In the example of Table 10-2, the foreign manager is assumed to act in such a way to mini-

Table 10-2. The Preferred Actions of the Foreign Manager Who Is Given the Translated Profit Responsibility.
Situation 1: Depreciating Foreign Currency (with real threat of devaluation) and Rising Prices (local inflation).

	Without Price Level Adjustment			With Price Level Adjustment[c]
Balance Sheet Items	Current Asset Method	Financial Asset Method	Net Asset Method[a]	Net Asset Method[b]
Current Monetary Assets (cash receivables)	Minimize	Minimize	Minimize	Minimize
Inventory	Minimize	Maximize	Minimize	Maximize
Fixed Assets	Maximize	Maximize	Minimize	Maximize
Current Liabilities (notes, long-term debts)	Minimize	Maximize	Maximize	Maximize

a. All assets are translated at the spot rate.
b. Concentration in physical assets results in maximum reported net income after price level adjustment.
c. Replacement value accounting is used by the parent.

mize either foreign exchange loss or price adjustment loss for this translated financial report to the parent.

It would require extensive research to determine how closely the foreign manager in fact conforms to the theoretical behavioral biases inherent in the translation method. To be sure, foreign managers do not have much freedom to manipulate balance sheet items. They are often constrained by the competitive situation of their local markets. Much as they might like to keep the accounts receivable and inventory at the bare minimum, local trade customs and competitive marketing conditions may force them to carry large receivables and inventories. Therefore, it may be reasonably speculated that the foreign manager might not be such a fool as to sacrifice his business by ordering his sales managers to provide credit for far fewer customers than local competitors do.

However, if the prime purpose of management control is to aid the foreign manager to do what the parent company believes is best for the long-run interest of the multinational corporation as a whole, the parent company might be wise to be aware of the differences in the possible built-in biases of foreign managers' behavior, given the translation method and a key evaluative measurement like translated profit.

Therefore, the translation method must be selected by the parent to motivate foreign managers to act in the manner deemed optimal for the goal of the company as a whole. Their performance might be measured by other performance indicators when the parent company knows standardized measurement of the foreign manager by the translated profit alone tends to motivate the foreign manager to act, where possible, differently from the desired goal of his operational unit. For example, if the target assigned to a manager is an increase in the market share of his products, his performance may be judged by an indicator that shows how well he achieved this assigned task.

Very few countries recognize foreign exchange losses as deductible expenses or losses. In particular, when a foreign exchange loss is charged to the foreign subsidiary by the parent, the foreign government rarely accepts such a loss as a legitimate tax deductible loss. Foreign exchange gains often receive different treatment by governments whose objective is to maximize tax revenues. One thing that international managers must keep in mind is that, given the strength of foreign currency relative to that of the parent's nation, the national differences in the tax treatment of foreign exchange loss and gain may influence the selection of the appropriate translation methods. When foreign subsidiaries are maintained under the branch status, even translation losses caused by the devaluation (and depreciation) of foreign exchanges are often wholly tax deductible.

4. TRANSFER PRICING OF INTERNATIONAL BUSINESS

A transfer price is defined as the price that is attached, for the purpose of management control, to goods and services moving from one profit or cost responsibility center to another. When such movements of goods and services within the corporation encompass more than one national boundary all the economic and political forces governing the movement of goods and services across national boundaries come to affect transfer pricing decisions.

In addition, it should be noted that a multinational firm uses transfer pricing for the purpose of shifting liquid funds from one operation center to another. When multinational managers are concerned with flows of their own liquid funds from one country to another, they naturally act to minimize the outright costs associated with such movements of funds. So, instead of using solely dividend

259

remittances, multinational managers often resort to underinvoicing or overinvoicing the goods and services that move from one of their foreign subsidiaries to another or to their headquarters. Besides, frequent use of "royalties," "technical assistance fees," and "management fees" have been made vehicles of transferring liquid funds from one country to another.

Even when the parent company in fact invests in a foreign subsidiary, it often extends such investments under the name of "long-term loans" and charges the subsidiary for interest on them. A foreign host country that is concerned with tax revenue often reacts by disallowing such interest payments from tax exemptions. When such long-term loans from parent to subsidiary do not carry a specified term and repayment schedule, and when a contractual provision of such loans enable the parent to convert these loans into equity, a number of host countries in fact deem such loans as equity investments by the foreign parent. Consequently, a withholding tax on dividends is often charged to the interest paid by the subsidiary to the parent company.

(1) International Factors That Influence Transfer Prices

Costs and Means of Transportation from One Country to Another: These factors influence considerations far more than do domestic transactions. Besides, far greater attention must be paid to delivery of goods from one country to another. The suppliers and users of goods must clearly spell out who is responsible for their delivery. The one who is responsible for delivery should be keeping an eye on costs as well as availability and shipment time for such diverse transportation as air cargo, ocean cargo, ocean freighter (tramper and regular charter), and overland transportation.

Tariffs: Tariffs even more importantly affect the costs of goods to buyers. Tariff schedules of imported goods not only vary from nation to nation, but even the application of the tariff schedule often varies with the country of origin of the imported goods. So, even if the market price of similar goods in the buyer's country is used as a guide price for the transfer price, the seller should calculate the upper limit of the f.o.b. price of his goods by considering tariffs and transportation costs.

There is no guarantee that either the f.o.b. or c.i.f. price of the imported goods forms the basis of the tariff calculation. The customs office sometimes substitutes its own estimates or the wholesale prices of comparable goods in the importing country for the reported landed price of imported goods. For example, the U.S. customs use the wholesale price of U.S.-made chemicals to compute duties on many imported chemicals.

(2) Additional Problems of International Transfer Pricing

Often, such nontariff trade barriers as import quotas, administrative delays of processing import permits, and arbitrary reclassifications of the imported goods for tariff purposes are real hindrances to the smooth movement of goods from one country to another. Where import quotas are in effect, there may be a limit of the quantity placed on the goods that a buyer-subsidiary wishes to bring in from the other country. When administrative delays and arbitrary reclassifications by one host country inhibit the importation of goods from another country, the parent company may be wise not to assign a key manufacturing task to a subsidiary in such a country. In this country, the parent should let its subsidiary operate on the sole basis of "local procurement" where possible, or it must face the decision of expanding the local manufacture of goods that are not locally available.

(3) Political and Economic Factors That Affect the International Transfer Price

Bilateral Trade Agreements Between Two Nations: These often make the movement of goods and the resultant payments easier for subsidiaries in such nations. Sometimes, it pays to ship goods from a third country to a country covered by such a bilateral trade agreement for re-export to a destination that happens to be a party to the same bilateral trade agreement.

National Differences in Corporate Tax Rates: These may influence the parent company's choice of a country to act as a financial pool center. In order to maximize the profits to be retained by the country of lower corporate tax, the transfer price attached to goods and services from a higher tax country to a lower tax country might be kept as low as possible so that the profits accrue to the lower tax country. However, the lower tax country's restrictions on capital have to be considered as well. Furthermore, the tax authorities of most countries often take a dim view of excessively low transfer prices that subsidiaries in their country charge to subsidiaries in other countries. Within these constraints, however, the parent might provide a guideline for transfer price in order to generate profits where the corporate income tax is low.

It should be pointed out that the United States in particular has already adopted the concept of "world income" for the corporate income tax of the U.S.-based firms. These firms are obligated to pay U.S. income tax on income generated and retained abroad. An exception is still made for funds that a parent company pools out of its earnings in developing countries for the purpose of reinvesting in developing countries. However, to the extent that the world income concept is enforced, U.S. firms lost much of their incentive to manipulate transfer prices to overcome tax barriers.

National Differences in Currency Strength: These should also be examined when the multinational corporation issues a guideline for international transfer pricing decisions. The parent's desire to take liquid assets out of a country threatened with devaluation might cause the subsidiary of such a country to charge a "low" transfer price to other subsidiaries that are not threatened by the currency devaluation.

(4) International Arbitration of Disputed Transfer Prices

When the parent lets each subsidiary negotiate the transfer price, it often becomes necessary to provide machinery for arbitration of the disputed transfer price. Apart from the possible complications of international transfer price mentioned, international arbitration is closely related to the organizational setup of the multinational corporation. Since corporate organizational arrangements are often changed to cope with the growth and diversity of domestic as well as international business, the arbitration machinery of disputed international transfer prices often finds itself caught in the midst of ever changing organizational arrangements among subsidiaries. Old areawide responsibilities are regrouped according to product lines, later decentralization by product lines is changed to the new arrangement of larger areawide responsibility encompassing more than one product line, and so forth. The parent company, therefore, must take care to provide efficient arbitration machinery at the scene closest to possible sources of dispute.

All in all, a useful guideline for transfer pricing decisions of multinational corporations is that the transfer price is neither more nor less than a means of management control. In the case of domestic operations alone, such economic and social factors as labor management relations, economic and monetary policies, price increases, and currency strength are assumed to be affecting all the operational units of the company within the same country. Therefore, even when the managers of decentralized operational units are judged and rewarded on the basis of a common yardstick like return on investment, they often accept such judgment without making much ado about regional differences in economics and politics. In the case of the multinational corporation, what are taken for granted for domestic operations and are therefore assumed to be uniformly influencing all the operational units suddenly become crucial variables that distinguish performance of one subsidiary from other subsidiaries.

The parent company is, therefore, wise to restructure its transfer pricing decision rules and the evaluation of the managers by considering the national differences in environmental variables that affect the performance of foreign operations. It may not be defensible any longer to evaluate the managers of foreign operational units across the board on a standardized measurement like return on investment (ROI). A more equitable measurement would be to judge the managers' performances against their expected performances. When the parent company draws up the expected performances of foreign managers, it should account for strategic decisions like the parent's decision to pool global profits in Country A. Naturally, the national differences in economic and social environments should also be accounted for when the parent draws up target performances.

5. TAXATION OF INTERNATIONAL BUSINESS

International business encounters great complexities in coping with the tax rules of the home and host governments that determine their taxable corporate income. Accordingly, international tax planning must be an integral part of international financial strategy. Taxation influences the firm's ultimate decisions as to (1) location of the foreign investment, (2) legal and managerial reporting relationships between the foreign subsidiary and the parent, (3) legal form of ownership of the foreign business such as branch status versus subsidiary, (4) method of financing foreign operations, and more importantly, (5) transfer pricing arrangement between the parent and the foreign subsidiary.

Although international tax planning requires the assistance of international tax lawyers, the following considerations will provide general guides to the tax constraints of international business of strategy:

Tax Havens: Ultimately, it is up to the home government whether or not tax havens can really benefit investing firms. Generally, a tax haven subsidiary is owned fully by the parent corporation and located in those countries that provide special tax considerations such as no corporate income tax. Countries like the Bahamas, Bermuda, the Cayman Islands, and Liechtenstein have no corporate income taxes. Countries like the British Virgin Islands and Jersey Islands have much lower corporate income tax rates than the United States and other industrialized nations. On the other hand, Hong Kong, Liberia, and Panama, tax income generated inside their countries but exempt income from foreign sources.

Tax havens are not limited to the countries mentioned above. In 1981, hoping to lure the headquarters of leading commercial banks away from New York, the state of Delaware in the United States passed a law to charge practically no state income taxes on banks' earnings. Many developing countries today make it a rule to exempt new foreign investments from corporate income taxes for a predetermined time period.

Tax Treaty: The history of taxation of the international business of the United States and other industrialized countries is replete with cat-and-mouse gamesmanship between taxing authorities and multinational firms that seek to legally avoid tax liabilities. By now, the taxing authorities have closed many loopholes concerning the tax treatment of foreign profits pooled into subsidiaries located in tax havens. However, multinational firms have legitimate concerns in avoiding double taxation. If they have paid income taxes in foreign countries, they would like to be given credit toward the total tax liabilities assessed by their home government.

Bilaterally, many nations concluded tax treaties that mutually recognize tax credits. Some tax treaties, such as the one between Singapore and Japan, even permit Japanese firms to consider exempted income tax in Singapore as "actually paid" to the Singapore authorities. The Japanese government provides full tax credit to this portion of the deemed income tax that the Singapore government granted as an incentive to the investing foreign firms.

Unitary Tax: California's is by far the most well-known unitary tax. Simply put, the unitary tax is devised by the state taxing authority to collect taxes from foreign and out-of-state firms operating inside the state. Even if these operating units record no taxable income, the state tax authority computes income taxes of these operating units on a pro rata basis according to the ratios of the number of employees, total assets in use, and total sales of subsidiaries to comparable figures of foreign firms' total operation. For example, if a subsidiary in California happens to employ 10 percent of the total employees of its parent-subsidiary's worldwide system, the state tax authority maintains that it is entitled to tax 10 percent of the reported income of the parent's consolidated performance.

Arm's Length Price: Multinational firms are suspected, wrongly or rightly, of evading taxes by home and host governments. These governments suspect that multinational firms avoid and evade taxes by: (1) treating dividends from their subsidiaries as loan repayments, technical fees, or interest payments to increase deductible expenses and obtain lower rates of withholding taxes; (2) not reporting salaries and wages paid by foreign subsidiaries; and (3) manipulating transfer prices charged to goods and services by the parent firm. The latter is the most common avoidance technique.

Accordingly, more and more countries—most notably the United States—are enforcing the rule of "independent price" or "arm's length price" as a rule of thumb to check transfer pricing arrangements between foreign subsidiaries and their parent firms. The independent price is the price that parent firms charge nonrelated firms for similar goods and services. The arm's length price is to be negotiated between parents and subsidiaries with reference to the independent market price, where applicable.

A celebrated study done by the Andean Group's Commission early in the 1970s showed that American pharmaceutical firms were exporting their fine chemical ingredients to their subsidiaries in the Andean Group member nations—e.g., Ecuador, Peru, Colombia, and Bolivia. These invoices always carried complex code names and high unit values. The chemists of the Andean Group Commission discovered that simple chemical ingredients such as salt and ordinary inorganic chemicals were being shipped by the American parents under complicated code names for three to seven times their market price.

Another example of foreign parent firms' manipulation of transfer prices involves the Ford Motor Company, which used to ship its complete knock-down parts of passenger cars to its Mexican subsidiary, at first on a full cost plus ordinary markup basis. Every time some parts were deleted from the shipping kit, only the variable cost of the deleted parts was deducted from the total shipment. In theory, according to this formula, Ford Motor Company would have recovered at least the fixed cost of the passenger car merely by shipping empty crates.

These particular abuses are now history, but similar ones could still occur. Therefore, in order to avoid political risks arising from tax disputes over the transfer pricing formula, parent firms and subsidiaries should keep independent pricing practices. Such arm's length business relationships should be spelled out in the contract between parent and subsidiary.

A SELECTED REFERENCE

Exposure and Transfer Pricing

Barrett, E.M. "Case of the Tangled Transfer Price." *Harvard Business Review* (May-June 1977).

Jones, C.S. "Transfer Pricing and Its Misuse: Some Further Considerations." *European Journal of Marketing* 15, no. 7 (1981).

Solomons, D. *Divisional Performance: Measurement and Control*, ch. 6. New York: Financial Executive Research Foundation, 1965.

A standard textbook exposition of intrafirm pricing considerations in the context of U.S. domestic firms.

Teck, A. "Control Your Exposure to Foreign Exchange." *Harvard Business Review* (January-February 1974).

Management Control of Headquarters-Subsidiary Relations

Alpander, G. "Multinational Corporations: Homebase-Affiliate Relations." *California Management Review* 20 (Spring 1978).

Brandt, W., and J.M. Hulbert. "Headquarters Guidance in Marketing Strategy in the Multinational Subsidiary." *Columbia Journal of World Business* (Winter 1977).

Doz, Y.L., and C.K. Prahalad. "Headquarters Influence and Strategic Control in MNCs." *Sloan Management Review* (Fall 1981).

Duerr, M.G., and J.M. Roach. "Organization and Control in European Multinational Corporations." In *Organization and Control of International Operations*. New York: The Conference Board, 1978.

Fischer, W., and J.N. Behrman. "The Coordination of Foreign R&D Activities by Transnational Corporations." *Journal of International Business Studies* (Winter 1979).

Robbins, S., and R. Stobaugh. *Money in the Multinational Enterprise*. New York: Basic Books, 1973.

A changing role of the financial control of MNC's headquarters.

Shetty, Y.K. "Managing the MNC: European and American Styles." *Management International Review* 19, no. 3 (1979).

CASE 4:
CHESEBROUGH-POND'S URUGUAY

In early August 1968, the Western Hemisphere Area Controller of Chesebrough-Pond's Incorporated was reviewing the operations of the firm's Uruguayan branch. Although this review was a routine evaluation of long-term prospects to which every Chesebrough-Pond's foreign manufacturing operation was periodically subjected, this was one of the very few times when the alternative of recommending that the company pull out of a country had seriously presented itself to him. Chesebrough-Pond's had never previously sold or phased out one of its foreign operations. It was company policy to stay in a market for the long run where at all practicable. Nevertheless, he knew that two other U.S. firms had recently closed down their sales operations in Uruguay, a country that had experienced a 135 percent inflation during 1967 and seemed doomed to endless devaluations. Moreover, Chesebrough-Pond's itself had recorded a $152,000 exchange loss on its Uruguayan operations in 1967, a result of the entries associated with the devaluation of the peso by 50 percent. Yet another loss of $22,000 was recorded when the peso was again devalued in April 1968.

On top of this, the controller had received news from Uruguay to the effect that all transfers of funds outside the country thenceforth would require the approval of the Central Bank and that wages and prices could not be increased over the level as of June 26, 1968. According to Chesebrough's Uruguayan management, the price freeze was being enforced. On the other hand, social unrest might force the government to rescind or modify the wage freeze.

The telegram informing Chesebrough's controller of these developments had arrived on July 5, 1968, four days after the revised 1968 budget for the branch. It noted that the government measures had rendered the budget obsolete. It did not state when a revised budget based on new assumptions might be available, nor did it speculate on what might happen to costs, margins, or sales volume as a result.

Chesebrough-Pond's Incorporated

Chesebrough-Pond's Incorporated is a large multinational manufacturer and marketer of cosmetics, toiletries, and hospital products, with headquarters in New York. In 1968, it had plants in sixteen countries and sales branches or subsidiaries in sixteen others around the world. Consolidated corporate sales in 1967 were $165,725,000, of which 39 percent were foreign sales. Reported after-tax earnings in 1967 were $14,783,000, of which $5,000,000 came from abroad. These figures represent a 5.4 percent increase in sales and a 17.8 percent increase in earnings over 1966. Stockholders' equity and total assets in 1967 equaled $71,117,000 and $109,587,000 respectively. Foreign sales were accounting for roughly 40 percent of total sales. Both of the company's last two presidents had had extensive international experience.

The company has placed great emphasis on marketing. Advertising, selling, and administrative expenses came to 45 percent of net sales in 1967. This pattern of expenditure was fairly consistent the world over.

The company's domestic product line could be classified into the four product groups, each of which was represented by a domestic product division. These groups were, first, the Cosmetics Division, which handled Pond's creams, Cutex lipstick and nail polish, and Angel Face powders and creams; second, the Proprietaries and Special Toiletries Division, which manufactured and sold Vaseline, Q-tips, men's hair grooming products, and Pertussin cold products; third, the Prince Matchebelli Division, which handled fragrances and eye makeup; and, finally, the Hospital Products Division, which manufactured and marketed surgical dressings and thermometers.

Chesebrough-Pond's international product line consisted almost exclusively of the items handled domestically by the Cosmetics and the Proprietaries and Special Toiletries Divisions. Responsibility for foreign operations and U.S. exports were centered in an International Division which in turn divided general management responsibility among regional vice-presidents for Europe, for Latin America and Canada, for the Far East and Pacific, for the United Kingdom and West Africa, and for South Africa and central Africa. Chesebrough-Pond's management believed that it sold more cosmetics abroad than any other U.S. firm.

The individual country branches and subsidiaries within each regional general management center were run as investment centers. "Return on assets employed," based on local currency calculations, were used as the primary basis for evaluating subsidiary managers. All of the company's eighteen manufacturing subsidiaries were wholly owned. Almost all of the country general managers were nationals of the country of operations. Subsidiary managers were given great latitude in local product introduction, purchase of machinery, hiring, setting and revising of standard costs, pricing, and drawing up budgets. Control was exercised through yearly local currency budgets prepared in October of each year for the following calendar year and revised in August of that year. The budget was prepared by the controller's staff in the foreign subsidiaries and branches and was reviewed in New York. No international or regional planning offices had been set up.

Operations in Inflationary Environments

Chesebrough-Pond's has conducted manufacturing operations in countries undergoing rapid inflation ever since the Pond's Extract Company, one of the firm's predecessors, started producing in a leased plant in Argentina in 1939. Chesebrough-Pond's had to cope from time to time with inflationary situations in Europe after World War II. Its plants in the Brazilian and Uruguayan markets, established in the late 1950s, provided additional experience with inflationary conditions.

Although Chesebrough-Pond's management had occasionally felt qualms about committing additional dollar funds to operations in Argentina and Brazil, the management felt that, by and large, dollar profits had been adequate despite devaluation losses and political risk. The Uruguayan branch, on the other hand, was sometimes spoken of as being a "dead loss." Of the $540,000 that Chesebrough-Pond's had recorded as a loss on foreign exchange in 1967, $152,000 was due to devaluations in Uruguay. The remainder was due to the larger Brazilian and Argentinian operations. The devaluation of the pound sterling in that year had been fully hedged.

Among the special accounting and control procedures that the company has adopted for operating in such environments was the use of a monthly average cost figure for charging inventory into costs of goods sold, the quarterly or even monthly revision of standard costs, and the use of the "current assets" method for translating balance sheets from local currencies to dollars. By this method of translation, current assets and liabilities in local currency terms were translated by dollar exchange rates prevailing at the time of translation, while long-term assets and liabilities were translated by dollar exchange rates prevailing at the time of their acquisition, that is, by "historical rates." In the budgeting process, a "best guess" estimate of the likely rate of inflation was incorporated by the local country manager in the budget prepared by his staff.

Chesebrough-Pond's Uruguay

Chesebrough-Pond's activities in Uruguay consisted of both manufacturing and sales and were conducted through a branch of the parent corporation. Pond's had marketed certain of its products in the Uruguayan market from the late 1940s; in 1959 manufacturing operations were begun in a leased plant in Montevideo. The original dollar investment in 1959 was $25,000. Subsequent investments—made primarily for working capital—had been financed from retained peso earnings; indeed, until 1967, the branch was entirely free of local debt. As can be seen from Exhibit 4, which presents the branch's December 1967 and June 1968 balance sheets, the parent company's investment in Uruguay was carried at $133,786 on the latter date. Despite continuous rapid sales growth between 1959 and 1966, unit sales volume declined in 1967.

The products produced and marketed in Uruguay included the following: Pond's cold cream, vanishing cream and dry skin cream; Angel Face powder and face cream; Cutex nail polish and lipstick; Odorono deodorants; and Lord Cheseline Hair Fixer.

Most of the raw materials used in making these products were purchased locally from indigenous manufacturers; the cost of materials generally amounted to less than 25 percent of the cost of goods sold. Packaging materials also were largely local though 10 percent of the cases in which creams and lipsticks were sold were imported from the United States. Some packaging materials were also imported from Chesebrough-Pond's Argentine plant. All told, packaging materials represented another 40 percent of cost of goods sold.

The Uruguayan branch faced scarcely any competition from local or international firms. Cosmetics in Uruguay were distributed to the public primarily through small pharmacies and supermarkets.

Until the wage and price freeze of 1968, the Uruguayan branch had always been able to adjust prices without having to submit any documentation to the government. After the devaluation of November 6, 1967, the government fixed maximum prices for goods such as cornmeal, rice, detergents, various construction materials, paper, and pharmaceuticals, though cosmetics prices were not affected at that time.

Despite the freedom to raise prices, other problems had arisen from the inflationary situation which had made it hard for the Uruguayan branch to hold its head above water. Whereas the Brazilian and Argentinian operations had been able to borrow locally, the Uruguayan branch had found local borrowing virtually impossible. Interest rates had been running upwards of 48 percent per year. And, even at those rates, loans were exceedingly difficult to obtain. Chesebrough-Pond's relationships with more than ten different banks had not solved the problem. Second, although Argentina had facilities for undertaking 180-day renewable swaps of dollars for local currency at rates of around 7 to 8 percent per year, and although Brazil had similar facilities for much of the time, no such facilities were available in Uruguay. Third, customers had been taking more and more time to pay their bills as the inflation went on.

Other problems also affected operating in the inflationary environment of Uruguay. Prior to the wage freeze, it had been Chesebrough-Pond's practice to increase all wages and salaries every three months by the amount of increase in the Finance Ministry's Cost-of-Living Index. Personnel Department officials noted that Chesebrough-Pond's was one of the very few companies that granted such across-the-board quarterly increases; most companies granted increases only on a semiannual or even annual basis. This policy was credited with the peaceful relations that existed between the company and its unions.

Apart from wage increases, there had been sudden increases, particularly extraordinary post devaluation increases, in raw material and packaging prices. Producers did not inform Chesebrough-Pond's management when they were about to raise prices. The sudden changes in the government's import control policies were of even more concern to management. To hedge against these uncertainties, Chesebrough-Pond's carried more than a year's inventory. Moreover, inventory was continually increased during 1967 and 1968. (This can be seen from Exhibit 4.)

Because of the difficulty of borrowing and the constant need for additional working capital, Chesebrough-Pond's has brought back virtually none of its Uruguayan earnings to the United States.

Exhibit 10-1.   Uruguay: Cost of Living Index (August 1962 = 100).

	1965	1966	1967	1968
January	205.4	385.2	588.8	—
February	—	—	—	—
March	222.2	404.4	689.1	1,707.0
April	227.3	423.3	706.1	—
May	—	—	—	—
June	248.9	463.2	762.2	2,123.0
July	—	—	—	—
August	273.0	481.0	941.0	—
September	296.1	493.7	1,023.8	—
October	308.3	509.7	1,076.9	—
November	—	—	—	—
December	373.8	558.3	1,317.0	—

Uruguay's Official Selling Rate for Foreign Exchange, Dollars per Peso

	1965	1966	1967	1968
January	—	—	— .013	0.005
February	—	—	—	0.005
March	0.042	0.017	0.012	0.005
April	—	—	—	0.004
May	—	—	—	0.004
June	0.042	0.015	0.011	0.004
July	—	—	0.011	—
August	—	—	0.010	—
September	0.042	0.015	0.010	—
October	—	—	0.010	—
November	—	—	0.005	—
December	0.017	0.013	0.005	—

Sources: Bank of London and South America, *Review*, various issues; IMF, *International Financial Statistics*, various issues.

Exhibit 10-2. Chesebrough-Pond's Income Statement, Uruguay Branch, in Local Currency.

| | Budgeted Six Months Ending June 1968 | | Six Months Ending June | | | | Year Ending December | | | |
| | | | 1968 | | 1967 | | 1967 | | 1966 | |
	mills. pesos	%	mills. pesos	%	mills. pesos	%	mills. pesos	%	mills. pesos	%
Net sales	32.1	100.0	31.9	100.0	16.8	100.0	42.7	100.0	30.3	100.0
Cost of goods sold	11.0	34.2	9.2	28.7	5.8	34.6	13.7	33.6	9.2	30.4
Gross profit	21.1	65.8	22.8	71.3	11.0	65.4	29.0	66.4	21.1	69.6
Advertising and selling	9.2	28.6	7.8	24.5	3.4	20.1	11.3	25.9	9.0	29.5
General and administrative expenses	6.4	19.7	7.6	23.9	3.3	19.5	9.2a	21.5	4.8a	15.8
Total expenses	15.5	48.3	15.5	48.4	6.6	39.5	20.5	47.4	13.8	45.3
Operating profit	5.6	17.5	7.3	22.9	4.3	25.8	8.5	19.0	7.3	24.3
Other income	0.5	1.7	0.4	1.3	b	2.0	0.7	1.8	0.9	2.8
Other expenses										
Exchange loss	b	0.1	0.7	2.1	b	0.3	0.7	1.6	6.0	19.7
Interest	2.8	8.8	0.7	2.2	b	0.3	0.5	1.2	b	0.1
Profit before income tax	3.3	10.3	6.4	19.9	4.6	27.2	8.0	18.9	2.1	6.9
Provision for income tax	0.6	1.8	1.3	4.0	1.2	7.5	0.7	1.7	0.8	2.5
Net income	2.7	8.5	5.1	15.9	3.3	19.7	7.3	17.2	1.3	4.2

a. Includes "Home Office Expenses," 2.8 million in 1967, and 1.3 million in 1966.
b. Less than 500 pesos.

Exhibit 10-3. Chesebrough-Pond's Income Statement, Uruguay Branch, in Dollars.

	1967		1966		1965	
	(thousands of dollars)					
	$	%	$	%	$	%
Net sales	399	100.0	428	100.0	190	100.0
Cost of goods sold	134	33.6	130	30.4	67	35.3
Gross profit	265	66.4	298	69.6	123	64.7
Advertising and selling	105		125		52	27.2
General and administrative expenses	84[a]		69[a]		33[a]	17.5
Total expenses	189	47.4	194	45.3	85	44.7
Operating profit	76	19.0	104	24.3	38	20.0
Other income	7	1.8	12	2.8	2	1.1
Other expenses						
Exchange loss	152	38.1	14	3.3	53	27.9
Interest	4	1.0	—	—	—	—
Profit before income tax	(73)	(18.3)	102	23.8	(13)	(6.8)
Provision for income tax	(4)	(1.0)	15	3.5	15	7.9
Net income	(69)	(17.3)	87	20.3	(28)	(14.7)

a. Included "Home Office Expenses," $24 thousand in 1967, $20 thousand in 1966, and $11 thousand in 1965.

Exhibit 10–4. Chesebrough-Pond's Balance Sheet, Uruguay Branch Balance Sheets.

	June 1968		December 1967		June 1967
	Pesos (thousands)	Dollars	Pesos (thousands)	Dollars	Pesos (thousands)
Assets					
Cash	4,419	17,677	2,415	12,076	1,612
Accounts receivable: Trade	20,954	83,815	14,735	73,675	10,696
Other	4,180	16,718	1,343	6,716	421
Inventories:					
Raw materials	9,807	39,229	5,972	29,860	—
Packaging	10,744	42,977	8,221	41,107	—
Work in process	323	1,291	321	1,605	—
Finished goods	2,450	9,799	1,972	9,861	—
Total	23,324	93,296	16,487	82,434	14,240
Prepaid expenses	1,075	4,299	—	—	—
Total current assets	53,952	215,778	34,979	174,901	27,954
Fixed assets	1,246	56,547	1,106	55,989	1,021
Less depreciation	479	34,980	416	32,597	351
Net fixed assets	766	21,567	690	23,392	670
Other noncurrent	19	76	114	569	499
Deferred expenses	—	—	1,121	5,604	—
Total	54,737	237,421	36,905	204,466	29,123

Liabilities

Notes payable	3,418	13,672	2,540	12,700	1,185
Accounts payable: Trade	11,990	47,960	7,593	37,800	4,944
Current intercompany	6,259	[Incl. Interco.]	3,215	[Incl. Interco.]	1,822
	[Incl. Interco.]				
Accrued expenses	1,369	5,476	473	2,366	749
Accrued taxes, misc.	6,733	26,932	2,967	14,836	1,425
Accrued income taxes	2,069	8,275	1,400	7,000	—
Total current liabilities	31,838	102,315	18,188	74,702	12,021
Reserve for deferred comp.	196	784	—	—	674
Capital	6,527	—	6,527	—	6,527
Retained earnings	11,075	—	{12,189}	—	4,906
Current profit	5,101	—		(63,706)	3,314
Total net worth	22,703	536	18,716	10,996	14,747
Total liabilities	54,737	103,635	36,905	193,470	27,442
Balancing item		133,786			
		237,421		204,466	

STUDY GUIDE QUESTIONS

1. Is the Uruguay branch manager performing well? Is the Uruguay operation a dead loss to Chesebrough-Pond's?

2. Will Chesebrough-Pond's competitors move into Uruguay if the firm leaves the country?

3. Why do you think the controller of Chesebrough-Pond's singled out the firm's Uruguay operation? Other subsidiaries in Latin America have also run up a translation loss. Is the controller trying to use the Uruguay situation to draw the corporate attention to something else?

4. What should Chesebrough-Pond's do with its Uruguay branch?

11 COMPARISONS OF AMERICAN AND JAPANESE CORPORATE CULTURE

As one American firm after another sought a quick fix for its declining competitive strength against Japanese firms inside and outside the United States, there arose a stampeding movement to "Learn from Japanese Management" in 1981 in the United States. Just as terminal cancer patients are often driven to try any esoteric and superstitious remedy even against their rational judgment, many American businesspeople rushed to nearby bookstores to snap up cut-and-paste quickies on "Japanese management" put out by unscrupulous, fly-by-night specialists on the topic. Management seminars featuring these specialists flourished for a while.

By the fall of 1982, there arose a predictable backlash against the Japanese management boom in the United States. Many American managers tried some quick-fix prescriptions offered in commercially successful but academically questionable books and vented their resentment about the treatment failures on anything Japanese. At the same time, the rising trade deficit of the United States with Japan amid the rising unemployment throughout the United States swung American emotions around to blame Japan for all the evils and problems of the American economy. The popular theories of "Japanese conspiracy" and "unfair competition" gained instant acceptance among American business managers threatened by the Japanese competition. Fortunately, however, there also remained in the United States management scholars and practicing business managers who became seriously interested in sorting out the myths from the realities in the "Japanese lessons for the American corporation" saga.

1. A CLOSER LOOK AT JAPAN'S "LIFETIME" EMPLOYMENT SYSTEM

Of all the facile generalizations about the Japanese system of industrial management, none is more erroneous than the superficial characterization of it as being traditional rather than quite modern and contemporary. Many elements of Japan's current management system are of a distinctly post–World War II vintage. In the American quest for the secret of Japan's success, no other aspect of this system has been so misunderstood as the Japanese system of lifetime employment.

Lifetime employment is, in itself, a great misnomer. For those employees who do not attain the rank of corporate officers, that "lifetime" merely refers to the span of time leading up to the age of mandatory retirement—about fifty-seven or, at best, sixty. Lifetime employment is not a legal contract, it is more like a psychological contract between the company and its members to mitigate as much as possible the difference in social and economic status between management and the rank and file.

Everyone, from the president to the lowest rank of factory worker, is paid according to the monthly salary system. The "egalitarian ratio" of the lowest salary paid to the highest salary paid within a Japanese firm is around 1 to 15. Even a ratio between 1 to 8 and 1 to 10 is not uncommon. A comparable ratio in the United States would be between 1 to 50 and 1 to 70 and can often exceed 1 to 100. This usually means that a manager is not able to dangle the threat— implicit or otherwise—of firing his subordinates as a device for controlling their behavior. It also means that a Japanese manager is much less likely to shift the blame for his own managerial errors, such as misreading market trends or giving approval to shoddy workmanship in new products, to his rank and file employees by laying them off when the impact of those mistakes is felt by the company. Further, it means that when a firm encounters economic hard times, the economic sacrifices are to be borne from the top down through, first of all, cuts in executive salaries, bonuses, perquisites, and even corporate dividends. This pecking order of sacrifice is accepted by the labor unions and by the employees, who, during severe economic crunches, are asked to cooperate with management by agreeing to wage cuts and even layoffs of nonmanagement employees.

A psychological contract of this kind is common in most Japanese firms, large or small. This is why the unemployment rate in Japan doesn't change markedly even during periods of economic downturn. A Japanese firm's way of cushioning the effects of economic decline is to maintain steady employment while making downward adjustments of various other forms of income payments (the opposite of the American way).

In a hierarchical society such as Japan, the large and powerful companies often soften the effects of an economic downturn by asking their small and medium-sized suppliers to trim prices and by cutting back the wages or hours on the job (often both) of their temporary and part-time workers and individual sub-subcontractors. Female workers constitute the majority of such part time workers. Postretirees make up the bulk of the temporary workers, who often hold unskilled manual labor positions, even in the plants of the larger firms.

Remember, the mandatory retirement age in most Japanese companies is around fifty-seven. The average life expectancy in Japan today is about seventy-eight for men and eighty for women. Social Security and company pensions (or lump-sum superannuation allowances) are often too meager to permit retirees to sustain their postretirement life without some additional source of income. What is more, the traditional ways of the Japanese family, by which the sons and daughters felt obliged to care for their aging parents, are gradually breaking down.

On the whole, though, the psychological promise of "lifetime" employment—which is of a distinctly post–World War II vintage—has served to minimize the resistance of ordinary workers to automation and other changes that took place in their jobs. A strong case can be made for the contention that the relative job security of the Japanese worker ultimately was recognized as a key element in Japan's industrial productivity and technological growth. It is a corporate culture that encourages informal but effective interdepartmental communication that has made it possible for Japanese firms to pursue a strategy of maximizing their global market shares. This kind of "interface" helps to motivate both management and ordinary employees to take an interest in the long-term survival of "their own" firm and to stay alert for dynamic changes in its marketing and technological environment.

In the United States, what is often achieved informally within a Japanese firm may have been tied to a formal arrangement such as the employee stock ownership plan (ESOP). According to the results of a study published in the Spring 1981 issue of *The Journal of Cor-*

poration Law (University of Iowa Law School), firms offering ESOP achieved noticeably higher productivity and stronger economic performance than comparable firms without ESOP. Recently, Bethlehem Steel, U.S. Steel, Firestone, Intel, National Semiconductor, and Caterpillar have all instituted practices akin to the Japanese way of absorbing economic shocks by reducing the salaries of executives and managers or by cutting back across the board on work hours rather than trimming their work force.

2. A GENERAL (UNIVERSAL) THEORY OF JAPANESE MANAGEMENT SYSTEM

From 1981 to 1983, as the economic depression deepened in the United States, there appeared manufacturing firms, airlines, and retail stores that successfully sought from their labor unions important changes in the time-honored work and seniority rules harmful to their productivity growth. More often than not, these changes were obtained in exchange for the management's de facto commitment to the job security of the rank and file union members. The moment American managers abandoned their propensity to disavow management's responsibility for protecting the job security of the rank and file, they found that the adverse relationships between management and employees often gave way to cooperative ones.

(1) Two Models of Corporate Organization

Let us call one model of corporate organization Model A and the other Model J. A priori, it is impossible to determine which model is superior and more efficient for effecting a given task. The only difference between the two models lies in the manner in which they accomplish their corporate goals.

Model A. Such strategic decisionmaking as choosing a firm's growth goals and new investments or performing long-range planning is the prerogative of very high echelon executives (executive functions). At this level, executives are encouraged to think approximately ten years ahead of their firm's present activities. This expected time horizon as a principal guide for the day-to-day execution of assigned tasks tapers off rapidly as we descend the levels of the firm's hierarchical organization. At the lowest level of the hierarchy— the rank and file level—a one-day or even half-day time horizon would be sufficient for performing a given assignment.

The Model A believes that according to its need, there are few idiosyncratic skills unique to the firm. This firm takes the expression "hired hands" quite literally. Any particular skill required to accomplish given tasks within the firm can be easily added to the general skill that each employee has already developed outside the firm, through his or her general and vocational schooling or prior job experience. Such procurement of necessary skills from outside markets influences the promotion and selection of people even for the highest rung of the corporate ladder.

Once the long-range strategic goals are determined by executives in the highest echelon, the implementation of these goals is subcontracted to the next level which includes operational units such as production divisions; functional units such as marketing, manufacturing, and R&D; or general administration units, including fiance and accounting. In turn, these subunits are assigned explicit performance goals (objectives) in terms of such quantifiable variables as profit targets, costs, production units, financial costs, and an assortment of indices designed to measure performance. Even human factors, such as employee job dissatisfaction or manager leadership, are measured by such indices as employee turnover ratios, absenteeism, and overtime hours logged.

The Model A corporation patterns the intrafirm relationships of its operational subunits as much as possible after the theoretical model of the competitive market mechanism. According to this mechanism, the market price becomes the signal to which all the actors in the market readjust their goals and performance. The actors' performance will be judged, after the fact, by the bottom line profit and loss. A Model A corporation relies, therefore, on the administered price mechanism, called the transfer price, for disciplining and rewarding the behavior and performance of its various subunits. A Model A corporation believes that individual managers and employees are motivated, in the main, to satisfy their economic needs by selling their job oriented skills to the highest bidder inside their firm. This assumption of homo economicus is the guiding principle in the designing of explicit performance measurements and in the resulting reward and punishment systems for managers and rank and file employees.

Model J. Strategic decisionmaking is considered the collective responsibility of the middle echelon management and above. Even rank and file employees and newly recruited college graduates are encouraged to take an active interest in the long-range goals of their firm. Accordingly, in the most successful examples of Model J corporations, the expected time horizons, which act as each member's principal performance guide for assigned tasks, from the top rung to the lowest rank and file, do not taper off as we descend in the hierachy.

The Model J firm believes that both managers and employees must acquire the skills unique to that firm in order to accomplish their assigned tasks. This firm hires the whole human being not merely a pair of hands. Through on-the-job training that often emphasizes job rotation to various divisions, not only requisite and idiosyncratic skills but also specific corporate ideology and culture are inculcated in the company's workers. Where possible, the company recruits college and high school graduates and trains them internally. Rarely does a Model J firm hire middle to higher echelon managers or specialists in mid-career from the outside. All necessary skills are developed, replenished, and accumulated within the firm, through the continuous training and acculturation of its employees.

The Model J corporation encourages even those young employees fresh out of school to develop strategic projects for the firm. Certainly, the long-range goals of the firm must be the concern of middle echelon and higher ranking managers. But even when certain strategic projects are developed by the highest level managers, the plans would not be made final until the middle to lower echelon managers have had the opportunity to refine and often revise them to fit their own execution of such plans. Since extensive consultation between implementors scattered throughout the subunits of the firm takes place before any strategic decision is made final, the division of tasks among various subunits of the firm is well understood by corporate members. This implicit understanding among the corporate members of each individual's task and of the relationships of this task to other jobs replaces the explicit performance goals that the Model A corporation uses for its subunits involved in strategy implementation.

The Model J corporation relies on shared goals and shared responsibilities among its members in the development and implementation of strategic decisions. It believes that its individual members are motivated to obtain psychological as well as economic satisfaction from contributing to the overall well-being of their corporation. Since all the members of a firm are expected to make contributions to the company's shared goals, their rewards at any given time are difficult to tie too closely to any specific role played by a single corporate member. Both economic and noneconomic rewards are likely, therefore, to be distributed among the corporate workers by criteria other than job performance—e.g., gender, age, seniority, family needs, and educational background.

The Model A company believes that special skills embodied in managers and employees can be procured from outside markets. The explicit rules and manuals that codify an individual's job tasks are written so as to permit newly recruited strangers to perform at least 70 percent of their maximum efficiency from their first day on the job. If the newcomers do not meet the grade, they are replaced by other recruits.

On the other hand, the implicit rules and modus operandi of a Model J firm rarely enable new recruits to perform even at 20 percent of their top efficiency. Their inefficiency results from not knowing the implicit rules influencing the give and take of personal relationships inside the firm. New recruits have to earn their way into the organization. They have to live in the organization for a long time to learn the implicit and idiosyncratic interdependency among various tasks and subunits.

As stated at the outset of this chapter, there is no telling a priori, which model is superior for performing a given task. Each can be equally efficient by merely applying different approaches. The situation in which frequent conflicts of interest arise between marketing and manufacturing departments can be used as an example. The marketing managers and their sales force wants as many varieties of products as possible to be sufficiently stocked so as to meet random requests from their customers. On the other hand, the manufacturing managers and their plant workers would like to produce a minimal variety of products so as to exploit the economy of scale of a long production run (a large lot size for a given production run). The latter think the customer should wait until production is completed and also note the critical economic tradeoffs that arise concerning quality, delivery, and price of product.

The solution to the above problem in a Model A corporation would be to place both marketing and manufacturing managers on the same group bonus incentive plan, which forces horizontal interaction and the discovery of suitable tradeoffs concerning product quality, delivery, and price of product. A Model J corporation, on the other hand, would solve this problem by developing a corporate culture that disciplines both marketing and manufacturing managers to share the responsibilities and goals of their firm.

(2) Corporate Cultures of Model A and Model J

As can be deduced from the preceding accounts of the two corporate organization models, Models A and J are principally distinguished from each other by the respective corporate cultures (atmosphere) that permeate their corporate hierarchy. In contrast to their Model A firm counterparts, even the rank and file employees of a Model J firm are very much aware of their organization's long-range goals. They are encouraged to participate actively in the performance of their company and, most notably, to contribute to its growth and potential. In order to nurture the corporate members' long-term orientation, which in turn fosters a strong personal identification with the company, the Model J corporation expends great effort and expense to keep even its rank and file employees informed of the firm's growth goals and of its new achievements in R&D, marketing, and manufacturing.

In order to compare corporate organizations in the United States and Japan, we should first identify some of the major contrasts between the types of organizations found in these two countries. In general, we can make the following observations about American and Japanese firms.

Key Characteristics	Japanese Firms	American Firms
1. Business orientation	Global: toward long-term growth	Domestic: toward short-term growth
2. Business target	Market share at home and abroad	Quarterly profit
3. Management attitude toward job security of rank and file employees	Seen as efficient means to ensure employees' long-term commitment to growth and technological innovation	Considered inefficient and an obstacle to growth
4. Staffing of executive positions	Promotion from within	Hiring from outside
5. Internal control of organization	Through implicit rules and shared goals among managers and employees	Through explicit rules and management by objective

Purely theoretical models of Japanese and American corporations are best illustrated in Figure 11-1. The triangle in the middle of the figure denotes the ordinary hierarchy from top echelon down to the rank and file employees. The very highest echelon of management in both Japanese and American firms is expected to maintain the broadest commitment to the firm's long-range goals. In most American firms, the lower the individual's position is in the hierarchy of the firm, the more markedly his commitment to the goals of the firm

Figure 11-1. Japanese and American Corporate Structure.

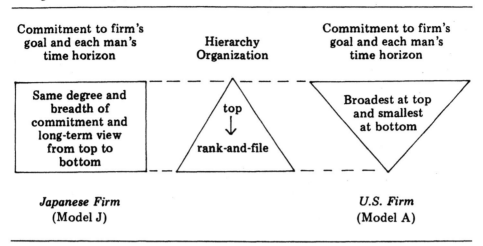

Commitment to firm's goal and each man's time horizon	Hierarchy Organization	Commitment to firm's goal and each man's time horizon
Same degree and breadth of commitment and long-term view from top to bottom	top ↓ rank-and-file	Broadest at top and smallest at bottom
Japanese Firm (Model J)		*U.S. Firm* (Model A)

Source: *The Japanese Are Coming*: A Multinational Interaction of Firms and Politics (Cambridge, Mass.: Ballinger Publishing Company, 1976), ch. 9.

tapers off. In most Japanese firms, even employees at the lowest level are encouraged to maintain a long-term interest in their firm's future.

Implicitly, the job security of the Model J corporation members becomes the foundation of the long-term orientation of the firm's workers. Job security also serves to support cooperative rather than adverse relationships among various subunits of the firm or between management and rank and file members. The job security of Model J members often negates the need for cumbersome measures of arbitrating job grievances or policing individual member's behavior— measures potentially damaging to a firm. Mutual trust between management and employees and among individual members is thus not only a cost-saving device but also a source of organizational productivity.

The management's ideological commitment to job security of the rank and file employees keeps it alert to dynamic changes in the firm's business environment. Inasmuch as a manager's misjudgment concerning the market or the competition that produces a decline in sales and profits is not counterbalanced by expedient layoffs of rank and file employees, managers must always concern themselves with their organization's flexibility to cope with rapid shifts in the business environment.

Unlike the Model A type, the Model J firm practices internal promotion of its members. Managers and specialists trained by the Model J firm often leave the company and join other organizations.

285

Rarely, however, does the Model J firm bring outsiders into its higher echelons. This asymmetry of job mobility—from the Model J to, perhaps, the Model A firm, but not vice versa—may be caused by a Model A firm's active bidding for the human talents trained by a Model J organization. A Model J firm attempts to train new recruits rigorously for a breadth of job skills and experience. A long apprenticeship, characterized by person-to-person training, is often the rule for a Model J firm. Accordingly, when Model A and Model J firms coexist in the same industry or in the same country, Model J firms are found serving as de facto vocational training institutes for Model A firms.

For specific job assignments inside the Model J firm, the talented candidates with a breadth of requisite skills and experience are recruited and trained internally. An individual member's advancement to a higher position is often determined by his cumulative mastery of requisite job skills and experience. This kind of promotion practice, based on an individual's acquired job skills and experience, is a substitute for the kind of open-market recruiting practiced by a Model A firm at all levels of its hierarchy.

Model J company workers are likely to identify socially with their own firm members rather than with outsiders. This kind of institutional identification erases the social distance between the firm's management and the rank and file, and between its professionals, such as engineers and production workers. The Japanese manufacturing firms, characterized in large part as Model J corporate environments, often go so far as to require all company members, including the president, to wear the same kind of "worker uniform"—the only distinction being the name and job title printed on the uniform's tag.

When this kind of conscious invisibility of social distinction between professionals and the rank and file is carefully nurtured within a firm, corporate goals are easily shared by both groups. This permits professionals to mingle socially and professionally with technicians and production workers on the production floor. Indeed, the ubiquitous presence of engineers and their close interactions with production workers is common in many Japanese manufacturing plants. Professionals are on the floor and in the yard to help workers improve production process technologies and performance. This close interaction has been the driving force behind Japan's rapid increase in manufacturing productivity and her subsequent international triumph in mass production activities, such as shipbuilding, steelmaking, and the manufacture of electronics, household appliances, and automobiles.

The impact of the Model J firm on the manufacturing productivity of Japanese plants caught the interest of a British shipbuilding industry executive and, as early as the mid-1950s, he predicted Japan's rising threat to the British shipbuilding industry. After touring a few Japanese shipyards, he commented approving that in contrast to the British shipyards of comparable size, where too many engineers locked themselves up in their offices and spent all their time drawing sketches, the Japanese counterparts mingled freely with workers in the yard, working with them to improve production processes. He also said that the overall ratio of engineers to ordinary yard workers in Japan appeared to be about three times as large as that in Britain. In 1978, an American researcher, after making extensive field surveys to find the cause of the superior product reliability of Japanese color television sets and of the industry's superior manufacturing productivity, made a similar observation: "In a Japanese production plant, the ratio of engineers and technicians to ordinary workers is about four times as large as that of comparable American plants. These professionals freely interact with their fellow production workers in order to improve their production processes for more reliable products. . . . In a comparable television plant in the United States, one cannot see any engineers assigned to production work."

In a similar vein, Mr. Akio Morita, chairman of Sony Corporation, stated in 1978 that he had found it very difficult to assign good engineers to the production floors in Sony's San Diego plant because "American engineers seem resentful of being reduced to working on production floors and having to interact daily with non-professional production workers."

(3) Model J Corporations in Japan and Elsewhere

Conventional wisdom states that the lifetime employment system and the resulting job security are unique to Japanese corporations and that the Model J characteristics of Japanese firms are deeply ingrained in the Japanese culture. In reality, nothing is further from the truth.

Contrary to popular myth, the type of lifetime employment erroneously thought to be unique to Japanese firms did not emerge in Japan until after World War II. Nor was management's commitment to job security and the well-being of the rank and file practiced at the beginning of Japan's industrialization. Only after the 1920s, with the threats of unionization resulting from crude and harsh labor practices inside Japanese plants, did industrial leaders begin to advocate reviving the old and traditional values of one large family. This revival was their collective response to militant unionism, which they considered an alien ideology.

Furthermore, the increasing scarcity of skilled workers during World War II forced Japanese management to extend salaried status and job security to production workers. Wartime collaboration between management and rank and file workers inside the plants further contributed to the erasing of social distance between professionals and rank and file workers. The Japanese industrialists' subsequent adoption of job security for their employees was further enhanced, moreover, as they discovered that a seniority-based wage system helped retain skilled workers and trained professionals. Japanese management learned that the Model J's kind of implicit modus operandi was an economical means of helping corporate members work hard toward a shared goal of long-term growth for the firm.

That Japanese industrialists found many remnants of Japanese feudal values and their social legacies to be fertile ground for fostering a paternalistic and even clanish corporate atmosphere cannot be denied. Thus, the old values of superior-subordinate interpersonal relationships were successfully reawakened by Japanese managers, who wanted to design their corporate organizations relatively free of outside union influence.

Nevertheless, it cannot be emphasized too strongly that it was the corporate need for developing and retaining job-related skills unique to the firm, rather than the paternalistic benevolence of Japanese industrialists, that led Japanese firms to refine many of the Model J firm's attributes. The wartime experience of reducing social status between managers and rank and file workers, as well as the immediate postwar needs for rebuilding the Japanese economy, merely facilitated a widespread practice of Model J type management-employee relations. Unfortunately, both foreign and Japanese students of Japanese corporations were dazzled by the successful and yet idiosyncratic mechanisms of Japanese corporate organizations. They did not separate the universal factors, such as a corporation's need to develop and retain unique job skills, from the enduring old values of feudal Japan still to be found in the corporate atmosphere of many Model J type Japanese firms.

Less culture-bound requirements, such as a firm's need for developing and retaining specialized job skills, might be considered likely to produce a Model J kind of corporate organization. Accordingly, in Japan, interindustrial differences regarding job security accorded to rank and file employees can be explained as differences in the requisite skill content required even of rank and file production workers. For example, the construction industry provides the least job security to unskilled workers because their skills can be easily procured in quantity from the open markets.

Japanese management's ideological commitment to job security for rank and file employees became increasingly apparent as Japanese manufacturing industries upgraded their technological capabilities. Up until the 1930s, when Japanese industries were characterized by such low-skill-intensive products as spun cotton yarn and standard industrial products, high rates of interfirm job mobility among both skilled and unskilled production workers existed. In fact, plant managers made it a rule to raid other plants for necessary workers. Because the standard level of technology was adequate for plant operation, firms did not need to develop and retain unique production or institutional skills.

It might also be concluded that job security itself is hardly sufficient to produce the dynamism of a successful Model J type firm. When corporate members are mindful of outside threats to their communal entity and when job security of corporate members from the top down does not preclude intense but friendly competition and cooperation, the job security of lifetime employment will usually produce the best kind of dynamic, Model J type firm. Indeed, when job security is emphasized to the exclusion of the corporate members' dedication to surviving tough technological, market, and managerial competition, the Model J type firm always runs the risk of sinking into rigid and lethargic bureaucracy—like, for example, the stifling bureaucracies at all levels of government and in some university administrations.

Of late, recognition of the success of the Model J type corporate organization has increased in the United States. In addition to the good results obtained by adapting Japanese management practices to Japanese subsidiaries in the United States, such native American corporations as IBM, Lincoln Industries, Delta Airlines, Texas Instruments, Dow Chemical, Hewlett-Packard, and leading investment banks and commercial banks, to name but a few, are practicing many of the attributes of Model J management–employee relations. Furthermore, there are a number of successful Model J type organizations—ones relying more on an implicit understanding of shared goals and responsibilities among corporate members than on a rigging of the transfer pricing mechanism to extract desirable behavior from corporate members.

Like their Japanese counterparts, American Model J firms are characterized by a widely shared understanding among their corporate members of what is vitally important for the well-being of their organization. This mutual comprehension of the critically important criteria for an organization's survival produces a conditioned response from corporate members that is highly effective and predictable. For example, highly disciplined police forces in any city or country respond most readily to calls for "scrambles," all-out crisis situations endangering the lives of fellow police officers.

Similarly, loyal members of the Model J type of corporation share an understanding of what constitutes the critically important factors that determine success in a competitive business environment. This shared understanding helps corporate members put aside their differences and agree on the priorities of tasks. The shared values and goals of the corporate members guide their specific actions at any given moment. Referring to codified instruction details in manuals or to predetermined explicit rules and regulations is unnecessary.

Perhaps this reasoning was the cause for highly professional organizations, such as investment banking firms in the United States, to increasingly emphasize Model J kinds of group assignments and job rotation. Promotion of investment bankers is governed on the surface by their explicit performance. An investment banker only performs well, however, when he can obtain cooperation from fellow bankers working on different aspects of the same job for the same client. The job skills of investment bankers are difficult to codify since they can be learned only by doing.

Accordingly, a strong group norm consisting of on-the-job training (trainee-apprenticeship) and team work is fostered among professionals of the same firm. It is no accident that leading investment banks recruit new MBAs from a short list of leading graduate business schools, mainly on the basis of the recruit's personal fit to the existing staff. Having attended similar, if not the same, schools, recruits at least possess similar vocabularies, analytical paradigms, and even personal styles. All of these attributes facilitate their acceptance into the tightly knit social groups of high-powered professionals.

Large or small, the Model J type of corporation invariably emphasizes job rotation, in-house training, apprenticeship, and corresponding respect for seniority and job security of corporate members. Such idiosyncratic interpersonal skills and managerial know-how can only be imparted to corporate members through their long years of adaptation to a given firm's corporate culture.

In comparison to a Model A firm, the Model J company attaches significantly greater importance to the recruiting of its employees. Even for the recruitment of rank and file employees, a high level of management is likely to be involved. The intrafirm prestige and the influence of the personnel manager in a Model J firm are measurably higher than that of his Model A counterpart. In fact, it is often considered a vital part of a high-level executive's functions to get involved personally and deeply in the recruiting of new college graduates. In successful Japanese companies, it is very common for the president of a firm with over 3,000 employees to conduct personal interviews of college graduates and frequently even of high school graduates wishing to join the firm. Since human resource management is considered vital for the Model J firm, the position of personnel director is not only a prestigious assignment but is often considered a mainstream avenue to the top level of the corporate ladder.

3. DECISIONMAKING PROCESSES OF JAPANESE CORPORATIONS

(1) "Top-down" versus "Bottom-up"

Such oversimplifications as "bottom-up" and "consensus building" are often used by both Japanese and foreign observers of Japanese firms' decisionmaking processes. What is missed by such simplifications is the real "top-down" decisionmaking processes that are at work in parallel with the bottom-up processes. The top management is entrusted with setting and resetting the overall goals of the firm. Accordingly, under a crisis situation, the Japanese top management is expected to take charge and clearly direct the organization to the new recovery path of the corporate activity.

Even under a noncrisis situation, you would find many Japanese top management subtly planting ideas and suggestions among the key decision initiators in the middle to lower management echelon. In fact, the art of the top management is to nudge his or her subordinates toward the ideas that he himself entertained. At the same time, true to the Model J type of Japanese firm, the top management is required to keep an open mind to new suggestions, changes, and other ideas to be offered by subordinates involved in the implementation of the agreed on decisions. Unlike typical Model A types of American firms, Model J types of Japanese firms do not automatically require the top management to "tell" and the lower echelon to "listen." The listening skills are the most important prerequisites of Japanese corporate members from the top to the bottom.

The commitment of individual employees to the widely accepted goals of their firm has produced an often mentioned decisionmaking system in Japanese firms that is called *ringi seido.* Observers of this decisionmaking process will note that new proposals—marketing or investment decisions, for example—are often initiated at the lower or middle echelons of the firm. These proposals are passed along through the hierarchy, collecting seals of approval or undergoing minor revisions on their way up to the president. The initiators or collaborating parties of such proposals are busily engaged on an informal basis in pinpointing key personalities whose support is needed. Some proposals die on their journey to the top echelon, but those that do survive cannot be attributed solely to their initiator(s). By the time a proposal is accepted by top management, there will be a corporate consensus concerning its feasibility.

This process of building a consensus among the individuals who will be affected by a decision takes the decision out of the hands of any specific initiator or implementor. The decisionmaking process in Japan is inextricably intertwined with the later process of implementation. This explains why American managers often complain of the length of time it takes Japanese managers to reach decisions. It is inconceivable to Japanese managers that any decision could be made without consulting those individuals who are directly responsible for the internal workings of the organization. To list the specifics of such a procedure would be too time consuming to do here. Ultimately, when a decision is made and communicated to a third party such as a customer, that may be deemed tantamount to the commencement of its implementation.

Consensus building practices in the decisionmaking process of Japanese firms have created two characteristics that are distinctly Japanese: a substantive involvement of middle management (section chiefs up to department heads) in strategic decisionmaking, and the expectation that presidential leadership will confine itself to coping mainly with crisis situations or with abrupt, clear-cut changes in the direction of the firm. Once the firm's general direction is communicated to middle management, both operations decisions and incremental changes tend to be entrusted to the initiative of lower to middle management echelons.

In actual practice, the conceptual demarcation of the roles of upper and middle echelons in a Japanese firm is often blurred. In general, one may view the upper and middle echelon as a group that concerns itself with not only the day-to-day fine tuning of the company's accepted strategies but also with the search for new strategic moves. In this context, members of the middle management level of a Japanese corporation act as planning aides and advisors to upper echelon management as well as day-to-day supervisors in the implementation of agreed upon strategies. In turn, the upper echelon is expected to take an active interest in the details of middle management's activities while remaining one step removed from any actual involvement.

(2) Who Holds Power in Japanese Corporations?

As it is with their American counterparts, the influence of Japanese executives generally stems from their position in the company hierarchy. The only marked difference between Japanese and American corporate power structure lies in the influence of a Japanese executive vice-president in charge of personnel affairs and his office. In American corporations personnel managers are often treated as glorified file clerks who screen routine application forms and other personnel matters. In view of the Japanese firm's emphasis on human resources development, the personnel department works closely with the company's president and manages all aspects of human resources management. The position of personnel manager is often considered to be one of the most important positions in the company. This management skill is deemed one of the managerial skills vital to anyone desiring to reach the upper echelon of the corporation.

The other difference between Japanese and American corporations is the inability of managers to fire their subordinates. It is the collective entity known as the firm that hires all employees and decides on their fate. Individual managers assume responsibility for training their staffs, evaluating their personal performance, and acting as their personal counselors. They do not have any right, however, to fire their subordinates. They can only influence their promotion.

(3) Middle Management: Center
of Meaningful Influence

A deep-rooted feeling exists among Japanese employees and managers that the Japanese corporation belongs to all of its members. This accounts for the substantive influence and authority that is delegated, de facto, to middle management. At minimum, middle management is expected to initiate questioning when it is not convinced of the wisdom of a specific decision reached by the upper echelon.

In the case of American subsidiaries I have studied in Japan, this conception of the roles of middle management in relation to upper echelon authority has caused considerable conflict between Japanese employees and American managers. These employees, working for the long-term goals of their firm, tended to challenge actions on the part of their superiors that they might have deemed detrimental to the good of the firm. The Japanese employees expected explanations from their superiors with regard to how certain actions would benefit the firm over a longer period of time than that which American managers would care to consider. Most American managers took such requests to be personal affronts to their management prerogatives.

293

American managers, bred in American corporate culture, expected the Japanese middle management to follow their decisions. Little did they expect their subordinates to confront them with questions concerning their decisions.

In my studies of Japanese subsidiaries in the United States, American plant and sales managers have often been bewildered when they discovered that they were expected to resolve problems among themselves without bothering Japanese top executives. American managers would report on problems to the Japanese president of the firm and would offer suggested solutions. The Japanese president would politely suggest in turn that if American managers were able to identify the problem and knew the solution, they should have quietly gone ahead and solved it. Once American managers learned that de facto delegation of managerial authority was materially prevalent in the Japanese corporate environment and that this culture was far more tolerant of managerial mistakes than was the American culture, they began to enjoy a position of managerial authority that in their former American companies had belonged only to a higher level of management.

(4) Management "Soft" and "Ambiguous" Techniques

Both in Japan and the United States, Model J types of firms are dominantly found among the industries that are confronted with three distinct environments: (1) global competition, (2) growth, and (3) technological innovations. The survival of firms surrounded by such uncertain environments as these three situations is dependent upon the organizational flexibility offered by Model J types of corporate culture. Unlike Model A types of firms, Model J types of firms respond to competitive challenges more often by rebuilding the corporate human resources and their thinking rather than by declaring new strategies and overhauling corporate structures and personnel. The management control systems of Model J firms are lubricated by the "soft" and "ambiguous" realms of job responsibilities and assignments between different jobs and functions. By relying on the shared goals of the firm, everyone is encouraged to fill in the ambiguous areas of job responsibilities.

The ambiguity of job responsibilities is superimposed on the corporate culture that encourages and rewards the informal but effective lateral communications across different functions and jobs as well as vertical communication between superiors and subordinates. Under these circumstances, the ambiguity of job responsibilities permits every ambitious manager and employee to try to fill in the ambiguous area. It also permits anyone to withdraw from this area without losing face when the task turns out to be beyond his or her liking or capability. Thus, it leaves the most capable individuals to absorb the once ambiguous areas into their work domains.

The corporation rewards those individuals who continue to prove themselves by expanding their job domains through helping the people around them to attain the shared goals of their firm. This is why the international division structure of Japanese multinational firms remains stable as compared with their American counterparts. Unlike Model A types of American multinational firms, Model J types of Japanese multinational firms do not force their members to see their intrafirm competition for promotion and other rewards as the zero-sum game — one's gain being perceived as someone else's loss.

4. INTERNAL WORKING OF JAPAN'S WHITE COLLAR ORGANIZATION: A CASE OF *SOGOSHOSHA*

(1) Recruitment of *Sogoshosha* Professionals

As in the case of other organizations dominated by white collar professionals and clerical employees, a *sogoshosha* consists basically of two groups of recruits: many male college graduates and an equal number of female graduates of junior colleges or four-year universities. Whereas the latter group provides clerical and auxiliary services, the former group performs the core functions of the firm. The remaining part of this chapter will concentrate on the personnel management practices of recruiting and subsequent promotion of *sogoshosha*'s managerial candidates — the majority of whom are male college graduates.

As is the case in other growth-minded Japanese corporations, *sogoshosha* compete aggressively for the brightest and most vigorous graduates of the leading colleges and universities. Given the job security of the Model J type of firm which characterizes *sogoshosha*, this college recruiting market is the only free and competitive arena in which *sogoshosha* compete with other Japanese firms. On the basis of a college or university's general reputation and the past performance of graduates of certain universities or particular departments of universities, each *sogoshosha* draws up a short list of designated universities that will serve as a guide for recruiting efforts.

In addition to the two or three private universities, there are about a dozen designated universities or national (public) universities. These designated universities are noted for their severe competitive entrance examinations. Since national universities charge only nominal tuition, the financial capabilities of middle and higher income families, which supply the bulk of college-bound students, play a lesser role in determining who enters leading universities than they do in the United States.

By concentrating on designated universities, *sogoshosha* and other Japanese firms believe they are interviewing only the brightest and most diligent young people—those who have proven not only their intellectual tenacity but their goal-oriented dedication by passing tough university entrance examinations. Furthermore, the *sogoshosha* and other firms often prepare their own guides for interpreting the students' academic records and extracurricular activities. Some firms have developed a rule-of-thumb criterion by which a B grade given by such and such a professor at one university is translated into an A grade for other courses offered by other professors. These kinds of meticulous efforts are often expected of *sogoshosha*. The procedure of selecting their future managers and professionals resembles the detailed evaluation of large-capital projects by manufacturing firms. Inasmuch as recruiting firms realize that they are hiring human resources for a long time period, their recruiting of young college graduates becomes just as, if not more, serious as the key investment decisions regarding plant expansions, R&D projects, and new market development.

All the firms carefully note the student's grades in his or her first foreign language, English, and in his second or third foreign language studied at college (German, French, Chinese, and so on). Given the distinct international focus of Japanese firms, their attention to foreign language proficiency is understandable. These firms know, moreover, that a mastery of any foreign language requires not only intellectual diligence and self-discipline but also a cultural sensitivity to foreign ways of life. This self-discipline coupled with cultural sensitivity constitutes the quality that *sogoshosha* and other Japanese firms expect from their future managers.

From the student's point of view, it is a lifetime career choice made at a tender age—the early twenties. Given the student's vague notion of what awaits him in any corporate life, he or she is liable to be influenced strongly by the public images of the firms to which he may apply. A student's line of study and general interest help him or her to draw up a short list of possible firms. School record allows him or her to weed out those firms that have rarely hired anyone with a standing below, for instance, the top third of his graduating class. Given Japan's major orientation toward international competitive strength, the bulk of college graduates develop a strong preference for international business careers. Someday, they keep telling themselves, they will represent Japan in the "Olympics" of business activities.

The *sogoshosha* and other firms accordingly take pains to cultivate their public images as international and growth-minded firms. They openly boast of their export and international activities and their plans for sending young college graduates on overseas study assignments. Indeed, those question and answer sessions held by recruiting firms at colleges are dominated by students' probing inquiries about international career paths for white collar professionals of recruiting firms. Rarely do students ask about such trivial details as starting salaries, fringe benefits, or other economic benefits. Nor do they ask about the specific job assignments that await rookie recruits. They are merely concerned as to whether the firm of their choice is really committed to continuously training its human resources.

The *sogoshosha*'s obvious identification with international activities places the "best nine" in the higher ranks of desirable firms. Mitsui and Mitsubishi, in particular, have always ranked as two of the "best five" firms, as rated by graduating students of leading universities. Thus, the best and brightest of the young cadres of the Japanese economy gravitate toward a career with leading *sogoshosha*. Only an elite career with national government services such as the Ministry of International Trade and Industry (MITI) or the Ministry of Finance outranks a career with the leading *sogoshosha* as a first choice for graduates of law and economics departments of the foremost national universities.

(2) The Life of Rookie *Sogoshosha*-Men

Each fall, each *sogoshosha* chooses 100 to 200 fourth-year college students as tentative candidates to join the firm on graduation in March of the following year. The first hurdle, the written examination, is merely designed to weed out the weaker candidates. For those students who pass the written examination, a series of rigorous personal interview tests lay in store with *sogoshosha* managers as well as with those rookie *sogoshosha*-men who themselves went through a similar grinding process the year before.

Just as in other Japanese firms practicing seniority-based promotion and job assignment for the first five to ten years of a college graduate's corporate life, the cadets joining a firm in 1979 will be identified as the Class of 1979. This is the vintage label that will accompany Japanese managers until retirement.

With the beginning of the Japanese fiscal year on April 1, hundreds of new cadets of the *sogoshosha* attend a *nyusha-shiki* (meaning, literally, the "ceremony of joining the firm"). Here the highest echelon of each *sogoshosha*, from president to managing directors, extend their personal welcome to the new family members. The orientation period, in which recruits are drilled on the history, philosophy, general organization, and general activities of their *sogoshosha*, varies in length from one to three months depending on the firm. During these months, the recruits often receive intensive classroom training in the rudimentary skills of foreign exchange transactios, export–import procedures, typing, computer programming, and other clerical skills deemed necessary for their immediate job assignments. They are expected to comprehend the clerical procedures for in-house sales and trading functions long before they are given actual sales assignments. Invariably, however, at the end of the orientation period, the cadet is assigned to a specific section of certain departments of a chosen product or functional division of the *sogoshosha*. In nearly all cases, the cadet has no say whatsoever about his or her new assignment.

Depending on the manpower needs of each section, and depending on each *sogoshosha*'s current and future strategy, the new people from the year's intake are allocated unilaterally by the personnel department. Rarely is the department head even consulted as to whom he might wish to have issued by the central personnel department. He is asked to submit a request concerning how many new people are needed, but beyond this he must wait until the end of the orientation period to find out how many new recruits will be granted and who might actually be sent.

Once the cadet is assigned to a specific product division or a staff function such as finance, personnel, communication, or area coordination, he is likely to stay with that division for at least the first ten years. Job rotation within the same division or function is the way of life for cadets during their first five to ten years. Job rotation outside of their first assigned division is rare, except for cross-job rotations between, for example, a product division and an area coordination, such as the North American section of the general affairs division and the personnel department.

Once assigned to a specific section, a cadet is expected to learn the trade by doing and by imitating. He will be assigned to help individuals who have been with the firm for two or three years to perform such menial tasks as preparing basic data sheets, running errands, and otherwise generally observing and acquiring the tricks of their trade. Each product division covers a wide range of activities from actual project planning, sales, and customer relations to such logistics as transportation, documentation, billing, warehousing, and record keeping. A cadet is likely to be assigned first to such routine work as logistics, telex communications, and record keeping. As he masters the details of trade logistics, he is then shifted to assist his seniors in dealing with customers.

The practice of starting cadets on routine and logistical support functions before they are permitted to deal with customers is no accident. Routine and repetitive as these tasks are, such logistical support as telex communications, shipping, billing, and record keeping provide the cadets with quick exposure to the core functions of a *sogoshosha* – the linking of diverse business deals abroad with equally diverse business deals in Japan. Cadets have to tune themselves in to the internal market dynamics of their own firm before they are capable of cultivating business deals outside it. Hourly telex communications and daily logistical details of each product section or area department contain summaries of hundreds of feelers, offers, deals, and prospects of the many trade, finance, and investment dealings that the *sogoshosha* is cultivating around the world.

A strong sense of timing and competition is likely to be inculcated in cadets, who are exposed to the hourly joys and frustrations of striking deals and chasing even the remotest business feelers. By observing the successes and failures of the senior members, and particularly by noting how they are rewarded or punished formally by the superior and informally by the people in the same section, cadets are expected to learn what is important for their section and firm. Only when this shared understanding of what is important is grasped are the cadets gradually allowed to deal with their peers and seniors – first, outside their own section but within the same firm, and later, with people outside the firm. This learning process takes at least one year and sometimes two.

(3) Rigorous Competition within the Firm

At this point, the leading *sogoshosha* have formalized their evaluation of an employee's performance. The heads of various subunits such as the section, department, and division are annually required to rate the subordinates who report directly to them. In addition to the overall rating, which carries a letter grade such as AA, AB, BB, and so forth, each person is rated in over one dozen evaluative performance categories.

Management by objectives? Far from it. Even a cursory glance at these categories of employee performance would reveal that each employee is rated for his or her attitude and personality rather than for his or her specific job performance or contribution to the firm's profits or sales. Each supervisor is expected to interpret the way his

299

subordinates carried out their assignments, so as to judge whether they are developing as desirable *sogoshosha*-men with all the desirable attitudinal qualities. Naturally, *sogoshosha* professionals work hard to strike business deals and make profits for their firm. Nevertheless, their superiors are expected to evaluate the manner in which these sales and profits are made.

What are the desirable attitudes of a *sogoshosha* professional? In Chapter 4, the major behavioral characteristics of *sogoshosha* were appraised. Its organizational flexibility, which enables it to cope with sudden shifts in its market environments at home and abroad, was established as its most important strength. In order to develop this organizational flexibility, which also permits it to exploit its internal market transactions and economies of scale in worldwide communications networks, it has cultivated the following two corporate atmospheres for shaping professional conditional reflexes.

The first is competition and cooperation. Individual initiative and competitiveness are encouraged within the constraints of give-and-take trading of personal favors and cooperation. Even as the recruits are becoming aware of the intricate interdependency among different sections of their firm, the formal and informal evaluations of their performances by their superiors and peers soon teach them that the most serious misbehavior is not following the accepted procedures for keeping peers and superiors informed of their new business initiatives. Such procedures ascertain organizational consent for their actions. *Sogoshosha* frequently penalize individual employees whose actions, despite having produced spectacular profits for the firm, were not in accordance with the accepted procedures for obtaining organizational consent. Conversely, an individual's mistakes are generally condoned if his actions are judged to have been motivated by a dedication to the shared goals of the firm and if these actions were cleared informally or formally in advance, with his peers and superiors. In this regard, the firm attempts to attain two apparently opposing goals: (1) encouragement of individual initiatives and learning by doing, and (2) protection of the firm from disasters that are likely to be caused by an unchecked overcommitment of the *sogoshosha*'s resources to uncertain and unevaluated business deals.

The second atmosphere relates to group versus individual incentives. The seniority-based pay scale and promotion inside Japanese firms are group incentives in their extreme form. Since it is not unusual for the breadwinner division of today to become the dead wood of tomorrow, *sogoshosha* cannot jeopardize economies of scale in organizational flexibility by tying individual rewards too closely to ongoing performance. Such a practice is intended to avoid fierce and destructive rivalries among different sections.

Accordingly, each spring a *sogoshosha* places all its recruits from colleges that year on the same rank at, for instance, Grade Nine. This is called the "intake's" starting rank. Some firms practice an ascending order of ranking for promotion of their male college graduate professionals and place their new intakes at Grade Three. In the case of one leading *sogoshosha*, which practices a descending order of ranking, Grade One is reserved for those professionals intended as candidates for the ranks of corporate officer. Usually it takes twenty to thirty years to rise through the ranks from Grade Nine to Grade One, or from Grade Three to Grade Ten, depending on the descending or ascending direction of ranking practiced by the firm.

At the beginning, all intakes are automatically promoted, for instance, from Grade Nine to Grade Six, purely on the basis of seniority. It might take them eleven years from entry date to advance together from Grade Nine to Grade Six. In the first five years they may advance from Grade Nine to Grade Eight and the next two ranks might require three years each. Beyond this grade, however, *sogoshosha* professionals are released for individual scrambling. Their goal is Grade One and, hopefully, further into the ranks of corporate officer. From Grade Five through Grade One, each rung becomes increasingly tougher to reach. After fifteen years out of college, there appear among the intakes of the same year, say vintage 1969, two to three years' difference in reaching Grade Three. The next rung, from Grade Three to Grade Two is almost a quantum jump. Many do not make it. Grade One is reserved for managers in charge of product divisions and major branch offices.

This process of ranking *sogoshosha* male professionals is akin to the competition among students entering the same college in the same year. By the time they graduate, students have ranked, among themselves, their fellow classmates as "A," "B," or "C" students. Having been given the same examinations and assignments, and having gone through comparable tests, some continuously fared better than others. These are the "A" students, who have gradually dominated that group of students who would be permitted to enter postgraduate schools.

(4) *Ringi Seido* and Collective Evaluation of Individual Initiatives

Individual performance is evaluated mainly by two criteria: (1) the innovative quality of business projects proposed by individuals and

(2) the implementation and management of such projects. In the *sogoshosha* that thrives on the interdependency among various units of its internal market, one can particularly observe the well-known tendency of Japanese firms to make business decisions final only after their implementation is painstakingly arranged. Conceptually, a *sogoshosha* rarely separates decisionmaking from its implementation. Basic ideas on specific business projects may well be generated by alert individuals at any level of the corporate hierarchy. Their implementation, however, requires the willing cooperation of the people around them. Unless successful implementation is assured in advance, no decision is made to go ahead with a new individual initiative.

Accordingly, to assist individuals in obtaining their group's sanction, *sogoshosha* have formalized the well-known procedure of *ringi seido*, a vehicle that enables all relevant comments and criticism to be duly solicited from those involved in implementing new projects and business deals. Procedurally, *ringi seido* refers to a formal system by which a given proposal is routed both horizontally and vertically through the hierarchy of the firm for comment and approval.

It is customary, however, for individual initiators informally to sound out in advance those key persons who will be involved in approving and implementing given proposals. The formal procedure of collecting seals of approval can only be started when the initiator has already touched the crucial bases and ascertained their active consent or their agreement not to oppose. Accordingly, it is not uncommon that the chart with names for routing a given proposal carries no space to indicate a denial, but only a place to note concurrence and comment. Any denials identified in this routing process are expected to be ironed out by intense negotiations among the people involved. Thus, the formal procedure of *ringi seido* permits the project initiator to identify potential blockages to its implementation and, at the same time, to benefit from a multiangle scrutiny of the proposals. After all, both the formal and informal aspects of routing and sounding out, which characterize the *ringi seido*, have evolved to allow all individuals concerned with a given proposal to participate actively in the collective decisionmaking process. Thus, when the new project is approved, their active commitment is assured.

The proposals that have survived the collective evaluation of formal routing are submitted to at least two more formal screenings from the viewpoint of firmwide interests. *Sogoshosha* have formal committees for investment and project evaluation that screen proposals submitted by various departments. The proposals surviving this screening are then submitted for formal scrutiny by a decisionmaking board comprising corporate officers holding the rank of managing director and above.

All in all, an individual's promotion, for instance, from Grade Four and beyond, is specifically related to his repeated successes in initiating innovative projects, expediting their approvals and, finally, organizing other fellow professionals to implement them. Active cooperation with successful projects is also likely to be recognized as a desirable attitude for a *sogoshosha* professional, thus bringing in some "Brownie points" or personal credits, which will subsequently be incorporated into the individual's overall performance evaluation.

Cumbersome as it seems, *ringi seido* and its resultant corporate atmosphere often augment the individual professional's limited experience and expertise. He is expected not only to solicit comments and suggestions but, more importantly, to listen to them. Recently, the department manager of a leading *sogoshosha* successfully steered through a critical deal concerning the acquisition of a sizable firm in the United States. Reflecting on his thousands of hours of negotiations with his American counterparts across the negotiation table, he observed,

> Because of our *ringi seido*, throughout the negotiations I had ready access to a range of expert advice and evaluations from my fellow corporate members. They always helped me to avoid serious mistakes and correct others in the budding. However, many times I noticed my American counterparts making questionable concessions and trade-offs whenever their expertise was overstretched. Legal and financial departments and other key product divisions of their firm were consulted only when we had initialled our tentative agreements. Then, sometimes, it was too late.

(5) Summary

Japanese *sogoshosha* show many characteristics of typical Model J firms. Just like investment banking houses in the United States, *sogoshosha* that rely solely on their professional members' interdependency have begun to balance the individual professional's initiatives with his necessary observance of the group's norm of mutual cooperation.

Once a candidate is admitted into a *sogoshosha*, his movement upward through the hierarchy depends more or less on his accumulated credits with the firm. Such a seniority basis enables the training of newer and younger recruits without seniors fearing they will be upstaged by them. Since each *sogoshosha*'s survival depends on a widespread and open sharing of its members' experience and expertise with one another, it cannot afford to risk the unchecked and destructive competition that often leads more senior members to fear a trampling by their younger co-professionals. The sense of equity and order provided by a seniority-based promotion practice has therefore been actively cultivated by *sogoshosha*.

How, then, do *sogoshosha* reward the departments having a high performance level and punish those with a poor performance record? How do they discriminate among high caliber individuals who consistently put in good performances and those average or poor individuals?

Even when all the male college graduates are advancing, for instance, from Grade Nine through Six solely on the basis of their seniority, the annual bonus of the best and the poorest of the same intakes, often equivalent to five or six months salary, might vary after five years by up to 15 percent. The reason for this variance is that every year the overall performance of each individual is rated by department managers. The scale might consist of five ranks. Rank One might denote the highest overall performance, with Rank Five reserved for those unfortunate individuals absent from the firm because of long-term illness. Those individuals placed in Rank One would then be assigned slightly larger salary points than the others. Under no circumstances, however, would the highest level of salary accorded to the top performer of, perhaps, Grade Six be more than the lowest level of salary accorded to the next grade level, Grade Five. The cumulative differences in salary points, which individual employees collect from Grade Nine through Grade Six, therefore produce the difference in annual bonuses between individuals, although outwardly all hold the same grade.

As college instructors are required to follow a grade distribution curve when assessing their students' performances, managers of the *sogoshosha*'s respective departments are annually given rank distribution curves for their departments. This rank distribution curve varies from one department to the next, depending on the overall economic performance of a department. Department managers whose units continue to outperform other departments are likely to be given a rank distribution curve that is skewed to Ranks One and Two. The departments whose performances persistently lag behind others would be given a curve skewed to Ranks Three and Four.

Sogoshosha, however, are careful not to reward fortunate departments too generously at the expense of the unfortunate departments whose businesses were unduly affected by adverse market conditions. Since individual members of a *sogoshosha* have very little to say regarding their job assignments, it would be unfair to tie an individual's economic rewards and promotions too closely to the unfortunate vicissitudes of his department's economic performance.

An individual's promotions are accordingly screened by a central evaluation committee, whose task it is to iron out interdepartmental inequities. This firmwide evaluation becomes increasingly important when employees are being evaluated for higher grades. As he approaches the end of the ranking ladder, the individual is evaluated by more than one superior. The manner in which a group of corporate officers perceives an individual thus becomes a critical factor in determining the promotion of any manager.

One leading *sogoshosha* has developed a voting method. Each year, managing directors and higher ranking officers vote to select the new corporate officers from a limited number of candidates. These officers are asked to select and rank perhaps three persons for promotion to the rank of corporate officer. Only those candidates receiving a distinct majority are then invited to enter the lowest rank of corporate officer and become a director. Those voting officers recommending individuals who were rejected by a majority of votes are also often sternly asked to explain to the chief executive officer of the firm why their selection criteria differed from that of the others. Accordingly, one man's "fair-haired boy" could not become a corporate officer unless he had also won the respect of a majority of the voting officers. The message is loud and clear. Whatever the limits of automatic promotion, moving up beyond Grade Six requires that an individual work closely with peers and higher ranked individuals outside his own department. This rule encourages individuals to interact horizontally and vertically with people throughout the corporate hierarchy.

The *sogoshosha* has taken years to evolve its system. Only within the last ten years, however, have many *sogoshosha* established the formal promotion systems described above. Until that time, the basic ingredients of today's formal systems have been evolving informally and formally in the respective *sogoshosha*. Through trial and error, however, the formal promotion and evaluation practices of *sogoshosha* employees have been taking on many aspects of the selection, initiation, and promotion practices of standing members of the American fraternal and professional societies.

Nevertheless, the *sogoshosha* are confronted in the 1980s with new challenges at home and abroad. All the leading *sogoshosha* are now, in fact, groping their way toward a revision of their internal working systems so as to elicit a better response to the dynamic changes in their market conditions.

12 SUCCESSFUL NEGOTIATIONS OF JOINT VENTURES

One skill that multinational managers must acquire is the art of negotiations in foreign culture. Unlike the business negotiations in a familiar home country, negotiations in foreign cultures require multinational managers to become ardent students of the political and economic history, culture, language, and social customs of the host country. This has a direct bearing upon not only the success of business negotiations but, more importantly, upon the ongoing success of the negotiated business deals.

Although businesses anywhere are interested in profits, the manifestations of that interest vary widely from one culture to the next. Accordingly, multinational managers must be able to reconcile their own notions of corporate profits with their foreign business partners' notions of profits.

Contrary to popular belief, the business negotiations in Japan and other East Asian cultures are in substance far more similar to the American and European practices than those in the cultures of Southeast Asia, the Middle East, Africa, and even Latin America. However, the styles of business negotiations in Japan may strike American and European negotiators as alien and nebulous. To this extent, the style might be also a substance. However, this style can be easily overcome if you know the underlying corporate culture of Japan.

Foreign firms' motives for entry into Japan are naturally diverse, and not all the foreign investments turn out to be successful. A number of manufacturing operations that came originally to tap "cheap Japanese labor" for export markets in the United States have long since retreated into Korea, Hong Kong, and Taiwan. General Motors' acquisition in the early 1970s of a sizable minority interest of Isuzu Motors, a fledgling Japanese automobile firm, remains a conspicuous example of the foreign oligopolist's tactic of "exchange of threats" with Toyota and Nissan—the Japanese oligopolists that were making rapid inroads into the American automobile market.

In 1975, Dow Chemical's entry into the alkali-related industry (causaic soda), a large market fragmented by rivalries among medium-sized and inefficient Japanese manufacturers, signaled the new phase of foreign entry into Japan. Despite political outbursts in Japan, the "reciprocity" principle (fear of foreign retaliation against Japanese multinational firms abroad) prevents the Japanese government from stopping Dow's entry outright. Dow's technological and financial capabilities, superior to those possessed by the feuding medium-sized firms in Japan, help Dow overcome cultural and political barriers to entry into a potentially lucrative market. If Dow proves to be successful, its competitors in the United States and Europe may follow suit. And Japanese alkali and other nonorganic chemical firms may be scrambling for tie-ups with these foreign entrants.

In the future, Japan will continue to offer one of the largest markets for many products and services. Japan now operates one of the most active and well-managed equity capital markets in the world, along with a variety of other well-developed financial markets. Of late, Japan has become a source of diverse manufacturing technologies for foreign businesses. Both the new and standard technologies amassed by Japanese manufacturing firms are now being actively sought by foreign businesses.

Needless to say, Japanese firms abroad are posing formidable competition to foreign businesses. The multinational managers of the 1980s can no longer afford not to study the modus operandi of Japanese firms if they are to compete successfully with Japanese firms inside and outside Japan. The following comments will help multinational managers develop their own keys in unlocking the esoteric behavior of Japanese government and business entities that have long baffled foreigners.

1. ENTRY FORMAT: JOINT VENTURE VERSUS FULLY OWNED SUBSIDIARY

As was pointed out in Chapter 9, the ownership of foreign subsidiaries is strongly influenced by both the strategy and the internal structure of the parent firms. Other things being equal, the joint venture format is often utilized for the sake of speed of entry into foreign countries. Foreign entrants obtain ready access to distribution channels, the market share, suppliers' contacts, management, and banking and government contacts through joint ventures with established local businesses as well as through a partial or total acquisition of established local businesses.

In the past, American firms have tended to place an inordinate amount of faith in legal ownership—hopefully fully owned or, at worst, 51 percent ownership—as the guarantor of effective control of their foreign subsidiaries. However, of late, as developing nations maneuver to have their own nationals own a majority of the equity of the foreign subsidiaries, even American firms are learning to separate the concept of legal ownership from that of effective control—that is, maintaining effective influence over the scope and direction of their subsidiaries abroad.

In the case of foreign firms entering Japan, the joint venture format has not only provided a speed of entry but has often been accepted as the only feasible format. This is mainly because the necessary human resources—rank and file employees and managerial talents alike—still exhibit a rigid disinclination to move from one firm to the next. Foreign firms often find it especially difficult to recruit capable middle management, skilled workers, first-line supervisors, and engineers, upon whose dedication the success of the ventures depend, particularly in the context of the Japanese corporate culture.

In the case of the foreign manufacturing firm whose entry into Japan is based on distinct technological leads over Japanese competitors, the firm might first form a joint venture sales firm with a Japanese manufacturer and, in the beginning, entrust the manufacturing tasks to the Japanese parent firm of the joint sales operation. However, as students of the product life cycle (PLC) model can readily predict, a closer communication between manufacturing and marketing operations as well as manufacturing cost-cutting efficiency will become crucial as the market competition stiffens with the entry of other foreign and Japanese firms into the same product fields. For example, the joint venture Fuji-Xerox, which emerged in 1965 as a sales firm, found it necessary in 1975 to vertically integrate its manufacturing operations by bringing the manufacturing facilities and personnel of the Japanese parent firm, lock, stock, and barrel, into the joint venture. With the expiration of Xerox's patent, and with the proliferation of new photocopying technologies, three Japanese competitors entered the market, and price and other competition soon followed. Fuji-Xerox needed a closer link between its marketing and manufacturing operations in order to cope with these mounting competitive pressures. The joint venture format with an established Japanese manufacturing firm can provide this strategic alternative to foreign firms entering the Japanese market.

Furthermore, the mastery of the intricate divisions of industrial and commercial tasks that prevail in Japan require close contacts with banks, trading firms, distributors, suppliers, and above all, with the Japanese government. These contacts are maintained through personal ties that corporate managers from top echelon to middle echelon have long cultivated. Again, the joint venture or the outright acquisition of ongoing Japanese firms is often the only alternative open to foreign firms. Given the fierce nationalistic posture of Japanese managers and entrepreneurs, however, the outright acquisition of ongoing Japanese firms by foreigners is usually out of the question, leaving the joint venture as the most sensible option.

2. SELECTION OF JAPANESE BUSINESS PARTNERS: IMPORT AGENT

If foreign firms wish to export their products to Japan without allotting too many personnel or capital resources to the development of their own sales subsidiaries, they must find suitable "import agents." The unplanned selection of importing agents can prove to be a costly mistake. Our research findings of both the success and failure of foreign firms exporting to Japan provide the following general rules, if one is looking for either Japanese import agents or reviewing current agreements with import agents.

Need for Planning. With the PLC model of international trade in mind, you must plan for the scope of your own involvement in Japan. As your first product loses its novelty in the Japanese market, marketing and sales efforts should be increased so that your position remains competitive in terms of advertising, distributor relations, and sales management. At the same time, you might be forced to bring new products into the market so that these newer products provide the cover of product novelty for the old ones. Does this make common sense? Yes, yet we found that many foreign firms selected their import agents *without* evaluating their flexibility in coping with the changing needs of the marketing environment.

Manufacturing Firms as Import Agents. As in the case of technical licensing agreements or joint manufacturing ventures, Japanese manufacturing firms should be selected mainly for their product and market compatibility with your own products. Technical capability, manufacturing competence, and coverage of the Japanese and export markets should also be considered. Foreign firms may find eager partners among Japanese firms seeking to diversity their own product lines and market coverage through business tie-ups with foreign firms. Given the fierce rivalry among the top five or ten Japanese firms in a given industry, foreign firms may find the fourth or even tenth largest firms eager to rely upon foreign technologies and products in their moves to catch up with the industrial leader. Here again, foreign firms must study both the industrial structure and specific behaviors of the Japanese firms involved.

Trading Firms and Wholesale Distributors as Import Agents. Very few wholesale distributors possess national market coverage. Therefore, if you choose to use this approach, you would need to select a few strong regional wholesale distributors. This may be the reason why many foreign manufacturing firms enter into licensing and import agent agreements with Japanese manufacturing firms, thus exercising influence over distributional channels on a national scale.

Trading firms are a different matter. There are nine leading general trading firms (*sogoshosha*) in Japan which deal in a variety of products and services for both domestic and international distribution. In addition, there are over five thousand special trading firms (*senmonshosha*) which specialize in a limited range of products and services, for either importing or exporting activities. Trading firms provide finances, warehousing services, and even missionary sales activities. Since they are always looking for potential businesses abroad, you may have already been contacted by a number of them for possible business tie-ups.

Large general trading firms can often provide you with a speedy entry into the Japanese market. In order to penetrate the Japanese market, however, your products must have the full attention of a missionary sales outlet. Fortunately, many specialized trading firms exist, some of which are subsidiaries of large leading general trading firms. Accordingly, if you plan to penetrate the Japanese market you should consider a two-step entry move—first through a large trading firm, and then, through the services of specialized trading or manufacturing firms as your sales needs change.

3. SELECTION OF JAPANESE BUSINESS
   PARTNERS: JOINT VENTURE

This is essentially the same process as concluding import-agent or licensing agreements with manufacturing firms. Here, however, the need for planning in coping with the changing relationships between you and Japanese partners will be far greater than in the case of import-agent agreements. Our research findings uncovered the following three potential sources of conflicts that might arise between Japanese and foreign business partners.

Inclusion of Trading Firms. Many Japanese manufacturing firms continue to rely on their related trading firms not only for export and import purposes but for domestic distribution of their products as well. In particular, it is not uncommon for Japanese firms to suggest including the trading firm as a third partner in the joint venture. Foreign firms' reactions are always: "why bother?" But before rejecting the suggestion to include a trading firm in the joint venture, you might analyze what motivates your prospective partners to make such a suggestion. You will soon discover that they depend on trading firms for supplies, domestic distribution, both long- and short-term finances and, above all, international trade. More simply, it might be that your prospective partners feel psychologically secure in letting their trading firms negotiate with unfamiliar foreign firms.

Once you are able to identify the specific concerns of your prospective partners, you can help them negotiate with trading firms for specific arrangements. Trading firms can be engaged as special negotiating agents for specific fees. And your joint venture will indeed need to purchase a variety of services provided by trading firms.

When a prospective partner insists upon bringing in a trading firm as the third partner, you may suggest that the Japanese portion of the ownership be split between the manufacturing firm and the trading firm. However, you would be wise to agree on a review of the entire arrangement in three to five years. Chances are that the Japanese manufacturer will find it cumbersome to have a trading firm as the third partner once a close working relationship is established between your firm and the manufacturing firm. The trading firm would not have much aversion to relinquishing its equity ownership of the joint venture so long as its services continued to be utilized at an appropriate fee.

Selection of President of Joint Venture. Regardless of the legal equity ownership of the foreign partner, the joint venture is often expected to obtain its human resources from management to rank and file employees in Japan. As a result, not only is the president of the joint venture to be selected according to the Japanese notion of leadership, but the management-employee practices must conform to the general expectations of the Japanese employees.

This does not mean, however, that administrative personnel innovations cannot be attempted with the introduction of foreign practices. But personnel "change agents" must be selected who will adapt foreign practices to Japanese practices.

Concerning the selection of the president, managers, and first-line supervisors of the joint venture, you may have to have a specific understanding with your Japanese partner that the joint venture will not be treated as a dumping ground for incompetent rejects and deadwood of the Japanese parent firm. It is one thing to have such an understanding; it is quite another, however, to police the quality of the Japanese personnel sent into the joint venture by the Japanese partner.

Instability of Joint Venture. The case Fried Chicken in Japan Chapter 6 points out the importance of obtaining a capable Japanese manager who understands the viewpoints of both Japanese and foreign partners. This is indeed critical for the success of any joint venture. As it stands, any joint venture possesses an inherent element of instability as the business environment and resultant strategies of one or both partners inevitably change.

Joint ventures are often loosely compared to "marriage." In reality, however, they should be treated more as "contractual cohabitation," where mutual relationships are subject to predetermined schedules of review and constant servicing. In the context of the Japanese corporate culture, which places a heavy emphasis on human relationships within the firm, the importance of constantly reinforcing the specific goals of the joint venture and, above all, communicating these goals even to the rank and file employees cannot be stressed too strongly.

We have found that informal but intensive annual "study sessions" between Japanese and foreign business partners are an effective tool in nurturing the necessary mutual understanding of the goals of the joint venture. At the same time, these study sessions test the intellectual and managerial capability of the participants. High-level managers from the Japanese parent could do the same.

Then, by comparing notes about the world and the Japanese situation, Japanese and foreign business partners could discuss the ranges of future actions open to their joint venture in Japan.

Foreign firms can offer to have promising young manager candidates of the Japanese parent firm and the joint venture spend some time (three months to one year) at the headquarters and plants of the foreign firms. Given the lifetime commitment system of employment of Japan, these young manager candidates are likely to remain with their firms indefinitely—usually until the age of mandatory retirement. The time, money, and personal attention that you invest in their personal growth would be long and warmly remembered. In turn, these Japanese managers could help you bridge the communication gap that is bound to arise between your firm and your Japanese partners over the direction of the joint venture in Japan.

Term of Foreign Managers' Residency in Japan. We have found that the five-year term of senior management residency in the joint or wholly owned venture in Japan provides an optimal balance. At any rate, senior managers should be in residence for no less than three years. Too frequent and sudden rotation of the senior managers by foreign parent firms are inevitably interpreted by the Japanese business community (not only by the Japanese partners) as a slight. On the other hand, if the residency becomes longer than five years, many foreign managers begin to feel they might have been assigned to their outposts in the Far East forever.

On the junior level, however, foreign management trainees can be rotated every two to three years. These trainees, who may later be candidates for senior positions in the Japanese operations, should be assigned to work for the Japanese managers in the joint or wholly owned ventures. In this way, once established, the mutual trust between Japanese managers and promising management candidates can provide an informal communication link even after foreign trainees have left their Japanese assignment.

4. NEGOTIATING WITH JAPANESE FIRMS

Japanese banks, foreign banks, and Japanese trading firms can often supply prospective leads to Japanese firms interested in negotiating joint ventures, import agencies, and technical licensing agreements with you. Chances are that you have already been contacted by Japanese firms for a variety of business tie-up possibilities. As indicated by the case at the end of this chapter, Picard Printing Product (B), the negotiation process is often strewn with many obstacles. More often than not, foreign businesses lack a clear-cut policy objective toward the Japanese market. This leads the potential Japanese partner into a prolonged negotiation and to an increasing mistrust of you on the Japanese side.

In the case of foreign businesses negotiating with Japanese firms, mutual ignorance of the parties' corporate culture and business situation can pose a critical blockade to negotiation. Before either party develops a mutual understanding of the size and shape of the "pie," which can only be accomplished by joint efforts by both parties, each party is prone, consciously and unconsciously, to scramble for dividing the pie. The end result is inevitable: a hopeless deadlock in the small details (often legalistic hagglings) of the prospective joint venture format and operations, without a clear-cut understanding of the joint goals.

Facing a Japanese Negotiating Team. As in the Japanese social structure, the divisions of social and industrial tasks permeate the Japanese firm. As a result, your Japanese negotiating partner would most likely consist of a team of specialists in each functional business line, headed, often ceremoniously, by a high-level manager holding officer's rank in the firm. Such a team approach is unavoidable in the context of the Japanese corporate culture if the negotiation is to be taken at all seriously. In order to implement the agreements of the negotiation, several departments of the Japanese firm will be involved. Indeed, in the Japanese corporate culture, the act of decision-making cannot, even theoretically, be separated from the painstaking rearrangement of both vertical and lateral working relationships within the various suborganizations of the firm. This rearrangement is vital for implementing the agreement.

Given the great degree of de facto delegation of decisionmaking authority to the middle management echelon of the Japanese firm, you will discover that one able person in his later thirties or mid-forties would emerge as the chief negotiator for the Japanese team. At this point, your success depends on whether you are able to develop a close and personal rapport with this person. The best way to achieve this rapport is over a glass of wine or beer, where you should exchange your views with him in a mock negotiation session. Here you should try to understand the problems that the Japanese negotiator faces, as he should try to comprehend yours.

Use of Intermediary or Arbitrator. There are many foreign and Japanese consulting firms in Japan that act as intermediaries for negotiations. Japanese banks and trading firms often fulfill such functions. If you can engage the services of respected individuals from academic circles (this is rare) or from banking communities as the arbiters of your negotiations, you can have delicate matters and problems communicated to the Japanese side and vice versa.

In the context of a culture that wishes to avoid personal confrontation and rejection, the judicious use of the intermediary can make a difference in the success or failure of the negotiation. Once you have established mutually satisfactory relationships with your Japanese partners, you will be in a position to identify delicate problems at the outset and diffuse them. Until then, you might have to rely on an intermediary-consultant to fill the communication gap between you and your Japanese partner.

Use of Lawyer. As the case of Picard Printing Product (B) shows, it is a good idea to keep lawyers out of negotiations. You can consult them in private, out of sight of the Japanese negotiators. But you should not bring the attorney into the negotiation. For one thing, lawyers are oriented toward saving you from cases of failure and dispute. Therefore, if you consult them, you might be unduly influenced by the note of inordinate caution that lawyers tend to bring into any negotiating atmosphere. You would soon find yourself more concerned with methods for cutting the joint venture pie than with development of mutual understanding of the goals of the joint venture. Also, in Japanese society, where litigation is rare except for extreme cases of dispute, the presence of lawyers in a negotiation conveys an inadvertent impression that you do not trust your Japanese counterparts.

Last, we have found that foreign managers unknowingly ask their lawyers the wrong questions. Instead of telling them, "This is what I want to do. How can I do it?" Foreign managers, who are often victims of their sense of insecurity in an alien culture ask, "What should I do?" Lawyers are paid to give advice, but their advice is naturally that of lawyers, not accomplished and seasoned business managers.

5. SIX "DON'TS" OF NEGOTIATIONS IN JAPAN

(1) Selling the Deal and Not the Seller

No American would enter into an agreement with a fellow American who seemed to be untrustworthy. This rule of human relations need to be expanded by an order of ten when negotiating with the Japanese. The Japanese must be convinced that you are trustworthy, just as you have the right to expect the Japanese to prove themselves to you.

Unlike in the United States, where legalistic and contractual bondings are prevalent in business relationships, personal trust between negotiators is one major guarantee in Japan that business agreements will be honored by each firm. Accordingly, Japanese negotiators instinctively attempt to assess whether their foreign counterparts are well respected by peers and superiors within their firm and whether their foreign counterparts are individually trustworthy.

Haste on the part of a foreigner to sell a specific deal before selling himself is often interpreted by the Japanese as the sign of a small person with whom dealing would be too risky. To avoid this unfortunate stereotyping by the Japanese, foreigners should at least take the following two precautions: First, they should obtain a very good introduction to the executives of their targeted Japanese firms, preferably by Japanese or foreign executives who have successfully done business with the targeted firm in the past. Japanese banks and trading companies can often provide such introductions. Second, before they explain the specific business deal they have in mind, they should take time to introduce themselves, their educational and vocational background, their family heritage (perhaps even including who their grandfathers were), and their position and functions within their firm.

The Japanese attitude toward the business negotiation is very personal in that the negotiation is merely one process to test their counterparts' trustworthiness. On the other hand, the American attitude toward the negotiation tends to be very legalistic in that the negotiation process is a legal sparring to make as many points as possible with their opponents. Thus, Americans often assume that nothing is binding until the final signing of the detailed legal documents. Any agreements that are reached in the process of negotiations are assumed to be subject to subsequent changes as the new phases of the negotiation unfold new circumstances. This is why Japanese negotiators often see American counterparts try to change promises and agreements reached the day before. To Japanese who are not familiar with the Americna legalistic attitude toward the business negotiation, this sudden reversal of American positions unfortunately signals untrustworthiness. The only way to avoid such unfortunate misunderstandings would be to set the negotiation rule from the outset that permits both parties to change any interim promises and agreements until the final agreement. One should never assume that the other side will understand his or her position and rule.

(2) Ignoring the Hidden Economics
of Japanese Business Relationships

When American managers attempt to sell their products or services they are prone to speak to their prospective customers only in narrow economic terms of such product- or service-specific variables as price, delivery, quality, or sales promotion. This narrow view of things will suffice in simple over-the-counter deals. But in negotiating with Japanese businesses, they should be more sensitive to such hidden but nevertheless vital economic factors as whether the deal in question will require Japanese businessmen to alter their business relationships with other Japanese firms.

What to an uninitiated foreigner might seem a simple supplier-client relationship often masks important considerations such as an outside supplier's cumulative favors to its client through its hiring of surplus or retired employees of the client firm. As a result, a narrow economic advantage such as price or quality differences between your product and that of a Japanese competitor may have to be extremely distinctive to motivate your prospective Japanese clients to forgo the hidden benefits associated with their existing relationships with other Japanese firms.

(3) Lack of Semantic Sensitivity

Unfortunately, there are still too few American business executives who possess even a rudimentary knowledge of the Japanese language, not to mention a crucially important sensitivity to the Japanese mode of interpersonal relationships and communication. American firms desiring to establish lasting business relations with Japan would benefit considerably from the development of a cadre of their own managers and specialists who are well versed in the Japanese language and culture. Until this happens, however, American business managers or government officials who negotiate with Japanese firms or government ministries should stay alert for three typical areas of miscommunication between Japanese and American negotiators.

First, the implied meaning of the Japanese phrase that is translated as "in principle" (*gensoku to shite*) is the opposite of the English meaning. If your Japanese negotiators agree to a certain point "in principle," that is tantamount to their declaring that they will abide by it 90 percent of the time (the remaining 10 percent being subject to acts of God). I have seen situations in which American negotiators nearly blew an entire deal merely because of their mental block against the Japanese use of the phrase "in principle." The same holds true for the Japanese interpretation of "gentleman's agreement." In a society in which one's trustworthiness (gentlemanliness) carries high social and economic value, a gentleman's agreement—especially one that is witnessed by a respected third party—is, again, almost unbreakable. Third, Japanese have a tendency to say *"hai, hai"* (yes, yes), the equivalent of "I understand," or even "I agree," while they are listening to you. These phrases merely mean that they are listen-

317

ing and that they understand your positions. Semantic miscommunication is often compounded by an innate Japanese propensity to avoid saying "no" directly. Instead of saying "no," they prefer to say "I will consider it." This makes it difficult for you as a negotiator to distinguish between their actual intention to conisder your proposal and a polite but firm refusal. At a time like this you might rely on a trustworthy third party to find out for you. The judicious use of a third party is a basic skill you will need to master. Often, the individuals who gave you a good introduction to your prospective Japanese clients are able to act as a third party for you.

(4) Insisting on Detailed Discussions With High-Level Executives

In Japanese firms, the degree to which de facto authority to formulate strategic decisions is delegated to middle echelon executives is usually far greater than in American firms. High-level executives in Japanese firms are often present at negotiations only to arbitrate various decisions recommended by their middle level management personnel. They also often do not carry overly impressive formal job titles. Many American negotiators overlook this factor and insist upon negotiating on details with their "formal" Japanese counterparts, to the latter's inordinate discomfort.

(5) Rushing the Negotiations

With the exception of instances in which a sense of urgency is already shared by your Japanese counterparts, there is no use in rushing through the negotiation process. Americans often complain that it takes an eternity for the Japanese to make up their minds on something. In turn, Japanese often complain that it takes Americans forever to implement decisions once they have been mutually agreed upon. It is standard Japanese business practice not to finalize a decision unless its implementation is also ensured and prepared for. This is why your Japanese counterparts often need time to contact key bases within their firm and prepare their colleagues to help implement the deal emerging between you and them.

At the same time, you need to educate your Japanes negotiating counterparts so that they will fully understand that decisionmaking is often separated from implementation in American firms. To avoid any distrust that may arise through mutual ignorance of respective corporate cultures, you should budget ample time for concluding negotiations with Japanese firms. You cannot hope to wrap it all up in just a few days. As your negotiation makes positive progress, it would be advisable to work out a timetable for implementation of the deal. In this way you would also ascertain what will need to be done to prepare your colleagues back home so that they can help you implement the new business decisions.

(6) Assuming Lasting Stability of the Agreement

Since the needs of the parties in a joint venture change over time, it is strange for Japanese and foreign negotiators to enter into a business agreement without working out in advance the procedures and criteria by which their mutual relationship will be reviewed on a periodic basis. According to my research findings on questions of stability in joint ventures, I have to conclude that there are inherent instabilities in any joint venture, let alone one between Japanese and foreign business partners.

In order to ensure the stability of your business agreements with Japanese partners, you would be well advised to agree on procedures and criteria for periodic review of the arrangement once the initial agreements for your business deals are concluded. With the establishment of formal procedures for such reviews, you can also handle your own corporate politics that might at least imply an evaluation of your predecessors who were involved in the initial agreements pertaining to the business deals.

6. JAPANESE AND EUROPEAN MULTINATIONALS IN AMERICA: A CASE OF FLEXIBLE CORPORATE SYSTEMS

Summary

Japanese and European multinational firms reveal that they are expanding their manufacturing activities in the U.S. while their American competitors are cutting back their manufacturing operations inside the U.S. This "Japanese and European Paradox" is to be explained by the product life cycle of foreign trade and the corporate culture as a firm-specific determinant.

1. Japanese and European Paradox

Of late, the Pacific Age of the U.S. has produced important changes in the international environment of the American economy (Tsurumi 1984). Ever since 1978, more American trade and investment have crossed the Pacific Ocean than the Atlantic, ending the 350 years of the Atlantic Age for the U.S. scarcely a decade ago, Western European countries and Canada dominated the U.S. trade and investment, with Latin America and Asia competing for the distant third position. In 1983, in two-way trade flows alone, of $461 billion of the U.S. trade, the Pacific trade ran up $183 billion, leaving further behind the Atlantic trade of $113 billion and the Canadian trade of $87 billion.

In direct investment areas, from 1979 to 1983, American investments in Japan and other Pacific countries were increasing at an annually compounding rate of 20%, about three times as rapid as American investments in Europe. In turn, increased American investments in Japan and other Asian countries have increased the tempo of Japanese firms' investments in the U.S. From 1979 to 1983, Japanese direct investments in the U.S. have increased by about 340% from $3.4 billion to $15 billion. In 1982, Japan's investments in the U.S. surpassed investment positions held by Germany and France. By the mid-1984, Japan's investment positions in the U.S. were estimated to have surpassed comparable positions held by the U.K. and the Netherlands, former leaders of foreign direct investments in the U.S.

Meanwhile, partly to offset slower growth of the Atlantic trade, European direct investment positions in the U.S. have doubled from about $40 billion in

1979 to about \$78 billion in 1983. Together with increasing Japanese investments in the U.S., steady increases in European investments in the U.S. have contributed much to closing the asymmetrical gap between American investments abroad and foreign investments in the U.S. As late as in 1979, foreign investment positions in the U.S. were merely about one-fourth of American investments abroad. By the end of 1983, however, foreigners had closed this gap to about two-thirds of American investments abroad. By the year 1990 the familiar asymmetry in the cross investment features between America and the rest of the world, most notably, Japan and Europe, will be easily reversed and foreign investment positions in the U.S. will exceed American investment positions abroad. Between Japan and the U.S. alone, this reversal already occurred in 1982.

More importantly, even a cursory analysis of Japanese and European multinational firms active in the U.S. reveals that they are expanding their involvements in manufacturing activities in the U.S. This is happening at a time when their American competitors are even cutting back their own manufacturing operations inside the U.S. This is what I call the "Japanese and European Paradox" in the U.S. When many American manufacturing firms are fleeing the U.S. to countries where wages are lower, their Japanese and European competitors are coming ashore to the U.S. to manufacture their quality products with high cost American labor. Some Japanese firms have taken over even unionized plants which their American competitors have abandonned as uneconomical and have turned them around successfully (Y. and R. Tsurumi 1984).

What does then enable Japanese and European multinationals to succeed where their American multinationals have failed in their own home territory? In particular, the three-way competition inside the U.S. among American, European and Japanese firms is moving into even high-tech fields in addition to steel, auto, machine, tools, tires, und pharmaceuticals. This situation challenges us to freshly review two theoretical paradigms of foreign trade and investment: namely (1) product life cycle theory of foreign trade (PLC) and (2) corporate culture as a significant firm-specific determinant of foreign direct investment.

2. A Revised Theory of Product Life Cycle (PLC)

In February 1983 Atari Corporation in the so-called silicon valley of California suddenly laid off 2,000 American workers, engineers, and managers and shifted its production operations of home computers and games to Taiwan. Over the past two decades or so, this sort of reaction to the first sign of intensifying price competition even in the growing U.S. market has gripped one American manufacturer after another. In order to meet their budgeted profits, American managers have ditched their employees and salvaged their equipment by moving familiar production processes to lower wage countries.

Many American economists and business executives, using a prototype PLC theory of international trade and investment (Vernon 1966), still defend the behavior of the "Atari Syndrome". According to them, the profit maximization goals of any firm would logically dictate an international migration of manufacturing operations of mature and standard products from the U.S. to low wage countries in a search for lower production costs. The mythology of the free enterprise system reinforces the effects of the Atari Syndrome to the extent that economists, business executives, politicians, and even labor leaders seem to equate the Atari Syndrome behavior with the sacred rights of management.

U.S.-trained economists and business scholars in particular still cling to the assumption that the rate of firm- and industry-specific technological innovation will decline as products enter the mature phase of the product life cycle. Accordingly, the behavior of the Atari Syndrome fits the prognosis offered by this prototype paradigm of the PLC theory. If firms do not achieve innovation in their production processes and upgrade the skills of their workers, they have little choice but to seek lower wage rates to cut average production costs. The Japanese and European Paradox in the U.S. confronts us with the task of revising the PLC theory. For example, in the U.S. automobile industry, in addition to earlier manufacturing investments by Volvo of Sweden and Volkswagen of Germany, Renault's partial acquisition of American Motors have brought the three European auto manufacturers to face off with three Japanese auto makers, Honda, Nissan, and Toyota, in the U.S. productions of subcompact cars. In the product development and subsequent production of subcompacts, all American auto manufacturers have all but conceded to their Japanese and European competitors. Although Volkswagen has somewhat stumbled, Honda, Nissan and Toyota have already shown that quality subcompacts can be profitably manufactured in the U.S. How did this happen?

Using the example of the Japanese automobile industry, I would like to demonstrate conclusively that even after the product reached its maturing stage in Japan the rate of technological innovation in the industry continued to grow. To ascertain this empirical proposition econometrically, I used the Bayesian estimation method of the production function (Y. and H. Tsurumi 1980). The results are summarized in Table 1. The methodology of the relevant econometrics is summarized in the Appendix to this paper. (Cf. 35 et seq.)

The Japanese automobile market reached the maturing stage around the second quarter of 1970. But even after 1970, the industry continued to register

Table 1: Coefficients of Technological Progress of the Japanese Automobile Industry*

Growth Stage	
1st Quarter of 1962 to 2nd Quarter of 1966	0.022
Maturing Stage	
2nd Quarter of 1970 to 2nd Quarter of 1980	0.035

* Estimated on the basis of quarterly production data, with the use of CES production function.

technological progress, as shown by the significantly larger coefficient of technological progress for the latter of the two periods indicated in Table 1. As market competition in Japan intensified throughout the 1970s among seven major firms, the Japanese invented and perfected flexible manufacturing systems (FMS). In addition, these technological innovations in both production processes and corporate management knowhow soon spread to other batch-system production operations, such as consumer appliances, IC chips, machine tools and electronics and precision equipment. These advances enabled many Japanese firms to attain two goals simultaneously – higher productivity and zero-defect production – which would enable the firms to cope swiftly with whimsical shifts in market demand at home and abroad without loosing production efficiency. These FMS-related management skills are now helping Japanese manufacturers to succeed in doing in the U.S. what their American competitors often failed to do: namely, to produce mature products in a high-wage country like the U.S.

Although Japanese auto makers have produced a number of product innovations such as the transversed front wheel drive engines of Honda Accord, their distinct technological innovations have been related to their manufacturing processes and institutional skill. Contrary to a popular belief in the U.S., the productivity and quality of Japanese firms do not stem from a static economy of scale like a longer production run of the same model than their American competitors (Garvin 1984). As shown in Table 2, when one compares the production systems of subcompact cars of General Motors and Toyota, for example one must notice that Toyota's system is radically different from that of General Motors.

In short, the manufacturing processes of Japanese firms like Toyota are not only far more productive but more importantly far more flexible than a typical manufacturing process of American firms like General Motors. As shown by the smaller number of quality inspectors inside their plants, Japanese manufacturers have integrated their quality control into their production processes. Whereas, their American competitors still try to "inspect quality" mainly after products are finished. Rather than using inventories of finished goods, parts,

Table 2: Comparisons of Manufacturing Systems of General Motors and Toyota, 1981 (Subcompacts)

	GM	Toyota
Average production run	10 days	2 days
No. of parts stamped per hour	325	550
Worker per press line	7–13	1
Average time needed to change dies	4–6 hours	5 minutes
Daily absenteeism	11.8%	3.5%*
No. of quality inspectors	1 per 7 workers	1 per 30 workers
Time needed per finished car	59.9 hours	30.8 hours
No. of outside suppliers	3,000	300
Inventory/sales ratio	17%	1.5%
No. of worker job categories inside plant	26	4

* This number includes people away from work on business and training assignment that make up most of Toyota's absenteeism rate.

and work-in-process products to cushion uncertainties of market demand, suppliers, and production operations, Japanese firms use frequent changes in the number of production shifts and the flexibility of production runs to cushion cyclical demand fluctuations. Rather than playing one supplier off against another, Toyota and other Japanese firms have long built up their organic and cohesive relationship with those fewer suppliers that operate equally flexible production systems to meet rigorous delivery schedules and quality standards (Y. Tsurumi 1982).

We can easily recognize the economic superiority of the flexible manufacturing system like the one developed by Toyota over the typical rigid manufacturing system of many American firms. More importantly, we need to acknowledge that the economic superiority of the flexible manufacturing system does not stem so much from such "hard ware" as robots – important as they may be – as from such "soft ware" technologies as the firm's abilities to obtain workers' willing cooperation for incessant retraining and rotational assignments. In 1981, a similar comparison of Ford and Mazda manufacturing systems revealed that Mazda's overall production cost was about $1,300 lower per car than Ford's comparable subcompacts (Y. Tsurumi 1983). The difference in the degree of automation and product engineering was found to contribute only 17% of the overall cost differences. The wage rate differential was found responsible only for 4% of the total cost difference. The rest originated from the difference in the production process yields and human resource management factors between Mazda and Ford. After all, the fact that over three-quarters of advanced industrial robots installed today in the world are found inside Japanese factories in Japan reflects their management-employee relations conducive to workers' total cooperation with introduction of new machines into their factories. In fact, one prevailing fallacy of American management today is to equate the flexible manufacturing systems mechanically with the robotization. Many American managers disregard the corporate culture underlying the successful robotization of manufacturing processes.

More dramatic comparisons of Japanese and American firms can be made with the example of 64 K RAM integrated circuits (IC chips). This comparison includes European-owned factories of Fairchild Camera in California which Schlumberger, a French firm, acquired in 1980. Japanese semiconductor makers in Japan pay roughly the same price as their American and European competitors in the U.S. for raw silicon materials. However, Japanese firms have to pay about four times as much as their American competitors for energy and chemicals and twice as much for direct labor. As a result, Japanese production costs per wafer are today about $159 as opposed to American competitors' costs of $94. However, Japanese firms dominate the American and European market of 64 K RAM IC chips. How is this possible?

In 1984, Japanese semiconductor firms were voluntarily restraining their supply quantity to the U.S. and European markets in order to maintain the price of $4 per IC chip. This price level provides a protective umbrella to higher-cost producers in the U.S. and Europe. Naturally, Japanese firms are found to be making 50% to 90% more profit contribution per IC chip over the cost of its wafer than their American competitors. The difference is due to the higher chip yields per wafer of Japanese firms. When American and European firms are making only 176 good chips per the same sized wafer, their Japanese firms are found making anywhere from 264 to 380 good IC chips per wafer.

Accordingly, once transplanted to the U.S. by Japanese firms, their flexible production processes make Japanese semiconductor firms far more competitive when they can work with cheaper labor, cheaper chemicals and energy in the U.S. Unlike the semiconductor operations, however, Japanese auto firms have to pay about 50% more for American labor than for their Japanese labor. Yet, the higher monetary wage rates in the U.S. are more than offset by the higher productivity of Japanese auto assembly systems. Today, General Motors is counting on its joint venture with Toyota in California for learning Toyota's superior manufacturing systems (Reich 1984). In Europe where the wage rates are already generally lower than Japanese rates, the flexible manufacturing systems of Japanese multinational firms have helped them more readily to overcome start-up problems.

All told, manufacturing firms can continue to pursue the technological innovations as they ride their product life cycle well beyond the growth stage. The innovation of production processes and management skills – institutional technology – often turn out to become the ultimate competitive strength of firms operating in the worldwide markets.

3. Corporate Culture as a Firm-specific Technology

The Japanese and European Paradox needs one additional explanation. Otherwise, we are still left with one mystery that Japanese plants of high-tech related products in Japan, Korea, Taiwan, Malaysia, Singapore, and Europe have been able to cope with dynamic shifts in U.S. market demands for IC chips, consumer electronics, and other high-tech related goods better than American plants located in the same areas.

The Atari Syndrome would not have placed American operators of off-shore supply bases at a disadvantage vis-à-vis their Japanese competitors if the mature demand in the U.S. market had remained rather static. In reality, however, maturing markets for many consumer durables and industrial products continued to reflect dynamic changes in the tastes and requirements of the users of those items. As seen in the case of color t.v. sets in the U.S., the maturing market demand often showed sudden surges of rejuvenated growth when new product innovations were added to what until that point had been considered standardized products.

Cut-off geographically from the American market, many of the manufacturing systems that American firms had moved overseas frequently proved too inflexible to cope with dynamic shifts in demand in the American market. For example, when U.S. demand for IC chips shifted from 16 K RAM to 64 K RAM during the period from 1980 to 1983, American suppliers failed to respond quickly. This void in the U.S. and European markets were filled by their Japanese competitors. Moreover, American IC chip manufacturers with off-shore plants in low wage countries frequently found themselves faced with new problems of defective product quality. Loosing out in the market to their Japanese competitors, American chip manufacturers ran to the U.S. government for protection from Japanese competition.

In order to remain competitive in dynamic markets firms must be able to supply newer products quickly in ample quantity to their markets. This move requires closer and simultaneous coordination among R & D, product development, marketing and manufacturing operations (Fraker 1984). This kind of corporate flexibility is only sustained by free and instantaneous flows of necessary information back-and-forth among diverse operational units of the same firm. Many American manufacturers could not cope with dynamic market changes because of not only vast geographical distance but more importantly, fatal communication gaps between their R & D and marketing centers in the U.S. and their manufacturing centers abroad. Unlike their Japanese competitors, manufacturing operations of many American firms abroad were informationally isolated from American markets.

In contrast, Japanese executives when encountering similar market competition invariably move to save their human resources. They tend to seek technical rather financial or legal solutions. If they must cut personnel costs immediately, they cut their own salaries first. They strive to lower production costs and improve product quality by building more flexibility into their production processes, through automation and worker retraining. The offshore plants of Japanese firms are closely linked with their parent plants and suppliers in Japan, all of which are alert for market changes worldwide.

Theoretically the Japanese solution is available to American firms. But it requires closer coordination of such diverse functions as research and development, manufacturing, and marketing. Such coordination demands that the corporate culture nurture an atmosphere of comraderie among different individuals so that they can develop a shared commitment to the same corporate goal. Unfortunately, to many American executives, management leadership means the manipulative power to pit one profit or cost center against another, or one individual against another. They are quick to take credit for their firms' financial success, yet equally quick to find someone else – often foreigners – to blame for their failures. Accordingly, production managers are told to cut the costs of production within their own limited means. As a result, one company after another falls prey to the deadly "Atari Syndrome". Their offshore plants are informationally and managerially isolated from the U.S.

Successful transfer of Japanese manufacturing systems and Volvo experiments of factory management to the U.S. have shown that even the production of mature products can be made economically feasible in a high wage country like the U.S. A strong case can also be made to show that sustained successes in the high-tech related markets of industrialized areas like the U.S., Japan, and Europe require multinational firms to develop flexible corporate and manufacturing systems to cope with dynamic shifts of such markets. Elsewhere, I have shown that successful Japanese and American firms in such markets have developed rather similar corporate structures and cultures and that corporate cultures of firms can be generally divided into two dominant types, namely Model J and Model A (Y. Tsurumi 1976 and 1979).

Model J type firms are found predominantly among Japanese, European and American firms whose business environment is characterized by technological innovations, global competition, and rapid growth. Unlike Model A type firms which include many American firms involved in mature technologies and markets in the U.S., Model J firms share such internal characteristics as (1) management commitment to the job security of employees; (2) a shared corporate goal as the effective management control device; (3) lateral and informal communication across different departments and individuals of the firm; (4) strong identification of both management and employees with their firm; and (5) management emphasis on continued training of corporate members.

Implicitly, the job security of Model J corporation members becomes the foundation of the long-term orientation of the firm's employees. The job security also serves to support cooperative rather than adversarial relations among various subunits of the firm or between management and rank and file members. The job security of Model J firms often negates the need for cumbersome measures of arbitrating job grievances or policing individual members' behavior. Because of the job security, few resist the introduction of new machines and changes in work rules that are necessary to remain competitive in dynamic markets. Inasmuch as a manager's misjudgement concerning the market or the competition that produces a decline in sales and profits is not offset by expedient layoffs of rank and file employees, managers must always concern themselves with their organization's flexibility to cope with rapid shifts in the business environment.

The Japanese and European Paradox in the U.S. has demonstrated that Model J corporate structures are far more flexible than Model A corporate structures in their ability to make high-speed adjustments to dynamic changes in technological and market environments. Similarly, even after having acquired unionized factories in the U.K., the successes of Hitachi and Toshiba, two leading electronics firms of Japan, have shown that even militant British trade unions moderate their adversarial behavior and accept no-strick clauses in their contracts under Model J types of management of Hitachi and Toshiba. Michelin's success in transplanting its plant management know-how to South Carolina in the U.S. also underscores the fact that the firm's emphasis of training American labor and honoring the job security of its rank and file employees has enabled Michelin to develop superior production systems to those rigid manufacturing systems of its American competitors in Ohio and other mid-western areas of the U.S. In fact, Model J corporate culture has shaped its corporation to be "a learning entity" which encourages much experimental adaptation to their new technological and competitive environment.

Structural and cultural differences between Model A and Model J types of corporation can best be observed by the following four components of the corporate structures. All these four components are interrelated with one another.

3.1 Management Leadership Style and Ideology

Ideologically, management treats human labor as most important and renewable assests of the firm. Management leadership style is expressed in management's keen attention to actual details of manufacturing and sales operations of the firm. Management is not prone to shift the blames for management mistakes to the lay-off of rank and file employees. The costs of adjustments are absorbed, often first by the top management echelon, through temporary reduction of salaries and wages rather than through reduction of employment level. In shaping Model J types of firms after World War II, the Japanese brand of Confucian ideas of moral courage, self-sacrifice, and benevolence was consciously applied to enriching the management leadership style and substance (R. Tsurumi 1983). In fact, Japanese management's conscious efforts from 1949 onward were devoted to combining the Japanese Confucian notion of managerial leadership and entrepreneurship with the best of American industrial ideologies of efficiency, quality, and growth (Kodansha 1983).

3.2 Human Resource Development

In order to develop the corporate culture to turn the firm into a learning entity, continual training of management and rank and file employees is emphasized. Many individuals are often rotated among different jobs so that they could develop their own views of how different functions of their firm are intertwined with one another. Each corporate member is encouraged and even required to share his or her job skill, knowledge, and even work assignments with fellow employees.

3.3 Personnel Rewards and Job Performance Evaluation

In order to ease job rotations and frequent changes in job assignments, wages and salaries are tied more to such personal factors as the seniority and training backgrounds than to specific job categories. When one links job categories to wages and benefits, one should maintain as few job categories as possible to facilitate job rotations. As shown in Table 1, Toyota's four job categories were far less than General Motors' 26 job categories inside a comparable auto assembly factory. Rather than relying on strict job descriptions for guiding individuals' job performance, their shared acceptance of their firm's goals and their assigned tasks is emphasized to guide individuals' job performance. In order to reward the cooperative work among employees as well as to help develop every member's commitment to the corporate goals, various forms of profit sharing plans are actively maintained (Marsh and McAllister 1981).

3.4 Management-Labor Relations

Both formal and informal information sharing about the firm's goals and operations between management and labor (employee) is extensively practiced. This shared information serves to reduce conflicts and tensions between management and labor. In addition to management's sharing the responsibility of honoring the job security of rank and file employees, the extensive and frequent sharing of information between management and labor was carried out by both Hitachi and Toshiba when they needed to avoid destructive labor relations developed under former British owners. In 1971 when Hitachi Metals acquired a special alloy plant in Edmore, Michigan in the U.S. from its former owner, General Electric Corporation, Hitachi Metals faced the militant labor union (the United Auto Workers) that had grown distrustful of the management under conflict-ridden relationships with GE management. By sharing the responsibility for the job security of rank and file members with the UAW, and by sharing the management information and operational information with the UAW and rank und file employees, Hitachi Metals rebuilt the management-employee relationship toward more cooperative mode. During the economic recession of 1974–76, Hitachi Metals opened its books to the UAW and asked the employee (union members) to choose between a temporary but across the board wage cut with no lay-off and the lay-off of about 25% workers with no wage cut for the remaining group. By an overwhelming margin, the union members decided to accept the wage cut across the board.

4. Conclusions

Flexible manufacturing systems of many Japanese firms and some American and European firms are integral parts of their flexible corporate systems. The Japanese and European Paradox in the U.S. is made possible by the flexible corporate systems of Japanese and European multinationals. Flexible corporate systems are already found more suitable for uncertain global competition in the 1980s and the 1990s. Accordingly, the final outcome of the global competition among multinationals of different nationality will depend on their ability to develop their flexible corporate systems with their own employees of different nationalities worldwide. The firms will have to learn to integrate even those foreign managers, specialists, and employees, not born and trained in the home country of the firms, into their informal and formal communication networks across different functions and locations of the same firm (Y. Tsurumi 1978; Japanese Business 1978).

In this regard, increasing successes of Japanese and European direct investments in the U.S. are confronting many American multinational firms in auto and other mature industries to reconsider their global strategies and corporate structures. Besides, as exemplified by IBM, there are already some American multinational firms in computers and other high-tech fields which have developed their own flexible corporate systems beyond those prototypes offered by their Japanese and European counterparts. The three-way competition among American, Japanese, and European multinational worldwide will take on far greater complexities as they grope for cooperation and competition among them through innovative business tie-ups and defensive manoeuvers in one another's territories.

More immediately, the Japanese and European Paradox in the U.S. helps us answer one tantalizing empirical question of multinational firms' investment behavior: why are many American multinationals prone to move their manufacturing operations to lower wage countries even before their products reach their maturity stage in the U.S.? Why do their Japanese and European competitors often wait until the end of the maturing stage of their products at home before they transfer the production of standard products to lower wage countries? Hypothetically, if American firms learn to behave like their Japanese competitors, they would collectively offer at least 4 to 5 years of additional employment time to their employees. Since this is no small matter for the U.S. struggling to ease employment adjustment problems, a host of public policy issues will be further illuminated by further analysis of the Japanese and European Paradox in the U.S.

Just as Japanese managers have successfully combined the Confucian entrepreneurship values of human resources with the modern capitalism based on the Judeo-Christian mores, European multinational managers have much to contribute to the ideological enrichment of flexible corporate structures. Many of them have already been bred in the tradition of humanistic and social democracy and have been exposed to pragmatic management-labor codetermination. Their successes in the U.S. will add a new dimension to the modern management of multinational firms.

Bibliography

Fraker, S.: High-Speed Management for High-Tech Age. *Fortune*, March 5, 1984.
Garvin, D.: Comparisons of American and Japanese Manufacturing Systems. *Columbia Journal of World Business*, Winter 1984.
Japanese Business: Annotated Bibliography and Research Guide. Praeger, New York 1978.
Kodansha Encyclopedia of Japan, Vol. 1. Harper & Row, New York 1983.
Marsh/McAllister: ESOPs Tables. A Survey of Companies with Employee Stock Ownership Plans. *Journal of Corporation Law*, Spring 1981.

13 INTERNATIONAL TRANSFER OF TECHNOLOGY
National and Corporate Productivity

In the discussion of the theories of international trade and direct investment (Chapters 4 and 7) it was assumed that the dynamically changing international flow of manufactured goods was caused by the successful transfer of requisite manufacturing technology from country to country. Indeed, this process of international technology transfer underlies all of the current crucial geopolitical issues – e.g., the North-South conflict, revitalization of American manufacturing industries, economic development, U.S.-China trade, East-West trade, and above all, the roles of multinational firms throughout the world and the U.S.-Japan productivity gap.

Technology has been internationally the most mobile factor of production. The agents of this international transfer are individuals who through their learning and training represent new technical skill, scientific knowledge, and innovation in their ability to create new products and production processes. The most common international carriers of technology are the products themselves. The fact that certain new products are successfully manufactured reduces the inherent uncertainties for those who attempt to create new products through trial and error. Furthermore, today, as international communication and transportation become increasingly efficient, new scientific, technological, and commercial discoveries travel through journals and other printed media from country to country.

No longer is the absorption of new technology the prerogative of the large multinationals. Alert international entrepreneurs can readily scan the world for the necessary technology. More often than not, they can purchase such technology through technical licensing agreements from individuals and firms that choose to make incremental profits by exporting (selling) technology to others. Nowhere is this situation more dramatically manifested than in the recent demise of large international steel mills and the corresponding rise of mini steel mills in the United States.

From 1979 to 1981, such large, integrated American steel companies as U.S. Steel, Bethlehem, and Kaiser were busy lobbying the U.S. Congress in Washington as well as in state capitols of such key states as New York, California, and Pennsylvania for increased protection from Japanese and European competition. In previous years, their failure to modernize steelmaking facilities and their tendency to divert investment funds from steelmaking to nonsteel businesses resulted in the inability of large American steelmakers to compete with efficient Japanese producers.

Large U.S. integrated steel producers lagged considerably behind their Japanese competitors in adopting a wide range of new steel and ironmaking technology. For example, to convert iron ingots into steel, an obsolete technology is the open hearth process, invented in the nineteenth century. The modern technology is the basic oxygen furnace (BOF) converter. In Japan, the last open hearth was destroyed in 1976; in America, as late as 1979 about one-half of American steel was still made using the open hearth process. In Japan, in 1981 the average size blast furnace produced 3 to 4 million tons a year; in the United States the capacity of 1 to 2 million tons a year was still considered large. All told, in 1980 steel imports garnered about 20 percent of American markets.

In 1980 ARMCO turned to Nippon Steel, the largest steelmaker in the world, for technical assistance. This Japanese steel company agreed to help ARMCO increase its steel productivity by applying Nippon Steel's proprietary know-how. Meanwhile, in 1979 Kaiser Steel broached the subject with another Japanese steel producer, Nippon Kokan, offering sales of all of Kaiser's steel plants. Nippon Kokan, however, eventually declined the offer because Kaiser's steel production facilities were too antiquated to be saved by an infusion of Nippon Kokan's technology.

Instead, in 1982 Nippon Kokan tried to purchase the Rouge Steel Plant of Ford Motor Company together with two leading general trading companies of Japan—Mitsubishi and Marubeni. The infusion of the Japanese steelmaking technologies was expected to revitalize the somewhat outdated steel plant in Michigan. In 1982, General Motors formed a manufacturing and sales joint venture in the United States with Fujitsu's industrial robotic subsidiary. General

Motors was counting on this joint venture as one effective way to diversify its business lines away from the automobile.

In contrast to lethargic productivity of large U.S. integrated steel mills from 1978 onward, dozens of new mini steel mills sprang up in Florida, North Carolina, and other southeastern states. They operated electrofurnaces that, by recycling scrap iron, turn out 1.5 to 2 million tons of iron and steel products per year mainly for use as small construction material such as ferroconcrete reinforcers, wire rods, and small-gauge pipes and structures. In 1980, it was estimated that about 15 percent of total U.S. steel output consisted of the products of the new mini mills. By 1990, this portion is expected to easily increase to 25 percent. These mini mills have already begun to pressure the large integrated steel mills to modernize their facilities for those products that compete directly with those of the mini mills.

Furthermore, these new mini mills compete head on with imports from Korea, Brazil, and Europe. The success of the mini mills was due to their adoption of the newest electrofurnace technology and the continuing casting process, which had been perfected in Japan and was widely known in steelmaking circles. Soaring fuel and other energy prices made the mini mills far more cost effective than the large integrated steel mills. Mini mills only used 9.9 million Btu's per ton of steel recycled from scrap while the integrated steel mills needed 35.2 million Btu's per ton of steel made from iron ore. More importantly, the entrepreneurs of these new mini mills applied such new management-labor practices as guaranteed job security for rank and file workers and the abolishment of restrictive work rules on production floors. Both guarantees were considered essential to the adoption of the continuous casting process used widely by the Japanese.

1. DEFINITION OF TECHNOLOGY

The preceding accounts illustrate how important it is for forward looking entrepreneurs not only to search for requisite technology worldwide but also to adjust their management philosophy to fit the new technology. For instance, one American manufacturer of industrial machinery tried to apply licensed (imported) Japanese technology to his factory only to discover that high turnover by rank and file workers made it impossible to utilize the licensed technology. What, then, is technology?

Technology is, of course, based on scientific principles and discoveries. However, technology that is the commercial application of such scientific principles and discoveries can only be elevated to proprietary skill and know-how by those who are intent on refining the commercial application of scientific principles usually treated as public knowledge by scientists and engineers. For an analysis of the international transfer of technology, it would be useful to classify technologies into the following three categories.

(1) Product-related Technology

It emanates from identifiable products that are new to host countries. This technology is often the proprietary possession of investing parent firms. Although specific production-related processes are an integral part of such proprietary products, the investing parent firm's technological advantage is that it alone owns the products in question.

(2) Production Process-related Technology

It originates from identifiable manufacturing processes. This technology is also often a proprietary holding unique to the investing parent firms. Although specific products accompany specific production processes, the technological advantage of investing parent firms is that they possess the unique manufacturing processes not held by indigenous local firms or other foreign investors.

(3) Institution-related Technology

This technology results from the body of the firm's organizational expertise that has grown out of a specific technology related to products and to production processes of investing firms. This operational experience is difficult to separate from the firm and employees affecting it. The firm's way of organizing and motivating employees and managers to produce specific products and services of high quality is but one example of such technology. The proper flow of management information within a given firm across different functional areas and proper communication between an investing parent firm and its subsidiary form the part of institution-related technology unique to firms.

Naturally, the distinctions between the three categories of technology are often blurred. However, they do require different methods of transfer from country to country. In particular, production process-related technology is closely related to institution-related technology, which determines the man-machine interaction on the production floor as well as the organizational effectiveness in maintaining lateral and vertical flows of management information within the firm. In terms of difficulty of international transfer, product-related technology is the most easily transferable to a foreign country. Institution-related technology is the most difficult to exchange internationally across different managerial cultures.

2. NATIONAL DIFFERENCES IN TECHNOLOGICAL FOCUS

Since technology is a product of entrepreneurs' conscious efforts to apply scientific principles to their perceived commercial opportunities, it is strongly influenced by societal characteristics of the entrepreneurs' business environment. It is no accident, therefore, that for some time after the turn of the twentieth century, the United States dominated such product innovations as the sewing machine, television, other large consumer durable items, passenger car automatic transmissions, and numerically controlled machine tools. All of these products were designed to respond to American society characterized by a mass market, high income (high wages), a relative shortage of skilled and household labor, and a relative abundance of natural resources.

By the same token, Japanese manufacturers have for some time excelled in perfecting compact and energy efficient household appliances, passenger cars, precision optical instruments, the single reflex camera, and mass production steelmaking know-how. All of these technological innovations of Japanese manufacturers were a response to the Japanese market and consumers' idiosyncratic preferences for intricate, reliable, miniature gadgets and to the acute shortage of industrial raw materials.

Thus far, the United States has been noted as the birthplace of product-related technological innovations while Japan has put significant focus on production process-related technologies. European nations have shown a relative balance between product innovation and production process innovation.

Table 13-1 shows national differences in profiles of technological innovations. The United States exhibited an emphasis on labor-saving types of technological innovations while Europe and Japan emphasized raw material savings.

Furthermore, technological innovations are very much the products of specific corporate cultures. The firm that elevates product quality to being the supreme guide of its business strategy naturally emphasizes production processes and requisite institution-related technology conducive to product quality. On the other hand, the firm that only tinkers with marginal and cosmetic changes in prod-

Table 13-1. Innovations in the U.S., Europe, and Japan—1945–1974.

Innovations	U.S.		Europe (U.K. included)		Japan	
	No.	Percentage	No.	Percentage	No.	Percentage
Labor saving	331	40.1	120	12.7	6	6.4
Material saving	175	21.2	444	46.9	32	34.1
Capital saving	58	7.0	104	11.0	7	7.4
Novel function	106	12.8	83	8.8	12	12.8
Safety	50	6.1	60	6.3	7	7.4
Others	106	12.8	135	14.3	30	31.9
Total	826	100.0	946	100.0	94	100.0

Source: W. H. Davidson, "Patterns of Factor-Saving Innovation in the Industrialized World," *European Economic Review* 8 (1976): 214.

uct style and appearance tends to ignore the modernization of its production processes.

The firm that is run by managers bred in the short-term orientation of financial profit maximization naturally ignores those R&D activities that will have five- to ten-year payoff periods. The firm that encourages R&D specialists, marketing personnel, production personnel, and human resource training specialists to interact freely with one another finds it easier to introduce new R&D innovations to the production floor and into the market.

Judging from the nationalities of Nobel Prize winners and from a number of internationlly recognized scientific breakthroughs, the United States has for some time outperformed other industrialized nations. Despite its sagging economy, the United Kingdom still continues to produce outstanding scientists. And yet, the decay of British manufacturing industries and their decline in international trade and investment performance point out that British firms have somehow failed to utilize readily available scientific and technological information to their industrial and commercial advantage. The United States shows similar symptoms. Even in the steel, automobile, and electronics household product industries the R&D units of American firms have produced remarkable prototypes of new products and production process innovations. And yet, they have increasingly failed to commercialize them.

On the other hand, Japanese firms have developed internal organizational systems that effectively utilize the world market's technological and scientific information. Although Japan's overall scientific and technological level is rapidly increasing, she is still lagging behind the United States and the United Kingdom in terms of generating scientific breakthroughs. And yet, since the end of the 1960s many Japanese firms have increasingly demonstrated their capability to apply new scientific and technological information to new products and production processes. For example, the prototype of television video recording (VTR) systems was invented in the United States late in the 1950s for broadcasting and industrial use, but Sony and Matsushita—two Japanese firms—were the ones that actually succeeded in improving the product and came up with the compact, reliable, easy-to-operate VTRs for consumer markets.

3. MULTINATIONAL FIRMS AS AGENTS OF TECHNOLOGY TRANSFER

There is no question that multinational firms act as effective agents of international transfer of technology from their home country to foreign host nations. On the other hand, developing countries regard foreign direct investment as an expedient package of the necessary ingredients for their industrialization, which include: capital, technology, export contact, managerial know-how, and entrepreneurship. And yet, especially in developing countries, critics say that foreign firms bring in the wrong technology or that foreign direct investments do not function well as implementers of international technology transfer.

When similar technology is licensed outright to indigenous firms in developing nations by foreign firms there are few complaints about foreign multinationals supplying inappropriate technology. This apparent contradiction shows that the ensuing controversies over multinational firms as agents of technology transfer are compounded by questions of foreign ownership of new manufacturing companies in developing nations and by the fear of developing countries that they may become economically, politically, and technologically dependent upon foreign multinationals.

Using the examples of overseas transfer of Japanese manufacturing technology either through licensing agreements or by direct investments of Japanese firms, we will examine a number of issues surrounding international technology transfer. We will see that in the real world, the conventional economists' prescription for technology transfer does not hold true.

(1) International Transfer of Japanese Technologies
Since the 1870s, Japan has succeeded in overcoming her shortage of manufacturing skills and experience and has rapidly caught up

with the advanced nations, mainly by division of tasks among many individuals and firms. Firms in Japan have organized their employees, subsidiaries, and subcontractors to allow one person or company to perform essentially a single function. Therefore, they did not have to wait for a single worker or firm to master the total breadth of skills needed for particular tasks. To compensate for the shortage of skilled workers in Japan, production processes, imported from the West, have often been broken down into a series of simple standard operations to be put together again by specialists in Japan. Because Japanese wage rates were much lower than those in the West, even this kind of division of labor involving many people permitted economical and rapid assimilation of diverse manufacturing technologies in Japan.

Convincing historical documents point out that similar adaptive efforts were accomplished during the nineteenth century by U.S. manufacturing industries. The United States was relatively low on skill, compared to the United Kingdom, the major source of imported manufacturing technologies to the United States at that time. The case of Japan remains a curiosity at present, however. Her adaptive efforts extended right into the 1950s. She is the only developed country today where one can still find vintage 1950s process technologies and related products, particularly in small to medium-sized firms.

Efforts in individual specialization have also been accomplished in the field of clerical and administrative works. This group or "human sea" (*jinkai senjutsu*) approach in shortening the time required for a Japanese firm to attain a given level of technological and managerial competence has remained very much intact in the older technologies still in use.

Accordingly, Japanese industries have produced individual engineers, skilled workers, and technicians who possess a distinctly narrower breadth of expertise than their counterparts in the United States. For example, a typical Japanese journeyman machinist can often perform only a specialized job on one machine, such as a lathe, while an American machinist can perform jobs on several different pieces of equipment, from lathe to milling machines. Such extreme forms of specialization have been perpetuated by the educational and vocational institutions, which historically have been the products of Japan's concerted efforts to attain a high level of industrialization in a short period of time.

Within the typical Japanese environment, process-related technology, in particular, has grown closely intertwined with the institutional idiosyncrasies of Japanese corporate culture. Accordingly, the international transfer of Japanese technologies to foreign licensees and to Japanese subsidiaries abroad often required, at least at the outset, the simultaneous grafting of the critical mass element of institution-related technologies onto the economic and cultural roots of host countries.

Japanese technology, which has found eager buyers in developing countries, most notably in Asia, is distinct from that purchased by developed nations. The recent fruits of Japanese R&D efforts in electronics and chemical and petrochemical products and processes have been mainly exported to the United States and Europe. New semiconductors and other new development, such as synthetic paper, are being licensed to American and European firms. And newer production processes such as the operational know-how of cold strip milling by steel plants are also sold by Japanese firms to U.S. plants. In contrast, older techniques such as drawing wires and producing power transformers are purchased by firms in India and Taiwan. Standard machine tools and their production know-how are also purchased by firms in Asia.

A classification (by their entry date into Japan) of the 689 technologies that Japan sold to other nations during the years 1950–1969 reveals that the newer the licensed technology, the greater its chance of being purchased by American and European firms.[1] In fact, as measured from the time of its first commercial application in Japan to its final export, the average age of Japanese technology licensed to U.S.- and Europe-based firms was about two to three years, while the average age of both product- and process-related technology purchased by Taiwan, Singapore, and India were from five to fifteen years.

Developing nations in Asia bought manufacturing technologies held by small to medium-sized firms in Japan. Countries such as Taiwan, Singapore, and India were the most frequent purchasers of old technologies that had only recently begun to lose their dominant presence in Japan. Other Asian countries, such as Thailand, Malaysia, and Indonesia, appeared technologically too weak to absorb Japanese technology merely through licensing agreements. As a result, they bought older, simpler technology from Japan mainly through the direct investments of Japanese firms.

A country like Japan emphasizes the improvement and adaptation of process-related technologies, which were developed earlier by foreign innovators, for the production of new products. As relative late-

---

1. Y. Tsurumi, *The Japanese Are Coming: A Multinational Interaction of Firms and Politics* (Cambridge, Mass.: Ballinger Publishing Company, 1976), pp. 169–78.

comers to the competitive scene for new products, Japanese firms often had to design cheaper ways of producing the same products in order to survive price-cutting battles on the world market in direct competition with earlier arrivals to the industrial scene.

When Japanese manufacturers succeed in developing technology that permits the reduction of unit production costs or the improvement of product quality or both, a number of manufacturers in the United States and Europe become potential purchasers of these innovations. Perhaps these foreign firms are already feeling the prick of price competition in their domestic and foreign markets as their products become mature, standard items in these markets. As a result, they often attempt to prolong their competitive positions by purchasing Japanese products and production processes that are economically superior to their own. Both increased steel product exports from Japan and higher sales of steelmaking technology from Japan to American and European steel firms followed this pattern. From 1981 to 1983, as Japanese imports captured about 30 percent of the U.S. machine tool market, Bendix, Acme, and other leading machine tool firms rushed to purchase products and technologies from Japan.

(2) Japanese Technology in the United States and Europe

As we saw in Chapter 7, Japanese direct investments in the United States and Europe continued to rise rapidly from the latter half of the 1970s to the early 1980s. In particular, Japanese manufacturing firms frequently opened manufacturing subsidiaries in the United States and Europe to avoid moves by protectionists to restrict Japanese imports. Although such protectionist actions triggered Japanese investments, the success of these investments depended upon Japanese firms' transfer of some unique competitive strength to American and European markets. The combination of Japanese production process-related technology and institution-related technology appears to enable Japanese manufacturing subsidiaries to overcome the handicaps of operating factories in direct competition with American and European firms on their own turf.

For example, even when the hardware production technology is ostensibly the same in General Motors' Lordstown auto assembly plant and Honda's assembly plant in Japan, Honda's plant demonstrates greater manufacturing productivity. Both are highly automated and designed to produce subcompact cars. And yet in early 1970s, when GM's Lordstown plant in Ohio fell short of its maximum production speed of 75 cars per hour, it ran into workers' sabotage, wildcat strikes, and an increase in product defects. At approximately the same time, Honda's assembly plant was easily turning out 100 to 120 cars per hour with impeccable workmanship. This productivity disparity must be due to differences in the two plants' institution-related technology, governing the efficiency of production processes.

Japanese manufacturers' production processes are more efficient not only in Japan but also when they are set up in the United States. Sony's San Diego plant is evidence of that fact. In 1979, this factory set a record of 200 consecutive days of no product defects, surpassing the previous record of its Japanese counterpart. After taking over the Quasar color television plant in Illinois from Motorola in 1975, Matsushita of Japan soon cut the annual warranty repair bills from about $16 million to less than $2 million a year.

This does not mean, however, that all Japanese manufacturing and nonmanufacturing subsidiaries in the United States and Europe are meeting with unqualified success. In fact, available research data indicate that Japanese subsidiaries in the United States can be classified into two groups.[2] On one end of the spectrum of economic and managerial success measured by profits and workers' turnover rates, is a small group of firms; on the other end of the spectrum are many firms experiencing increasing hostility and failure on the part of American supervisors and rank and file employees.

The preceding episodes indicate that Japanese production process-related technology is transferable to advanced nations such as the United States and Europe. However, this transfer requires special attention by both Japanese and foreign managers involved in the adaptation of Japanese production processes to American and European environments.

Illustrations of the operations of the GM and Honda plants are schematically presented in Figure 13-1. For the same of simplicity, both assembly factories are represented by five mechanically similar substations. Products flow from Station 1 through Station 5 before they are moved to the final quality control inspection station (QC). Like other American industrial plants, the GM system has a large QC staff, whose function it is to pass or fail the assembled products depending upon how they stand up under the visual or other testing procedures. In order to make sure that the production workers at Stations 1 through 5 pay attention to product quality, the QC department often stations sub-QC inspection personnel in between

2. For example, see Richard T. Johnson-Pascale, "Success and Failure of Japanese Subsidiaries in America," *Columbia Journal of World Business* (Spring 1977): 30-37.

Figure 13-1. Two Types of Factory Management (Model A and Model J).

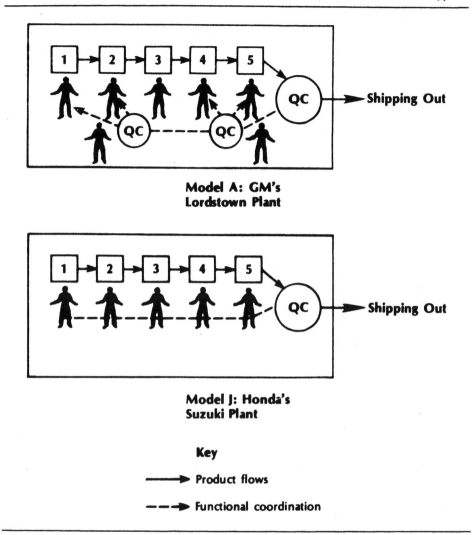

**Model A: GM's
Lordstown Plant**

**Model J: Honda's
Suzuki Plant**

Key

→ Product flows

--→ Functional coordination

production stations. These sub-QC personnel oversee production workers.

On the other hand, the Honda plant has, if any, a very small QC inspection staff at the end of the assembly line. This staff just attaches "OK (passed)" labels on each product that has already been produced. There will be no special sub-QC inspections scattered though the assembly line to look over the shoulders of production workers.

At the GM plant, management emphasizes, through QC inspectors, the notion of adequate quality level (AQL). No one knows how this level has been determined. In reality, the AQL concept is used as the euphemism for tolerating product defects at each production station up to 2 percent (98% reliability). Since there is no guarantee that the five different production workers from Stations 1 through 5 build the permitted 2 percent defects (two out of a hundred products) into the same product cumulatively, it is highly probable that by the time the product passes Station 5, up to thirty-one products out of a hundred—a 31 percent defect rate—will contain some product flaw.[3]

3. Let us think that there are n processes to make a product. Let A_f be the no-defect region in process f ($f = 1, \ldots, n$). For a product to be without defects, we have to have in symbols

$$S = \left\{ A_1 \cap A_2 \cap A_3 \cap \ldots \cap A_n \right\}$$

and if we want to have, say, 95 percent of products without defects, then

$$Pr(S) = Pr\left[A_1 \cap A_2 \cap A_3 \ldots \cap A_n \right] = 0.95. \qquad (13\text{--}1)$$

1. *Case Where A_f ($f = 1, \ldots, n$) are mutually independent:* Let α_f be the probability of defects (or the significance level) for process f. Then

$$Pr\left[A_1 \cap A_2 \cap \ldots \cap A_n \right] = (1 - \alpha_1)(1 - \alpha_2) \ldots (1 - \alpha_n). \qquad (13\text{--}2)$$

Example: Let $n = 5$ (5 processes). $\alpha_1 = \alpha_2 = \ldots = \alpha_5 = \alpha = 0.05$. Then

$$Pr\left[A_1 \cap A_2 \cap \ldots \cap A_5 \right] = (1 - \alpha_1)(1 - \alpha_2) \ldots (1 - \alpha_5) = (1 - \alpha)^5$$

$$= (1 - 0.05)^5 = 0.774 . \qquad (13\text{--}3)$$

Hence if we want, say, 95 percent of products without defects we have to set each significance level α (for each process) by

$$(1 - \alpha)^5 = 0.95$$

$$\text{or} \quad 5 \log(1 - \alpha) = \log 0.95 , \quad \alpha = 0.0102.$$

If there is n processes α is to be found by

$$(1 - \alpha)^n = 0.95.$$

For a large n, we have

$$\alpha \sim \frac{1 - 0.95}{n} . \qquad (13\text{--}4)$$

Even for $n = 5$, the approximate formula (13–4) produces a fairly accurate estimate as long as α is small:

$$\alpha \sim \frac{1 - 0.95}{5} = 0.01 .$$

The exact α value is 0.0102.

At Honda's plant each worker assigned to a production station is trained to strive for zero defects. A mere one percentage point reduction in the defect rate at each station dramatically reduces the maximum defect rate from ten to thirty, to a mere 5 percent. Of course, total productivity of a Honda style plant will also be greater than a GM style plant.

Nowhere has this difference in emphasis of manufacturing operations between the GM style American automobile firm and the Honda style Japanese auto company been more evident than in the persistently high rate of recalls of defective products by American automobile firms. During the 1970s, it was not uncommon for American automobile firms to recall just as many cars each year as their annual production. As indicated by such terms as "adequate quality level" and "planned obsolescence," the American automobile industry has loosened its quality standard and has lost the confidence of Americans in American cars. The same fate has befallen the American TV manufacturers.

GM style American factories have come to treat productivity and product quality as economic tradeoffs. The function of checking product quality was delegated to quality control inspectors, who try

---

Remark: Equation (13-3) shows that if we set the probability of defects at each process to be 5 percent ($\alpha = 0.05$), then the probability of products without any defect becomes 0.774 (77.4%), not 95 percent.

2. *Case Where A_f (f = 1, ..., n) are not mutually independent:* In this case we no longer have Equation (13-2), which is given by equality, but the so-called Bonferroni inequality

$$Pr\left[A_1 \cap A_2 \cap \ldots \cap A_n\right] \geq 1 - \alpha_1 - \alpha_2 - \alpha_3 - \ldots - \alpha_n. \tag{13-5}$$

Example: $n = 5$ and $\alpha_1 = \alpha_2 = \ldots = \alpha_5 = \alpha = 0.05$,

$$Pr\left[A_1 \cap A_2 \ldots \cap A_5\right] \geq 1 - \alpha_1 - \ldots - \alpha_5 = 1 - 5\alpha = 1 - 5\,(0.05) = 0.75.$$

Remark: Equation above says that the probability of products without any defect is greater than or equal to 75 percent. Notice that compared to the independence case – Equation (13-3) – we have an inequality sign rather than an equality sign. The lower bound 75 percent is less than 77.4 percent, as in the case of independent events.

When there are n processes, then to have *at least* 95 percent products without any defect we have to set the significance level at each process by

$$1 - n\alpha = 0.95$$

$$\alpha = \frac{1 - 0.95}{n}.$$

$$\text{For } n = 5, \quad \alpha = \frac{0.05}{5} = 0.01.$$

345

to "inspect quality into" manufactured goods. Ordinary workers are pushed to increase physical hourly output while QC inspectors look over their shoulders to catch some products at less than AQL standard. Factory purchasers of raw materials and parts rarely confer with production personnel or QC inspectors. They are trained to reduce the total costs of products purchased from outside suppliers. Worse yet, factory managers and QC inspectors are often under strong management pressure to ship out, regardless of quality, anything that is produced by the factory.

In 1981 when the U.S.–Japan trade conflict over automobiles was heating up, both Japanese and American automobile firms and their consultants began to compare extensively the difference in the unit production cost of subcompact cars between Japanese and American automobile plants. In Table 13–2, one of such comparisons is summarized for Mazda and Ford. It should be noted that 49 percent of the net cost difference came from the difference in the production process yields and that the next most important factor, 34 percent, was the human resource factor. All told, 83 percent of the unit production cost difference between Ford and Mazda, which was a typical case of such comparisons, were due to the combination of production process- and institution-related technologies of Japan.

Table 13–2. Production Cost: A Comparison of Mazda and Ford.

Labor per Vehicle	47.0 (Mazda)	112.5 (Ford)
Cost Difference per Vehicle	$1,304[a]	
Sources of Cost Difference		
Plant Engineering		49%
Process yield	40	
Quality control	9	
Technologies		17%
Automation	10	
Product engineering	7	
Human Resources		34%
Absenteeism	12	
Broader job categories		
and lesser supervision	18	
Production rates	4	
Total		100%

a. This was computed when the yen/U.S. dollar rate was ¥210/$1.00 in 1981.

Similarly, in 1982, as the new U.S.–Japan trade conflict emerged over the integrated circuits (IC chips), Japanese producers were found to have product yield records twice as good as their American competitors. In the cases of automobiles and IC chips, the product quality of Japanese products were also judged to be significantly superior to American products.

On the other hand, Japanese mass production process-related technology has been based on the idea that product quality ultimately determines physical productivity and that production workers know best how to build (not inspect) quality into their products. At each factory, purchasing departments freely consult and plan together with production workers, quality control specialists, engineers, and supervisors concerning the quality of products purchased from outside suppliers. Suppliers with quality problems are dropped. Inside their factory, engineers, quality control specialists, foremen, and other factory managers are trained to listen to production workers' suggestions for improving product quality and productivity at the same time.

Neither factory managers nor QC inspectors are under management pressure to ship out everything that is produced by their factory. On the contrary, they are motivated not to ship out any defective product.

Even in the fields of production scheduling and inventory control, American plant managers are trained to maximize given production runs and adjust the required length of machine setup time to the length of production runs. Japanese workers and managers are trained to minimize the machine setup time regardless of the length (size) of their production run. With the cooperation of outside suppliers, the buffer level of inventories of parts and materials purchased from outside is also kept to the hours (not days or weeks) of reorder cycles. Production workers at each production station are trained to consider their fellow workers down the production line as their "customers." Just as they demand zero defects from their outside suppliers, each production worker is expected to supply zero defect products to his or her customer down the production line.

This difference in factory operations was aptly described by Mr. Takemoto of Sanyo. Sanyo (U.S.A.) was persuaded by Sears Roebuck to take over the Warwick Co. in Arkansas in 1976. Warwick was about to be dropped by Sears Roebuck as a supplier of private brand color television sets because its rate of product defects was running at 20 to 30 percent.

When Takemoto walked into the Warwick Plant for the first time, he said he was struck by the spacious QC station at the end of the production line. The plant manager was proudly pointing out how much personnel and equipment were allocated to this QC station and how fast the assembly line was moving. Takemoto's immediate remedy was to abolish the spacious QC station. He told each worker to take as much time as he or she needed to make the products right from the start rather than pushing slipshod products down the assembly line. These steps alone cut the factory's defect rate from 30 percent to less than 5 percent in less than a month from Sanyo's takeover. This move was coupled by Sanyo's decision to abandon Warwick's habit of laying off production workers during the slack season. It was ridiculous, Takemoto argued, for the firm to lay off its workers and then incur the costs of rehiring and retraining them in a few months. The resultant job security of Warwick workers made the unionized factory workers cooperate with the many changes in production procedures. Besides, workers' cumulatively learned skill and operational know-how were retained and improved upon even during off-season production.

One American labor unionist was struck by the turn around in the Sanyo plant and wrote as follows:

> The Sanyo people said they had two requests: they wanted the union committee to talk with the management about production policies, methods and goals and they wanted it to join in a start-to-finish quality control program that would guarantee that not a single defective TV set left the plant.
>
> The union committee was shocked by the first proposal and overwhelmed by the second. The old American management never missed the chance to remind the union that production policy was the prerogative of the boss, all the while winking as imperfects TV sets were slipped into the market.[4]

4. "QC CIRCLE" AS JAPANESE PRODUCTIVITY KNOW—HOW

Workers must be taught to think statistically and scientifically about the ways to improve product quality and productivity. Such standard statistical techniques as scatter diagrams, histograms, and even ordinary time-and-motion studies can be taught to workers. Some simple random sampling techniques are also the workers' tools.

For example, the fishbone diagram shown in Figure 13–2 is used extensively by production workers to pinpoint the many causes of product defects and low productivity.

The "QC circle movement" of Japan showed that ordinary production workers could become enthusiastic participants in quality-

4. The *New York Times*, February 11, 1982, OpEd.

Figure 13-2. Five Causes of Product Defect and Poor Productivity.

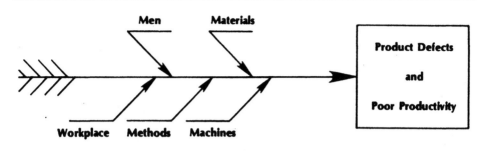

Note: This diagram is popularly known as the "Ishikawa Diagram" after Dr. Kaoru Ishikawa of Japan, whose works in quality control are widely recognized.

first activities. They are given a schematic diagram (Figure 13-2) as an analytical method of separating many plausible causes of product defects. Simple statistical tools that show economic tradeoffs between various causes (4M and 1W of Figure 13-2) are emphasized as the workers' own tools to improve their own work quality.

From the end of World War II and throughout the balance of the 1940s, concerted efforts were made by Japanese industrial engineers, academics, and managers that emphasized the improvement of Japanese product quality as the cornerstone of industrial recovery for the postwar era. By 1950 these movements were already spreading from one factory to another. From the outset, the foreman and other small group leaders on production floors were encouraged to emphasize product quality as their own central supervisory responsibility. Systematic infusions and subsequent diffusions of various methods of statistical quality control were then introduced into the Japanese industrial scene. These methods and the accompanying management philosophy of the quality-first approach, taught by Dr. W. Edward Deming and Dr. J.M. Juran in the early 1950s, were adopted as the central tools of such small group activity as the QC circle movement.

The QC circle movement was further fueled by the characteristic fierce Japanese competition among different firms. This rivalry was intensified by the occurrence of the Deming Prize—the gold medal of the industrial quality Olympic Game. On the production floor, workers were organized into small groups, each of which was called a "QC circle." It was the circle's task to identify specific quality control problems of its group's work place and proceed to solve them. The plantwide or the firmwide annual competition of QC circles further motivated them to excel in their tasks.

Any student of product quality control and inventory control knows that, generally speaking, 80 percent of the causes (often more serious causes) of product defects can only be solved by changes in basic engineering design and management. The remaining 20 percent of the causes can be remedied by the QC circles themselves. In fact, the QC circle activities not only solve 20 percent of the problems but, more importantly, signal 80 percent of the other causes to engineers and management. All told, managers, engineers, and workers alike develop the attitude that quality cannot be inspected into their product but must be built and engineered into it.

Zero defects begins with no defects in the supplies and materials purchased from outside the firm. Accordingly, Japanese firms check the quality of all supplies and materials purchased from outside. The purchasing manager is held responsible not only for the cost of these supplies and materials but for their quality. Purchasing managers and quality control engineers evaluate the production processes and work place atmosphere (management–employee relations) of prospective outside suppliers. They are interested in the process of man-machine interactions of outside suppliers, which determine not only the quality of their supplies but also their ability to deliver these supplies frequently and on time. In order to meet the demanding conditions of their customer factories, prospective suppliers are also forced to adopt the total quality approach to their products and they demand the same from their outside suppliers. This is how the quality-first approach and the QC circle movement spread rapidly from one factory to the next.

QC circles are also found among office workers. In this way, the notions of quality, productivity, cost reduction, and grassroots teamwork are adopted by office managers, clerks, sales personnel, and other office staff.

Obviously, the total quality control system of a firm is but one reflection of the corporate culture upholding the company's commitment to total quality as the nondelegable responsibility of top management. Likewise, the success of this total quality system is rooted in the implicit but strong psychological contract between rank and file employees and the management. Workers are assured that management will not shift the blame for managerial mistakes to rank and file employees. If the firm is caught unprepared by a shift in market demand or by stronger competition and is forced to absorb such adverse economic effects as a substantial decline in sales and profits, these economic costs will be shared from the top management down. Management's commitment to the job security of the rank and file employees is the linchpin of the total quality system.

The gains of the total quality system are also shared by management and employees alike. The Japanese wage system has placed both management and rank and file employees on monthly salaries. This erases the social status discrepancy between salaried staff and employees paid on an hourly basis. In addition, biannual bonus systems, which evolved in Japan after World War II, function as a total group bonus incentive par excellence. Both management and employees are keenly aware of the close relationship between the size of the bonus and their firm's economic performance. Every six months, the firm tallies its economic results to date and shares a sizable portion of the gains, if any, with both management and ordinary employees.

QC circles and related manufacturing know-how and plant management are transferable to the American scene. Once top management convinces rank and file workers that it will not shift the blame of its managerial mistakes to them, it can take the nine steps listed below. Of course, management should be concerned with the safety and welfare of the rank and file workers and reward them for their attendance and work record. A reduction in worker turnover and absenteeism is a necessary condition for the successful introduction of the total quality system on the production floor.

1. . The chief executive officer (CEO) assumes the ultimate responsibility for the quality-first approach.
2. Operationally, Quality Inspection (QI) first rejects even the slightest product flaws.
3. Quality Inspection and Material Purchasing (MP) report functionally to the CEO and are held jointly responsible for the total quality of materials purchased from outside suppliers.
4. QI, MP, Production Scheduling (PS), and foremen will all be held responsible for production scheduling.
5. Foremen should be trained to pay attention to product quality, not to mere physical output per worker.
6. QI, and in-plant engineers encourage foremen and production workers to offer suggestions for improving product quality. (Use Figure 13–2 as a problem-solving guide.)
7. Foremen and production workers should be given in-plant training in simple statistical quality control methods (economic trade-offs among the elements of Figure 13-2, scatter diagram, frequency distribution of product defects, and other simple observation and analytical tools).
8. Foremen and production workers will be assisted by industrial engineers to drastically minimize the machine setup time regardless of the size of the production run (continuous flows).

9. Work incentive bonus, piece rates, and other economic compensation for workers, foremen, QI, MP, and PS should be tied to the total product quality and steady flows of work-in-process products.

5. SELECTION OF REQUISITE PRODUCTION PROCESS—RELATED TECHNOLOGY

Once we understand that proprietary production process-related technology is a product of a specific corporate culture, investors' selection of technology and factory management style for their overseas subsidiaries is more a cultural than a scientific or engineering decision. This explains why local nationals trained in Germany prefer German machines, just as their competitors trained in Japan prefer Japanese machines.

Furthermore, we have found that economists' broad recommendations about adjusting appropriate technology to local economic conditions are not followed at all in the real world of fierce competition among foreign subsidiaries from various nations. If anything, the available empirical studies of selection of production process-related technology for manufacturing subsidiaries in the developing economies show that foreign investors tend to show a distinct preference for more automated and mechanized (capital intensive) production processes than do their comparable home plants.[5] This tendency is particularly strong when the investing firms are concerned with product quality. They seem to count on the automated processes as a built-in compensation for the lack of production and maintenance skills of local labor and engineers.

Investors' preoccupation with product quality and resultant mechanized processes are not limited to foreign investors. This tendency was shared by indigenous manufacturers striving to overtake foreign competition in their own home markets. These indigenous manufacturers and foreign firms try to position themselves in the highest product quality market segments of the market. In this way, they try to avoid the dreaded possibility that latecomers may preempt the quality segment of the market and prevent early entrants from upgrading their product quality. A mechanized operation is insurance against such a risk.

5. For an econometrically rigorous study, see Hiroki Tsurumi and Yoshi Tsurumi, "A Bayesian Estimation of Macro and Micro CES Production Functions," *Journal of Econometrics*, no. 4 (1976): 1–25.

In complicated operations required for high-quality products, plant engineers tended to rely heavily on semiautomatic and continuous processes rather than risk the possibility of production breakdowns and the deterioration of product quality by using unskilled workers. In the dyeing processes of textile operations, for example, automatically controlled, continuous processes are often used rather than manually controlled batch systems, which require skilled artisans to produce quality products. Most notably among the indigenous textile mills in Indonesia, I found firms switching over to automatic processes once management decided to upgrade product quality.

After product quality and production scales were determined, the parent company's engineers and cost accountants took over the final selection of manufacturing technology and equipment. In this regard, my field investigations in Indonesia among foreign manufacturing subsidiaries—forty-two of Japanese origin, five of other—revealed the following constraints on the selection of manufacturing technologies and processes.

(1) Local Laborer's Work Habits

Even when Indonesian workers are assigned to jobs that flow in sequence from one worker to the next, their ingrained attitude of minding one's own business tends to cause bottlenecks in the production flow. Rather than helping a fellow worker who lags behind, a fast-paced worker simply rests, and, perhaps out of extreme reluctance to antagonize, an Indonesian supervisor often fails to prod workers into maintaining a quick, continuous flow of work. As a result, many foreign plants have installed conveyor belts and semiautomatic machines to handle vital flows of materials. Even when labor-intensive production methods were feasible with the extensive use of simple manual tools (knives, for example), initial attempts to employ them were often abandoned when such tools kept disappearing. Foreign managers have tended to solve these control problems by using machine-paced production processes. Foreigners substitute their lack of training and supervising skills with capital (machinery).

(2) Insufficient Managerial Skills of Japanese Managers Operating in a Foreign Culture

Japanese managers fear that their ignorance of Indonesian customs and manners might inadvertently cause negative reactions from native employees. As a way of avoiding this problem, Japanese expatriate managers often prefer machines to labor. Their hidden rationale is that the fewer people there are to deal with, the less chance there will be for personal conflicts.

(3) Local Availability of Maintenance and Repair Service for Equipment

Developing countries are characterized by a severe paucity of skilled maintenance and repair technicians and independent maintenance and service workshops. As a result, foreign engineers and technicians must train and develop teams of local maintenance crews inside their own plants and maintain and repair their equipment themselves. These obligations invariably lead foreign plant engineers and technicians to select for their plants processes and machines with which they are most familiar.

(4) Market Uncertainty

When market conditions are uncertain, manufacturing firms are willing to pay a premium for flexibility in production volume. In this regard, labor-intensive processes, which complicate firing or reassignment of workers, are generally not as flexible as machine-intensive processes in adjusting production volume or production varieties. Foreign managers who prefer to avoid, at almost any cost, the possibility of confronting or antagonizing the labor force, government officials, or politicians of the host country are likely to prefer machine intensity over labor intensity.

The picture that has emerged from the preceding accounts is that of vulnerable foreign managers and engineers trying to minimize various political and business risks in an unfamiliar environment. According to one study of foreign manufacturing operations in Thailand, foreign subsidiaries became suddenly keen on automating and mechanizing their operations after the political upheaval in October 1973. Even the firms that, before the upheaval, had preferred workers to machines changed their preference after being exposed to the militancy of Thai workers.

These examples are also applicable to foreign direct investment in developed economies. In the United States and the United Kingdom, since foreign investors fear militant labor unions, they find it advantageous to automate their plants as much as possible. Automation not only reduces the need for high-cost labor but, more importantly, makes for fewer employee training and management problems.

6. NATIONAL POLICIES OF PRODUCTIVITY GROWTH

Since one nation's productivity growth is critically tied to the behaviors of its firms as well as to the general quality of the work force, the national policies of productivity growth must be related closely to the educational and industrial policies of the nation.

354

For instance, even in the midst of the 1981–1983 economic depression of the United States, which also produced a worldwide economic collapse, the American debates over lamentable productivity declines ignored two glaring flaws of the United States. First, in 1982, the United States produced only 58,000 new college graduate engineers. In the same year, Japan, with one-half the U.S. population, turned out 74,000 college graduate engineers. Also, the spending cutbacks that the Reagan administration initiated in education supports were aggravating the shortage of skilled workers and engineers. Second, the United States' tax reliefs to American corporations were not tied to specific behaviors deemed desirable to the growth of corporate productivity such as increased investments in research and development as well as in retraining workers and managers.

In the general educational fields, the situation in the United States is even more alarming. In 1983 more than one-half of all high school graduates tested were found seriously deficient in the basic skills of reading, mathematics, and science. In fact, it was not uncommon for undergraduate business and economics students in many state universities to possess the mathematical and science skills of an eight or ninth grader (14-year old) in Japan. If this situation persists, it will be tantamount to the unilateral economic disarmament of the United States against its international competitors.

No concept has been more misunderstood by American managers, academics, workers, and politicians than productivity. For workers, a call for increased productivity carries with it the threat of layoffs. Managers treat productivity as an economic tradeoff with product quality. Economists simple-mindedly equate productivity with mechanization and automation of production processes. Business school courses on corporate productivity are often watered down to numerical games of inventory control and production flow in which financial budgeting methods are oversold as effective management tools. To them, the corporate productivity is synonymous with office automation. Politicians' approach is to throw more tax money at defense and economic problems. What is completely ignored in these futile debates is how to restore the management leadership and culture that once pushed the United States to the apex of the world economic power.[6]

6. See Rebecca R. Tsurumi, "American Origins of Japanese Productivity: The Hawthorne Experiment Rejected," *Operations Management Review* 1, no. 3 (Spring 1983): 48-49.

Multinational managers must, therefore, concentrate on the ways to transfer across national boundaries the critical mass of the corporate culture that produced product-, production process-, and institution-related technologies to be moved from one country to the next.

More often than not, such international transfer of the critical mass of corporate culture and institution-related technologies require a large number of core production workers and first-line supervisors to be immersed in the original work situations that produced production process-related technologies earmarked for international transfer. This is why the NMB, a miniature ball bearing manufacturer of Japan, brought over 200 Singaporean workers and supervisors to its plant in Karuizawa, Japan, from 1972 to 1973, prior to NMB's commencement of the manufacturing operations in Singapore. From 1981 to 1982, Nissan Automobile Co. of Japan sent over 200 workers and supervisors of its light-truck assembly plant in Smyrna, Tennessee to the plant in Japan for three to six months of on-the-job training. This approach presupposes that these trained foreign employees will remain with their firms for a long time.

In 1982, Honda Motors' plant in Maryville, Ohio was sending its winning QC circle team to the companywide presentation of QC circle results in Japan. Similarly, from 1980 to 1982, Westinghouse and General Electric, which wanted to acquire the total quality approach of their Japanese competitors, sent inspection teams to Japan. These teams consisted not only of plant managers but also of first-line supervisors and labor unionists.

Meanwhile, many Japanese multinational firms were sending their own teams of engineers, supervisors, and core production workers to Africa, Asia, Latin America, Europe, and the United States. Their missions were to train their counterparts in their overseas subsidiaries. More and more multinational firms were recognizing that it was not enough to send one or two managers and engineers to their overseas manufacturing plants.

This means that multinational firms must also train a vast number of skilled workers, engineers, first line supervisors, and middle managers to become attuned to the social and cultural environments of their overseas factories. Otherwise, these trainers will fail to help their foreign counterparts adapt production-process technologies to various work situations found locally. Long gone are the days when a handful of linguistically and culturally sophisticated multinational managers were able to act as effective international transfer agents of various technologies.

356

14 NATURAL RESOURCE INDUSTRIES AND WORLD POLITICS

The earth is endowed with an almost countless variety of minerals and organic substances. The geographical distribution of these natural resources is, however, very uneven. Some portions of the globe are virtually barren of economically usable natural resources while others yield one resource or another in copious quantities. Very often natural resources are found far from where the products made from them will be consumed. In such situations, the multinational corporation often plays a key role.

1. VERTICALLY INTEGRATED FIRMS

In several industries in which supply sources of raw materials are geographically distant from major markets, a special type of multinational corporation has evolved—the corporation whose operations are vertically integrated across national boundaries. The domain of activities of such a corporation is often quite large. The corporation typically engages in exploration to locate and develop new sources of raw materials. Once the resource is developed, the corporation engages in extractive operations, transportation operations, and refining operations. The corporation may engage in additional "downstream" activities, including additional manufacturing operations to upgrade the product further, and distribution and marketing operations. Schematically, the activities of the vertically integrated multinational corporation may be depicted as shown in Figure 14-1.

Figure 14-1. Activities of the Vertically Integrated Multinational Corporation.

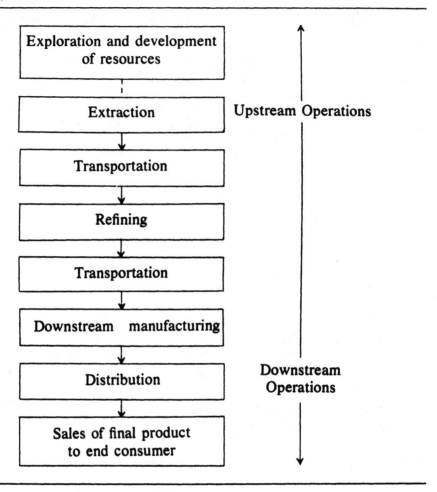

Note: Arrows indicate flow of product.

Vertically integrated multinational corporations exist in a number of natural resource-based industries, including iron and steel, oil, most nonferrous metals and, to some extent, paper and pulp. Recently, large food-processing firms have increasingly become vertically integrated, extending their activities from food growing to final marketing. In most of these industries there are also firms that are neither vertically integrated nor multinational. In the steel and oil industries, for example, there are vertically integrated firms whose operations are limited to the United States, specialized firms that operate at only one or a few levels, and vertically integrated multinational corporations.

358

Firms' quest for vertical integration would not be great if upstream operators could easily market their products, and if downstream firms could have uninterrupted access to raw materials. The industrial structure of vertical integration is produced by many market imperfections. So long as downstream firms can obtain competitive edges over other downstream firms by acquiring sources of raw materials at lower costs, these downstream firms will tend to seek their own sources of raw materials. On the other hand, upstream firms that face downstream bottlenecks limiting their ability to dispose of raw materials will try to integrate forward by developing downstream operations that provide them with their own captive outlets.

When raw materials are found in areas remote from consuming countries, firms' quests for vertical integration take on multinational activities. Nowhere has this situation been more clearly demonstrated than in the raw material processing industries of Japan. Until the early 1970s, none of the large Japanese firms processing raw materials found it necessary to become vertically and multinationally integrated. Their sizable markets were tightly shielded by the Japanese government from the direct competition of foreign multinational firms. Under general glut conditions, fierce competition among about ten leading Japanese trading companies made it certain that Japanese processing firms would acquire from the world export markets whatever raw materials they needed at competitive prices. Of course, this situation has already changed. And during the balance of the 1980s, Japanese trading and raw material processing firms will continue to seek their own captive sources of raw materials.

2. VERTICAL INTEGRATION AND BARRIERS TO ENTRY

There are three industries in which vertically integrated multinational corporations have played especially prominent roles. These are the oil, aluminum, and copper industries. Although there are major sources of raw materials within the major consuming nations in each of these industries (oil and copper are produced in large amounts in the United States, for example, and bauxite is produced in France), these sources are inadequate to meet more than a fraction of the consuming nations' demand in the middle 1980s. Consequently, the bulk of the raw materials must be obtained from sources outside of the consuming nations. In the case of oil, copper, and aluminum a few nonconsuming nations hold most of the known supplies of these raw materials.

In each of these three industries, a relatively small number of firms historically have extracted raw materials from the resource-rich countries and transported them to the consuming countries. In most cases, these same firms have been vertically integrated, carrying on the bulk of the downstream operations of refining, manufacturing, and distributing within the consuming countries, albeit often in competition with domestic firms.

In order to operate multinationally, a firm must have some advantage over its nonmultinational competitors. It is obvious that in the case of the multinational vertically integrated oil, copper, and aluminum companies, access to scarce raw materials is the major advantage. What is not so obvious is why relatively few companies are vertically integrated multinationals. Alternatively put, one must explain what are the barriers to entry that prevent other firms from imitating the vertically integrated multinationals.

Several barriers to entry have been hypothesized. Some of these are:

1. The multinational firms possess specialized proprietary knowledge at the exploration stage. This knowledge gives them an edge over potential new entrants when it comes to locating economically viable deposits of the raw materials.
2. The multinational firms possess long-term concession agreements with countries in which raw materials deposits are located. The terms of these agreements are such as to blockade new entry.
3. The capital costs and risks associated with development of new raw materials ventures are both high. Only the largest companies, the established multinationals, are capable of accepting these high costs and risks.
4. The established multinational firms control downstream markets for the raw materials through their vertically integrated operations. A new entrant at the raw materials level is unable to find markets for its output, and a new entrant at the downstream level is unable to find sources of supply of raw materials.

Each of these hypothesized barriers to entry is probably partially true. The first barrier was of great significance earlier in the twentieth century, when many of the major deposits of raw materials were first discovered and developed. In the copper industry of the early twentieth century, the oil industry of the 1920s and 1930s, and the aluminum industry of the 1950s, the technological and logistical expertise needed to locate and develop sources of supply in remote areas was limited to very few companies. Those companies that established an early stake in overseas extractive ventures are most often the ones that became dominant in their respective industries. In the mid-1970s, however, the necessary technical knowledge became so widely disseminated that it no longer constitutes a major barrier to entry.

Companies that early on were able and willing to venture into remote countries to develop extractive operations were, in fact, in many cases able to obtain from local governments concession agreements that, among other things, gave the companies a broad range of exclusive rights to develop each country's resources. Since the initial concession agreements were struck, however, most host nations have been able to modify or even abrogate these agreements. These modifications have tended to allow new entrants to come into the countries. New entry, however, has not generally been the primary objective of host governments in modifying concession agreements, as will be seen later in the chapter. In many cases, the company (or companies) that originally developed a host country's natural resources, even after renegotiation of concession agreements, still have exclusive contracts to manage these resources, albeit on terms more favorable to the host government than originally.

Although it is true that the capital costs and risks of developing new raw materials ventures are high, it is probably also true that the number of firms that might be able to accept these costs and risks was much greater in 1983 than it was, say, in 1925 or 1955. Only a finite number of such ventures are available, and as the world's largest oil, copper, and bauxite deposits were first discovered, the number of firms able to assume the costs and risks of developing them was relatively small. The costs and risks of developing a new minerals venture thus have historically posed a major barrier to entry, but over time this barrier has been declining.

It is true that the major vertically integrated multinational firms in the oil, copper, and aluminum industries do process a large portion of the natural resources they extract, and the vertical structure of these industries does pose a barrier to entry. At virtually every stage of these industries, however, there is a "competitive fringe"—some flow of the product outside of the operations of the large firms. Most of the new entry that has occurred in these industries has consisted of firms that operated on the competitive fringe, integrating their activities forward and backward and thus becoming vertically integrated themselves.

In fact, in all three industries there has been a substantial amount of new entry in the decades following World War II. In 1950, for example, eight major oil companies controlled production of 96 percent of the world's crude petroleum outside the United States and

Table 14-1. The Major Vertically Integrated Multinational Firms in the Oil, Copper, and Aluminum Industries.

Oil

Firm Name	Nationality of Parent	Percentage of Production of Oil, Non-U.S. and Non-Communist, 1969[a]
Exxon	United States	14.4 (16.5)
British Petroleum	Great Britain	14.1 (16.2)
Royal Dutch/Shell	Netherlands–Great Britain	11.6 (13.3)
Gulf	United States	8.5 (9.8)
Texaco	United States	6.9 (8.0)
Standard Oil of California	United States	6.6 (7.5)
Mobil	United States	4.2 (4.8)
Cie. Francaise de Petroles	France	4.1 (4.7)
		62.0 (80.8)

Copper

Firm Name	Nationality of Parent	Percentage of World Copper Production, 1969, (Non-Communist Countries)
Kennecott	United States	13.1
Anaconda	United States	10.9
Anglo-American	South Africa	7.9
Union Miniere	Belgium	7.5
Roan–Amax Grove	Zambia–Great Britain–United States	6.9
Phelps Dodge	United States	5.3
International Nickle	Canada	1.5
Total		54.0

Aluminum

Firm Name	Nationality of Parent	Percentage of World Primary Aluminum Capacity, 1973 (Non-Socialist Countries)
ALCOA	United States	15.0
ALCAN	Canada	14.3
Reynolds Metals	United States	10.8
Pechiney Ugine Kuhlmann	France	8.8
Kaiser Aluminum and Chemical	United States	8.5
Alusuisse	Switzerland	4.6
Total		62.0

a. Numbers in parentheses indicate percentage of exported crude oil produced by each firm.

Sources: For oil statistics, M.A. Adelman, *The World Petroleum Market* (Baltimore: Johns Hopkins University Press, 1972), pp. 80–81; for copper statistics, Ann Seidman, *Natural Resources and National Welfare: The Case of Copper* (New York: Praeger, 1975), p.10; for aluminum statistics, E.M. Graham and Y. Tsurumi, *The World Aluminum Industry* (Cambridge, Mass.: Harvard Business School, 1975), p. 17.

the Communist countries. By 1969, these same eight companies produced only two-thirds of the world's petroleum outside the United States and the Communist countries. (In 1969 these companies still controlled perhaps as much as 80 percent of exported crude petroleum.) The deterioration in the position of these eight firms reflected new entry into the industry. Many of the so-called new entrants, however, were vertically integrated U.S. oil firms that ventured abroad during the 1950s and 1960s in response to a decline in U.S. domestic oil reserves as a percentage of world reserves. Whether or not these firms can truly be thought of as new entrants is a matter of debate. In the aluminum and copper industries also, new entry caused the position of the major firms to erode in the post–World War II period. In aluminum, six firms held 100 percent of the world's primary aluminum capacity in 1950; in 1973, the same six firms held about 60 percent. In the copper industry, the large firms have historically been neither as dominant in terms of collective market share nor as vertically integrated as have been the oil and aluminum firms. In 1948, the seven largest copper firms controlled 70 percent of world production, but by 1969 this had dropped to 54 percent.

During the 1970s, the extractive sites of several of the largest copper and oil companies were nationalized by the host governments. These nationalizations will be discussed in a subsequent section of this chapter.

Table 14-1 identifies the major firms in the oil, copper, and aluminum industries by nationality of parent.

Analyze the attached case, AMAX–Mitsui (A). In addition to the study guide questions at the end of the case, you should consider the following questions;

a) How can AMAX–Mitsui's alumax make sure that it would continue to obtain alumina from the present supplier even after the present long-term purchase plan expires? Is Mitsui's ownership necessary and useful for this guarantee?

b) Why did AMAX choose to sell its aluminum subsidiary? How is this sale related to the new growth strategies of AMAX?

CASE 6:
AMAX-MITSUI (A)

In August 1973 AMAX, Inc.[1] was negotiating with the Mitsui Trading Company the sale of 50 percent of AMAX's equity interest in its aluminum subsidiary. If the sale was consummated, it was agreed that AMAX would assume the existing long-term debt of the aluminum subsidiary, and a jointly owned independent entity, the Alumax Company, would be formed to operate the aluminum business under its former management. The new company would be headquartered in San Mateo, California. The transaction would represent the largest direct investment in the United States by a Japanese corporation in history, and the first sizable major equity position ever assumed by a Japanese interest in a large U.S. corporation.

In 1973 Mitsui was the second largest trading company in Japan, having a total annual turnover of over $16 billion. The trading company is a phenomenon unique to Japan. Historically, a number of trading companies were the "flagship" organization of the *zaibatsu*, the pre–World War II industrial combines of

1. From 1957 to 1974, the legal name of AMAX, Inc., as The American Metal Climax Company. Although the name was legally changed to AMAX, Inc., in 1974, after most of the events of this case took place, the company is referred to as AMAX, Inc., throughout the case.

Copyright © 1975 by the Corporation of the Massachusetts Institute of Technology and the President and Fellows of Harvard College.

Written by Edward M. Graham and Yoshi Tsurumi.

Japan. In the pre-World War II era, the Mitsui *zaibatsu* was by far the largest of these (Mitsubishi was second largest, Sumitomo third largest). The Mitsui *zaibatsu*'s major activities included banking, insurance, retailing, iron and steel fabricating, fabrication of heavy machinery, nonferrous metals refining and fabricating, shipbuilding, fertilizer, coal mines, chemicals, textiles, nonferrous mines, food processing, beverage, and real estate.

The historic role of the trading company in the *zaibatsu* was to handle the foreign trade as well as domestic wholesale marketing activities of the constituent firms of the *zaibatsu*, including the all-important procurement of raw materials from foreign sources. Japan, as has been often noted, is a nation not well endowed with raw materials, and hence raw material procurement has been an especially important aspect of Japanese business. In addition, the trading company was often the "information center" and coordinator of the *zaibatsu*. It often spearheaded creation of new industrial ventures by providing necessary financial and managerial resources.

Although the Mitsui *zaibatsu* was dissolved during the American occupation, the separate companies into which it was split continued to work together in an informal group, and the Mitsui Trading Company continued to be the informal leader of this group. In 1973, the Mitsui Trading Company continued to be the principal vehicle through which the foreign trade of the Mitsui companies was conducted, including raw materials procurement. In addition the Mitsui Trading Company emerged as a major holder of Japanese direct investment in foreign lands.

AMAX, Inc. described itself in its 1973 annual report as "a highly diversified natural resources company with a broad base in minerals and energy resources." 1973 sales were over $1.3 billion while after tax earnings were $105 million.

AMAX was formed by the 1957 merger of the American Metal Company, Ltd. and the Climax Molybdenum Company. The larger of the two, the American Metal Company, Ltd., was a miner, processer, and trader of nonferrous metals and minerals, including copper, lead, zinc, precious metals, and potash. The company held major investments in two large African copper-mining concerns, the Rhodesian Selection Trust, Ltd. and the Roan Antelope Copper Mines, Ltd., but it did not manage these concerns directly. A subsidiary of the American Metal Company, Ltd., the United States Metals Refining Company owned and operated the largest secondary copper-smelting facility in the United States. The company also owned oil properties in Oklahoma. At the time of the merger, about 25 percent of the common stock of the American Metal Company Ltd. was owned by Selection Trust, Ltd., of London, and about 10 percent by Phelps Dodge, Inc.

In terms of sales, the Climax Molubdenum Company was barely a tenth the size of the American Metals Company, Ltd. at the time of the merger, but Climax's earnings were almost 90 percent of those of the American Metals Company. The source of Climax's earnings was the huge Climax, Colorado molybdenum mine, which in 1957 supplied almost half the non-Communist world demand for molybdenum. Molybdenum was a vital ingredient for many types of high-strength hard steel alloys. Climax Molybdenum Co., in addition to owning the Climax mine, owned downstream facilities to process the molybdenum concentrates from the mine into usable molybdenum products. By-products from these operations included tungsten, pyrite, tin, and monazite, all of which were commercially salable. At the time of the merger, Climax also held investments in oil, uranium, thorium, and vanadium-bearing properties.

Merger discussions between the American Metal Company and the Climax Molybdenum Company were initiated in the middle 1950s. In mid-1957, the discussions were terminated as a result of failure of the two parties to agree on a valuation of Climax relative to American Metal. As a consequence of the break-down in the talks, the chairman of the board of Climax, Mr. Arthur Bunker, decided to hire a person with broad industrial and managerial experience to take over the diversification program. The person hired was Ian MacGregor, who was to play a major role in the future of the AMAX company.

In the autumn of 1957, at the behest of American Metal, talks between the two companies were renewed, and the merger was consummated in December of that year. Following the merger, major new activities were added to AMAX's portfolio of operations.

In 1962, AMAX entered the aluminum industry. Building up operations by means of acquisition and internal expansion, by 1966 AMAX had emerged as a major integrated aluminum producer. (The details of this are covered in the next section.)

In 1963, AMAX gained claim to a major deposit of high-grade iron ore at Mt. Newman in Western Australia. By 1965 it was determined that at least one billion tons of iron ore were recoverable from this location. In 1967 final agreements were made for a consortium of American, Australian, British, and Japanese companies to create a joint venture to exploit Mt. Newman. AMAX would hold 25 percent equity participation in the venture. One of AMAX's partners in the consortium was Mitsuitoh Pty., a joint venture of two Japanese trading companies, Mitsui and C. Itoh. Mitsui was two-thirds owner of the venture. Mitsuitoh held 10 percent of the project. This was the first time in history that Japanese interests participated in a major Australian minerals venture.

In 1969 AMAX acquired the Ayrshire Collieries Corporation, an independent coal-producing company in the United States. The acquisition of Ayrshire, accomplished by exchange of AMAX preferred stock for Ayrshire common, gave AMAX control over large reserves of coal located largely in the Midwest and in Wyoming and the Rocky Mountain area.

In 1973, by exchange of AMAX preferred stock for the acquired companies' common stock, AMAX acquired the Banner Mining Company and the affiliated Tintic Standard Mining Company. These companies owned a large body of copper ore in Arizona. The ore body was leased by the Anaconda company, which operated a large mine to exploit it. AMAX for years had sought to engage in copper mining in the United States. With the acquisition of Banner and Tintic, AMAX would form a partnership with Anaconda, named the Anamax Company, to expand and operate the mine.

An AMAX executive who played a major role in the expansion and diversification of AMAX's activities was Ian MacGregor. Following the merger, Mr. MacGregor was made vice-president in charge of new business development, and in this role he led AMAX's efforts to enter and establish itself in the aluminum industry. Later, as chief executive officer, he played a key role in the formation of the Mt. Newman consortium and oversaw the acquisitions of the Ayrshire, Banner, and Tintic Standard companies. MacGregor grew up in the Scottish West Highlands. His father was an employee of British Aluminum, and MacGregor's first job was in British Aluminum's management training program. His early experience with the British aluminum industry was to be very valuable to him in his career with AMAX.

The Entry of AMAX into the Aluminum Industry

During the first years of its existence, AMAX was able to generate earnings faster than it could reinvest them. In 1960, for example, earnings after tax were $41.3 million; dividends and capital expenditures less depreciation were $24.6 million. Long-term debt was less than 10 percent of total capitalization at the time of the merger, and over the next several years the long-term debt was reduced while shareholder's equity increased.

In order to utilize effectively the growing liquid assets of the company, AMAX management asked MacGregor in 1960 to create a group to investigate new businesses that the company might enter. The objective was to find businesses that would provide the company with greater long-term growth potential than existing investment opportunities but that were congruent with the company's expertise in minerals and metallurgy. On account of the latter condition MacGregor ruled out the possibility of the company entering into such then fast-growing industries as electronics, fast foods franchising, and other industries totally alien to AMAX's existing competence.

MacGregor accepted the prior conclusion of the analysts that the long-run growth potential of the integrated aluminum industry was greater and the prospective return on investment higher than those of other major metals and minerals industries that he studied. This judgment was confirmed by new economic studies, which indicated that: (1) the growth rate for aluminum and aluminum products was high, and these high rates of growth would persist throughout the 1960s; and (2) the existing integrated aluminum companies in North America were more highly leveraged than were most other American manufacturing companies, and the possibility existed that these aluminum firms would experience difficulty in financing the expansion of capacity required to serve a growing demand for aluminum and aluminum products. Thus, MacGregor believed that new entry could occur in the aluminum industry without disrupting the stability of the industry.

Entry into the industry did pose some problems, however, for the following reasons:

1. Upstream aluminum operations (bauxite mining, alumina production, and primary aluminum reduction), which were generally more profitable than downstream operations, were highly specialized and capital intensive, and, additionally, the minimum scale for economic operations was very large.

2. Entry into the industry at the level of bauxite mining or alumina production appeared virtually impossible. The known reserves of bauxite in the early 1960s were almost entirely controlled by the established companies—

ALCOA (U.S.), ALCAN (Canada), Reynolds (U.S.), Pechiney (France), Kaiser (U.S.), and Alusuisse (Switzerland)—and these companies did not appear eager to share their bauxite operations with a major new entrant into the industry.

3. Entry into the industry at the level of primary reduction was only slightly less problematic. Over 85 percent of primary reduction capacity in North America was controlled by ALCOA, ALCAN, Reynolds, and Kaiser. There was no free market for alumina, and hence the alumina for a primary reduction mill would have to be purchased from the integrated producers. Because a primary aluminum reduction facility must be operated continuously, even a brief interruption in the supply of alumina could result in severe adverse effects on the economics of operating the facility.

4. The aluminum industry had historically been subject to cycles of undercapacity and overcapacity. Were AMAX to construct and operate integrated upstream facilities but fail to establish a secure market for its output of ingot, during a period of overcapacity AMAX might have to "dump" its ingot at distress prices.

A tentative conclusion of MacGregor was that if AMAX were to enter the aluminum business, it should initially enter downstream operations via acquisitions of existing businesses rather than attempt to enter at the upstream end of the business. Downstream, the industry was less concentrated and less capital intensive than upstream, but also less profitable. Once, however, a downstream market share had been firmly established, the company could integrate upstream.

An impetus to the plan for entry via downstream acquisition came in 1962, when the U.S. Department of Justice blocked the acquisition of the Kawneer Company by Kaiser Aluminum and Chemical Company and the acquisition of the Apex Smelting Company by ALCAN. Kawneer was one of the nation's leading fabricators of architectural aluminum products supplied to the commercial construction industry. The company was partially integrated—that is, it converted aluminum billet into extrusions, and the extrusions were assmbled into finished architectural products. Thus, while Kawneer was mainly a secondary fabricator, it produced many of its own mill products. Apex was a leading secondary smelter of aluminum whose main business was to produce aluminum alloys from processed scrap.

In 1962, AMAX was able to reach an agreement with the owners of Apex and Kawneer to merge their companies into AMAX, exchanging AMAX convertible preferred stock for common stock of the acquired companies. Kawneer and Apex not only provided an initial entry for AMAX but also provided AMAX with staff and technical personnel experienced in aluminum operations.

Expansion of downstream aluminum operations was accomplished in 1963, when AMAX acquired the Hunter Engineering Company for $22 million in cash. Hunter was a major producer of aluminum siding to the mobile-home industry, other sheet and building products, and other mill products. Hunter was also a leading producer of machinery for aluminum rolling mills (this line of business was sold by AMAX in 1970).

Having secured a downstream base in the aluminum industry, Mr. MacGregor began to consider backwards integration. Of paramount importance was to secure a supply of alumina, and to this end he directed his efforts in 1963 and 1964.

The first effort failed. A consortium of companies led by Kaiser was being formed in 1963 to exploit the underdeveloped Gladstone bauxite deposits in Queensland, Australia, but MacGregor was unable to convince the partners in the consortium to allow AMAX to join or to grant to AMAX a long-term contract to buy alumina.

A second chance to gain access to the Gladstone alumina came about through a complex series of events. Through a personal friend, MacGregor learned that the Howmet Corporation—a primary and secondary fabricator of aluminum which was, in 1963, in the process of being acquired by Pechiney—was interested in the possibility of backwards integration into primary aluminum production. Howmet, however, had a problem. New developments in the technology of primary reduction were resulting in new levels of scale economies. It appeared that whereas the minimum efficient size for a primary reduction mill had historically been 65 to 90 thousand tons per year, new technology would raise the new minimum efficient size to 120 to 150 thousand tons. If Howmet were to build a plant with such a large capacity, it would be unable to utilize the full output.

Approaching Howmet, MacGregor was able to ascertain that Howmet would be interested in constructing a large primary reduction facility as a fifty-fifty joint venture with AMAX. It remained, however, to convince Pechiney, the French parent of Howmet, of the wisdom of creating the plant. Initially, the management of Pechiney was reluctant to approve the venture. After several trips to Paris with the president of Howmet, however, MacGregor was able to convince them to go ahead. Early in 1964 MacGregor proposed formally to the AMAX board of directors that AMAX join with Pechiney and Howmet to construct a large primary aluminum reduction plant in Ferndale, Washington. A new company, the Intalco Aluminum Corporation, to be owned 50 percent by AMAX, 25 percent by Pechiney directly, and 25 percent by Howmet was created to construct and operate the reduction facility. Fifty percent of the output of Intalco would go to AMAX and the other 50 percent to Howmet. Initial capacity was to be 76,000 tons of aluminum ingot per annum, ultimate capacity 228,000 tons. Initial investment was $60 million.

Pechiney was a participant in the Gladstone bauxite and alumina consortium, and, as a partner with Pechiney in Intalco, AMAX was able to gain access to Gladstone alumina. However, a new source of Australian alumina unexpectedly became available to AMAX. ALCOA of Australia, a joint venture between ALCOA and local Australian partners with the support of the Western Australian government, was developing a bauxite mine and alumina plant in Western Australia, but was unable to contract to ship enough alumina to run the complex profitably. This was of concern to ALCOA's Australian partners. Approaching ALCOA of Australia, which was anxious for prompt expansion, Mr. MacGregor was able to obtain a long-term contract for delivery of alumina at favorable prices to Intalco for AMAX's share of the output.

In 1965, to capitalize on scale economies and clear market opportunities, it was decided that the Intalco plant's start-up capacity should be increased from 76,000 tons of aluminum per annum (one pot-line) to 152,000 (two pot-lines).

By the time the plant actually began producing aluminum in 1966, work had already begun to construct the third pot-line to increase capacity to the full 228,000 tons. Total investment in the facility exceeded $150 million.

The creation of Intalco marked the emergence of AMAX as an integrated producer of aluminum. To round out downstream operations, AMAX in 1965 acquired the Johnston Foil Company of St. Louis, a manufacturer of aluminum foils and other metal foils. Inside the United States, fabricating operations were expanded from 1963 to 1966, and overseas fabricating plants were established and acquired in the United Kingdom, continental Europe, Australia, and Japan.

In 1965, the Amax Aluminum Company was organized as a subsidiary within which all aluminum activities of AMAX were to be situated. The subsidiary included an international division. In 1966 domestic operations were reorganized into seven divisions based on product lines: mill products, building products, extrusions, Kawneer (architectural products), foil products, Apex, and Hunter Engineering (aluminum rolling mill machinery). Intalco continued to be run as a separate company, 50 percent owned by Amax Aluminum Co. Early in 1966, Stephen Furbacher, formerly an executive of Kawneer, succeeded Mr. Mac-Gregor as president of the Amax Aluminum Company, and MacGregor became president and chief executive officer of the parent company, AMAX, Inc.

By late 1966, AMAX was, on the basis of dollar sales of aluminum and aluminum products, the fifth largest aluminum company in North America, although on the basis of primary aluminum capacity AMAX was in a tie for eighth place. The growth of AMAX's aluminum business as a percentage of AMAX sales is documented in Exhibit 14-1. Although growth in the earnings of the aluminum business did not keep pace with sales, it was believed by AMAX management that this was largely due to start-up costs of the many new facilities to come online. As the business matured and as AMAX emerged as a major force in the U.S. aluminum industry, it was believed that earnings would grow.

The Kimberley Project and Expansion
of AMAX Aluminum

Although in 1967 AMAX did not own upstream bauxite mining and alumina production facilities, efforts to integrate backwards into bauxite and alumina had begun in the middle 1960s. In 1968 AMAX announced that it had discovered and gained legal claim to a huge deposit of high-grade bauxite located at Kimberley, in Western Australia. In 1970, announcement was made of a tentative consortium to exploit the Kimberley bauxite reserves. Members of the consortium would be AMAX, the Sumitomo Chemical Corporation, and Showa Denko—two leading aluminum ingot producers in Japan—Vereinigte Aluminum of West Germany, and Holland Aluminum of the Netherlands. The project would include a bauxite mine on the Mitchell Plateau, a railroad to transport the ore to the Australian coast, and a large coastal alumina plant with deep port facilities to load alumina onto ocean-going freighters.

The total development cost of the Kimberley project was estimated in 1970 to be between $400 and $500 million including all such necessary infrastructure as town site roads, railways, port facilities, water supply, and power plants. Later, the estimate was revised to about three-quarters of a billion dollars. To be economic, for this size of initial investment, annual output of alumina would have to be large enough to equal, for example, the annual demand of Japan in 1975.

At about this time, a minor recession was being felt in Australia and the recently elected labor government of Western Australia expressed a desire for new projects to be begun in the bauxite-alumina industry. In discussions between Western Australian government officials and AMAX, it became clear that uncertainties in the world alumina market made it doubtful whether AMAX could put together a large enough consortium to get the Kimberley project going. At the same time, the Australian federal government's desire for major Australian participation in such a venture found no interested takers.

Expansion by ALCOA of Australia was also in danger of being shelved because of a lack of alumina buyers. AMAX decided that if the Western Australian government would give them a twelve-year moratorium on the Kimberley development, AMAX would provide firm contracts for alumina on which the stalled ALCOA project could go ahead at once. This would provide some immediate employment prospects in Western Australia, and the government of Western Australia was amenable to this plan.

Renewal of alumina contracts with ALCOA of Australian to supply AMAX with alumina eased pressure for AMAX to develop the Kimberley reserves. Long-term contracts and options with ALCOA of Australia not only would continue to supply Intalco with alumina at economic prices but would also supply future AMAX primary reduction plants when and if they were built.

In 1973, the Kimberley project still had not advanced beyond the planning stage. The late 1960s saw the aluminum industry as a whole go into one of its periodic periods of overcapacity. Between 1969 and 1972 primary aluminum production capacity in the United States grew from 3.88 million short tons per annum to 4.77 million, while primary production climbed from 3.79 million short tons in 1969 (98% of capacity) to only 4.12 million in 1972 (85% of capacity). As a result, the list price of primary aluminum actually declined slightly, from 27 cents per pound on January 1, 1969 to 25 cents in May 1972. During the 1969 to 1972 period, there was substantial discounting by primary aluminum producers. Thus, the actual market price was somewhat lower than the list price. By contrast, the composite published price of steel during the same time span rose from 9.2 cents per pound to 11.9 cents, nickel from $1.28 per pound to $1.53, and electrolytic copper from 47.4 cents per pound to 51.4 cents. In Europe and Japan new primary capacity had been added in the late 1960s and early 1970s and overcapacity also became a problem in these areas.

Despite the overall industry picture, AMAX continued to expand its aluminum operations from 1967 to 1973, although not as rapidly as from 1962 to 1966. Intalco capacity in 1968 was boosted to the full 228,000 tons (Actual production at Intalco reached 263,000 short tons in 1972.) A rolling mill was constructed in 1967–68 in Illinois, extending AMAX's sheet-producing capability to include the entire range of no-heat-treatable aluminum alloys. New extrusion and fabricating facilities were opened in the United States and abroad in 1968, 1969, and 1970.

By early 1971, it was believed by AMAX executives that AMAX would be able to utilize additional primary aluminum capacity by the mid-1970s when the industry would be in a cycle of undercapacity. Two opportunities arose to increase primary capacity.

The first opportunity arose when AMAX learned that the Mitsui Trading Company was interested in establishing a primary aluminum reduction facility in the western United States. Mitsui had in fact been investigating the possibility of building such a plant since 1967. Both for Mitsui and for the Japanese economy such a move appeared to make sense. From Mitsui's point of view, the Mitsui group of companies was in a weak position in the light metals industries relative to other groups within Japan, and a U.S. reduction facility would help close the gap between Mitsui and competing firms. From the point of view of the Japanese economy, the availability of power and environmental considerations within Japan were putting a limit on the ability of the aluminum industry to grow internally. The expectation was that much of the growth of Japan's aluminum supply would have to come from facilities outside of Japan.

A site for a primary reduction plant was located in northwestern Oregon, and a contract for power was received from the Bonneville Power Administration. A tentative decision was reached to construct a 187,000 ton per annum plant, the cost of which, by the time estimates were worked out in 1972, was estimated to exceed $250 million. In 1972, it was publicly announced that the facility would be 50 percent owned by Mitsui and 50 percent by AMAX. Each company would, in exchange for its equity participation, receive 50 percent of the facility's aluminum output.

Steps to construct the Oregon plant were not begun by AMAX until 1973, and then a dispute with the government of Oregon over environmental aspects of the plant delayed plans further. Late in 1973, the issue of whether or not the facility would be built at all lay in the hands of the government of Oregon, and the matter lay unresolved.

The second opportunity for AMAX to expand primary aluminum capacity was consummated when agreement was reached between David Mayers, the aluminum group's new president who succeeded Stephen Furbacher in 1972, and the Howmet Metal Corporation. The agreement stipulated that AMAX would eventually become half owner of Howmet's Eastalco primary aluminum facility, located in Frederick, Maryland. During 1973 and 1974, Eastalco rated capacity would be increased from 86,700 short tons to 173,400 short tons, half of which would go to AMAX. It was contemplated that at some future date capacity might be boosted to 260,100 short tons to be shared equally between AMAX and Howmet. The total cost to AMAX of participation in Eastalco (excluding costs of future expansion) was estimated to exceed $150 million.

Expansion of AMAX's Nonaluminum Activities
From 1967 onward, substantial capital commitments were required in AMAX's operations other than the aluminum subsidiary. The Mt. Newman iron ore mine began operations in 1967 and over the years 1967–71 required well over $100 million dollars from AMAX, 25 percent owner of the mine. By 1971 the mine was the largest single supplier of iron ore to Japan. In 1967 the Urad

Mine, an old molybdenum mine located about thirty miles north of Climax, Colorado, was reopened, requiring $25 million in capital investment over the years 1967–71. The Urad mine exploited a relatively small molybdenum deposit to supplement the Climax mine's output. In the longer term, AMAX was developing a third Colorado molybdenum mine to exploit reserves discovered in 1965. This mine, Henderson Mine, when it came on-stream in the mid- to late 1970s, would rival the Climax mine in yearly output. The Henderson Mine, located very near the Urad Mine, would require capital expenditures of over $400 million over a five- to eight-year period beginning in about 1971. Climax itself would need capital funds for expansion as the opportunity presented itself to develop an open-pit mine to exploit lower grade ores at the surface. Also, downstream molybdenum processing facilities were in need of modernization and expansion. Through the 1970s the expansion and modernization of molybdenum operations was expected to cost AMAX at least $500 million.

Additional capital was needed to expand coal production. By 1972 AMAX had become the fifth largest producer of coal in the United States. In 1973, shipments began from the new Belle Ayr South mine in Wyoming and the new Ayrshire and Wabash mines in Indiana. At the end of 1973, over $65 million had been spent on coal mine expansion and development of new mines, and through the remainder of the 1970s over $200 million more were due to be spent.

AMAX expected to incur other capital costs through the 1970s. Purchase and rehabilitation of a zinc plant in Illinois was budgeted at $26 million. AMAX had long sought entry into the nickel business and acquisition and rehabilitation of a nickel refinery in Louisiana was budgeted at $53 million.

The effect of so much expansion resulted in AMAX's capital expenditures almost tripling between 1967 and 1973, as shown in Exhibit 14–2. As is indicated by Exhibit 14–3, total yearly capital expenditures exceeded net cash flow after dividends during these years, thus requiring AMAX to raise outside capital. Resultant changes in AMAX's capitalization are shown in Exhibit 14–4.

By 1969, the capital requirements for AMAX's various operations were beginning to tax the company's ability to raise funds from outside sources. The situation was compounded in the following years by depressed securities prices and rising interest rates. The net result was a steady climb in the cost of capital to the company throughout the early 1970s.

Late in 1972 the board of directors of AMAX began to put pressure on I.K. MacGregor, now chairman of the board as well as chief executive officer, to limit future capital investment to only those areas of the business that were resource based and had the highest potential return on investment. The perception of the board was that throughout the 1970s, investment opportunities available to AMAX would simply outstrip the ability of the firm to raise capital.

Reviewing AMAX's operations, MacGregor concluded that return on investment on mining operations had been higher than return on manufacturing operations. Furthermore, he concluded that the potential return on investment in bauxite mining was not competitive with that of other minerals that AMAX mined. This latter conclusion was somewhat academic in view of the fact that in 1972 AMAX's aluminum operations were not integrated back into bauxite mining and alumina production, but the point stood that even if AMAX were to be able to develop the Kimberly bauxite complex, the future expected rates of return in the aluminum subsidiary would be lower than those of AMAX's other operations.

The Decision to Sell Equity in the Aluminum Subsidiary

One evening in the spring of 1973, MacGregor was sitting in a Manhattan restaurant with Robert Marcus. Mr. Marcus was the executive vice-president of the Amax Aluminum Company, and he had worked with MacGregor in the early 1960s in putting together the aluminum operations. The two executives were discussing the capital needs of the aluminum subsidiary over the next five years. Mr. Marcus was well aware of the fact that AMAX might not in the future be able to supply all of the capital to the aluminum subsidiary that the subsidiary might require.

"You know," MacGregor told Marcus, "the board of directors just isn't going to allow me to give you the sort of money you want. Frankly, I doubt that we could raise the total sums that you require. Even if we could, the needs of the molybdenum and coal operations are substantial, and many board members just simply feel that these must take priority over aluminum."

Marcus pondered the situation. He had previously discussed with MacGregor the possibility of the Amax Aluminum Company becoming a quasi-independent company with its own capitalization. MacGregor had agreed that if this were to happen, AMAX would absorb the Aluminum Company's existing debt, and the Aluminum Company would then be able to raise its own capital through the issuing of debt and equity. This question was, who would be willing to buy a large share of AMAX's equity in the company at a reasonable price? In 1973, stock market prices were generally depressed, and shares of major aluminum companies such as ALCOA, Reynolds, and Kaiser were selling at price/earning (P/E) ratios of from seven to thirteen times earnings, which meant that the market value of each was below net book value. From a number of points of view, sale of the Amax Aluminum Company to another domestic aluminum firm might have made sense, but this alternative had to be ruled out on the basis of the probable reaction of the Antitrust Division of the Department of Justice. MacGregor and Marcus began to discuss other possible buyers.

"I have considered the possibility of approaching Pechiney," stated MacGregor. "The problem is, I am not sure that they would be able to buy in cash. We would want cash—we need it—and they are not extremely liquid. Besides, I am not sure but what the Department of Justice would object to Pechiney's taking a major ownership position in our aluminum company."

"Maybe a Japanese firm would be willing to buy us," ventured Marcus.

"Why would one want to?" asked MacGregor.

"Well, when I was over there talking to Mitsui about the Oregon plant, I had the distinct feeling that they really badly wanted to secure sources of aluminum outside of Japan," said Marcus. "They're a big company, they have access to funds, and their government is giving top priority to the securing of raw materials. I think that aluminum is rather high on the Japanese government's list.

"Besides, our State Department has been putting pressure on the Japanese for several years now to do something about the surplus trade balance Japan has been running with the United States. If Mitsui were to buy us, it certainly would do something about the balance of payments."

"I also have thought about Mitsui as a possible buyer," said MacGregor. "My impression is that the Mitsui Trading Company wishes to integrate into overseas manufacturing, and it wants to do so in big chunks.

"Who did you talk to at Mitsui when you were discussing the Oregon smelter?"

"A Mr. Hisachi Murata, who is a managing director of Mitsui, and a Mr. Smuio Takahashi, who is in charge of Mitsui's light metals business," replied Mr. Marcus.

"I know one of Mitsui's executive vice-presidents very well," said Mac-Gregor. "His name is Tatsuro Goto. Look, you go home, pack your bags, and leave for Japan as soon as you can. I'll send a wire to Mr. Goto, telling him that you are coming and have important business to discuss."

"One question," interjected Marcus. "Suppose for a second that they say 'yes.' How much do you want for the company?"

"Well, most aluminum companies are selling in the market about at book value. Our aluminum business achieves a higher return on investment than do our competitors, however, and I think that we should sell substantially above book value. Use your own judgment when you are in Tokyo as to how best to present an offer."

Mr. Goto was an executive vice-president and member of the Executive Committee of the Mitsui Trading Company. When, on the following Friday, Mr. Marcus met with Mr. Goto and Mr. Murata in Tokyo, both were enthusiastic about the proposal. Learning that several other members of the Mitsui executive committee (there were six in total) were tied up on the golf course over the weekend, Mr. Goto arranged for a meeting of the full committee for Monday. On Monday, the commiteee met and quickly agreed that it was extremely interested in the possibility of buying in cash 50 percent of AMAX's equity in the aluminum subsidiary. The committee also indicated that it agreed that the Amax Aluminum Company was worth more than book value.

Several days after Mr. Marcus returned to the United States, the AMAX board of directors approved the transaction in principle. Permission to consummate the deal was required from Japan's Ministry of International Trade and Industry (MITI), but permission was expected to be forthcoming. During negotiations in August, the final terms of the transaction were to be set.

Exhibit 14-1. Sales, Earnings, and Capital Expenditures of AMAX, 1964-1966, by Lines of Business (in miilions of U.S. dollars).

	1964	1965	1966
Sales			
Molybdenum and specialty metals	98	111	123
Copper, lead, and zinc	169	161	200
Aluminum	139	170	217
Petroleum and chemicals	32	33	33
Earnings (before tax, exploration, corporate overhead)			
Molybdenum and specialty metals	34	39	40˙
Copper, lead, and zinc	11	15	20
Aluminum	4	4	9
Petroleum and chemicals	5	8	4
Capital Investments			
Molybdenum and specialty metals	13	25	24
Copper, lead, and zinc	2	6	9
Aluminum	9	27	40
Petroleum and chemicals	11	7	12

Source: Annual Reports.

Exhibit 14-2. Capital Expenditures of AMAX, by Product Line, 1967-1973 (in millions of U.S. dollars).

	1967	1968	1969	1970	1971	1972	1973
Molybdenum and specialty metals	25	17	11	29	49	39	51
Copper, lead, and zinc	13	15	15	8	8	10	110[b]
Aluminum	29	27	10	21	13	11	11
Coal, petroleum, and chemicals	5	4	83[c]	19	36	52	64
Iron ore	14	29	18	24	30	8	10
Overseas investments[a]	—	—	—	84	—	12	1
Other	—	—	10	4	6	25	18
Total	86	103	147	189	142	157	265

a. These largely consist of investments in African mining companies.
b. Includes $85 million in connection with purchase of Banner Mining Co.
c. Includes $76 million in connection with purchase of Ayrshire Collieries.
Source: Annual Reports.

Exhibit 14-3. Capital Deficit of AMAX, 1967-1973 (in millions of U.S. dollars).

	1967	1968	1969	1970	1971	1972	1973
Earnings after tax	56.6	68.7	82.0	72.6	55.1	66.2	105.1
Dividends paid	29.5	29.8	32.5	36.3	36.5	37.3	45.1
Earnings after tax and dividends	27.1	38.9	49.5	36.3	18.6	28.9	60.0
Depreciation and amortization	21	25	27	37	39	42	48
Total cash flow after dividends (rounded)	48	64	77	73	58	71	108
Capital expenditures (including acquisitions)	86	103	147	189	142	157	265
(Cash flow) – (capital expenditures)	< 38 >	< 39 >	< 70 >	< 116 >	< 84 >	< 86 >	< 157 >

Exhibit 14–4. Capital Structure of AMAX, 1967–1973 (in millions of U.S. dollars).

	1967	1968	1969	1970	1971	1972	1973
Long-term debt (interest bearing)	157	190	201	261	392	457	441
Reserves, deferred taxes, and other noncurrent liabilities	23	28	56	64	102	138	172
Total long-term debt and deferrals	180	218	257	325	494	595	613
Preferred stock[a]	14	10	1	1	1	1	2
Common stock[a]	107	111	24	24	24	24	24
Capital surplus	8	10	168	177	177	177	264
Retained earnings	287	324	361	408	423	490	550
Total stockholder's equity	417	456	554	610	626	693	841

a. After 1968 values of preferred and common stock stated at nominal value.
Note: Figures no not include minority interests.
Source: Annual Reports.

378

Exhibit 14–5. Summary Income Statement, AMAX, Inc., 1967–1973 (in rounded millions of U.S. dollars).

	1967	1968	1969	1970	1971	1972	1973
Sales	478	571	754	859	767	876	1.337
Earnings from operations	44	56	73	86	60	88	145
Dividends from nonconsolidated investments	22	28	33	14	11	8	14
Net interest[a]	2	2	2	2	–	< 5 >	< 10 >
Taxes: federal and foreign income	< 12 >	< 17 >	< 25 >	< 30 >	< 17 >	< 25 >	< 44 >
Net earnings	57	69	82	73	55	66	105
Earnings per share of common stock ($)	2.47	2.95	3.47	2.93	2.19	2.62	4.03
Depreciation, amortization, and depletion	21	25	27	37	39	42	48

a. In 1971, 1972, and 1973 respectively, the following amounts of interest were capitalized: $3.8 million, $11.6 million, and $14 million.

Source: Annual Reports.

Exhibit 14-6. Summary Balance Sheet, AMAX, Inc., December 31, 1973 (in thousands of U.S. dollars).

Cash, time deposits, marketable securities	287,900
Accounts receivable, net	193,370
Inventories	177,450
Other current assets	13,300
Total current assets	672,020
Plant and equipment, net	889,940
Other long-term assets, net	150,210
Total assets	1,712,170
Current liabilities	256,610
Long-term debt	440,680
Other long-term liabilities	174,530
Total long-term liabilities	871,820
Preferred stock (nominal value)	1,770
Common stock (nominal value)	23,790
Paid-in capital	264,150
Retained earnings	550,890
Treasury stock	< 250 >
Total equity	840,350
Total liabilities and equity	1,712,170

Note: Figures do not reflect effects of Mitsui purchase of 50 percent of AMAX, Aluminum, Inc.
Source: Annual Reports.

Exhibit 14-7. Income Statement, AMAX Aluminum Company, 1969-1973 (in rounded millions of U.S. dollars).

	1969	1970	1971	1972	1973
Sales	279.9	276.7	286.8	310.8	373.0
Costs and operating expense	217.0	219.2	232.3	249.1	296.1
Selling and general expenses	25.2	26.6	28.0	29.9	31.1
Depreciation and amortization	9.4	10.3	10.8	10.7	10.7
Taxes other than federal and foreign income taxes	3.7	42	4.3	4.6	5.4
Earnings from operations	24.6	16.5	11.4	16.5	29.6
Interest on loans to AMAX	1.3	1.4	1.6	1.5	1.5
Other income	0.2	0.6	1.1	0.7	0.5
Other expense	0.2	0.3	0.4	0.3	0.4
Taxable income	23.3	15.4	10.5	15.4	28.2
Federal and foreign income taxes, net	12.1	7.3	4.4	6.2	11.9
Net earnings	11.2	8.1	6.1	9.3	16.3

Source: Company Prospectus.

Exhibit 14-8. Balance Sheet, AMAX Aluminum Company, December 31, 1973 (in thousands of U.S. dollars).

Cash and equivalent	2,732
Accounts receivable	71,462
Inventories	59,225
Other current assets	3,117
Total current assets	136,536
Investments in 50% owned companies at equity	9,884
Net fixed assets	119,377
Other assets	3,613
Total assets	269,410
Current liabilities	48,753
Long-term debt	7,449
Other long-term liabilities	12,519
Total shareholders' equity	200,689
Total liabilities and shareholders' equity	269,410

Source: Company Prospectus.

STUDY GUIDE QUESTIONS

1. Why did AMAX choose a Japanese firm? And Mitsui?

2. How much should AMAX ask for the 50 percent interest in its aluminum division? What should be the criteria? A market value of the firm? A present value of the expected earning streams? A book value? The amount that Mitsui would have to invest if it started its own aluminum operation?

3. Will the AMAX–Mitsui tie-up pose a threat to other Japanese aluminum firms? To multinational majors? What can AMAX and Mitsui do together better than alone?